For Reference

Not to be taken from this room

ENCYCLOPEDIA OF

Victoria Sherrow

ABC-CLIO

Women and Sports

Library of Congress Cataloging-in-Publication Data

Sherrow, Victoria.
    Encyclopedia of women and sports / Victoria Sherrow.
       p.   cm.
    Includes bibliographical references and index.
    ISBN 0-87436-826-X (alk. paper)
    1. Women athletes—Encyclopedias.   2. Sports—Encyclopedias.
   3. Women athletes—Biography. I. Title.
   GV709.S44   1996
   796'.082—dc20   96-19600
                                               CIP

02 01 00 99 98 97 96 95   10 9 8 7 6 5 4 3 2 1

ABC-CLIO, Inc.
130 Cremona Drive, P.O. Box 1911
Santa Barbara, California 93116-1911

This book is printed on acid-free paper ∞.
Manufactured in the United States of America

ENCYCLOPEDIA OF

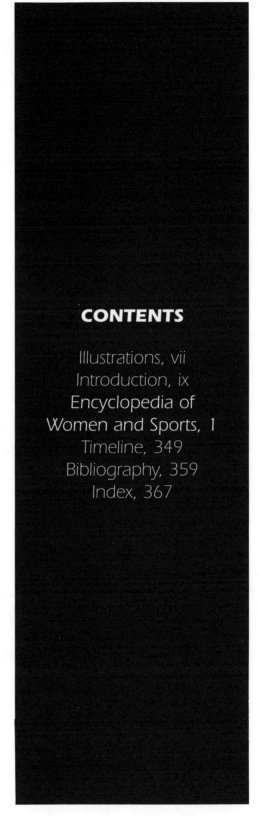

CONTENTS

Women and Sports

ILLUSTRATIONS

INTRODUCTION

When the Virginia Slims Tennis Tour for women was launched in 1970, many women objected to the slogan, "You've come a long way, baby." Some resented the patronizing sound of the word "baby," while others disliked the idea of linking athletics with smoking and cigarette ads. However, people agreed with the first part of the slogan. Women athletes have indeed come a long way in sports, making a place for themselves in a world that was dominated by men so completely and for so long.

Consider the status of women back in ancient Greece, in 776 B.C., with the first Olympian Games: Not only were women banned from the competition, but any woman caught watching the games faced the penalty of being thrown to her death from Mount Typaion.

Longstanding Prejudices

The Greeks were not alone in their attitudes about women and sports. For centuries, the words "sports" and "athletics" were viewed as synonymous with men and with manly activities and attributes. Sports required strength, speed, power, and a muscular physique; competition in

sports required one to be outgoing and aggressive. These traits were traditionally considered to be masculine and manly.

In addition, sports and athletic contests were public pursuits that put the physical body on display. Again, this was something that most societies deemed appropriate for men but not women, who were relegated to the home, where they carried out domestic roles and duties.

Underlying these negative attitudes and prohibitions about women and sports were certain fears and concerns. Men did not want their roles and superiority in the physical realm to be challenged or usurped. And sports, especially team sports, had become a cherished male domain. Many men enjoyed being in an all-male setting where they were free to behave differently than they would if ladies were present.

People also worried about the sexual consequences of women displaying themselves in physical ways. They believed such activities might arouse sexual feelings in the women themselves and in spectators, leading to immoral activities that would disrupt the social order. They also feared that if women became too physical or sports-minded, they might develop confusion about their sexual identity.

To justify their attitudes or because they sincerely believed what they were saying, physicians, educators, and others who wanted women to avoid sports claimed it would damage their health. Traditional views held that women were frail and delicate compared to men. Their bodies were not built to withstand the same kind of training and exertion.

Besides, women were child-bearers and thus had a special duty not to damage their reproductive systems. Through the years, various "experts" explained how athletic activities would harm a woman's organs and put her at risk for injuries. Jumping, running, or horseback riding might jar or displace her pelvic organs. Team sports might lead to blows on the breasts or abdomen.

Strenuous exercises were also believed to lead to nervous diseases, and women were regarded as mentally and emotionally less stable than men. In all ways— physical, mental, and emotional—they were considered "the weaker sex."

Women themselves had doubts about how they would look while engaging in sports. Moving quickly, playing aggressively, and sweating, for example, were regarded as "unladylike." Vigorous activity could lead to a disheveled, and therefore undesirable, appearance. Seeking to win and showing off one's skills went against the idea of modesty, deemed a desirable feminine trait. Fears of being called unladylike were especially strong among middle-class women. Many upper-class women had the means and social status to defy conventions, and lower-class women often had less to lose.

Around the world, through laws and social pressure, women were kept out of sports or discouraged from taking part. Women who defied local customs risked criticism and other negative consequences. They might be considered unsuitable mates, which was a serious matter in those days when marriage was the major or only acceptable means of economic support for women.

Making Inroads: Sports Appropriate for "Ladies"

It is not surprising that the first sports to gain acceptance among women were golf, croquet, and archery. These sports did not involve physical contact among participants and could be played without straining. They allowed women to wear conventional clothing.

Most women engaging in these sports were members of the upper classes, since wealthy people had the leisure time to pursue sports, as well as more money for equipment. Also, they had access to the kinds of facilities needed to play sports like golf. Golf developed an elite following and was popular among members of country clubs. Mary, Queen of Scots, is known to have played golf during the 1500s, but more than three centuries passed before many women took up the sport or were officially allowed on golf courses. Archery, popular with Queen Victoria during the 1800s, attracted a number of women, again, generally the wealthy. It was possible for women to shoot arrows at a target quietly while maintaining the accepted feminine demeanor and attire.

Lawn croquet was the first game played by both men and women together in North America. The "gentle game of croquet," as it was called, became popular at picnics and garden parties and was also played at exclusive clubs or on manicured lawns at private homes. As more and more people took up croquet during the 1860s, croquet clubs were formed and less affluent people also took up the game.

New ideas about the health benefits of physical fitness brought more women into sports and exercise classes conducted in educational settings. In the early 1830s, Catharine Beecher, director of an all-girls' school in Hartford, Connecticut, advocated physical education and exercise for women. The calisthenics program at Beecher's school became a model for other private girls' schools and colleges around America. Beecher advised all Americans to engage in vigorous exercise at least one or two hours each day.

During the late 1880s, women were taking up new sports in their leisure time. Girls and women of different classes enjoyed roller skating and ice skating. Roller skating became so popular during the 1880s that businessmen across the United States invested more than $20 million into building rinks, and most cities and towns had at least one rink. Lawn tennis was considered appropriate for women so long as they did not play too aggressively and wore clothing that covered their bodies. Like golf, tennis was often played at private clubs or country homes where people had the space and money to build courts and the leisure time to play.

Bicycles and Bloomers

With the arrival of the bicycle in the late 1800s, women of all classes found new freedom and pleasure in a sport. Bicycling became both an important form of transportation and a popular pastime for individuals, families, and groups. Working girls, representing an increasing percentage of the American population, delighted in the mobility they gained from their bicycles.

However, an immediate problem presented itself: What was the female cyclist to wear, since the long skirts of that era were bound to get tangled in the pedals and spokes of the wheels?

For centuries, women had been dressed for inaction, not physical movement. Until recent decades, women's clothing covered most of their bodies and styles restricted freedom of movement. During the mid-1800s, women wore voluminous, hooped skirts that reached the ankle, wide long sleeves, and layers of undergarments. Cumbersome clothing also often aimed to influence a woman's shape. Whalebone corsets pinched women's waists to make them unnaturally small. Tight-waisted garments caused many women to experience episodes of faintness, dizziness, and shortness of breath, and long skirts were inconvenient for certain activities. The rumblings of discontent grew louder as women sought more comfort and freedom of movement.

Then, some women openly rebelled and spoke out for change. In 1851, Amelia Bloomer and her supporters suggested that women should adopt a freer style of dress consisting of wide pants beneath a loose-fitting dress. They were ridiculed by other women as well as men. However, a number of women embraced the "Bloomer Costume" and the newfound freedom it gave them.

The bloomer was welcomed by women's rights advocates as well as women who enjoyed cycling, horseback riding, gymnastics, and skating. Thousands of women in the United States and Europe adopted the new style, and some formed Bloomer Clubs where they discussed politics and other issues of the day.

Amelia Bloomer had clearly struck a

nerve. Both cycling and bloomers came to symbolize a new spirit in America and were linked to the broader social efforts of the suffragist movement as women struggled for the right to vote. Suffragist leader Elizabeth Cady Stanton said, "Many a woman is riding to suffrage on a bicycle."[1] Women now were free not only to move around on their own power, they also had defied conventions about what women should wear. The bicycle, bloomers, and politics had become connected, just as women's pursuit of athletic equality would be tied to their pursuit of equality in other arenas during the years that followed.

In 1891, Frances Willard, a leader in the women's suffrage movement, addressed these issues while speaking to the National Council of Women of the United States:

> Be it remembered that until woman comes into her kingdom physically, she will never really come at all. She has made of herself an hour-glass, whose sands of life pass quickly by. She has walked when she should have run, sat when she should have walked, reclined when she should have sat.... She is a creature born to the beauty and freedom of Diana, but she is swathed by her skirts, splintered by her stays, bandaged by her tight waist, and pinioned by her sleeves until...a trussed turkey or a spitted goose are her most appropriate emblems.[2]

The progress of women in sports paralleled the liberation of women in other spheres. As women began to question old ideas about their roles and to insist that they had certain rights—to vote, to own property, to pursue higher education, to choose jobs and professions outside the home, to plan the size of their families—so, too, did they question the old ideas about what kinds of physical activities were open to women.

Testing New Limits

By the late 1800s, women who loved bowling, tennis, and golf increasingly sought places to enjoy these sports, as well as the chance to compete. In 1891, the Shinnecock Hills golf club on Long Island, New York, permitted women to come to the course along with their player-husbands. Wives who wanted to play golf themselves convinced the club's owners to build a women's nine-hole course. In 1894, women competed in the first tournament to determine a U.S. women's amateur golf champion.

Women took up more taxing sports as well. Rowing either alone or in groups, "lady scullers," as they were called, often took part in races sponsored by their colleges or in their communities. In one 1870 race outside Pittsburgh, Lottie McAlice, winner of a one-mile rowing race, received a substantial prize—a gold watch and $2,000 in cash. On the East Coast, two baseball teams called the Blondes and Brunettes attracted fans to their exhibition matches during the 1880s.

A sport called pedestrianism also attracted many people during the 1870s. These long walking contests allowed women to demonstrate their endurance as they covered distances of several miles, both in city and rural areas. Some of these walking races pitted women and men against each other.

During these years, women founded their own sports organizations, sometimes aided by men, other times on their own. Women bowlers were among the first to organize. Many bowling alleys of the early 1900s were dingy places where men smoked, drank, and placed bets. Other owners maintained clean, reputable alleys and tried to attract bowlers of both sexes. In 1907, Dennis J. Sweeney, a proprietor in St. Louis, Missouri, started the first women's bowling leagues. Nine years later, Sweeney held an informal national women's tournament. Bowling became a popular way to spend an evening out. Married couples bowled together, often eating at the bowling center's restaurant. Women also bowled together during the daytime.

Although bloomers had become more acceptable by this time, sports clothing for women was still often restrictive and uncomfortable. Women tennis players wore clothing that might startle and amuse young people of today. Player Violet Sutton describes the required dress: "It was a wonder we could move at all. We wore a long undershirt, pair of drawers, two petticoats, white linen corset cover, duck shirt, shirtwaist, long white silk stockings, and a floppy hat. We were soaking wet when we finished a match."[3]

Physical education for women, conducted in same-sex classes only, now included dancing and movements resembling dancing. Gymnastics, which fit this ideal, grew to be an acceptable form of exercise for women. Of course, women taking part in gymnastics were covered from head to toe in costumes that might consist of a sailor blouse, knee-length bloomers, and tights.

Women in tennis and gymnastics eventually adopted clothing that enabled them to move more freely, as did other pioneering women in bowling, swim-ming, and other sports. Their efforts required courage and determination. Change did not come easily.

A few daring women attempted feats that nobody, male or female, had tried. In 1901, Annie Edson Taylor, a 43-year-old widow and schoolteacher from Bay City, Michigan, decided to go over Niagara Falls in a barrel. The oaken barrel was about four and a half feet high, bound on the outside with metal hoops and lined with leather. When Taylor emerged alive after her trip down the falls, she was somewhat dazed and had suffered cuts and bruises. Despite her amazing and courageous achievement, Taylor never became wealthy or famous and died in poverty in 1921.

During the early 1900s, team sports for women increased as well. More women were playing basketball in teams organized by the Young Men's Christian Association (YMCA) and Young Women's Christian Association (YWCA), city recreation departments, churches, and industry. Young women were invited to join their companies' industrial basketball leagues and play against teams from other companies.

Minority Women Break Barriers

African Americans, excluded by law and by custom from national competitions and organized white athletic programs, formed their own teams and leagues. Basketball games and track-and-field competitions became regular community events, drawing large, enthusiastic crowds.

Track-and-field events were especially popular in low-income communities, since they cost less for participants than many other sports. By the late 1920s, African American colleges, trade schools, and other schools had organized inter-scholastic leagues, such as the Georgia–Carolina College League.

A group of African American women played baseball on a team called Madame J. H. Caldwell's Chicago Bloomer Girls. The team "barnstormed," playing against any team, black or white, male or female, who wished to challenge them. Spectators paid 25 cents a ticket to see the Bloomer Girls, and this money was used to help the team travel to other states.

Some middle-class black citizens built private clubs where they played tennis and other sports. Amateur matches for both men and women players were held during the summer in Chicago, New York, and other cities.

Newspapers in the black community covered women's sports, exalting in the success of local athletes. Like the white-dominated media, black newspapers gave women less attention than they devoted to male athletes and men's events. However, a number of black women athletes were well-known to the public. In 1927, a newspaper for African Americans, *The Defender,* asked readers to name the most popular athletes, and 5 of the top 17 were women. They included Mrs. C. O. ("Mother") Seames, a tennis player and instructor, and a basketball player named Virginia Willis.

Not only did African Americans enjoy the chance to develop their skills and compete in organized sports, they welcomed the chance to show that they were as capable as whites when given an equal chance. As black and white track teams in northern states began competing against each other and black athletes competed on U.S. Olympic teams, African American leaders pointed to athletics as a key element in the struggle toward equality in all areas of life. Inroads on the playing field might lead to progress in other areas, they declared.[4]

Trailblazers

Between 1900 and 1930, the number of Americans participating in sports increased greatly. Most of these athletes were men, and some, like baseball player Babe Ruth and golfer Bobby Jones, reached the status of national heroes.

During these years, women were bowling and competing in track-and-field and figure-skating events. They played golf, tennis, and basketball, in the latter case following different rules than those in the men's game. As more and more women of all ages took up sports, American magazines and newspapers began to take notice of what they called "the new athletic girl."[5] Journalists praised her rosy glow, healthful appearance, and easy movements.

One of the most original and determined of these new athletic women was Eleonora Sears, a member of a prominent and wealthy Boston family. There seemed to be no sport "Eleo" would not try on land or sea—tennis, polo, race-car driving, swimming, diving, fishing, shooting, canoeing, horseback riding. She did so many things well that in 1910 a magazine called Sears "the best all around athlete in society."[6]

With her secure social position, self-assurance, and rare physical talents, Sears was well-situated to flout convention. Yet through the years, she endured severe criticism. For example, in 1912, while traveling through Burlingame, California, Sears tried to join a practice session being held by a men's polo team. When she rode onto the field astride her horse and wearing jodphurs, spectators gasped to see a woman dressed in men's-wear and who had, furthermore, abandoned the accepted side-saddle position. The polo team refused her requests to play with them.

After the incident, ministers around the country derided Sears in their sermons. The Burlingame Mothers' Club passed a resolution urging that Sears "restrict herself to the normal feminine attire in the future."[7] True to form, Sears did not comply but took to wearing trousers not only on horseback but on other occasions. She developed her own manner of dress for other sports as well. Later in her life, Sears distinguished herself as a squash player and marathon walker.

Women of more modest means were pursuing sports in larger numbers, too. Organized competition in swimming, track, tennis, golf, basketball, riflery, and bowling sponsored by industrial leagues provided inexpensive entertainment in rural areas and other communities across America. During these years, the work week was becoming shorter, so people had more leisure time.

In the sport of bowling, women used the same alleys men did and followed the same rules and scoring system. Talented Floretta McCutcheon of Denver, Colorado, was among those who defeated male competitors. In 1927, at age 39, she won a well-publicized match against top men's bowler Jimmy Smith, considered one of the greatest bowlers of all time. In six games she earned 1,377 points to his 1,376. McCutcheon traveled around America giving bowling demonstrations and taught classes where a number of other women learned the sport.

During these years, it became clear that many women rejected the physical limits that traditionally had been placed on them. They broke down barriers in other areas, too. In 1919, future Olympic medalist Ethelda Bleibtrey was cited by police at Manhattan Beach for "nude swimming" after she removed the stockings women were then expected to wear at the beach and in the water. Bleibtrey received a great deal of public support. Soon stockings were no longer part of women's bathing costumes. During that same decade, Annette Kellerman had spurned the long, billowy bathing suits of the day for streamlined suits without sleeves or skirts so that she could move faster through the water. Tennis player Mary K. Browne wrote articles describing how sports and exercise would help women to develop slim, fit bodies that suited the short, revealing fashions of the "Roaring Twenties."[8]

Some people were horrified at the competitive atmosphere that was developing in organized sports for women. They disliked the idea of girls or women competing with men or being watched by audiences that included men. They also criticized sports events where women were featured in beauty contests as part of the festivities.

Among those who protested girls' basketball teams playing at the same events as boys' teams was Lou Henry Hoover, wife of Herbert C. Hoover, who would serve as U.S. president from 1928 to 1932. In 1923, Lou Hoover headed a national committee to investigate these mixed-gender sports events. She worked to end the practice of double-headers and the presence of male spectators at women's events. Later, Hoover directed the Women's Committee of the National Amateur Athletic Federation, which believed that strong competition in women's sports would lead to commercialization and exploitation of women.

Among the public, however, there was more acceptance of women athletes. By the 1920s and 1930s, tennis player Helen Wills, golfer Glenna Collett, and swimmer Annette Kellerman were among the athletes viewed as heroines, much like popular movie actresses. The media favored swimmers, tennis players, figure skaters, and golfers. Some were photographed and featured in newspapers and magazines endorsing commercial products.

Women had other athletic role models during the 1930s. The Norwegian figure skater and three-time Olympic gold medalist Sonja Henie started a boom in her sport and became a multi-millionaire, starring in Hollywood films and ice shows that toured the world. The pioneer aviator Amelia Earhart had replicated the daring cross-Atlantic solo flight of Charles Lindbergh and was often in the news. A popular series of mystery novels for young girls featured Nancy Drew, a lively, independent teenage detective who was also an accomplished athlete.

Women athletes offered new opinions about women and sports. In 1932, Helen Wills wrote, "The feminine mind in sports reflects the general trend of feminine thinking of the day. The ideas and, along with them, the inhibitions imposed upon us by previous generations are being dispelled."[9]

Critics continued to advocate moderate exercise for women in a non-competitive atmosphere. People also expressed fears that the boundaries between men and women were being blurred and would lead to social problems. When women pushed for more rights in various areas of life, it challenged old ideas about the proper roles, traits, and balance of power between the sexes. These concerns were reflected in the media. For example, a 1912 issue of *The Ladies Home Journal* featured an article titled "Are Athletics Making Girls Masculine?" The debate went on into the 1920s, as shown by many articles from those years. One article in the November 1928 issue of *Hygeia Magazine* listed the ill effects of competitive sports for women, saying, "Girls are nervously more unstable than men and are consequently more affected in the way of distraction from their studies, in the loss of sleep before and after games, and in general nervous injuries."[10]

The Struggle for Olympic Glory

When a French sports lover, Baron de Coubertin, revived the Olympics and organized the first modern games in 1896, it was, like the ancient games, for men only. Women were, however, allowed to watch. De Coubertin echoed the sentiments of many people when he said, "Let women practice all the sports if they wish, but let them not show off."[11]

Even in ancient times, some women had rejected the idea that sports should remain outside their realm of interest or their abilities. When they were banned from the ancient Olympics, some Greek women organized their own events in honor of the goddess Hera, queen of the Olympian gods. Every four years, the women athletes, wearing tunics, competed in a foot race. The winners received crowns of olive wreaths.

By the 1920s, the Amateur Athletic Union (AAU) broke its former men-only policy and began developing programs for women and girls in swimming, track, and other sports. Many women also wanted to take part in more events at the Olympics. Critics had difficulty justifying keeping them out as more and more women showed that they would not accept their second-class status and began achieving athletic feats that had once been thought impossible.

Aileen Riggin, who won gold medals in diving and swimming at the 1920 Olympics, later recalled,

We learned that women might participate in the Games in the spring of 1920. The American Olympic Committee and the various affiliated groups were not in favor of sending women at all. In those days women did not compete in strenuous athletics. No one swam very far. It was not considered healthy for girls to overexert themselves or to swim as far as a mile. People thought that it was a great mistake, that we were ruining our health, that we would never have children, and that we would be sorry for it later on. There was a great deal of publicity against women competing in athletics at all. We had to combat this feeling at every turn. Many of the coaches on the Olympic team for men decided that they did not wish to be "hampered" by having women athletes on the team, and many of the officials felt the same way. It took a great deal of persuasion by the American women to convince them to let us participate in the Olympics at all.[12]

As the years went on, more events for women were added to the Olympic Games. Women competed in track and field for the first time in 1928, and the amazing Babe Didrikson first gained national prominence four years later at the 1932 Olympics in Los Angeles. Starting with high-jumper Alice Coachman

(1948), African American women would win numerous medals in track and field, especially top athletes from Tuskegee Institute and Tennessee State's Tigerbelles. Among the most famous Tigerbelles were Wilma Rudolph, who won three gold medals at the 1960 Games, and Wyomia Tyus, who won gold medals in the 100-meter race in both 1964 and 1968.

Toward Recognition and Equal Pay

By mid-century women were well-accepted at the Olympics and had made inroads in many sports. However, some still struggled to break new ground, even in male-dominated sports like bullfighting and wrestling. Horse racing and auto racing were among the sports that continued to reject women, and several women fought for the chance to compete in these arenas.

At the local level, girls who wanted to play on Little League baseball teams or on school-sponsored soccer, baseball, tennis, or basketball teams were usually disappointed. The vast majority of money allocated to sports programs in elementary and secondary schools and colleges and universities went to men's programs. Most women were also excluded from fields related to sports, such as coaching, training, administration, sportswriting, and sportscasting.

A glance through magazines, newspapers, and books written in the 1950s and early 1960s shows that male athletes still received far more acclaim and attention than women. For example, in a 1965 book, *Pictorial History of American Sports*, fewer than a dozen pages in the 307-page volume deal with individual women athletes, women's teams, or the history of women and sports. One section of the book on women athletes refers to them as "the fair ones" and focuses as much on their physical traits as their athletic achievements.

Women athletes resented getting short shrift from the press. In the early 1970s, a high-school student complained to the *Washington Post:* "Girls' high school basketball scores are completely ignored in your paper while boys' high school basketball is given 500-word articles.... [Girls' basketball] is an exciting spectator sport with a four-month season that is of interest to thousands of Washington-area students, including boys."[13]

Besides not receiving as much attention, women athletes complained about the limited number of tournaments and the low earning potential in various sports. For instance, in 1972, the top woman bowler earned $11,200, while the men's top winner bagged $69,000. Men had five times more tournaments to compete in annually. This imbalance existed in tennis, golf, and other sports, too. At some national and international tournaments, women winners received less in prize money than men who won corresponding titles.

These inequities prompted women athletes to organize. They were aided by the growing women's liberation movement. During the 1950s, African Americans had built a nationwide movement for civil rights and an end to segregation and discrimination in housing, education, public transportation, and other areas of life. In the wake of this movement, other groups, such as Native Americans and women, also spoke out against the unjust ways in which they had long been treated. Federal laws, including the Civil Rights Act of 1964, were passed to end some of these injustices.

Tennis player Billie Jean King became one of the most vocal and devoted spokespersons for women and sports. King led protests against unequal treatment, organized women tennis players, and helped to found the Virginia Slims tour, as well as World Team Tennis. In addition, she was one of the founders of *womenSports*, the first magazine devoted exclusively to women's athletics, and the Women's Sports Foundation. Reaching out to women in other sports, King helped to start a professional women's basketball league. She managed to do all this in addition to playing world-class tennis until she retired in her late thirties.

Women activists were gratified when Congress passed Title IX as part of a broader education bill in 1972. Discrimination on the basis of sex was thus banned in educational institutions receiving federal funds. Changes made it possible for more girls and women to compete in school-sponsored athletics, but such changes occurred unevenly throughout the country. Old walls came down as the Little League was reorganized to welcome girls' teams as well as boys'.

More athletic scholarships became available for young women, and their participation in high-school sports rose 500 percent between the early 1960s and the early 1980s.

The decade of the seventies would become remarkable for its many firsts— first woman to race at the Indianapolis 500 (Janet Guthrie); first woman in professional football (Pat Palinkas); first woman instructor at a municipal golf course (Helen Gilligan Finn, in New York City); first woman finisher in the Boston Marathon (Nina Kuscik); first girl to play with boys in the Babe Ruth Baseball League (Yvonne Burch); and many others.

Introduction

New Role Models

As the women's movement gained steam, the media offered new images of strong and athletic women in films and on television. During the 1970s, one of the top-rated television series, *Charlie's Angels*, featured attractive female detectives who not only caught criminals but showed off skills in tennis, skating, swimming, golf, the martial arts, football, basketball, and other sports. Popular actresses and models could be seen playing different sports and taking part in celebrity tennis and golf matches. The message was that sports could be "feminine."

During the fitness boom of the seventies, many celebrities marketed videotapes that showed their fitness routines. Clothing manufacturers also capitalized on the boom, offering women many choices and innovative designs in athletic attire. There was a profitable market for clothing to be used for exercising, skiing, swimming, cycling, and racquet sports. Besides the traditional white tennis dress, women could now choose pastels or bright colors for their one- or two-piece outfits. Warm-up suits that people could wear en route to the gym, club, or field also sold by the millions. Sports were not only fun, they were now quite fashionable. The pale, subdued, rounded woman of past centuries had given way to a new ideal: fit, trim, athletic.

The athletes of the late twentieth century were reaching out in other ways. Olympic gold medalist Jackie Joyner-Kersee used her influence to found the Jackie Joyner-Kersee Foundation, which developed community programs and funded scholarships for young people. Joyner-Kersee also worked with children's sports teams in her hometown, St. Louis, Missouri. She said that during her own childhood, she was inspired by athletes Wilma Rudolph, Babe Didrikson, and Flo Hyman, and by the great civil rights leader Rosa Parks.[14]

As the twenty-first century neared, women athletes were being interviewed more often on television and in the print media, and more women had become regular sportscasters and TV commentators, on the local level as well as for the major networks. In 1996, NBC-TV hired an all-woman team made up of Billie Jean King, Martina Navratilova, and Mary Carillo to commentate on the women's matches at Wimbledon.

More women also became coaches and administrators of sports programs in schools, colleges, and universities. In some cases, women coached teams made up of boys or boys and girls. Between 1971 and 1992, the number of girls taking part in interscholastic sports at high schools rose from 300,000 to more than 2 million.[15]

More women played intercollegiate sports, too, as these numbers rose from 16,000 in the early 1970s to more than 160,000 in the late 1980s. By the 1990s, women made up more than 34 percent of all intercollegiate athletes and received about one-third of all athletic scholarships. They were also well-represented in master's sports for older athletes and competitive events for athletes with disabilities. As a result, young women who came of age after the 1960s were used to seeing women athletes in various sports and related fields.

Recent Trends and Issues

Although women athletes continued to break new ground, there have been setbacks. Between 1980 and 1988, President Ronald Reagan's administration reduced the number of personnel who examined complaints and infractions relating to Title IX. As a result, there was less rigorous enforcement of this law. In the 1983 case *Grove City College v. Bell*, the U.S. Supreme Court ruled that Title IX only applied to those specific programs that received federal funds, even if the school received some federal funding for general use. This ruling disappointed advocates for women in sports.

While more women had become involved in more aspects of athletics than back in the 1960s, women were still not on par with men. As of 1993, college athletic departments still awarded about twice as much money in scholarships to men as to women, even though women made up at least half of the college population. Colleges were also spending more to recruit male athletes, and most programs were run by men. In many schools, female athletes did not receive the same quality of uniforms or equipment, and their facilities were inferior to those used by men.

During the 1990s, the Women's Sports Foundation, American Civil Liberties Union (ACLU), National Organization for Women (NOW), and other advocacy groups continued to watch out for inequitable treatment and illegal acts by schools and colleges. They were also concerned about discrimination against women on the basis of race. In 1995, when *Sports Illustrated* listed its "forty most influential athletes between 1955–1995," no African American woman was on the list. Black women athletes also have not been offered as many commercial endorsements, with only a few of the most remarkable achievers being chosen.

Speaking philosophically about this situation, Jackie Joyner-Kersee has said,

> I feel that as an African-American woman the only thing I can do is continue to better myself, continue to perform well, continue to make sure that I'm a good commodity. If doors aren't opened for me, then maybe it will happen for someone else. I hope someone who's watching me is also educating herself about what she can do to be consistent, what she can do to provide a message, what she can do to deliver a commodity as I've tried to do.[16]

Among those for whom doors opened in 1995 was basketball player Sheryl Swoopes. A star on the team at Texas Tech, she became the first woman to have a pair of athletic shoes named for her when Nike introduced its black-and-white, high-top design Air Swoopes. These shoes began appearing on gymnasium floors across America.

As a new century loomed, women were talking more about what they could contribute to sports that would be unique, redefining what is feminine and womanly to include physical strength and athletic prowess. Mary Jo Peppler, a top volleyball player and coach, is one who believes that sports and femininity can exist in harmony. She says, "Women must shape their own amateur and professional sports so that they are consistent with positive female values."[17] Peppler believes that certain traits common to women help them more in sports—for instance, the idea that movements contribute to skills rather than a common male view, that movements are a means of showing off and gaining recognition. "Women appreciate power more as it relates to performance of skill than to ego supremacy. As a result, I believe that women are easily channeled toward skills, finesse, and energy," says Peppler.[18] She also thinks women should strive to reach their personal goals in sports rather than viewing supremacy as the main goal. "Women should not have to be concerned with becoming 'equal' to men in sports. Women's sports should not mold themselves after male models. . . . Positive dynamics of the feminine contribution to sports must be identified and developed."[19]

Going along with this is the idea that in some sports, men and women may compete on the same terms, whereas in others, it is more fruitful to separate them. Among the sports in which women and men have often achieved similar results are bowling, golf, fox hunting, equestrian events, thoroughbred racing, shooting, auto racing, billiards, diving, and marathon running. These sports require various skills and do not rely just on physical strength.

Fitness expert Gordon Richards has developed different ways of blending and separating the sexes for different sports activities. Richards says, "I do this by designing, say, a day's hike where the girls and boys follow separate routes of different distances and degrees of difficulty in the morning. But then they meet up in order to finish off the day's activities together. I can't envision a mixed rugby team, but I can envision men and women's teams training together, especially on the basics of passing and kicking. . . ."[20]

Says author Paul Wade, "The liberation of women in sport is only a step towards complete integration, where men and women will learn to take part in sport in the most natural way possible—with their families."[21]

Advocates of sports for women point out that sports offer benefits to all people, regardless of gender: promoting physical fitness and skills, increasing self-confidence, building social skills and the ability to work with a team, and showing the importance of working toward a goal and improving one's personal best. Taking part in sports shows girls that they are as important as boys and can have an active, not just supporting, role.

Research shows that, on average, female athletes also have higher grades in school and attain higher scores on achievement tests, besides showing more self-reliance and self-confidence than girls and women who are not involved in athletics. They are less likely to become unwed teenage mothers or to abuse illegal drugs.

Many women athletes cite the feeling of self-confidence as one of the greatest benefits they have derived from their involvement in sports. Control over the body and physical strength, say sports advocates, are empowering. Women will never fully develop their potential in other areas unless they also develop their physical potential.

• • • •

Before he played in the famous televised "Battle of the Sexes" tennis match against Billie Jean King, Bobby Riggs said of his opponent, "She's a great player for a gal. But no woman can beat a male player who knows what he's doing. I'm not only interested in glory for my sex, but I also want to set women's lib back twenty years, to get women back into the home, where they belong."[22]

Introduction

On September 20, 1973, as millions watched the King-Riggs match on television, King won in straight sets, 6-4, 6-3, 6-3. Around the country, women cheered, and many collected on bets.

Billie Jean King chose not to stay home where Bobby Riggs said she belonged. Nor have the millions of other women who believe that they, too, belong on the playing fields, tracks, slopes, rinks, arenas, and courts, as well as in homes, schools, offices, operating rooms, halls of Congress, and other places.

The process of gaining acceptance for women in sports has been a slow but steady one. This book shows how women have fought against old prejudices to become contenders as individuals and on teams in national and international competitions. It describes the ways in which individuals and groups have fought for the chance to earn a living at their chosen sports and to gain recognition from the media and the public. That process is ever-evolving, as many women overcome social obstacles as well as the challenges of developing skills in their sports. Women have taken enormous risks and experienced the failure and success that go with competition, as well as exhilaration and satisfaction along the way.

Notes

1. Elizabeth Cady Stanton, *Reminiscences of Elizabeth Cady Stanton* (London: T. Fisher Unwin, 1898), p. 51.

2. Diana Nyad, *Other Shores* (New York: Random House, 1978).

3. Grace Lichtenstein, *A Long Way, Baby* (New York: Morrow, 1974), p. 138.

4. Charles Anderson, *The New York News*, 21 Aug. 1919: Editorial (From the Tuskegee Institute Archives, News Clippings).

5. Anna de Koven, "The Athletic Woman," *Good Housekeeping*, August 1912, pp. 151–152.

6. Phyllis Hollander, *American Women in Sports* (New York: Grosset and Dunlap, 1972), p. 59.

7. Ibid.

8. "Fit to Win," *Collier's*, 16 October 1926, p. 16.

9. Interview: *The Saturday Evening Post*, 28 May 1932, p. 29.

10. *Hygeia Magazine*, November 1928.

11. Audrey Osofsky, "Let Them Not Show Off," *Cobblestone*, August 1984, p. 18.

12. Lewis H. Carlson and John J. Fogarty, *Tales of Gold* (New York: Basic Books, 1987), p. 15.

13. George Sullivan, *Better Basketball For Girls* (New York: Dodd, Mead, 1981), p. 6.

14. Interview with Jackie Joyner-Kersee: *Women's Sports and Fitness*, Jan./Feb. 1995, p. 21.

15. "Shooting for Equality," *Scholastic Update*, 1 May 1992, pp. 24–25.

16. Interview: *Women's Sports and Fitness*, Jan./Feb. 1995, p. 22.

17. Mary Jo Peppler, *Inside Volleyball for Women* (Chicago: Henry Regnery, 1977), p. 5.

18. Ibid.

19. Ibid.

20. Paul Wade, with photography by Tony Duffy, *Winning Women: The Changing Image of Women in Sports* (New York: Quadrangle, 1983), p. 123.

21. Wade and Duffy, p. 127.

22. George Gipe, *The Great American Sports Book* (Garden City, New York: Doubleday, 1978), p. 345.

A

Aarons, Ruth Hughes (b. 1915)
One of the best table tennis (Ping-Pong) players in history, Hall-of-Famer Aarons won her first U.S. national women's singles title in 1934 and held that title through 1937. She and Anne Sigman won the women's U.S. doubles title in 1936. During four years of top tournament play, Aarons never lost a match.

In the early 1900s, Asian and Eastern European players dominated international table tennis competitions. In 1936 Aarons, a native of New York City, became the first American to win the world championship singles title. As of 1995, no one from the United States, man or woman, had since won a world singles title in the sport of table tennis. While competing in Europe, the teenage champion was impressed at how seriously Europeans played this sport.

Aarons was part of the 1937 U.S. women's team that won the Corbillon Cup, awarded to the team that wins the world championship. From 1934 to 1937, the versatile champion also won the world mixed doubles title every year, playing with four different male partners.

See also Table Tennis
Reference Boggan, *History of U.S. Table Tennis, Vol. 1* (1996).

Abbott, Margaret (1878–1955)
Called "a fierce competitor" and praised for her backswing, Abbott won the women's golf event in the 1900 Olympics, one of the two events that was open to women for the first time that year. She thus became the first American woman to win a gold medal at the Olympics. A native of Chicago, Abbott was attending art school in Paris, France, where the 1900 Olympic Games were being held. She and nine other women entered the nine-hole golf event and Abbott defeated her competitors with her score of 47. She received a porcelain bowl mounted in gold for her prize. The golf competition for women was discontinued after these Olympic Games, but Abbott continued to play recreational golf.

Reference Leder, *Grace and Glory: A Century of Women at the Olympics* (1996).

Ackerman, Phyllis (b. 1940)
In 1974, Ackerman became the first woman to provide professional sports commentary on a men's professional basketball team. A former schoolteacher, Ackerman had never appeared on television. She was chosen from among 178 other applicants by a local Indiana station to commentate on the Indiana Pacers, a team in the American Basketball Association (ABA).

Adamek, Donna (b. 1957)
Champion bowler Adamek earned the nickname "Mighty Mite" shortly after she began bowling at age ten. She went on to become one of only four women ever to bowl three perfect games. From

1978 through 1981, she was four times named Woman Bowler of the Year.

The native of Duarte, California, started on the women's professional bowling circuit at age 19. By 21, Adamek had been named Woman Bowler of the Year. She was the Women's International Bowling Congress Queens tournament winner in both 1979 (with an average score of 218) and 1980. She won the All-Star U.S. Women's Open tournament in 1978 and 1981 with an average score of 201.10 the latter year. Partnered with Dorothy Fothergill, Adamek won the Brunswick Great and Greatest titles in 1979. She captured her fifteenth Ladies Professional Bowling Tournament title in 1983.

See also Fothergill, Dorothy

Aerial Sports

During the early 1900s, a few women pioneers became pilots. Women have also taken to the air as balloonists, skydivers, parachutists, and in hot-air airships, among other things. One of America's top women balloonists, Denise Wiederkehr of Minnesota, broke both a time and distance record when she flew from Lakeland, Minnesota, to Waupon, Wisconsin. She covered the 228 miles in 11 hours and 20 minutes. The Kentucky Fried Chicken corporation hired Wiederkehr to promote its produce by flying a chicken-shaped balloon over cities throughout the United States.

The first woman to earn the U.S. Parachute Association's 36-hour freefall badge was Carolyn Clay of Williamsburg, Virginia. Clay achieved 100 hours of accumulated freefall time, earning her the nickname "the Queen."

During the early 1990s, American Cheryl Stearns, a US Air pilot from Raeford, North Carolina, was regarded as the world's top skydiver. By 1996, Stearns

had broken three world records: number of jumps in a 24-hour period, highest number of dead-center jumps in a 24-hour period, and highest number of jumps for women in a 24-hour period.

Dale Stuart, an aerospace engineer who graduated from the Massachusetts Institute of Technology, was the Women's Aerial Freestyle Champion from 1990 to 1994. Stuart wrote *The Aerial Freestyle Guidebook* and promoted her sport during television, movie, and video appearances, and in magazine interviews.

The Misty Blues, an all-woman demonstration team organized by Sandra Williams of Florida, have appeared all over the world at air shows. Williams has also organized five women's world-record skydiving events.

A number of women have taken up skydiving. In 1993, a group of South Carolina skydivers jumped from 18,000 feet. Among the 200 chutists were four husband-wife teams. The women were Cynthia Bigson, Amy Goriesky, Robyn Linaberry, and Suzanne Pike. On August 14, 1993, at Le Luc, France, an all-women, multinational skydiving team organized by American Alexis Perry broke world records. They achieved a free-fall parachutist star formation of 100 divers. On October 10, 1993, American Lillian Goodin was one of the leaders of a record-breaking group in Richland, Washington, in which 38 people completed a canopy formation, in which divers hold onto one another after chutes have opened. In 1994, several women were part of the Diamond Quest group of 46 skydivers who set a new record for canopy relative work in Davis, California.

See also Aerobatics; Air Derby, Women's; Crosson, Marvel; Earhart, Amelia; Stearns, Cheryl
References United States Parachute Association, "Skydiver Targets Five New World Records" (October 1995).

Aerobatics

The sport of aerobatics evolved from stunt flying. It requires pilots to perform complicated maneuvers in the air using specially designed, small, powerful aircraft. Since 1960, a world aerobatics competition has been held every two years in either Europe or North America. Judges at aerobatics competitions score pilots' performances based on their movements in the air and how well they stay within the designated space. There are four categories or stages in competition: known, freestyle, unknown, and 4-minute flights.

Pilots who finish as one of the top five women or men in the unlimited (most advanced) national competitions are chosen for U.S. aerobatics teams, sponsored by the U.S. Aerobatics Foundation. In 1986 Debby Rihn was one of nine pilots who competed at the world competition in South Cerney, England. Rihn had placed third at the 1984 championships. Rihn and her team members Julie Pfile and Linda Meyers won a silver medal for the United States at that event, held in Hungary. In the last round of the 1986 competition, Meyers and Pfile won gold and silver medals. Pfile finished second among all the women, while Rihn finished sixth. The U.S. women's team as a whole came in second, after the Soviet Union team.

Aerobics

During the late 1960s, Americans became more concerned about physical fitness, taking up individual and team sports and starting exercise programs. Many were drawn to a type of exercise called aerobics, which grew more popular after Kenneth Cooper's book, *Aerobics*, became a bestseller. Aerobic exercise aims to improve cardiac output—the amount of blood pumped each minute—by strengthening the heart muscle. Stronger heart muscle can pump blood more efficiently, thus delivering oxygen throughout the body and improving the body's aerobic power or capacity. A number of studies showed that athletes trained in aerobics have a higher oxygen uptake (ability to use oxygen) than those who are untrained.

Aerobics, or aerobic exercise, became especially popular with women. One of its forms, a type called "Jazzercise," reminded many people of dance movements. New fitness clubs sprang up in cities across the country, and women were among the first aerobics instructors. After leading successful aerobics programs in Puerto Rico and New Jersey, Jacki Sorenson developed the Aerobic Dance Corporation in 1972. She became one of the leaders of the aerobic exercise movement. Aerobics classes were scheduled at various times, including evening sessions to fit women's work schedules. Videotapes of aerobic workouts also became quite popular for home use, a trend that continued into the 1990s.
See also Physical Fitness

Air Derby, Women's

The first women's cross country air derby, also called the Powder Puff Derby, was held on August 18, 1929, with 20 competitors, 18 of them from the United States. Flying alone (without mechanics on board), pilots raced a distance of 2,350 miles, from Santa Monica, California, to Cleveland, Ohio. There were two divisions in the race, one for heavier planes and one for lighter planes. Louise McPhetridge Thaden of Pittsburgh, Pennsylvania, won the heavier-plane race with a time of 20 hours, 19 minutes, 10 seconds. Phoebe Fairgrave Omlie of Memphis, Tennessee, won the lighter-plane race, finishing in 24 hours and 12 minutes. Fifteen pilots finished the race.

Throughout the nation, these women were known as Petticoat Pilots and Flying Flappers. They included Amelia Earhart and Ruth Nichols.

See also Crosson, Marvel; Earhart, Amelia

Akers-Stahl, Michelle (See Soccer World Championship, Women's)

Albright, Tenley (b. 1935)
From her first skating lessons, Tenley Emma Albright showed real talent, and her family could afford excellent instruction. But it was dedication and hard work that turned her into the first American woman to win the world figure skating championship and Olympic gold medal.

The Boston native took up figure skating at age eight, but the next year, she suffered from an attack of polio, a disease that attacks motor nerve tissues. She was left weakened but without any paralysis. She resumed skating, which helped to rebuild the strength in her back muscles. Seeing her natural ability, her surgeon father asked champion Maribel Vinson Owen to coach her. Later, Albright would also work with a world-famous Swiss coach, Gustave Lussi.

She won the Eastern Juvenile Girls' Championship at age 12 and became novice champion the next year. By 1952, at age 17, Albright won a silver medal in Oslo, Norway, at her first Olympic Games. Skating with strength, grace, and maturity, she became America's first women's world champion in 1953. Her performance earned such adjectives as "sparkling" and "flawless." She was praised for her clean lines on the ice and the definition she gave to the numerous difficult moves in her program.

Albright was now pursuing two dreams: to win the Olympics and to become a doctor. She juggled skating and premed studies at Radcliffe College by rising each day at 4 a.m. Trying to defend her world title in 1954, Albright fell during her free-skating routine and placed second. With determination, she regained her title the next year and headed for the 1956 Olympics with high hopes. In Cortina, Italy, Albright badly cut her ankle, and her father came to Europe to treat the injury. Despite the pain, Tenley Albright skated brilliantly during the final free-skating program and became the first American woman to win the gold.

Albright finished college in only three years. In 1961 she graduated from Harvard Medical School, then trained as a surgeon. She continued to skate for pleasure while practicing medicine, rearing three daughters, and teaching underprivileged children how to skate. She also skated in exhibitions for charity but never as a professional.

In 1976 Albright achieved another "first" when she became the first woman ever named to the U.S. Olympic Committee (USOC). Later, she also served on the International Olympic Committee (IOC). A pioneer in many areas, Albright was also the first woman named to the Harvard University Hall of Fame. She was inducted into the Ice Skating Hall of Fame (1974), the U.S. Figure Skating Hall of Fame (1976), the Women's Sports Hall of Fame (1983), and the Olympic Hall of Fame (1988). Albright has said that her experiences as an athlete helped to teach her the concentration and discipline she needed to succeed as a surgeon.

See also Figure Skating; Olympics, Winter; Vinson Owen, Maribel
References Bass, *The Love of Ice Skating and Speed Skating* (1980); Bortstein, *After Olympic Glory: The Lives of Ten Outstanding Medalists* (1987); Hollander, *American Women in Sports* (1972); Van Steenwyk, *Women in Sports: Figure Skating* (1976).

Alcott, Amy (b. 1956)

Golfer Alcott, a native of Kansas City, Missouri, was still a teenager when she achieved a score of only 70 on the arduous Pebble Beach golf course in California and broke a course record set for women in the 1940s by the legendary Babe Didrikson Zaharias.

In 1973 Alcott won the U.S. Junior Girls' title, then placed second in the Canadian Amateur tournament in 1974. She joined the Ladies Professional Golf Association (LPGA) tour in 1975 and was named Rookie of the Year for an outstanding performance that included winning the Orange Blossom Classic.

Alcott won the U.S. Women's Open in 1980, a year in which she achieved her best scoring average—71.51, which earned her the Vare Trophy. In 1983, she won another major tournament, the Nabisco–Dinah Shore Invitational, which she would also win in 1988 and 1991. The next year, Alcott won the Lady Keystone Open and set a tournament record by achieving a round score of 65. Her victory at the San Jose Classic later that year brought her career victory total to 21. She topped off the season by finishing second at the LPGA championship and third in the Women's Open. In 1988, Alcott's career winnings topped $2 million. As of 1994, she had won 29 tournaments, tying for thirteenth place on the women's all-time list.

See also Didrikson Zaharias, Babe; Ladies Professional Golf Association; Vare Trophy

All-American Girls Professional Baseball League (AAGPBL)

More than 500 young women from the United States, Canada, and Cuba played professional baseball in the AAGPBL from 1943 to 1954. The league was conceived by chewing gum magnate Philip K. Wrigley, who owned the Chicago Cubs men's professional baseball team. After the United States entered World War II late in 1941, Wrigley realized that male players would leave to serve in the military. He thought a women's league could sustain interest in baseball and make use of the fields.

By the 1930s, baseball had become the favorite spectator sport in America. Millions of Americans were also playing softball, a version of the sport. At the beginning of the war, President Franklin D. Roosevelt himself had expressed a desire to "keep baseball going." In a letter dated January 16, 1942, to baseball commissioner Judge Kenesaw Mountain Landis, Roosevelt wrote, "I honestly feel that it would be best for the country to keep baseball going. There will be fewer people unemployed and everybody will work longer hours and harder than ever before. . . . Baseball provides a recreation which does not last over two hours or two hours and a half, and which can be got for very little cost."

During 1942, Wrigley organized the women's league, originally planned as a group of softball teams. He and his advisors later decided on a version of baseball that used the underhand pitch, from softball, but allowed runners to lead off and steal bases, as in baseball. Players would use a 12-inch ball. Besides playing competitive games in stadiums, the teams also played exhibition matches for American troops, visited military hospitals, sold war bonds, and took part in programs for young people.

Many Americans did not want women athletes to dress or act like male athletes, so Wrigley's group decided to encourage a "feminine" appearance. Players wore pastel uniforms with skirts, not pants. They were expected to have well-groomed hair,

Initially started as a way of filling baseball parks while male players served in the military in World War II, the All-American Girls Professional Baseball League played both competitive and exhibition games from 1943 to 1954. The league sought to avoid looking "masculine" by wearing pastel, skirted uniforms. In the early years, players were also required to attend charm school.

wear makeup, and to display good manners. In the early years, players attended a charm school run by Helena Rubinstein, head of a successful cosmetics company. The AAGPBL president told players, "Femininity is to be the keynote of our league."

The first cities to host teams were South Bend, Indiana, Rockford, Illinois, and Racine and Kenosha, Wisconsin. Players started at salaries of about $45 a week, more than many men earned at their jobs, and more than most teachers earned in a month. Their travel and living expenses were also paid.

To find top players, scouts traveled around America watching young women play in local leagues, often sponsored by businesses and companies. Those who were chosen attended tryouts in Chicago in May 1943. The final cuts were made on May 26, and those chosen for the South Bend Blue Soxx, Rockford Peaches, Racine Belles, and Kenosha Comets got ready to play 108 games in the next three months.

An emphasis on "femininity" as defined by white culture in America and fears about public reaction kept African-American women out of the AAGPBL. Although many extremely talented black players existed, leaders of the league did not even discuss hiring them until 1951. At that time, two African-Americans were working out with the South Bend Blue Soxx team in Indiana. The AAGPBL board talked about recruiting black players who showed "exceptional ability" but never made the effort to hire these players.

In 1944, the original four teams were joined by the Minneapolis Millerettes and Milwaukee Chicks. By 1945, the Chicks had relocated in Grand Rapids, Michigan, while the Millerettes left their home base to become a traveling group called the Minnesota Orphans. Most of the Orphans relocated in 1945 to Fort Wayne, Indiana, and became the Daisies, a team that won more games than any other in the league's history.

A competitive league was formed in 1944. The National Girls Baseball League (NGBL) began in the Chicago area with four semipro teams: the Parichy Bloomer Girls, the Music Maids, the Rockola Chicks, and the Match Corp Queens. When the war ended, Arthur Meyerhoff became the head of the league and teams continued to play. A new team, the Muskegon, Michigan, Lassies, was added in 1946; it would go on until 1951.

In 1946, new rules permitted a sidearm pitch. The mound-to-plate distance was increased to 43 feet, in light of the stronger pitches. The balls were also ½ inch smaller than in previous years. Racine won the league title that year, and player Sophie Kurys stole 201 bases, setting a new record. Joanne Weaver of the Fort Wayne Daisies had a batting average of .429 one season and led the league in batting for three years running.

In 1946 and 1947, the league began sponsoring junior teams in minor leagues to train young players. By 1948, the ball size had been decreased, from 11 inches to 10⅜ inches. The next year, the regulation size became 10 inches, the smallest yet, and overhand pitches were required. Games attracted thousands of midwestern fans, but the league was known throughout the nation. A New York City reporter described the games as "fast, tight, and professional" and wrote, "The girls play hard and for keeps."

Two new Illinois teams were formed in 1948: the Chicago Colleens and the Springfield Sallies. Both teams were disbanded at the end of the year. Fans and interest dwindled after 1948, and the league developed economic problems. In the conservative atmosphere of the 1950s, women were again urged into domestic roles, caring for homes and children. Baseball was again viewed as the domain of men. By 1954, only four teams remained in the circuit, and the women's leagues ended after that season. Some of the players went on to teach physical education or continued to play baseball as a recreational pastime.

For decades after it ended, the league was nearly forgotten and seldom mentioned in print. But in 1980, former player June Peppas started a newsletter so that former AAGPBL members could keep in touch. In 1982, the players met in Chicago for their first reunion. Author Sharon Roepke came to interview the players, whom she had read about in newspaper clippings. She created All-American Girls Professional Baseball League cards featuring photographs of the players in uniform, taken during the days of the league. She also led an effort to convince the National Baseball Hall of Fame in Cooperstown, New York, to induct the AAGPBL and recognize its players and teams. In 1968, the Hall of Fame had finally recognized the African-American men who played on the Negro Leagues. On November 5, 1988, the hall officially recognized the women baseball players and opened a display in their honor at the Cooperstown museum.

Besides the players, umpire Pam Postema and Cincinnati Reds owner Marge Schott were featured in the exhibit, which recognizes the women's contributions to the sport. In addition to photos, the exhibit features uniforms and equipment used in the games and a list of the 545 women who played professional baseball during the 1940s and 1950s.

See also National Baseball Hall of Fame; Postema, Pam

References Fincher, "The Belles of the Ball Game Were a Hit with Their Fans," *Smithsonian Magazine*, July 1989, 94; Gluck, *Rosie the Riveter Revisited: Women, the War, and Social Change* (1979); Helmer, *Belles of the Ballpark* (1993); Macy, "Wow, Can She Throw That Ball!" *Cobblestone*, July 1985, 32–34; Ward and Burns, *Baseball* (1994).

All-American Red Heads (See Basketball)

All-American Soap Box Derby

The derby is a coasting race for small, gravity-powered cars built by their drivers and assembled within strict guidelines regarding size, weight, and cost. Races are open to young people 9 to 16 years old who meet these guidelines. In the early years after the race began in 1934, most cars were made from wooden crates that previously contained soap, hence the name.

Races are held each year on the second Saturday in August at Derby Downs in Akron, Ohio. There are three competitive divisions: stock cars, in which racers use prefabricated cars that come in kits approved by the derby; kit cars, in which race cars are assembled from approved kits that do not include wood shells; masters (for ages 11–16), in which contestants use cars they have designed, then constructed with hardware approved by Derby officials.

The first girl to win a derby event was 11-year-old Karren Stead of Lower Bucks, Pennsylvania, in 1975. Since that time, others female winners have included Joan Ferdinand of Canton, Ohio, age 14 (senior winner, 1976); Tonia Schlegel of Hamilton, Ohio, age 13 (senior winner, 1981); Anita Jackson of St. Louis, Missouri, age 15 (senior winner, 1984); Tami Jo Sullivan of Lancaster, Ohio, age 13 (senior winner, 1986); Faith Chavarria of Ventura, California, age 12 (masters winner, 1989); Sami Jones of Salem, Oregon, age 13 (masters winner, 1989); and Kristina Damond of Jamestown, New York, age 13 (stock winner, 1994). In 1992 three girls reached the winners' circle: 11-year-old Carolyn Fox of Sublimity, Oregon, won the kit race; 12-year-old Bonnie Thornton of Redding, California, won the masters; and 10-year-old Loren Hurst of Hudson, Ohio, won the stock race. In 1994, Danielle Del Ferraro became the first girl to win two years in a row.

See also Del Ferraro, Danielle

All-American World's Champion Girls Basketball Club

Starting in 1936, this group toured the United States playing exhibition basketball, in a humorous version of the game. The team traveled thousands of miles entertaining spectators. When women basketball players began playing by the same rules as men, the club played men's teams. In 1971, they took the name "Red Heads," and all players dyed their hair accordingly. They mastered the fancy moves and dribbling techniques made popular by the Harlem Globetrotters.

Allerdice, Ellen Hansell (See Hansell, Ellen)

Allison, Stacy (See Mountain Climbing)

Amateur Athletic Union (AAU)

(American Amateur Athletic Association) Founded in the early 1900s, the AAU is "America's largest nonprofit volunteer service organization dedicated to the encouragement of amateur sports and physical fitness." In 1995, more than 7.7 million Americans were participating in AAU programs each year. Programs are conducted in high schools and colleges; through athletic clubs; and through civic, community, fraternal, and service orga-

nizations. Under AAU rules, members cannot accept money as a prize but may receive gifts of clothing or equipment as well as support from a sponsor for training and competition expenses—travel, food, and lodging, for example.

In the early years, the AAU did not include women in its programs. James Sullivan, AAU president in 1913, said that he did not want "to make girls public characters." (Letter to the editor, the *New York Times,* July 13, 1913.) The AAU was urged to change its policy and form women's teams for the 1922 Olympics but chose not to do so. Women were first admitted to the AAU in 1923, when a new president declared that women athletes were demonstrating their ability and interest and, therefore, the AAU would organize and standardize their sporting events. Women were allowed to compete in track and field, basketball, gymnastics, handball, and swimming.

In 1922, a new organization, the National Amateur Athletic Federation (NAAF) was founded, primarily to challenge the AAU's domination of amateur sports. Members of the NAAF included college and military sports leaders, scout leaders, school sports associations, and people who ran public recreation programs. They wanted to discourage commercialism and strong competition in amateur sports. The following year, a women's division of the NAAF was formed, made up of women physical education specialists and headed by Lou Henry Hoover, wife of Herbert Hoover, the man who would become president of the United States in 1928. For 17 years, the women's division fought to suppress highly competitive sports for women. The division said competition hurt athletes as well as athletic programs run by communities, schools, and colleges.

Eventually, the division disbanded, unable to stop the growth of competitive women's amateur sports.

In 1942, the AAU spearheaded a program to promote physical fitness among school-age children in America. Toward that end, it developed more programs for young people, leading to the first Junior Olympics held in 1967. During the 1970s, the AAU urged Congress to pass the Amateur Sports Act (1978), which established new national governing bodies for each Olympic sport. The AAU elected its first woman president, Gussie Crawford, in 1988.

Meanwhile, AAU programs grew throughout the nation. Today, the AAU sponsors some 1,500 competitive events and distributes several awards for athletes. Young people start out in divisions based on their age: bantams are ages 9 and under; midgets, ages 10–11; juniors, ages 12–13; and seniors, ages 16–17. The AAU also organizes open competitions for young people 14–17 years old.

After competing in local, state, and regional meets, an athlete may qualify to compete in the AAU's annual Junior Olympics. Young people may also attend developmental camps for each of the 17 sports that are part of these Olympics. Among the AAU sports for girls and women are basketball, Chinese martial arts, cross country racing, field hockey, gymnastics, judo, karate, multievent track and field, power lifting, soccer, softball, surfing, swimming, synchronized swimming, table tennis, taekwando, weight lifting, trampoline and tumbling, and volleyball. Programs and competitions for the physically challenged are also sponsored by the AAU.

Each year, the union also selects an amateur athlete to receive the Sullivan Award, or Sullivan Memorial Trophy. The AAU/Milky Way All American Awards, established in 1987, go to high school seniors who show outstanding commitment to academics, athletics, and community service. More than $230,000 in scholarships go to the recipients of these awards.

See also Junior Olympics; National Amateur Athletic Federation; Sullivan Award

Amateur Softball Association (ASA)

Organized in 1933, the ASA developed standardized rules and equipment for the game of softball. The teams that had competed at the national men's and women's softball championships in Chicago that year had followed different rules and used bats and balls that varied in size and weight. The ASA rules committee became known as the International Joint Rules Committee on Softball (IJRC). The IJRC sent representatives to different countries in order to teach the game around the world.

The ASA has continued to focus on the sport of softball, updating and revising rules through the years. It organizes tournaments for men and women at the local and national levels. In national competition, there are slow-pitch and fast-pitch tournaments. The ASA also provides information and printed materials about softball from its national office in Oklahoma City, Oklahoma.

Amateur Status

Amateur athletes are those who do not receive monetary compensation for performing their sport. Under the rules set by the amateur athletic associations, athletes who accept money for their sport or for endorsements or appearances are ineligible for college scholarships and may not compete on college teams.

Rules governing the Olympics changed somewhat after the 1988 Olympic Games, and the organizations that govern different sports have also changed their rules from time to time. For example, as of 1994, figure skaters are permitted to skate in certain professional events approved by the United States Figure Skating Association (USFSA) without losing their amateur status, although the events do carry monetary prizes. In some sports, athletes who have turned professional may later regain their status as an amateur by not taking part in any professional events for a specified number of months or years before a given amateur competition takes place.

America³ (America Cubed)

In 1995 the captain and crew of this yacht became the first all-woman group to race for the America's Cup, the most coveted international prize in yachting. Critics had said that yacht racing required more strength than most women have, pointing out that male sailors were typically 6 feet tall or taller and weighed more than 200 pounds. The crew was selected from 650 applicants. The 28 women chosen for the crew included veteran sailors, such as Jennifer Isler, who won an Olympic sailing medal; weight lifters; and world-class rowers, such as Olympic medalist Anna Seaton-Huntington. The crew began training in April 1994, often putting in 12 hours a day as they prepared for the preliminary races, which began in January 1995.

Bill Koch, a billionaire yachstman who had captained the crew that won the cup in 1992, organized the all-women effort and provided his yacht for the races. Commercial sponsors for the women's crew included Chevrolet, L'Oreal Cosmetics, and Hewlett Packard,

Inc. The women received much press and television coverage. But Koch said, "While this will enhance women's athletics, it is no female lib thing. Our only desire is to win."

During the challenge races held from January through May, the women's crew was in third place and thus did not get to compete against the foreign yacht for the cup. But the *America Cubed* won a preliminary race and showed that a non-male crew was up to the task. After the first four rounds, Koch provided a different yacht, the *Mighty Mary*. The women's crew won another race on March 20. One male crew member, David Dellenbaugh, was also added, replacing the ship's tactician. This change was very controversial.

See also America's Cup; Riley, Dawn

References Lloyd, "The Women of America Are On Board, for Now," *New York Times*, March 21, 1995, B17; Reed and Warner, "Sisters in Sail," *People*, February 20, 1995, 85–87; Starr, "A New Crew Rocks the Boat," *Newsweek*, January 16, 1995, 70–71; Whiteside, "A Whole New Tack," *Sports Illustrated*, February 1995, 40–43.

American Alpine Club (See Peck, Annie Smith)

American Amateur Bowling League (AABL) (See Bowling)

American Bowling Congress (ABC)

The all-male bowlers' organization regulates men's tournaments and leagues in the United States. Its counterpart for women is the Women's International Bowling Congress (WIBC).

See also Bowling

American Horse Show Association (AHSA)

This organization has established written rules for horse shows and officially

U.S. players celebrate a strike during the 1971 World Bowling Championships.

recognizes certain shows throughout the United States that meet its standards. Shows wishing to be recognized must register with the AHSA to be listed in their rule book that year. The AHSA sends officials called stewards to horse shows to ensure the correct conduct of a show and to help settle disputes over classifications or eligibility.

American Tennis Association (ATA)

The ATA was founded in 1916 as an organization for African-American tennis players. For years, black players had been barred from major tennis tournaments, which were often held at country clubs or tennis clubs restricted to "white members only." The ATA sponsored sectional and national tournaments for singles and doubles players in different age groups.

During the late 1940s, Althea Gibson won several national ATA titles. Gibson became the first black player to be accepted at a major U.S. tournament when she played in the U.S. Championships of 1950. Later, Arthur Ashe broke the color barrier for men, playing in top tournaments in the United States and around the world. Both Gibson and Ashe won the prestigious Wimbledon (all-England) tournament. After that, ATA tournaments continued but, like other major U.S. tournaments, were open to all players, regardless of race.

See also Garrison-Jackson, Zina; Gibson, Althea

America's Cup

This prestigious yachting race began in 1851 when an American yacht sailed to England and challenged 17 boats to a race. The yacht had been specially built by members of the New York Yacht Club and was owned by seven American businessmen. Members of England's Royal Yacht Squadron invited the Americans to bring their yacht to the Isle of Wight for a race. The *America*, as the yacht from the States was called, started the race in last place but reached the finish line 18 minutes before its closest competitor. A trophy called the Hundred Guineas Cup was given to the winning boat; this prize later became known as the America's Cup. The cup was placed on display at the New York Yacht Club.

The race is held every three years, and challengers try to take the cup from the previous winner. Americans won the cup each year until *Australia II* took the cup in 1983. In 1995 the first all-woman crew prepared to compete in the race on the *America³*.

See also *America³*; Sailing

Anders, Beth (b. 1951)

Anders succeeded as both a player and coach in women's field hockey. She was regarded as one of the best penalty corner scorers in the world, scoring six penalty corner goals in seven matches during the 1984 World Cup competition. In 1969, the Pennsylvania native became part of the U.S. national women's field hockey team. She played sweeper-midfielder and served as captain. From 1969 to 1984, Anders was the team's high scorer, and she also played on the World Cup team from 1971 to 1984.

Anders and her teammates did not get to compete in the 1980 Olympics because the United States boycotted the Games. In 1982, *Olympian* magazine named her and teammate Charlene Morett Co-Athlete of the Year. She scored four goals on penalty corners during the Four Nations tournament, where her team defeated Australia, Canada, and New Zealand to win the gold medal.

In 1984, Anders played her one-hundredth international field hockey match.

She captained the U.S. team that won a bronze medal in women's field hockey at the Olympic Games in Los Angeles. It was the best finish ever for the U.S. team. The team Anders coached at Old Dominion University won 28 of 33 games in 12 years.

Anderson, Jodi (b. 1957)
Chicagoan Anderson was in her first year of competition when she set a junior high record with a long jump measuring 16 feet and 7 inches. She attended high school in Los Angeles where she set state records in all four track and field events in which she competed. In college, Anderson won the national long-jump title in both 1977 and 1979. She won the national outdoor long-jump title in 1977, 1978, 1980, and 1981.

Competing in the multievent pentathlon, Anderson won the collegiate title in 1979. During the 1980 Olympic trials, she set a new U.S. long-jump record—22 feet, 11¾ inches. She also won the pentathlon event. But the United States boycotted the 1980 Olympics and Anderson and the other Americans were not able to compete. Knee injuries prevented her from completing the 1984 Olympics, for which she had qualified in the heptathlon. Anderson later appeared as the character "Pooch" in a feature film called *Personal Best* (1982), a fictional portrayal of women track and field athletes.
See also Heptathlon; Pentathlon

Anderton, Carol (See Bowling)

Angelakis, Jana (See Fencing)

Annual Empire State Building Run-Up
This running event was held for the first time in 1978. Competitors ran up the 1,575 stairs to the observation deck on the eighty-sixth floor of this famous New York City landmark. Fifteen people, including three women, attempted the race, which was won by Gary Muhrcke, with a time of 12 minutes and 32 seconds. Marcy Schwam, a physical fitness instructor from Ossining, New York, achieved the best time for a woman in the race: 16 minutes, 3.2 seconds. Schwam came in tenth among the racers.

Anorexia Nervosa (See Eating Disorders)

Applebee, Constance
(1874–1981)
Known as the "Queen of American Field Hockey," Constance Applebee was still coaching when she was 95. Applebee believed that field hockey promotes physical and mental strength and that it "develops strong nerves, will power, determination, discipline, and endurance."

A native of England, Applebee was a physical education teacher who helped to make her beloved sport, field hockey, popular in America after she moved to Cambridge, Massachusetts, in 1901. Applebee held the first demonstration of the game in a courtyard, then arranged for exhibition matches at various women's colleges in the area. Applebee coached thousands of young players in junior and senior high schools, colleges, and various clubs. While coaching at Bryn Mawr College in Pennsylvania, she became editor and publisher of the first sports magazine for women. The *Sportswoman* covered skating, swimming, archery, and lacrosse, as well as field hockey and other sports.

Applebee tried and failed to have a women's field hockey event held at the 1920 Olympics. In 1922, she helped to organize the United States Field Hockey

Archery

Association (USFHA) in Philadelphia. The USFHA became the governing body for the sport, promoting field hockey and arranging competitive events in the United States and abroad. The game remained popular throughout the 1990s, with many players continuing to play into their fifties and sixties.

See also Field Hockey

References Hollander, *100 Greatest Women in Sport* (1976); Sullivan, *Better Field Hockey for Girls* (1981).

Aquacades

Held annually, the Aquacades—aquatic exhibitions—were popular touring water shows created by the Broadway producer Billy Rose. The first of these theatrical performances featuring top swimmers and divers was held in 1930, featuring Olympic diving champion Aileen Riggin.

The Cleveland Aquacade, held in 1936, starred Olympic champion Johnny Weissmuller, later featured in a series of *Tarzan* movies, and backstroke gold medalist Eleanor Holm, who was married to Rose. Women swimmers wearing glamorous costumes performed individual and synchronized group routines against a backdrop of ornate sets.

The Aquacades, which continued into the early forties, were highly profitable. Top swimmers such as Holm earned as much as $4,000–$6,000 a week, while those in smaller roles received $400 or $500 a week—enormous sums for both women and men during the lean years of the Great Depression.

See also Holm, Eleanor; Riggin, Aileen

Archery

Archery, the use of bows to launch arrows toward targets, was one of the first sports to be taken up to any large extent by women. Initially a means of hunting and self-defense, archery is now more commonly pursued as a sport. Queen Victoria of England was a well-known enthusiast. The sport was one of those considered "appropriate" for women, perhaps because it involved no physical contact among competitors and a lady need not change her manner of dress while playing. In addition, it was quiet and could be performed at a leisurely pace without much commotion. In 1883, Alfred B. Starey echoed the feelings of many when he commented in the September issue of the *Wheelman*, "Archery, like tennis, is too refined a sport to offer any attractions to the more vulgar elements of society."

In the United States, the first archery tournament was held in Chicago in 1879, sponsored by the National Association of Archers, forerunner of the National Archery Association. The association had been founded in Boston that same year. Later, women's archery events were added to the national competition. In 1885 Mrs. M. C. Howell became the U.S. women's archery champion. The proficient Mrs. Howell would eventually capture this title 16 times between the years 1885 and 1907.

At the 1904 Olympic Games, archery events for women were featured for the first time. Women from the United States won all three events, although Americans were the only archers competing at those Games. After that year, archery was dropped from the Games. In 1972, it was reinstated and the competition was standardized so that both men and women completed two rounds consisting of 144 arrows, 36 shot from each of four different distances. In women's archery, the four rounds are shot from a distance of 70, 60, 50, and 30 meters. In the men's competition, rounds are shot from 90, 70, 50, and 30 meters.

At the 1972 Games, American Doreen Wilber won the gold medal. Wilber was the U.S. national women's champion in both 1973 and 1974. Four years later, at the 1976 Summer Games, another American, LuAnn Ryon, won the Olympic gold medal for archery. Ryon set a record with her point total of 2,499. The U.S. women's archery team won an Olympic bronze (third-place) medal in 1988. In 1992, South Koreans won both the individual and team women's archery events. Ryon held the national title from 1976 through 1978. In recent years, two Americans have won the national title three times apiece: Debra Ochs (1986, 1988, and 1989) and Denise Parker (1990, 1991, and 1993).

See also Wilber, Doreen

Arendsen, Kathy (See Softball)

Arlington, Lizzie (See Baseball)

Armstrong, Deborah (b. 1963)
Skier Deborah (Debbie) Armstrong, who won the first gold medal of the 1984 Olympic Games in the giant slalom race, grew up loving the sport. She told interviewers that for her, training and competing were always more fun than work, saying, "Skiing is my life. It's what I love to do."

Prior to the Olympics, the Salem, Oregon, native competed in downhill and slalom events both in the United States and internationally. In December 1981, she attended her first World Cup championship. During the 1982–1983 season, she skied in the World Cup giant slalom and downhill races, winning fifth place at a downhill competition held in Switzerland. She won third place early in 1984 at a World Cup supergiant slalom competition and took fifth in the giant slalom.

Improving her performance, she won her Olympic gold medal that year with a combined (averaged) time of 2 minutes, 02.98 seconds for the two runs of the giant slalom. The national giant slalom women's champion in 1987, Armstrong was also a member of the 1988 Olympic team but did not win a medal.

Ashford, Evelyn (b. 1957)
During the late 1970s, American sprinter Evelyn Ashford broke the East German women's decade-long hold on the 100- and 200-meter races. Although at 5 feet, 5 inches, Ashford was not as tall as many runners, she was called the "fastest woman in the world" in 1979.

Growing up, Ashford had trained on a number of school track teams around the country, following her father's various assignments in the air force. In 1972, while Ashford was living in Alabama, she traveled to Spokane, Washington, to participate in the Junior Olympics, sponsored by the Amateur Athletic Union (AAU). She finished sixth in the 100-yard dash and eighth in the 220-yard race. During her high school years in California, Ashford was invited to race against her school's star football player. She won the 50-yard sprint, and since there was no track team for girls at the time, she became a member of the boys' track team. Her idol during those years was Wilma Rudolph, who had won three gold medals in track and field at the 1960 Olympics.

In 1975 Ashford won an athletic scholarship to attend the University of California at Los Angeles (UCLA). By age 19, she was such an effective runner that she came in fifth in the 100-meter race at the 1976 Montreal Olympic Games. At national collegiate track and field events, she won both the 100- and 200-meter

Evelyn Ashford, pictured here during a 1991 relay race, was known as "the fastest woman in the world" in 1979. She became the first American woman to break the 11-second barrier in the 100-meter race with her time of 10.79 seconds. Ashford also set a new world record in the 60-yard dash in 1981.

races—a "double-double"—for two years in a row. Her training program included weight training and distance running, as well as sprinting.

In one 100-meter race at the national outdoor championships in 1979, Ashford became the first American woman to break the 11-second barrier with her time of 10.79 seconds. Only one other woman, Marlies Gohr of Germany, had run that distance in under 11 seconds. Ashford was the World Cup Winner in 1979 and looked forward to trying for an Olympic medal. But that year, the United States did not compete in the Olympic Games, as a political protest against the invasion of Afghanistan by Russia. "I felt as if my soul was ripped out," Ashford later said of that disappointment. For several months, she quit training and competing. But she came back to win the World Cup again in 1981, and as in 1979 was named woman athlete of the year by several sports authorities. In 1981 she set a new world record in the 60-yard dash with her time of 6.62 seconds.

A recurrence of a hamstring injury forced Ashford to withdraw from the finals at the 1983 world championship races. Returning to competition early in 1984, she looked forward to the Summer Olympics, to be held in Los Angeles. There, she won the 100-meter race and ran with the women's 4 x 100–meter relay team, netting two gold medals. A pulled muscle kept her out of the 200-meter event. Later in 1984, she broke her previous record in the 100-meter race with a time of 10.76 seconds, a new world record.

In 1979 Ashford had married athlete Ray Washington, a college basketball coach. They had a baby in 1985, but the demands of motherhood did not keep Ashford from new athletic achievements.

In 1986 she won the 50-meter dash at the Vitalis Olympic Invitational with a time of 6.6 seconds and won the 100-meter dash at the Goodwill Games. Ashford was also a reporter for *World Class Woman*, a cable television program about women and sports, and served as a spokesperson for the Mazda auto company's track team.

At the 1988 Olympics, 35-year-old Ashford placed second in the 100-meter race and captured gold once again when the women's 400-meter relay team turned in another winning performance.

See also Rudolph, Wilma
References "World's Fastest Mom," *Ebony*, June 1986, 155–156ff.

Ashworth, Jeanne (See Speed Skating)

Aspinall, Nan Jane
A gifted horsewoman, Aspinall was the first woman ever to ride on horseback alone across the country. She set out on September 1, 1910. It took her 301 days to cover the 4,500 miles between San Francisco and New York City.

Association for Intercollegiate Athletics for Women (AIAW)
The AIAW developed as a governing body for women's sports, functioning much as the National Collegiate Athletic Association (NCAA) did for men's athletics. In 1971 the AIAW began setting the rules for women's collegiate athletic competition at the local, state, regional, and national levels. It sponsored competitive events for college women who were amateurs rather than professional athletes. Prizes in the form of plaques were awarded to those who took top honors, including a Female College Athlete of the Year. Among the AIAW-sponsored events were an annual national

basketball championship and tennis tournaments with both singles and doubles events.

Until 1974, the AIAW opposed athletic scholarships to college for women athletes. This policy aimed to prevent women athletes at the collegiate level from being "commercialized or exploited." The AIAW stated that if such scholarships were allowed, the high-pressure tactics that colleges and universities used to recruit male athletes would be used on women as well. The AIAW later changed its policy and encouraged scholarships so that talented women could receive financial aid for their educations. The AIAW did set guidelines for the methods colleges could use to recruit athletes, stipulating that college recruiters must contact athletes through letters or telephone calls, not by direct visits to a home or school. Colleges were told not to pay the expenses of students when they visited the campus or when they took part in auditions there. These and other guidelines regarding eligibility, financial aid, and auditions were set forth in an AIAW publication, *High School Brochure.*

After the passage of Title IX in 1972, schools were required to equalize athletic opportunities and programs for men and women. Starting in 1980, the NCAA began sponsoring championships for women's sports, planning to take responsibility for both men's and women's collegiate athletic programs. The NCAA scheduled its events on the same dates as AIAW events, and there was television coverage for NCAA events. The AIAW was unable to compete, as its members left to join the more powerful, better-funded NCAA. In 1982 the AIAW ceased to function.

See also National Collegiate Athletic Association; Title IX

Athlete of the Year

In 1931, the Associated Press began giving this award each year to its choice for the best male and the best female athletes. Women from around the world are eligible for the award. In the years the award has been given, several women have been honored more than once, for example, Babe Didrikson Zaharias, who won in 1945, 1946, 1947, and 1950. Maureen Connolly won the award three times (1951, 1952, and 1953). Among the twice-honored U.S. athletes were Patty Berg, Alice Marble, Althea Gibson, Wilma Rudolph, Mickey Wright, Kathy Whitworth, Billie Jean King, Chris Evert, and Martina Navratilova.

See also Berg, Patricia Ann; Connolly, Maureen; Didrikson Zaharias, Babe; Evert, Chris; Gibson, Althea; King, Billie Jean; Marble, Alice; Navratilova, Martina; Rudolph, Wilma; Whitworth, Kathy; Wright, Mickey

Austin, Tracy (b. 1962)

The arrival of petite Tracy Austin caused a stir at the 1977 Wimbledon tennis tournament. This 14-year-old from Rolling Hills, California, was the youngest person to compete at that prestigious event since 1887. Ranked among the top ten women players in the world in 1978, she was the youngest ever on the U.S. Wightman and Federation Cup teams.

Austin had often found herself the youngest in a group of tennis players. She was not quite two years old when her mother enrolled her in tennis clinics for children ages three to eight. She had been able to play tennis nearly each day, since she accompanied her mother to the Jack Kramer Tennis Club where Mrs. Austin worked in the pro shop. All the Austins, which included five children, played tennis, and the family had collected many prizes and trophies. At age four, Tracy appeared on the cover of

Touted as the youngest Wimbledon participant since 1887, Tracey Austin's career was cut short by a tragic car accident in 1989.

World Tennis magazine, another "first" in her career.

Moving into the junior tournaments, Austin won the Los Angeles 10-and-unders and 12-and-unders on the same day. By age 10, she was winning national titles, too. In 1976 she won both the 14-and-under singles title and the 16-and-under indoor singles title. The next year, still an amateur, Austin became the youngest player ever to win a professional singles title (the Avon Futures in Portland, Oregon). Her parents insisted that she keep up with her schoolwork and not travel for more than one week at a time.

Austin turned professional just before her sixteenth birthday. She won the U.S. Open women's title that year, in 1979, defeating the great champion Chris Evert. Once again, Austin set a record, this time as the youngest woman to win that tournament and the youngest to win a Grand Slam event. Two years later, she captured the U.S. women's crown again. By then, she had earned over $1 million in prize money at her sport.

During four months in 1980, Austin achieved her long-standing dream of being ranked the number one woman player in the world. She looked forward to playing at Wimbledon. She did not win the women's title there, but she and her brother John won the mixed doubles. They won second place at Wimbledon the following year.

By then, Austin was experiencing recurrent leg muscle problems, which never fully healed between matches. For several years, she was plagued by back, leg, and foot injuries. After staying out of major tournaments for a number of months, Austin played some doubles matches. She also worked as a TV commentator, doing broadcasts for ABC from Wimbledon and from Barcelona during the 1988 Summer Olympics.

Returning to competition in 1989, Austin was planning to play mixed doubles with her brother John in a World Team Tennis event in New Jersey. En route to the match from New York City, her car was hit broadside by a van running a red light. Austin's right knee was shattered, her back was sprained, and her heart and spleen were bruised. Surgery and bone grafts, along with metal screws, were required to repair the knee. Doctors said she would never play professional tennis again. Austin embarked on a strenuous physical rehabilitation program that included boxing and weight training. She sometimes hit tennis balls from a chair. By 1991, she was able to play in some charity and corporate tennis events.

In 1993 Austin married mortgage broker Scott Holt and decided to make a comeback in professional tennis. She played in the Evert Cup tournament in Indian Wells, California, and defeated the twelfth-ranked woman player in the world before losing in the next round. In her 1992 autobiography, Austin expressed appreciation for her many opportunities and blessings but also described the pain of having been forced to leave the tour at age 21, when she was reaching her peak: "I am haunted by the thought that I had to leave the game so young."

References Austin, *Beyond Center Court* (1992); Gutman, *More Modern Women Superstars* (1979); Neill, "Pretty in White," *People*, May 10, 1993, 113–114.

Automobile Racing (See Racing, Auto)

Babashoff, Shirley (b. 1957)

Swimmer Babashoff set new records in the 200- and 400-meter freestyle swimming events in world competition and won eight Olympic medals in the course of two Summer Games.

Born in Whittier, California, Babashoff started swimming lessons when she was eight. She often trained with her two older brothers, both competitive swimmers. When she was 15, she was considered to be the best woman freestyle swimmer in America. In 1972, she was selected as part of the U.S. Olympic team. At the 1972 Olympic Games, held in Munich, Germany, Babashoff won silver medals in the 100-meter and 200-meter freestyle events and was part of the U.S. women's team that won a gold medal in the 400-meter freestyle relay. At age 15, she had three Olympic medals. Her time in the 100-meter race was 59.02 seconds; in the 200-meter race it was 2 minutes, 01.22 seconds.

Back home, Babashoff continued training at the Mission Viejo Swim Club. She worked on the backstroke, breaststroke, and butterfly, as well as the freestyle. Lifting weights helped increase the strength in her arms, back, and shoulders. During these years, women from East Germany dominated world swimming events, and Babashoff was regarded as the second-best in several events. Yet in 1974, Babashoff managed to set two new world records, for the 200- and 400-meter races. She won both of these races at a world meet in 1975.

Babashoff returned to Olympic competition for the 1976 Montreal Games. There, she added four silver medals and one gold to her accomplishments. Her strongest opponent was a remarkable East German named Kornelia Ender, who defeated Babashoff for the gold in four events, the first woman swimmer ever to win four golds. To save her energy for the 800-meter freestyle, Babashoff had decided to drop out of the race that preceded it. However, Ender competed in the two races and won them both, the first time any Olympic athlete had won two gold medals within a half hour. Babashoff came in third in the 800-meter race and was part of the winning 4 x 100–meter relay team.

In 1987, Babashoff was voted into the U.S. Olympic Hall of Fame, one of five women swimmers in the hall as of 1994.

Reference McWhirter, et al. *1986 Guinness Book of World Records* (1986).

Babe Didrikson Zaharias Trophy

This 4-foot-high trophy is awarded by the Associated Press to the female Athlete of the Year. The trophy was given on behalf of the remarkable athlete for whom it was named after her death from cancer in 1955. In 1972, George Zaharias, husband of Babe Didrikson, told a reporter for the *Los Angeles Times* that he and his wife had conceived of the idea of a trophy that would give women athletes a concrete symbol of their achievements in addition to press clippings.

Babilonia, Tai (b. 1960)

In 1979, Babilonia and her partner Randy Gardner became the first Americans in 29 years to win the world pairs' figure skating championship, long dominated by skaters from the Soviet Union. Some commentators said that Babilonia and Gardner had skated a "perfect program." Babilonia was praised for her long, graceful lines on the ice combined with great athletic strength.

Babilonia and Gardner, known for their elegant style and outstanding sit-spins, were favored to win the 1980 Olympic gold medal in pairs' figure skating. Then Gardner suffered an injury before the final free-skating event at Lake Placid, New York, and the couple had to withdraw. After this disappointing setback, Babilonia did some professional modeling and appeared in televised sports events as well as professional ice shows. She was in the news in the late 1980s when she came forward to discuss how she had conquered drug dependency. Audiences were pleased when Babilonia rejoined Gardner for professional skating appearances.

Reference "A Skating Star's Long Fall from Grace," *People Weekly*, April 17, 1989, 8–9.

Backhand, Two-Handed

Tennis star Chris Evert popularized this stroke during the late 1960s when she began appearing in major tournaments. As a young child, Evert had been too small to hit a strong backhand with just one arm. Her father and coach, Jimmy Evert, allowed her to use two hands, thinking she would later change to the traditional one-handed shot. Evert developed such power and accuracy that she kept the two-handed backhand.

A number of male players have also used the stroke. Though it may increase power, the two-handed backhand sometimes limits a player's reach.

See also Evert, Chris

Bacon, Mabel (See Powerboating)

Bacon, Mary (1950–1991)

Jockey Mary Bacon, the first woman to win 100 horse races, loved the track since she began riding and racing as a teenager. Although women jockeys were belittled and told they did not belong in a "man's sport," Bacon persisted, sure that she could succeed as a professional in the sport.

As a child, Bacon won prizes for her performance at horse shows, where she competed in dressage and other events. She began racing in the 1960s and won her first race in 1969. At age 19, on an Oklahoma track, Bacon suffered her first serious injury. For four days, she lay paralyzed in the hospital, the result of pinched nerves in her broken back. Six weeks later, she was riding again.

Although others might have given up racing after such an injury, Bacon was more eager to succeed than ever. She later described her philosophy: "Life is short, and you must make the most of it." Two years later, she broke her collarbone and leg during another fall. In 1972 after she was thrown during a race in Pittsburgh, another horse fell on her and she was left unconscious. Again, Bacon returned to riding a few days after her discharge from the hospital. Five days after regaining consciousness, she won one race and placed third in another.

The Philadelphia Sports Writers Association awarded Mary Bacon their Most

Courageous Athlete award in 1973. Accepting the prize before an audience of 1,000 men, Bacon said simply, "I ride because I love horses." The glamorous, blond Bacon also received attention for her looks, and her pictures were featured in *Playboy* magazine.

In 1974, with fellow jockey Joan Phipps, Bacon won the Daily Double at Aqueduct racetrack in New York, the first time women had done so. But she continued to suffer injuries during the last years of her career. A fall at an Albany, California, track left her in a coma for eight days. She developed cancer in the 1980s and was too weak to ride or race. Depressed and in pain, Bacon committed suicide in 1991. Her husband, Jeff Anderson, had her ashes scattered at Belmont Park on Long Island, New York.

During her career, Bacon raced 3,526 times, winning 286 races, placing second in 310 races, and third in 323. Her prize money totaled more than $1 million.

Badminton

Badminton, which evolved from an ancient racket sport, may have originated in China, though nobody is certain. These early racket sports may have had spiritual and prophetic significance: it is believed that people sometimes hit an object into the air with their hands or some sort of bat, thinking that the number of times it was hit up without touching the ground would predict the length of their life. Today's badminton is a game in which players hit a lightweight shuttlecock or "birdie" back and forth over a net with lightweight rackets.

By the 1800s, British officers stationed in India played the game. It became popular in England during the 1870s, where players used a shuttlecock made from a rounded piece of cork with feathers attached to its flat top. It was christened Badminton, after the residence of the sport-loving Duke of Beaufort, in southern Gloucestershire. The Duke had taken up the sport after he watched British officers on leave from India playing the game. The Badminton Association of England was formed in 1893, and the first All-England tournament was held in 1899.

Travelers who had visited the British Isles and India brought badminton to Canada and the United States in the late 1800s. It spread after English teams toured Canada in 1925 and 1930. The game was especially popular during the Great Depression of the 1930s, when many people were unemployed and sought inexpensive forms of recreation. Some people used a wooden ball rather than a store-bought shuttlecock. An International Badminton Federation was formed in 1934, while the American federation was organized two years later, in 1936. The name eventually changed to the United States Badminton Association. National championships were first held in 1937.

Among the top women players in the world was Judy Devlin Hashman (b. 1935). Some called her the best woman player in history after she won her tenth world singles title in 1967. Hashman was born into a family credited with influencing the development of the modern version of badminton. Canadian-born, she moved to the United States in 1936 and became an American citizen. She won the first of six national junior titles in 1949. After marrying British badminton player Dick Hashman in 1960, Judith Devlin Hashman moved to England and became a British citizen in 1971. Devlin Hashman and her sister Susan Devlin Peard were both elected to the Badminton Hall of Fame (in 1963 and 1976, respectively).

The United States produced another world champion in 1978 and 1983, when Cheryl Carton of San Diego, California, won the women's title. Some of Carton's stiffest competition came from Canadian women, who were becoming top players in the 1980s.

While male players compete for the Thomas Cup, women compete for the Uber Cup, the top international prize for women. In 1957, when the first cup match was held, the U.S. team defeated Denmark to win. Women from Great Britain, Denmark, and Canada once dominated international competition, but Asian teams were quite successful in the 1990s. In 1992, the Chinese women's team won the cup, the fifth time in a row they have won the world title. Teams from the United States and Canada also compete for the Devlin Cup. The Canadian team won the Devlin Cup away from the United States in 1983, winning all five games.

Before badminton became an Olympic sport, a demonstration took place at the 1972 Games in Munich, Germany. Twenty-five competitors from 11 countries took part. The game was a medal sport for the first time at the 1992 Olympic Games in Barcelona, Spain. South Korean women won both the individual and team gold medals. In 1996, no U.S. teams qualified for the final events.
See also Devlin Cup

Ball Boy/Girl

In tennis, boys and girls are both eligible to serve as ball persons, retrieving balls during the course of the match. They are chosen for their knowledge of the game and ability to move quickly and quietly on and off the court and throw the ball as needed. At the U.S. Open tournament, applicants must be 14 years or older.

Ballooning (See Aerial Sports)

Balukas, Jean (See Billiards)

Bancroft, Ann (b. 1955)

In 1986 Bancroft along with five other people and a team of 21 sled dogs walked to the North Pole from Ward Hunt Island, Canada. She and other members of the Will Steger International Polar Expedition walked, skied, and pushed dog sleds full of equipment over 1,000 miles of polar ice in –70°F weather. Their goal was to duplicate the trip made by the Peary team in 1909.

A physical education teacher, Bancroft left her job to train in Canada before the expedition, which took 55 days. After the expedition, she moved to Minnesota.

Bancroft, Jessie Hubbell (1867–1952)

Born in Minnesota, Bancroft became the first woman to head a physical education program in a large public school system. A frail and sickly youngster, Bancroft originally began reading books about diet, exercise, and hygiene in order to improve her own health. In 1888 she enrolled in the Minneapolis School of Physical Education, where she studied anatomy, physiology, and gymnastics. She planned a career in physical education, since she believed interest in the field was growing. But during those years, men dominated this field as they did other athletics-related activities and organizations. From her home, Bancroft started gymnastics classes for women and demonstrated exercises at schools and churches. She lectured on these subjects throughout the midwestern states. In 1891 Bancroft became one of the first people to attend the Harvard Summer School of Physical Education. She learned the latest theories about different systems of exercise, as well as more anatomy and physiology relating to body mechanics. In New York City, she embarked on a teaching career, finding only part-time positions in the beginning.

But in 1893, Bancroft was appointed director of physical training in the Brooklyn Public Schools. For nearly ten years, she oversaw a large, expanding program. Officials were so impressed that they asked her to serve as assistant director of the physical education programs in the New York City schools. From 1903 until her retirement in 1928, Bancroft held that post. She developed model programs for classroom teachers to use in teaching exercises to students of different ages. Bancroft also set up the first public school gymnasium and published many articles and five important books in her field.

For her achievements, Bancroft became the first woman to receive the Gulick Award for distinguished work in physical education. She died at age 85 of a heart attack.

See also Physical Education
References Gerber, *Innovators and Institutions in Physical Education* (1971); Scherman and Green, eds., *Notable American Women: The Modern Period* (1980).

Baseball

American baseball may have evolved from a game called "rounders" that came from England in the early 1880s. The batter in this game had to run around stakes set up at each of three bases. The opposing team threw the ball at the runner; once hit, he was "out." Later, bags of sand replaced stakes, and runners were tagged, not hit, by the ball.

As baseball gained popularity in the United States, girls and women joined teams and games in their yards and neighborhoods. During the late 1800s, schools set up boating, baseball, and other sports activities to encourage women students to exercise. In 1866 the Vassar Res-

olutes was the first women's college baseball team formed, and others followed. But parents feared that their daughters were engaging in too violent an activity and might be injured, and their complaints put an end to these organized games. It was not until 1880 that Smith College in Massachusetts again tried to establish a baseball team, which did not last long, for the same reasons.

Other women's teams developed during the 1880s, including the Black Stocking Nine, a team that was featured on an early set of baseball cards. But women were not welcomed on organized teams or as professional baseball players for decades. Some professional women players performed as part of novelty acts throughout the country. Hundreds of spectators showed up to watch two teams called the Red Stockings and Blue Stockings play against each other.

Occasionally, a professional men's team featured a strong woman player to attract publicity. Pitcher Lizzie Arlington was featured at games with a Reading, Pennsylvania, team from the Atlantic League. Arlington pitched so well that no man scored a run during the inning she pitched. A local sportswriter gave her cautious praise, saying that "for a woman, she is a success." In 1898, Arlington was hired to pitch in the old Atlantic league, part of the men's organized baseball system, thus becoming the first woman hired to play with the minor leagues. During the early 1900s, Ohioan Alta Weiss became a professional baseball player and later managed a men's ball team.

Some women entered throwing contests. Babe Didrikson Zaharias was among the top throwers of her day, winning the Women's Outdoor Baseball Throw in 1931 with a distance of 296 feet. Later, women pitchers played in exhibition matches.

Left-hander Jackie Mitchell managed to strike out the legendary Yankee hitters, Babe Ruth and Lou Gehrig, during an exhibition in 1931. Mitchell became the second woman hired by a minor league team (the Chatanoogo Lookouts).

When World War II interrupted play in the men's major leagues, more than 500 women played professionally for women's teams in the All-American Girls Professional Baseball League (AAGPBL), which operated from 1943 to 1954. In 1988, a permanent exhibit honoring the AAGPBL and women in baseball was placed in the National Baseball Hall of Fame and Museum.

In 1953, Toni Lyle Stone became the only woman ever to play in the highest level professional teams of the Negro baseball leagues. Black men had not played in the major leagues and so had been playing in their own segregated leagues for decades. Stone played second base with the Indianapolis Clowns and had a batting average of .243 for 50 games. After Jackie Robinson broke the color barrier in the modern major leagues when he joined the Brooklyn Dodgers in 1947, all the major league teams eventually became integrated.

During the 1990s, a women's professional baseball team called the Colorado Silver Bullets played against men's pro baseball teams. The women's team was sponsored by the Coors Beverage Company, based in Colorado. The team played its first season in 1994, winning two games and losing ten. One of the Bullets' pitchers was Gina Satriano. She had stirred controversy earlier in her life, too, when she and her father, a former major league pitcher, sued in California so that Gina could play in the Little League. Satriano says, "Baseball is a game where size doesn't have to matter."

See also All-American Girls Professional Baseball League; Croteau, Julie; Didrikson Zaharias, Babe; Little League; National Baseball Hall of Fame; Softball; Weiss, Alta
References Araton, "The Trials of a Woman Pitcher," *New York Times*, June 15, 1995, C3; Cahn, *Coming On Strong* (1994); Macy, *A Whole New Ball Game* (1993); Nelson, *Are We Winning Yet?* (1991); Peterson, *Only the Ball Was White* (1970).

Baseball Hall of Fame (See National Baseball Hall of Fame)

Basketball
Modern basketball was developed by a Presbyterian minister, Dr. James A. Naismith. In 1891, he introduced the game on the grounds of the Young Men's Christian Association (YMCA) in Springfield, Massachusetts. Naismith believed that youth would be healthier and better behaved if they spent their leisure time playing a sport that was possible at any time of the year, indoors or outdoors. A lover of history, Naismith had probably read about the ballgames played by Native Americans in Central and South America. He worked out the elements of a game, which required players to score points by throwing a ball into a peach basket suspended from each end of a balcony in a gymnasium. Although Naismith's players were all boys, it took only a few weeks for girls to observe the new game and begin playing together.

As basketball spread throughout America and the world, people changed the rules and developed their own versions of the game. These rules were standardized in the United States in 1934. Two sources for rules for women's basketball were the National Federation of High School Associations in Elgin, Illinois, and the National Association for Girls and Women in Sport in Washington, D.C. The Federation rules use the 30-second clock—if a team does not get a shot off within 30 seconds, a horn blares and they must give up the ball. The clock is used in women's collegiate play. It prevents teams from keeping the ball for extended periods of time without making an effort to score.

College women began playing basketball in 1892, a year after the game was invented. At Smith College, an all-women institution, physical education director Senda Berenson taught the game to her students and set up matches between groups of players within the school. Teams from different colleges competed against each other. The first women's intercollegiate match was held in April of 1896 between teams from the University of California–Berkeley and Stanford University.

Women's rules, different from men's, were first standardized in 1899 and put into book form two years later. Berenson played a key role in this process. Some people objected to the idea of women playing basketball at all. They claimed that women's hearts were much smaller than men's and that the sport involved ongoing movement that might strain the heart muscle and cause girls to faint. (*Hygeia Magazine*, November 1928.) Others believed that the sport was attracting "undesirable" people, those from the lower classes of society. They urged women of the higher social classes to avoid sports that attracted working-class women.

Outside colleges, women could play among themselves or on teams sponsored by social and business organizations. Talented players were often chosen for the All-American teams that played at amateur basketball tournaments. Babe Didrikson Zaharias, who played for a Texas team called the Golden Cyclones, was among the athletes who first received acclaim while playing team basketball.

Until the late 1950s, the women's game was slower and simpler than that played by men. There were more rules that limited the number of dribbles. Teams were made up of six players and only two were permitted to move about on the whole court. By the late 1960s, women's basketball adopted the five-player system used in men's basketball.

Basketball for women surged during the 1970s. More programs for women opened at summer camps, city recreation centers, and school and church leagues. The first tournament among college teams was organized in 1969. Coach Carol Eckman of West Chester State College brought 16 teams together for the event, and a national collegiate tournament has been played every year since. In 1975 the first Association for Intercollegiate Athletics for Women (AIAW) meet for college basketball teams was held. The competition was held in Madison Square Garden in New York City before about 12,000 fans, the first time women had played basketball at the Garden. The winning team, known as the "Mighty Macs" from Immaculata College of Philadelphia, also won national titles in 1972, 1973, and 1974. Mary Scharff was the high scorer during that 1975 game. Mississippi's Delta State defeated the Mighty Macs in 1975 and won the title again in 1976 and 1977. Since the late 1970s, women's basketball has been dominated by teams from UCLA, Louisiana State, North Carolina State, Tennessee, and Maryland.

Basketball became one of the fastest growing of all sports for women. Women players enjoyed the speed and excitement of the game, along with the challenge of playing well individually and with the team. The first professional league, the Women's Professional Basketball League (WBL), was formed in 1978, with eight teams divided into eastern and western divisions. Playing four quarters, each 12 minutes long, the WBL used a ball slightly smaller than that used by their male counterparts. By 1980, there were nine teams playing in the United States. Even so, by 1982 there was not enough support for the league to continue.

Interest in women's basketball, however, continued to increase. The National Collegiate Athletic Association (NCAA) conducted play-offs and organized a 32-team event for college women's teams in 1982. By 1994, the NCAA tournament included 64 teams. Attendance at the Final Four games grew from 153,014 in 1991 to 266,154 in 1994.

Women's basketball became part of the Pan-American Games in 1955 and was added to the Summer Olympic events in 1976. The U.S. women's team won the gold medal for basketball in 1984.

Among the members of the 1984 U.S. women's Olympic team was Denise Curry, a high-scoring forward at UCLA. She had also been part of the 1982 team that defeated top Soviet Union players during an international tour. Her teammates included Anne Donovan, Janice Lawrence, Ann Meyers, Cheryl Miller, and Lynette Woodard.

By the 1980s and 1990s, more college scholarships were being awarded to women basketball players than to those in any other sport. Basketball ranked as the high school sport with the most girl participants, a total of 387,800 in 1991, according to the National Federation of State High School Associations. Women college basketball stars were also receiving more attention. Rebecca Lobo, a top player with the University of Connecticut, and Sheryl Swoopes, at Texas Tech, were endorsing commercial products even before they finished college. Both were members of the 1996 U.S. women's basketball team that won the gold medal at the 1996 Olympics in Atlanta, Georgia. Called the women's "Dream Team," it was coached by Stanford's Tara Van Derveer, who led that school's team to two NCAA titles.

See also Association for Intercollegiate Athletics for Women; Berenson, Senda; Blazejowski, Carol; Didrikson Zaharias, Babe; Donovan, Anne; Lawrence, Janice; Lieberman, Nancy; Meyers, Anne; Miller, Cheryl; National Collegiate Athletic Association; Pan-American Games; Rush, Cathy; Wade Trophy; Woodard, Lynette

References Brasch, *How Did Sports Begin?* McKay, 1970; Dowling, "The Other Dream Team," *TV Guide,* July 22, 1996, 14–22; Rush, *Women's Basketball* (1976); Sullivan, *Better Basketball for Girls* (1978).

Battle of the Sexes

Also called the Superbowl of the Sexes, this was one of the most notorious tennis matches in history. On September 20, 1973, women's tennis champion Billie Jean King met a former men's tennis champion, 55-year-old Bobby Riggs, at the Houston Superdome. Riggs had defeated another top woman player, Margaret Smith Court, and King challenged him to a match.

More than 30,000 fans came to watch this unique match, some paying $100 for a courtside seat, while millions of others watched on television. King told a reporter, "I hear people are betting like crazy. . . . That adds something extra." The prize was $100,000—winner take all. But both players were to receive about $75,000 in television and film rights.

King entered the arena dressed dramatically in a tennis dress adorned with sequins and rhinestones, carried on a gold chair by four young men. Riggs arrived in a gilded rickshaw pulled by six male models. As fans cheered, the two exchanged points and reached five games apiece when King broke Riggs's serve to take the lead. King took the first set, six games to four. She continued to dominate the match as her supporters called out, "Bye, bye, Bobby." Leading easily in the third set, King was the winner.

Newspaper headlines the next morning declared, "BILLIE JEAN OUTLIBS THE LIP." King later said that the match did a great deal for women's tennis and women's sports in general, as well as boosting interest in tennis.

See also King, Billie Jean; Tennis

Baugh, Laura (b. 1955)

In 1971, at age 16, this Florida native became the youngest woman ever to win the U.S. Women's Amateur Golf Tournament. Baugh had begun hitting golf balls at age two when her father, an expert golfer, spotted her natural talent. As a young child, Baugh could name the various golf clubs and their uses. By age seven, she could send a ball more than 200 yards down the fairway, and she won a number of the Pee Wee and Junior championships held for children.

Forceful drive shots and carefully controlled puts helped her to win the 1971 title, surpassing nearly 100 older and more experienced golfers. At 18, Baugh turned professional. She tied for second place at the Lady Tara Tournament in Atlanta, Georgia. Blond and good-looking, she was nicknamed "Golden Girl" and brought new glamour and interest to her sport. Promoters of women's golf were eager to use competitors like Baugh

to attract the press, spectators, and more sponsors for the tour. Baugh was asked to endorse various commercial products, such as golf clubs, cars, and watches. She also modeled sportswear and made television appearances.

Reference Moffett, *Great Women Athletes* (1974).

Belote, Melissa (b. 1956)

Belote was one of the greatest swimmers of all time using the backstroke, a difficult stroke in which a swimmer is not able to look ahead and see the end of the pool.

As a young swimmer in Springfield, Virginia, Belote started practicing this stroke to keep the chlorine out of her eyes. Swimming hundreds of laps a day, she soon increased her speed and endurance. Belote became the best backstroke swimmer in her area and began amassing medals and trophies in regional competitions. By 1971, she was ranked as one of the top U.S. women in her sport.

Belote made the Olympic team and headed to the 1972 Munich Games. In her first event, the 200-meter backstroke, she won the gold medal and set a new world record: 2 minutes, 19.19 seconds. She and her three teammates won the 4 x 100–meter relay, with Belote getting the team off to a headstart. She set another world record in the 100-meter backstroke to win her third gold medal in the Games. Her outstanding performance was eclipsed that year by Mark Spitz, who took home seven gold medals in men's swimming events.

In February 1973, at the World Women's Invitational Swim Meet, Belote again excelled, winning the 100-yard backstroke, the 200-yard event, and a third gold in the 400-relay medley where she was teamed with Shirley Babashoff, Cathy Carr, and Deena Deardurff.

See also Babashoff, Shirley
References Stambler, *Women in Sports* (1975); Wallechinsky, *The Complete Book of the Olympics* (1984).

Benjamin Briscoe Trophy (See Motoring Club, Women's)

Benoit Samuelson, Joan (b. 1957)

A native of Cape Elizabeth, Maine, Benoit became the first woman to win an Olympic marathon. As a child, she was an expert skier, staying out on the slopes even after darkness fell. She played tennis and basketball in high school, as well as competing in track and field. At Bowdoin College she was a star field hockey player and trained by running, which became her major sport.

Although Benoit entered qualifying rounds for the 1976 Olympics, she did not make the team as a middle-distance runner. She developed an interest in long-distance running and began training for marathons. In 1976 she won a 7-mile race in Massachusetts.

Benoit amazed spectators by winning her first Boston Marathon in 1979, with a time of 2 hours, 35 minutes, and 15 seconds, a U.S. record for women. Her second and third victories came in 1982 and 1983. Her 1983 time set a world record at 2 hours, 22 minutes, and 43 seconds. She also won other marathons and a number of shorter races. By the early eighties, she was considered the country's best woman distance runner.

In 1984 Benoit felt knee pains while training for the Olympics. She was eager to go to these Games, since women would be running a marathon in the 1984 Olympics for the first time. In her 1987 autobiography, she described this as the "most frightening moment in my life." The pains came and went during the next few weeks. Benoit was told to rest, but that would mean stopping the training she needed to qualify for the Olympics. When the knee did not improve, she had surgery three weeks before the Olympic trials. Within days, Benoit doggedly began swimming and riding a stationery bicycle to develop strength in her leg. She made the team and headed for the Olympics.

The day of the marathon was unusually hot and muggy, so adverse that some runners became dehydrated and disoriented. Benoit concentrated hard during the race and was first heading into the tunnel that led into the Los Angeles Coliseum, the end of the marathon course, emerging as the winner with a time of 2 hours, 24 minutes, 52 seconds. That year, she shared the Sportswoman of the Year Award with Olympic gymnast Mary Lou Retton. In 1985 she won the Chicago Marathon. She was honored in 1986 with the Sullivan Award given to the year's most outstanding amateur athlete, and the Abibe Bikila Award, given for contributions to the sport of long-distance running.

See also Sportswoman of the Year Award; Sullivan Award
References Benoit, *Running Tide* (1987); Benoit, *Running for Life* (1995); Condon, *Great Women Athletes of the Twentieth Century* (1991).

Berenson, Senda (1868–1954)

A Lithuanian immigrant, Berenson grew up in Boston, where she attended the Boston Normal School of Gymnastics. At Smith College in Northampton, Massachusetts, she served as athletic director and taught physical education. The game of basketball had just been introduced, and Berenson organized a freshman-sophomore game that became a tradition.

Some newspaper articles criticized the game as having been loud and "wild," with aggressive play. They claimed the players' and spectators' behavior was too rough and aggressive. In response, Berenson developed the first set of rules for the game of women's basketball in 1893, rules that were followed for 70 years.

The rules were put into book form in 1901 and approved by the National Women's Basketball Committee, which Berenson organized two years before. The rules limited body contact. They also said that players could not hold onto the ball for longer than 3 seconds and that they could dribble no more than once (later changed to three times) with each possession of the ball. There were to be six players on the court at a time, each playing a particular position in a section of the court. This was in contrast to the men's game, in which there were five players who could move about on the full court.

From 1905 to 1917, Berenson served as chair of the rules committee for the American Association for the Advent of Physical Education (later the National Association for Girls and Women in Sports). She continued to teach and served as director of physical education at a private school for girls from 1911 to 1921. Berenson and Margaret Wade were the first two women elected to the Basketball Hall of Fame.

See also Basketball
References Barnes, *Women's Basketball* (1980); Sullivan, *Better Basketball for Girls* (1978).

Berg, Patricia Ann (b. 1918)
Like many girls of her day, Patricia Berg was discouraged from playing football, baseball, and other sports with boys. Told to find something more "ladylike" to do, the Minnesota-native took up golf, receiving her first full set of clubs at age 14. Berg won her state's championship in 1935 and repeated that victory in 1936

and 1938. She polished a strong, sure swing that often kept her score in the 70s.

At age 20, Berg won the National Amateur Women's title. She went on to win 26 amateur titles, and, throughout her career, qualified for every tournament she entered. Turning professional in 1930, Berg won the Women's Masters (for the first of seven times), and the international Tam O' Shanter tournament, which she would win four times. Berg won the Ladies Professional Golf Association's (LPGA) first U.S. Women's Open in 1946. Five years later, Berg captured the Western Open title. In 1959, at age 41, she hit a hole-in-one at the U.S. Women's Open, the only woman ever to do so.

Besides being named Athlete of the Year three times by the Associated Press, Berg received the Vare Trophy three times. She was also honored for her charitable work for such causes as the Cerebral Palsy Foundation. In 1978 the Patty Berg Award was established in her honor and is given by the LPGA to women who have made an outstanding contribution to golfing. Among those who have received it are Marilynn Smith (1979) and Betsy Rawls (1980).

One of Berg's greatest efforts was to help other women golfers. In 1946 she helped to found the Ladies Professional Golf Association (LPGA) and headed the organization for four years. The LPGA played a key role in developing the women's golf tour and increasing the prize money women could earn. Berg also taught thousands of golf clinics and exhibitions.

In 1951 Berg was one of the first four golfers chosen for the LPGA Hall of Fame. She was also named to the World Golf Hall of Fame, which honors top men and women in the sport. Berg was voted into the Women's Sports Hall of Fame in 1980.

See also Ladies Professional Golf Association; Vare Trophy
References Markel and Brooks, *For the Record: Women in Sports* (1985); Moffett, *Great Women Athletes* (1974); Pachter, et al., *Champions of American Sport* (1981).

Betz, Pauline (b. 1919)

A top player during the 1940s, Pauline May Betz was suspended from the United States Lawn Tennis Association (USLTA) for publicly supporting a professional tennis tour for women.

Born in Dayton, Ohio, Betz began playing tennis at an early age. Her style combined speed and strength with deft movements on the court. Many commentators described her as "ballet-like." In 1941 and again in 1945, Betz was the runner-up in the U.S. women's singles championship. She won that tournament from 1942 to 1944, securing her fourth title in 1946. That same year, she won the Wimbledon championship without losing a single set. She and her partner Budge (John Edward) Patty won the French mixed doubles title, and Betz won both her singles matches and her women's doubles event while competing on the U.S. Wightman Cup team.

In all, Betz earned 19 U.S. titles on both clay and grass surfaces, both indoors and out. She was ranked as the number one woman player in both the United States and the world in 1946 but was not able to compete after her suspension. Betz later took part in professional exhibition matches. She married Bob Addie, a sportswriter for the *Washington Post*, and became a teaching pro in Washington, D.C. In 1965 she was inducted into the International Tennis Hall of Fame.

Reference Collins and Hollander, eds., *Bud Collins' Modern Encyclopedia of Tennis* (1994).

Bhushan, Insook (b. 1952)

An American born in South Korea, Bhushan became a top women's table tennis (Ping-Pong) player during the 1970s. She captained the world champion South Korean team in 1973 before moving to the United States to settle in Aurora, Colorado, in 1974. As of 1977, she began competing as an American. Bhushan won six women's singles national titles (1976–1978; 1981–1983) and a number of doubles and mixed doubles titles.

At the National Sports Festival in 1983, Bhushan won four gold medals, in the singles, doubles, mixed doubles, and team events. She swept the same four golds at the Pan American Games that year and won all four events at the U.S Nationals in December. While winning the singles, doubles, mixed doubles, and team titles at the 1983 U.S. championships, Bhushan won every game. The U.S. Table Tennis Association named her its Amateur Athlete of 1983 and Sportswoman of the Year in 1986–1990.

Bushan, the mother of two sons, was a member of the U.S. Olympic teams in 1988 and 1992. She won the gold medal again at two more Pan American Games, in 1987 and 1991.

Reference USA Table Tennis Association, "Insook Bushan," *Fact Sheet,* 1992.

Biathlon

This winter sport is a race that combines target shooting with cross country skiing and is an Olympic event both for men and women. The men's event was introduced in 1960, though the women's event was not included in the Games until 1992. Women from Europe typically dominated world competition in the biathlon.

At the 1992 Olympics in Albertville, France, Myriam Bedard of Canada became the first North American woman to win a medal, the bronze, in the biathlon. At the 1994 Winter Games in Lillehammer, Norway, Bedard won the gold, the first North American woman to achieve such a win. The 24-year-old Bedard had competed in her first biathlon nine years earlier and became the Canadian junior champion in 1988. In 1993, she became the first North American woman to win a gold medal in world biathlon competition. The course at Lillehammer was 15-kilometers long.

The U.S. biathletes also turned in their best performances ever at the 1994 Olympics. Joan Smith placed fourteenth and Joan Guetschow came in seventeenth. Guetschow was one of only three skiers in the field of 68 women who hit as many as 19 of the 20 targets along the route.

References Clarey, "A Biathlon First for a Canadian Who Wouldn't Quit," *New York Times,* February 19, 1994, 27; Clarey, "11 Months after Heart Surgery, U.S. Biathlete Is Better Than Ever," *New York Times,* February 19, 1994, 28.

Bicycle Racing (See Cycling)

Billiards

Nobody knows for certain how the game of billiards originated. It probably developed from lawn bowling as people sought a way to play this game in a smaller space. The idea of a table on a platform evolved gradually, along with the use of one ball to hit another into a corner hole. Clubs used to hit these balls were replaced with sticks, the forerunners of modern cue sticks. The game of billiards is mentioned in Shakespearean plays and was known in both England and France by the 1400s. There were billiard rooms in men's private clubs as well as public billiard rooms in England. Queen Victoria had a billiard table set up in Windsor Castle. English and Spanish immigrants brought the game to North America in the 1500s.

In America, the game of pocket billiards also became known as pool. Men dominated the sport for a number of years, but some men believed women could play billiards. In 1915, a top male player, Maurice Daly, said billiards rooms should be open to women. A professional tour for women developed in the late 1900s. The Women's Professional Billiards Association (WPBA) sponsors the tour. Jean Balukas (b. 1959) was one of the top U.S. women players. Balukas took up billiards before age five, using the table her parents had bought for her brothers. She won her first title, the U.S. Open Billiards Championship, when she was nine years old, defeating the Michigan state women's champion. At 13, she won the U.S. Women's Open Pocket Billiards Championship, a title she held for six years. In 1978, Balukas was the world women's champion.

By 1995, the WPBA was sponsoring 18 major tournaments, and ESPN, the sports network, televised the national championships, held in December. Top players included Loree Lee Jones, Ewa Mataya-Lawrence (the number one player on the WPBA tour from 1990 to 1993), and Jeannette Lee, the number one U.S. women's player in 1994. Lee's parents emigrated from South Korea and settled in Brooklyn, New York, where she grew up. She began playing pool at age 18 and resolved to master the game. She started on the tour at 20 and had reached the top position in just three years, often practicing the sport 60 hours a week.

See also Jones, Loree Jon
References Berkow, "Jones Sinks, Then Soars," *New York Times,* August 12, 1995, 31.

Black (Bonfils), Winifred Sweet
(1863–1936)

Newswriter Black became the first woman to report on a prizefight. Under the pen name Annie Laurie, the Wisconsin native worked as a reporter for the *San Francisco Examiner* from 1890 to 1895. Black found resourceful ways to get unusual stories or interviews with important people. Two of her most significant stories were on the San Francisco earthquake of 1906 and the scandalous murder of the famous New York architect, Stanford White. In 1902 she became the first woman to report on a prizefight. Later, during World War I, this pioneer newswoman served as a foreign correspondent for the *San Francisco Observer*.

Blair, Bonnie Kathleen (b. 1964)

In 1994, having won six Olympic gold medals—five of them gold—Bonnie Blair became the top American Winter Olympian in history, as well as the top gold medalist among American women.

Born in Cornwall, New York, Blair grew up in Champaign, Illinois, the youngest of six. She and her siblings all skated in competition. Blair first skated at age two and focused on speed skating, earning a spot on the national speed skating team when she was 15 years old. A year later, she had achieved a national ranking and went to Europe to train for the upcoming 1984 Olympics. Although she made the team, Blair did not win a medal. Training intensively for the next four years, she won a gold medal in the 500-meter race at the Winter Olympic Games in Calgary, with a time of 39.1 seconds, her first world record. She went on to capture the bronze medal in the 1,000-meter race, the only American to win more than one medal at the 1988 Games.

Following the Olympics, Blair held on to her world record time in the 500-meter race until late 1987. She returned to the Olympics in 1992. At Albertville in France, Blair won the 500-meter race once again and won another gold medal for the 1,000-meter when she crossed the finish line two one-hundredths of a second faster than her nearest opponent. She defended her 500-meter title in 1993 and 1994, then captured two more gold medals in the 1994 Olympics in Lillehammer, Norway, for a total of five. Her 1994 Olympic time for the 500-meter race was 39.10 seconds. Her time in the 1,000-meter race held on February 23 was 1 minute, 18.74 seconds. Sportswriter Jere Longman praised Blair's aggressiveness and "impeccable technique," which included a low, crouch position and expert use of the piston stroke.

Blair's friendly manner and achievements led to more honors and product endorsement offers after the Olympics. Journalists called her an "All-American girl" and noted that she enjoyed eating peanut butter and jelly sandwiches before racing and that she wore no socks under her skates. Blair was named 1994 Babe Zaharias Female Amateur Athlete of the Year at a ceremony held in Beaumont, Texas, Zaharias's hometown.

Skating in February 1995, Blair broke her own world record in the 500-meter race in Calgary, Canada, with a time of 38.13 seconds. She broke another record in the 1,000-meter, where her time was 1 minute, 19.43 seconds. In March 1995, on her thirty-first birthday, Blair retired from competitive skating. She said, "I guess I've gotten to the point where I accomplished way more than I ever expected. It's getting more difficult to stay at the level I like to be on. It's time to go on with the rest of my life." She settled in Milwaukee, Wisconsin, where she continued her public speaking.

See also Olympic Medal; Olympics, Winter

Blazejowski, Carol "Blaze"

References Berkow, "Speeding Blair Captures Gold for Fifth Time," *New York Times*, February 24, 1994, C1; "Blair Holds Her Emotions for a Fifth," *New York Times*, February 24, 1994; "Blair Wins 4th Gold and Shows No Sign of Slowing," *New York Times*, February 20, 1994, C3; "Honored," *Women's Sports and Fitness*, March 1995, 29; Longman, "Retiring at Top Speed," *New York Times*, February 19, 1995, 1, 4; Rushin, "The Last Lap," *Sports Illustrated*, February 27, 1995, 52–55.

Blalock, Jane (b. 1945)

A native of Portsmouth, New Hampshire, Blalock was an outstanding young golfer who won her state's junior title and the New England junior title when she was 17 years old. Beginning in 1965, she won four consecutive New Hampshire Amateur titles. During those years, Blalock attended Rollins College in Florida. She won the Florida Intercollegiate title in 1965.

When Blalock joined the women's Ladies Professional Golf Association (LPGA) tour in 1969, she was named Rookie of the Year. From 1969 to 1981, Blalock competed in 299 tournaments, qualifying for every one she entered. She finished in the top ten three times in 1983. In 1972, Blalock won the Colgate-Dinah Shore Classic. One of her most exciting tournaments was the 1978 Bankers' Trust Classic in Pittsford, New York. Going into the last day of play, she led Nancy Lopez by three shots. Spectators watched as the two played head-to-head during the last nine holes. They were tied for the lead at the sixteenth hole, just two holes from the finish. Lopez managed to hit an amazing 35-foot putt for a birdie on the seventeenth hole and par for the last hole, winning the title.

In 1975 Blalock took part in the Superstars event, a televised sports competition for top women athletes. She went on to do sports commentary for television and to teach golf. Blalock has been described as a generous competitor who has praised and encouraged other golfers while boosting the sport. She has also been praised for her ability to play well under pressure and in all kinds of conditions. After becoming a full-time stockbroker in 1986, Blalock played few golf matches on the women's tour.

Blazejowski, Carol "Blaze" (b. 1956)

Basketball player Blazejowski, known to her fans as "Blaze," won the Wade Trophy as the outstanding woman collegiate player in 1978. She had set a scoring record that year by making 52 points in a single game.

A native of Cranford, New Jersey, Blazejowski played basketball on the street and school playgrounds. Later, she recalled that her parents had encouraged her: "When I began playing ball it was fine with [my father.] My mother was a tomboy when she was young. She had three brothers and was always out playing with them." She also watched basketball players on television and tried out the winning moves she observed. In high school, Blazejowski competed both with boy and girl players. She also played in local Catholic Youth Organization leagues. Besides playing basketball, baseball, and other sports, she earned excellent grades.

Blazejowski attended Montclair State College, where she became a top basketball player. During her first season, she scored an average of 33 points in 17 games. The team won 13 games that year and lost only 4. In 1975, under coach Maureen Wendelken, Montclair's team became one of the best in the country. Wendelken was impressed with Blazejowski's determination, discipline, and the pride she took in playing her best. She said that Carol moved so well on the court that she was often open and guards could give up the ball to her. During the 1975–1976 season, her team finished with 20 wins and 5 losses. Blazejowski was named an All-American and scored an average of 28.5 points a game.

The next year, she scored 919 points in 27 games—an average of 34 points a game. Her team finished eighth in the country. Playing at Madison Square Garden against Queens College, she scored 52 points of the 102 earned by her team. No woman had ever scored so many points at the Garden.

During her senior year, Blazejowski scored at least 40 points in each of her last three games and accumulated 1,235 points in 32 games. She led the nation in scoring for women's collegiate basketball, and some commentators said she could compete on a men's team. Blazejowski's career total was 3,199 points. She had looked forward to playing in the 1980 Olympics, but the United States boycotted those Games for political reasons.

In 1980, Blazejowski signed to play pro basketball with the New Jersey Gems, part of the two-year-old Women's Basketball League, but the League folded after one season. In 1984, she joined the New York team, part of the newly formed Women's American Basketball Association, which had taken the place of the Women's Basketball League.

As of 1994, Blazejowski's college career scoring average of 31.7 points was still a record. That year, she was inducted into the Naismith Memorial Basketball Hall of Fame, one of only five women to be so honored as of 1994.

See also Wade Trophy
References Anderson, *The Story of Basketball* (1988); Brown, *The Complete Book of Basketball* (1980); Gutman, *More Modern Women Superstars* (1979).

Bleibtrey, Ethelda (1902–1978)
The first U.S. woman to win the Olympics swimming competition, Bleibtrey set a world record with her time of 1 minute, 13.6 seconds in the 100-meter freestyle event. From 1920 to 1922, she won every race she entered.

Bleibtrey was born in Waterford, New York, and began swimming to gain strength after recovering from polio, a disease that attacks the motor nerves that control muscles. One of her friends competed in swim races, so Bleibtrey joined her and succeeded in winning every national amateur title in sprint racing. In 1919, Bleibtrey was cited by police at Manhattan Beach for "nude swimming"—she had removed the woolen stockings women were then expected to wear while on the beach and in the water. The public sided with Bleibtrey, and soon stockings were no longer part of women's bathing costumes.

Only two years after her first race, Bleibtrey competed in the 1920 Olympics held in Antwerp, Belgium. Conditions were grim, with the athletes practicing and competing in cold water that many of them later called "muddy." Nonetheless, Bleibtrey won a gold medal in the 100-meter freestyle, the 300-meter freestyle, and again as part of the women's 2 x 100–meter freestyle relay team. Since Bleibtrey was also the world backstroke champion, she would likely have won four medals had that event been offered at the time.

Bleibtrey was inducted into the International Swimming Hall of Fame in 1967. Of her sport, she once said, "Swimming is the best sport in the world for women. . . . After a girl has had a good swim, she feels relaxed, cool, and her muscles are in order, and her whole make-up, both physical and mental, is at rest and at peace with the world."

Reference Carlson and Fogerty, *Tales of Gold* (1977); Mallon and Buchanan, *Quest for Gold* (1984).

Bloomer, Amelia Jenks (1818–1894)

Born in Homer, New York, Bloomer was a teacher before marrying a Quaker magazine publisher. She became publisher and editor of the *Lily*, a newspaper for women. A women's rights advocate, Bloomer wrote articles about the right to vote, fair treatment in the workplace, and other social reforms.

In 1851 she promoted a style of dress she had admired on her cousin: full Turkish pantaloons worn beneath a short skirt. It became known as the Bloomer, Bloomer Costume, or simply bloomers. The outfit was especially popular with women athletes who needed more freedom of movement. Bloomer continued to promote this style of dress along with important social reform issues until her death in Iowa at age 76.

See also Bloomers
References Gattey, *The Bloomer Girls* (1967); Riegel, *American Feminists* (1963).

Bloomers (also "Bloomer Costume")

During the mid-1850s, women typically wore many undergarments, including several petticoats, and hoop-skirted gowns made of some 20 to 30 yards of fabric. Stiff corsets reinforced with steel and whalebone stays squeezed their torsos and kept them from taking deep breaths and moving freely.

In 1851, Amelia Jenks Bloomer, the publisher-editor of a prominent women's rights newspaper, suggested that women cast off this cumbersome clothing and adopt a bifurcated garment that covered the legs separately, like men's trousers. The outfit proposed by Bloomer consisted of very full pantaloons and a skirt that just covered the knee. The Bloomer, as it was called, was welcomed by women's rights advocates and those who felt trapped by their clothing or enjoyed sports such as cycling, horseback riding, gymnastics, and skating. Thousands of women, including many in England, France, and other countries began wearing bloomers, sometimes forming Bloomer Clubs. The style became associated with the growing women's suffrage movement. Critics called the wearers "Bloomer Girls" and "Bloomerites."

See also Bloomer, Amelia Jenks
References Gattey, *The Bloomer Girls* (1967); Riegel, *American Feminists* (1963).

Blum, Arlene (See Himalayan Expedition)

Boating (See *America*[3]; Powerboating; Sailing)

Bobek, Nicole (b. 1968)

A native of Chicago, Bobek began skating at age three. Her mother had fled from Czechoslovakia in 1968 when that country was invaded by tanks from the Soviet Union. In 1991 Bobek won the Vienna Cup in Austria and the Olympic Festival figure skating competition. But she had a reputation for being inconsistent and unwilling to train intensively and was criticized for being a smoker. Bobek also changed coaches every few years, more frequently than most skaters do.

Working with coach Richard Callaghan in 1994, she showed her ability to stick with a training regimen and skate consistently well throughout a competition. With determined effort, Bobek won the 1995 ladies' national championship in Providence, Rhode Island, with a performance that sportswriter Jere Longman called "mature, sophisticated." She also received high praise for her ability to interpret music and choreograph some of her own routines. At the world championships later that year, Bobek came in third.

At the 1996 nationals, held in San Diego, California, Bobek had expected to defend her title. She was in second place after Michelle Kwan at the end of the ladies' short program. But she had been plagued with an injury to her right ankle that became worse during the competition. Bobek was forced to withdraw.

References Howard, "Queen for a Day," *Sports Illustrated*, February 20, 1995, 26–31; Longman, "Another U.S. Champion Swirls in Controversy," *New York Times*, February 20, 1995, C3; Longman, "Bobek's Title Routine Silences Critics for Now," *New York Times*, February 13, 1995, C6.

Bodybuilding

Traditionally a male pursuit, bodybuilding—or working to attain well-defined muscles—is now a sport for women as well. The idea of heavy muscles on a woman is still controversial, despite the argument that bulky muscles do not make a woman "unfeminine" or masculine. Supporters of bodybuilding celebrate the idea that women can now explore new physical potentials. Others complain that in bodybuilding, women are on public display wearing skimpy swimsuits and are being evaluated for their appearance. There have also been cases of eating disorders and the use of anabolic steroids among female bodybuilders who attempted to sharply reduce body fat and increase muscle growth through artificial means.

Bodybuilding competitions are held on the local, national, and world level. At these events, the bodybuilders flex to display the various muscle groups, which are judged according to how well-developed and symmetrical they are, among other criteria. One of the most important bodybuilding events is the Ms. Olympia contest. In 1980 and 1982, American Rachel McLich won the Ms. Olympia title in her sport. McLich went on to become the Women's Professional World Champion in 1981 and 1982. A recent U.S. bodybuilding champion (1992) is Shelley Beattie. Beattie, who is deaf, also won a place on the women's yachting crew that sailed the *America*³ in its bid to compete in the 1995 America's Cup races. Beattie was a regular performer on the television program "American Gladiators."

See also *America*³; America's Cup

Boston Marathon

This 26-mile, 385-yard race began in 1897 as part of Boston's St. Patrick's Day celebration and has been run every year since then except in 1918. By the 1980s, it was one of the major marathons in the world.

Women were not officially allowed to compete until 1972, but some determined women joined the race anyway. In 1966, 24-year-old Roberta Louise (Bobbi) Gibb joined male runners on the course and completed the marathon that year and the next. The Boston Athletic Association acknowledged that she had finished the race but would not officially list her as a competitor, since women were not allowed to enter in the first place.

The next year, Kathrine Switzer entered the race using only her initials and was issued a number to run. She finished behind Gibb that year, but received a great deal of publicity when organizers noticed her running and tried to oust her from the race. Gibb and two other women ran the marathon in 1968, and Sara Mae Berman finished first among the group of women who ran the race in 1969. Her time was 3 hours, 22 minutes, 46 seconds. Five women, including Switzer, ran the marathon in 1970, and Berman repeated her victory of the previous year with a time of 3 hours, 5 minutes, and 7 seconds—a course record for women. She won her third marathon in 1971.

In the meantime, the Road Runners Club of America and other groups and individuals were pressuring the Amateur Athletic Union to permit women to run marathons. The next year, women were officially allowed in the Boston marathon.

Miki Gorman of the United States won in 1974, setting a new record time of 2 hours, 47 minutes, and 11 seconds. She won again in 1977, with a time about 1 minute longer than her 1974 time. Joan Benoit Samuelson broke Gorman's record when she won in 1982. She did even better when she won in 1983, achieving a new record of 2 hours, 22 minutes, and 43 seconds. Between 1986 and 1995, no American woman won the Boston marathon.

See also Switzer, Kathrine
Reference Higdon, *A Century of Running: Boston* (1995).

Bowling

Historians believe that bowling dates back to before 5300 B.C. People of the Stone Age rolled heavy, rounded stones at targets, perhaps as a training exercise for hunting. Originally, rolling of a ball down a lane to hit pin-like objects may have been a game or religious rite. Signs of bowling dating back to ancient times have been found in Egyptian ruins.

No one is sure how the idea of using nine pins then ten pins came to be. Dutch settlers brought the nine-pin version of the game to early America. It was played outdoors on areas called bowling greens. Some towns had special bowling greens that can still be located today. Around 1900, modern bowling developed with the ten-pin version of the game.

During the 1800s, bowling establishments tried to attract women to the sport by making the sport more genteel, as this paragraph from a Milwaukee newspaper in 1855 shows: "The ladies who passed through Burns' swinging doors took a shocked look at the joint and told the proprietor it would never do if he wanted the feminine trade. Spittoons went out, the genuine oil paintings of naked nymphs came down from behind the bar, curtains were hung and rugs laid. The help were ordered to shave at least twice a week. Signs went up asking gents to kindly refrain from profane language." Some bowling establishments were so well-maintained and respectable that women of the higher classes in society went bowling during the late 1800s.

As more people began to bowl, organizations were founded to govern the sport. The National Bowling Association (NBA) was formed in 1875 by 27 clubs in New York City. They established a standard ball size and rules for the game that defined the size of the lanes and ways in which pins would be removed. However, people in different geographic regions continued to play by different rules. The American Bowling League, which succeeded the NBA in 1890, also ended quickly, after just one year. The American Amateur Bowling League (AABL), which objected to prize money, was unpopular.

In 1895 a strong bowling organization called the American Bowling Congress finally began unifying the game and its many players. However, the bowling alleys of the early 1900s often were places women would not go for fear of losing their reputations. Alleys frequently were located in the same buildings as bars and billiard rooms. There, men smoked, drank, and gambled. Bookies frequently arranged for bets in these places and used them to collect and distribute bet money.

Some alleys were not troubled by such activities, or their owners made a big effort to clean them up. Women could be seen at some alleys bowling with their husbands. At many of these places, couples enjoyed a night out, paying 50 cents to eat large meals and bowl for as many hours as they wished.

In 1907, Dennis J. Sweeney, a proprietor in St. Louis, Missouri, started the first women's bowling leagues. He also arranged an informal national women's tournament in 1916, where women used the same lanes as men. The winner was Birdie Kern, whose father had won the national men's singles title in 1904. Kern, along with Addie Ruschmeyer of New York City, Goldie Greenwald of Cleveland, Ohio, and Floretta McCutcheon of Denver, Colorado, were the first women to distinguish themselves in the sport. They often defeated male competitors, as when Greenwald bowled a 300 in a men's game. At age 39, McCutcheon won a highly touted 1927 match against top men's bowler Jimmy Smith. For six games, she earned 1377 points to his 1376.

In 1915, Ellen Kelly of St. Louis organized the first women's bowling association. She urged women to organize in other cities and to hold tournaments. After the first "national" tournament was held at Dennis Sweeney's lanes in 1916, the women decided to form the Women's Bowling Congress (WBC), which later became the Women's International Bowling Congress (WIBC). The WIBC was incorporated in 1919. Its goal was to promote the sport and provide opportunities for women to play in tournaments. It also enforced rules of play. The first tournament sponsored by the WIBC was held

in 1917, and 100 women took part, both as individuals and as members of teams. As bowling establishments continued to be cleaned up, membership rose. From 1917 to 1927, the number of women in the WIBC increased from 641 to 7,757.

Some women even opened up their own alleys. In 1930 Violet Simon of Minnesota set up the first of her eight bowling centers. She later told author Herman Weiskopf, "The things that got women to bowl were that the places were cleaned up, classes were held so they could learn the game, and they were made welcome. *Knowing* they were welcome was very important to women." During the 1930s, Marie Warmbier dominated American women's competition.

Bowling surged during the 1940s, when it became a popular way to raise money for the war cause. Special matches were held to support war bonds, the Red Cross, and the USO. Sometimes bowlers donated blood after these events to inspire others to do the same. The Bowlers Victory League raised money to buy recreational equipment for the armed services. The WIBC backed many drives and purchased a bomber called the *Miss WIBC*, presented to the U.S. Army Air Force in 1943. Bowling leagues and activities kept up morale, too. Between 1941 and 1945, membership in the WIBC doubled.

After the war, people had more leisure time, and housewives were encouraged to take up bowling. Even prestigious Vassar College added bowling to the intramural sports played by its all-female student body. Young people of both genders were welcomed in bowling alleys. Mixed doubles matches and women's and men's tournaments appeared on television, boosting the sport. "Championship Bowling" was a popular program during those years. More tournaments were opened to women, and Marion Ladewig became the star woman bowler of the 1950s. In 1960 Sylvia Wene won the All-Star tournament for the second time and became the first woman to bowl a perfect game of 300 in that event.

During the 1960s, though, interest in bowling dwindled. By 1970, the All-Star tournament had ended, along with the Chicago Proprietors' World Invitational. But the sport revived during the 1970s, assisted by the debut of a program called "Bowling for Dollars" in 1968. Carol Anderton of Texas won the Brunswick Showdown in October 1975 at Caesar's Palace in Las Vegas, Nevada, and took home $50,000, the largest prize in the history of women's bowling. Fifty years after it was founded, the membership of the WIBC had risen from 40 people to some 3.4 million. About 125,000 local bowling leagues sponsored weekly games.

The Professional Women Bowlers Association (PWBA) was formed in 1959, with 23 women signing on as charter members. In 1960, 100 women participated in the first PWBA tournament, held in Miami, Florida. Yet, progress was slow. In 1963 there were only four PWBA-sponsored events all year.

Early in the 1970s, more tournaments were run for women, many gaining television coverage. The $85,000 Brunswick Red Crown Classic was the first nationally televised event for women. It was the best-funded tournament up to that point. In 1977, All-Sports Productions worked hard to bring more attention and prize money to women's bowling. The company, out of Chicago, hoped to promote events for the PWBA.

Also around this time, the Ladies Professional Bowlers Association (LPBA) was rising in importance. Founded by lawyer and businesswoman Janet Buehler of Akron, Ohio, the LPBA sought more sponsors to fund tournaments. Both groups operated tours for several years. By 1978, however, they had dissolved and given way to a new organization, the Women's Professional Bowlers Association (WPBA). Women members of both older groups automatically became members of the WPBA. In addition to the professional organization, semiprofessional groups were developed in the east, west, and other regions of the country.

Among the top women bowlers were Judy Cook, a Missourian who was runner-up for 13 years, then won the Pearl Cup in Japan in April 1973. She followed up with consecutive wins in the Ebonite Classic in August and the Cavalcade of Stars in November. Patty Costello is among the American women who have been named International Bowler of the Year twice. Other top competitors included Dorothy Fothergill, Betty Morris, and Judy Soutar. Morris was named Bowler of the Year in both 1976 and 1977.

In 1994 Aleta Sill won both the Bowling Proprietor's Association of America U.S. Open and the Delaware Open. Sill and Anne Marie Duggan both earned more than $100,000 on the tour that year. Duggan captured the WIBC Queen's title and Santa Maria Classic.

Surveys show bowling to be one of the most popular year-round activities in the nation. As of 1977, about 63.7 million people bowled at least annually. The WIBC had 4 million members in 1977. There were three divisions for women bowlers: open—for the best bowlers, and first and second divisions for those less skilled. Each division offered singles, doubles, and team competitions. A Queens tournament had replaced the American Bowling Congress Masters. The WIBC also sanctioned independent tournaments run by sponsors. By the 1990s, more women were involved in bowling than any other sport.

Young girls have also excelled as bowlers. In 1978, ten-year-old Wendy Jackson set a new record for girls in her age group when she bowled a 272 game. Jackson hit seven consecutive strikes in that game. Bowling has also been a sport in which people with certain disabilities can excel. There are special tournaments for bowlers who are blind or who use wheelchairs.

See also Adamek, Donna; Costello, Patty; Fothergill, Dorothy; Ladewig, Marion; McCutcheon, Floretta **References** Gipe, *The Great American Sports Book* (1978); Ladies Professional Bowlers Tour, *1994 LPBT Guide* (1994); Weiskopf, *The Perfect Game: The World of Bowling* (1978).

Boxing

Few women took up boxing until the 1900s. The combative nature and physical contact in the sport led to the idea that it was "unfeminine" and suitable only for men. Until 1867, when new rules were set up by the Marquis of Queensbury, fighters could engage in more violent tactics than today. Yet a few women became famous for their prowess in the ring. Elizabeth Wilkinson was an English boxing champion during the early 1700s. In 1795, Londoner Mary Ann Fielding won a 1 hour, 20 minute fight against her opponent after flooring her more than 70 times, according to written accounts of the match.

In the 1800s, boxing was outlawed in many parts of America. As a result, boxing matches were held in secret. But as English boxers performed in America, it became known as a respectable sport. The first official women's boxing match in the United States was held on March 16, 1876. After defeating her opponent

Rose Harland, Nell Saunders received a silver butter dish as a prize.

Still, women were discouraged from and even banned from attending men's boxing matches. Until 1974, no woman had ever been granted a license to act as a judge at such events. The New York State Athletic Commission granted such a license to Carol Polis that year. Other women also made inroads in judging boxing matches. Carol Castellano and Eva Shain were licensed next by New York State officials.

In 1975, about a thousand spectators watched the first women's boxing bout. Thirty-four-year-old Caroline Svendsen defeated Jean Lange 50 seconds into the first round. The match was held in Virginia City, Nevada, after the state's boxing commissioner agreed to allow the fight. In other states, women lobbied unsuccessfully for the right to hold officially sanctioned women's boxing matches.

During the 1980s, one of the top American women boxers was Jackie Tonawanda of New York City, who has been called "the female Muhammad Ali." Lightweight fighter Marian "Lady Tyger" Trimiar was one of the first women licensed as a boxer by the New York State Athletic Commission. Trimiar credited her sport with making her "more feminine, more mature" and called herself "a pioneer."

The sport has increased in popularity among amateurs as well as professionals. Boxing classes and clubs for women have sprung up in various cities in the United States, and some women celebrities claim they box to keep fit.

See also Shain, Eva

Bright, Patricia Ann (b. 1942)

A volleyball player, Bright played in two Olympiads and numerous other in-

American boxer Cathy "Cat" Davis receives a head-snapping right from German Uschi Doering in the 1979 women's lightweight championship.

ternational and national events before becoming a coach. She grew up in a volleyball-loving family and played the game with her mother as a child. She later attended Michigan State University where she practiced with the men's team, since there was no team for women. After transferring to the University of Southern California, Bright was able to compete on the collegiate level with other women.

At her first international competition, the Pan American Games in 1963, Bright was part of the U.S. team that won the second-place silver medal. Newly wed, she went to the 1964 Olympic Games in Tokyo, along with husband Mike who was a member of the U.S. men's volley-ball team. The U.S. women finished fifth that year. A remarkable Japanese team won the gold medal.

Bright returned to the Olympics in 1968, again as a setter/hitter. That year, the U.S. team finished eighth in Mexico City. However, Bright achieved a service ace against the team from the Soviet Union, which later won the gold medal.

After leaving amateur competition, Bright combined motherhood with her career as a volleyball coach at Santa Monica High School in California. History repeated itself as Bright not only played volleyball with her daughter but coached her high school team.

Brisco-Hooks, Valerie (b. 1960)

In 1984, sprinter Brisco-Hooks, from Greenwood, Mississippi, became the first woman to break 50 seconds in the 400-meter race, with a time of 49.83 seconds.

Brisco-Hooks had been a track and field star during her teens and at California State–Northridge but retired after her marriage and the birth of her son in 1982. She then returned to running to improve her fitness level and discovered she was running well enough to compete again. In 1984, Brisco-Hooks ran her best time ever—22.16 seconds—in the 200-meter race. She became national indoor women's champion in the 220-yard dash and won first place in the 400-meters at the outdoor national competition with her record-beating time of 49.83 seconds.

Brisco-Hooks was coached by Bob Kersee, husband and coach of the great track and field champion Jackie Joyner-Kersee. At the Olympic trials that year, she established a new record in the 400-meter race by running it in 49.79 seconds. Her time at the Olympics in Los Angeles was even better—48.83 seconds, which set a new Olympic record for the 400-meters and a new American record. In addition to that gold medal, Brisco-Hooks won the 200-meter race, setting another Olympic record with her time of 21.81 seconds, and she was part of the winning U.S. 4 x 100–meter relay team, bring home three gold medals. In 1985,

she set a world record of 52.99 seconds in the women's indoor 400-yard run.

References "After the Gold, Some Glitter," *Sports Illustrated,* June 3, 1985, 46.

Broadcasting (See Sportscasting)

Broadwick , Georgia "Tiny" (b. 1895)

In 1913, Broadwick became the first woman to free-fall parachute from an airplane that was flying at about 30 miles per hour. With an 11-pound silk parachute, intended for use by the U.S. army, she landed on a barley field in Los Angeles after falling about 100 feet. As a result of tests done by Broadwick and others, the 11-pound parachute, called a "life boat," was put into use by the military.

Broderick Cup

Annual award given to the most outstanding college woman athlete.

See also Caulkins, Tracy

Brooks, Lyn (See Triathlon)

Brough, Louise (b. 1923)

Champion tennis player Althea Louise Brough is one of the few players to win triple titles at Wimbledon in one tournament.

Born in Oklahoma City, Brough was raised in Southern California and dominated girls' junior events there during the 1930s. In 1940 and 1941, she won the national 18-and-under title.

The normal schedule of international tennis events was disrupted during World War II. Brough played in her first Wimbledon in 1946, when the tournament resumed, and thrilled spectators with her net-play based on a strong volley. The talented newcomer reached the finals in all three women's events, losing the singles to Pauline Betz but winning the doubles with her partner Margaret Osburne DuPont and capturing the mixed doubles title with Tom Brown.

For the next ten years, she played in 21 of 30 possible Wimbledon finals in those three events. Brough won the women's singles title in 1948, 1949, 1950, and 1955. She and DuPont captured the doubles in 1948, 1949, 1950, and 1954. She won the mixed doubles in 1947, 1948, and 1950. Thus 1950 became the year of Brough's "triple." That same year, Brough won the Australian singles title.

Brough was less successful as a singles player at the U.S. national championships, where she won only once, in 1947. However, she played in six finals there, and she and partner DuPont won 12 U.S. championships, with one winning streak that lasted from 1942 through 1950. Some commentators called them the best U.S. women's doubles team in history. The versatile team succeeded on clay surfaces as well, winning the French title three times.

With 35 major titles to her credit, Brough ranked behind four other women (Margaret Smith Court, Martina Navratilova, Billie Jean King, and DuPont) as of 1995. She was inducted into the Tennis Hall of Fame in 1962.

Brough married Dr. A. T. Clapp and retired from amateur competition. She sometimes played in the senior tournaments for players over 40 during the 1970s. In 1971 and 1975, she and her partner Barbara Green Weigandt won the senior women's U.S. Hard Court Doubles tournament.

See also Betz, Pauline; DuPont, Margaret Osburne; King, Billie Jean; Navratilova, Martina
References Collins and Hollander, eds., *Bud Collins' Modern Encyclopedia of Tennis* (1994); U.S. Lawn Tennis Association, ed., *Official Encyclopedia of Tennis* (1972).

Brown, Carol (See Rowing)

Brown, Earlene (b. 1935)
Before Brown's excellent performance at two Olympic Games, the United States had not been a contender in the shot put event at the Olympics. Women from the Soviet Union and Eastern Europe had dominated the event in world track and field competitions. But the 226-pound Brown was a surprise fourth-place winner in the women's shot put at the 1956 Olympic Games in Melbourne, Australia. Returning to the Games held in Rome, Italy, in 1960, Brown won a bronze medal in the shot put. Teammates recalled Brown's considerate, enthusiastic ways during the Games. Between 1956 and 1962, Brown won the women's U.S. shot put title eight times and was U.S. women's discus champion in 1958, 1959, and 1961.
See also Track and Field

Brown, Mrs. Charles S.
In 1893, Brown became the first winner of the U.S. national women's golf tournament, held at Meadowbrook Hunt Club on Long Island, New York. Her score for the 18-hole course was 132, which gave her a two-stroke lead over her closest opponent. That same year, she won the U.S Women's Amateur Championship.
See also Golfing

Bulimia (See Eating Disorders)

Bullfighting
A controversial pursuit and so-called blood sport, bullfighting has been dominated by men for centuries. It began in Spain and spread to Mexico and Central and South America when Spaniards colonized these areas after the 1400s. In most places, laws and custom kept women from officially fighting bulls or being paid bullfighters.

Conchita Cintrón, the first female bullfighter, confronts her fifty-first bull in Tijuana, Mexico.

During the 1900s, some female bullfighters gained recognition. Conchita (Verrill) Cintrón was a mounted bullfighter, and is thought to have slain 800 bulls during her career. In 1949, she broke the Spanish law that banned women from fighting a bull on the ground. Arrested by police, she was quickly released when the public protested. Cintrón moved to Lisbon, Portugal, where she married in 1951 and left bullfighting.

In 1951, Patricia Hayes, a musician in El Paso, Texas, was known for her bullfighting prowess, which she displayed both in Texas and Mexico. An article about Hayes noted that she received "repeated ovations" from the audience in Acapulco and that she was the only female bullfighter to set barbed hooks into the bull's shoulders before making the kill. It was said that she killed 15 bulls during her first year in the ring. Beginning in 1952, another Texan, Patricia McCormick, embarked on a bullfighting career that lasted several years.

American Georgina Knowles became famous as the Lady Bullfighter on Horseback. In 1955, she fought bulls in Mexico, using both hands while riding her horse.

Burchenal, Elizabeth (1876–1959)
Born in Indiana, Burchenal was a talented folk-dancer and musician who pro-

Eighteen-year-old Conchita Cintrón acknowledges praise from over 10,000 fans.

moted physical education in public schools. After graduating from Dr. Sargent's School of Physical Education in Boston, she taught physical education in Chicago and Boston. While working with immigrants in New York City, Burchenal decided that folk-dancing would be a valuable addition to physical education programs in schools.

Burchenal served as the executive secretary of the Girls' Branch of the New York Public Schools Athletic League from 1906 to 1916 and taught teachers how to use physical education with their students. As Burchenal traveled and worked with teachers in Canada and Europe, her ideas were adopted in other countries. Among her many honors was the Gulick

Award (1950) given to the individual who has made the most outstanding contribution to the field of physical education that year.

References Scherman and Green, eds., *Notable American Women: The Modern Period* (1980).

Burr, Leslie (See Equestrian Sports)

Butcher, Susan (b. 1954)
A native of Cambridge, Massachusetts, Susan Butcher grew up with a love of nature and animals. She enjoyed many sports, including sailing, field hockey, basketball, softball, and swimming. When Butcher was 15 years old, she received her first Siberian husky, named Maganak, as a gift from an aunt. Butcher

Named Sled-Dog Racer of the Decade by the Anchorage Times and Outstanding Female Athlete of the World by the International Academy of Sports in France in 1989, Susan Butcher poses with her lead dog, Granite, after placing second in the 1989 Iditarod race.

became fascinated with the history of sled dogs and attended sled-dog races. She also bought another husky.

When Butcher finished high school, she planned to become a ship-builder. She applied to a school in Maine, but they would not admit a woman. At age 17, Butcher moved to Colorado where she worked at a kennel, training and running dogs in exchange for room and board. She took veterinary classes at the University of Colorado. Sadly, she lost both her huskies during this time—one was hit by a car and the other was stolen.

After reading about the Iditarod race in a magazine, Butcher moved to Alaska in 1975. There she worked at the University of Alaska in Fairbanks in a program to save the endangered musk-ox. In the summer, Butcher worked at a salmon factory where she cut and chopped fish. She saved all the money she could to buy huskies for a sled-dog team.

In 1977, Butcher moved to the west coast of Alaska where she met sled-dog expert Joe Redington, who had helped to found the Iditarod sled-dog race. Redington owned a large kennel and let Butcher work there in exchange for dogs. She learned more about how to raise the dogs and train them to run in teams, how to spot a good leader, and how to develop a trusting relationship with the dogs in order to avoid danger on the trail. Often, she was in charge of caring for 150 dogs.

With Redington, Butcher took a team of sled dogs to the summit of Denali. It was the first time anyone had mushed a sled-dog team to that altitude (20,320 feet). They battled 100-mile-per-hour winds and swerved around 2,000-foot-deep crevasses to make their way to the top. Their team of seven dogs made the trip in 44 days.

Butcher dreamed of entering and winning the Iditarod. She moved to a wilderness area near the Wrangell Mountains, close to the Canadian border. There she raised and trained her dogs, 50 miles away from the nearest neighbor. She hunted wild game for food and chopped firewood to warm her log cabin.

In 1978, Butcher entered the Iditarod Trail Sled-Dog Race for the first time. Started in 1973, the Iditarod is an annual race more than 1,000 miles long that runs between Anchorage and Nome, Alaska. The race can take as few as 11 days or several weeks. Many people cannot complete the course at all. It covers rugged, frozen country with steep hills. Teams and their drivers, called "mushers," must cross frozen rivers and avoid stumps and wild animals that might be on the trail. Cold winds and below-zero temperatures threaten dogs and drivers alike. All competitors must complete one 24-hour rest period. After that, few rest more than four hours at a time during the remainder of the race. At rest stops, mushers feed and water their dogs, mend their harnesses, check their feet, and replace the booties they wear, if necessary. The winner receives $50,000.

Butcher was one of three women to enter in 1978. One of the others was Verona Thompson, who had finished the race in 1977, the third woman to do so. In that 1978 race, Butcher finished in nineteenth place, making her the first woman ever to finish in the top 20. As part of that group, she received a cash prize.

The next year, she improved her performance and reached ninth place. Doing steadily better, she finished fifth in the 1980 race. In 1983, despite a mishap along the trail in which she fell into icy water, she managed to finish second, as she had the year before.

With a top team and years of experience, she had a good chance to win in 1985. But disaster struck on the trail when the team ran into a large, angry moose. The moose became entangled in the dogs' harnesses and began stomping. It killed 2 dogs while injuring 11 others. As Butcher tried to free her dogs, the moose struck her shoulder. Another sled arrived, and the musher shot the moose. Butcher withdrew in order to seek medical care for her dogs in Anchorage. The 1985 race was won by a woman for the first time when Libby Riddles of Teller, Alaska, crossed the finish line in Nome.

Determined to try again, Butcher, now married to David Monson, rebuilt her team and entered the 1986 race. She won, defeating the team that had won the year before along with 70 other competitors. Her record-breaking time was 11 days, 15 hours, and 6 minutes. It was the first of three successive wins. Butcher received the Victor Award as Female Athlete of the Year and the U.S. Academy of Achievement Athlete of the Year. For the second year in a row, the Women's Sports Foundation named her Professional Athlete of the Year.

In 1989, her dog team weakened by trail virus, she still managed to place second. That year, she was named Sled-Dog Racer of the Decade by the *Anchorage Times*, as well as Outstanding Female Athlete of the World, an honor bestowed by the International Academy of Sports in France. She regained the top spot in 1990 and set a new speed record: 11 days, 1 hour, 53 minutes, and 23 seconds. It was the first time anyone had achieved four Iditarod victories. (Rick Swenson would reach the total the next year, when he won and Butcher came in third.) *USA Today* named Susan Butcher Top Professional Sportswoman of 1990.

In 1991, she worried that a blizzard at the end of the course might harm her dogs. At a rest stop, Butcher delayed, hoping for better weather, and did not win that year. But the record she had set in the 1990 Iditarod remained, as did some records she set in shorter (300- to 500-mile) races. She took second place in the Iditarod once again in 1992.

Besides competing in sled-dog races, Butcher and her husband run their Trail Breaker Kennels from their property near Eureka, Alaska, near the Arctic Circle. Often, mushers purchase Trail Breaker dogs for their own sled-dog teams.

See also Iditarod Trail Sled-Dog Race; Riddles, Libby

References Butcher, "A Women's Icy Struggle," *National Geographic,* March 1993, 411–422; Dater and Coman, *Body and Soul: Ten American Women* (1988); Mueller, "Making Time," *Outdoor Life,* February 1991, 18; Steptoe, "The Dogged Pursuit of Excellence," *Sports Illustrated,* February 11, 1991, 4.

Camp Fire Girls

The Camp Fire Girls was the first national nonsectarian and interracial organization for girls. Charlotte Vetter Gulick and her husband, Luther Halsey Gulick (a hygiene and physical educator for whom the Gulick Award was named), along with their friend William Chauncey Langdon developed the first program. Camp Fire Girls worked to develop character and good physical and mental health. Outdoor activities and sports were a major focus of the group.

It began in 1910 with a camp experience for 17 girls in Maine. By the 1980s, there were about 400 local groups and more than 600,000 members. Both boys and girls may now join the organization, which has changed its name to Camp Fire.

Canoeing

Canoes were used for thousands of years, especially by Native Americans and Alaska Natives, for transportation. During the 1700s, French trappers began racing in canoes, and in the 1860s, the idea of canoeing as a sport took hold in England. Clubs for canoe enthusiasts were set up around the country, and the Canoe Club was formed for male canoeists in 1866. In North America, competitive races were organized during the late 1800s. Canoeing was a demonstration sport at the 1924 Olympic Games, then became a full-medal sport in 1936, with races over 1,094 yards (1,000 meters) and 10,936 yards (10,000 meters) long.

In addition to competing in world and Olympic canoeing events, women have undertaken record-breaking canoe trips. Along with Verlen Kruger, Valerie Fons traveled down the Mississippi River from Lake Itasca, Minnesota, to the Gulf of Mexico, in 1984; the trip took 23 days, 10 hours, 20 minutes.

See also Kayaking

Capriati, Jennifer (b. 1976)

Born in New York City, Capriati moved to Florida at age four. Her parents believed she had so much aptitude for tennis that they arranged for her to study with Jimmy Evert, a well-known coach who had helped his daughter Chris Evert reach the top of the game.

A powerful game and the ability to run down balls all over the court brought Capriati the junior French Open and junior U.S. Open titles in 1989. The next year, she became the youngest player ever to reach the semifinals of the French Open. As a young star on the rise, she gained endorsement contracts with a racquet manufacturer and an Italian sports clothing company. When Capriati turned professional in 1990, she was a month shy of 14 and was already a millionaire. German player Steffi Graf was the only player to have become a professional at a younger age.

Capriati's early tournament play was

so impressive that people began predicting she would soon be number one. She was introduced in 1991 at the Italian Open as "the future of women's tennis." That year, in a startling upset, Capriati defeated Martina Navratilova in the quarterfinals at Wimbledon. At age 15, she became the youngest woman ever to reach the semifinals of that tournament. She also won the Pathmark Classic, the Mazda Classic, and the Player's Challenge. She reached the semifinals of the 1991 U.S. Open but lost to Monica Seles. Capriati later said that the loss was a big disappointment: "Just thinking that I was two points from the final of the U.S. Open. I'd give anything to go back to that moment and win." Her income for prizes and endorsements in 1991 exceeded $6 million.

At the 1992 Summer Olympics in Barcelona, Spain, Capriati won the women's tennis gold medal. Her opponent was Steffi Graf, then ranked number one in the world among women players. In 1993, Capriati lost in the first round of the U.S. Open. She took a break from the tour to attend to school full-time and recover from an elbow injury. During 1994, Capriati was charged with possession of marijuana, an illegal drug, and left the tennis tour in May.

References Finn, "Capriati's Quest Continues," *Tennis,* September 1993, 94; Preston, "The Unmaking of a Champion," *Tennis,* June 1994, 55–62; Trabert, "Capriati's Classic Backhand," *Tennis,* February 1993, 104–105.

Carner, JoAnne Gunderson (b. 1939)
A top junior golfer in the fifties, Carner went on to win five U.S. Amateur titles—in 1957, 1960, 1962, 1966, and 1968. Two years later, as a professional, Carner won the Wendell West Open, part of the Ladies Professional Golf Association (LPGA) tour. The next year, "the Great

Gundy" captured the U.S Women's Open for the first time, regaining that title in 1976. By 1988, the friendly golfer with the strong, consistent game had amassed 42 titles, the seventh highest number of titles ever won by a woman golfer.

Honored with many awards, Carner won the Vare Trophy five times (1974, 1975, 1981, 1982, and 1983). In 1981, she won the Bob Jones Award, named after the legendary men's champion golfer. She was inducted into the LPGA Hall of Fame in 1982, while still actively playing pro golf. That same year, she was named LPGA Player of the Year for the third time. In 1983 Carner was the top money-earner on the LPGA circuit, with $291,404 to her credit. Her career earnings had reached $1,644,348, making her the top money-winner in women's golf up to that point. Continuing to play pro golf, Carner came in third at the 1987 U.S. Women's Open and was runner-up at the 1989 Dinah Shore tournament. She has been inducted into the World Golf Hall of Fame, the LPGA Hall of Fame, and the International Women's Sports Hall of Fame.

See also Vare Trophy
Reference *Sports Illustrated 1996 Sports Almanac* (1996).

Carpenter-Phinney, Connie (b. 1957)
An expert road racer, Carpenter-Phinney was also an outstanding all-around cyclist. Like many cyclists, the Madison, Wisconsin, native was a strong speedskater and competed in the 1972 Olympics, placing seventh in the 1,500-meter speed skating race. When she entered cycling competition starting in 1976, she won the U.S. women's road race championship and the pursuit championship. She repeated both victories in 1977 and 1979.

Successful in world competition as

well, Carpenter-Phinney placed second in the 1977 world road race championship, winning a bronze medal in that competition four years later. She won a second-place silver medal in the pursuit event in 1982. Carpenter-Phinney also won three Coors International Classic competitions, in 1977, 1981, and 1982. In 1983, she won a first-place gold medal in the world pursuit competition and set a world record time of 3:49.53. She was named Colorado Sportswoman of the Year.

No American cyclist had won a medal in the Olympics since 1912. Going into the 1984 Olympics, Carpenter-Phinney looked like a strong contender. She had won more national and world titles than any cyclist, man or woman, before her. The Los Angeles Games featured a 79-kilometer road race for the first time, and Carpenter-Phinney capped her competitive career by winning the gold. She was inducted into the International Women's Sports Hall of Fame in 1990, the only cyclist as of 1994. She was also elected to the U.S. Olympic Hall of Fame (1992) and is, again, the only cyclist there as of 1994.

In 1996, Carpenter-Phinney was one of the first 40 Olympians chosen to be part of an elite group called "100 Golden Olympians." These athletes were gathered together in Atlanta on July 18, 1996, for a special tribute to the Centennial Olympic Games, celebrating the one-hundredth anniversary of the modern Olympics.

Reference "Los Angeles 1984," *Women's Sports,* October 1984, 36.

Casals, Rosie (b. 1948)

Born in San Francisco in 1948, Casals started playing tennis at age nine, using the public courts at Golden Gate Park. Casals later recalled, "I was good right away. I can't remember when I couldn't hit the ball." Her father, a native of San Salvador and former soccer player, coached Rosie and her older sister. On the junior circuit, Casals won the United States Lawn Tennis Association's (USLTA) Hard Court singles for girls 13 and under in 1961. She won the 14-and-under crown the next year. In 1964 and 1965, Casals won the 18-and-under title twice, along with the Women's Hard Court singles title in 1965. She reached the semifinals of the U.S. Open at age 17, where she battled the famous Maria Bueno in three lively, crowd-pleasing sets.

Like her friend and frequent doubles partner, Billie Jean King, Casals came from a lower-income home and often found herself playing at tournaments against wealthier opponents. They could afford the travel, entrance fees, and shoes and other equipment that was a strain on her family's resources.

Casals became known for her speed on the court and aggressive style of play. She was adept at executing different kinds of shots from anywhere on the court, hitting some that seemed impossible to run down. She could smash a powerful overhead or lob over opponents who came into the net. These shots made her an especially skillful doubles player.

One big win came in 1973 when Casals won $30,000 at the Family Circle Cup singles' title in Sea Pines, South Carolina. The prize-money in this tournament, part of the Virginia Slims circuit, was the largest single amount ever awarded in women's sports. Teaming up with King, Casals won the U.S. Indoor Doubles in 1966, 1968, and 1971, and the U.S. Hard Court Doubles in 1966. The two captured Wimbledon Doubles crowns in 1967, 1968, 1970, 1971, and 1973. Casals also played mixed doubles successfully, winning at Wimbledon with Romanian Ilie Nastase in 1970 and taking other titles with various partners. In 1973, her prize winnings were the second largest among those on the women's tour.

Along with friend and doubles partner King, Casals was a staunch advocate for women's tennis and for equal prize money. "Equal pay for equal play," became one of their slogans. On the court, Casals favored bright-colored clothing and bandannas. Her fellow players also knew her as a lover of literature who attended concerts and the theater while touring cities around the world. Casals has said she was privileged to be able to follow her chosen profession: "I'm doing what I love to do."

See also King, Billie Jean; Virginia Slims
References Lichtenstein, *A Long Way, Baby: Behind the Scenes in Women's Pro Tennis* (1974); Sullivan, *Queens of the Court* (1974).

Caulkins, Tracy (b. 1963)

During her competitive swimming career, Caulkins set 5 world and 61 U.S. records. She also won more national racing titles—48—than the legendary men's champion Johnny Weissmuller. The versatile Caulkins has won races using all types of swim strokes.

A native of Winona, Minnesota, Caulkins won her first national title at 14 in 1978: She won five gold medals and one silver at the world swimming championships. That year, she became the youngest athlete ever to win the Sullivan Award. The United Press International also named her their Female Athlete of the Year.

With two more golds and two silvers to her credit from the 1979 Pan American Games, Caulkins was well situated to win medals in freestyle, medley, and breast stroke events at the 1980 Olympics. However, President Jimmy Carter announced that U.S. athletes would boycott those Games to protest the Soviet Union invasion of Afghanistan.

In 1981 Caulkins performed well and was named Sportswoman of the Year by the Women's Sports Foundation. The next year, while a university student, she received the Broderick Cup as the top women's college athlete that year. Caulkins seemed to experience a slump at the 1983 world championships, winning no gold or silver medals. At the 1983 Pan American Games, she won the 200-meter individual medley and the 400-meter individual medley but did not equal her 1978 time.

By 1984, she was back in top form, defeating outstanding East German swimmers in the 200- and 400-meter individual medleys. She won the 200-meter event again at the national indoor championships later that year. Then came the Olympics, anticipated for so long. Captain of the team that competed in Los Angeles, Caulkins won three gold medals and placed fourth in the 100-meter breaststroke. Her time in the 200-meter individual medley set a new Olympic record: 2 minutes, 12.64 seconds. Caulkins also swam with the U.S. team that won the 4 x 100–meter medley relay.

Caulkins retired from amateur competition after the Games and was offered the chance to do commercial endorsements. She also commentated on swimming competitions and wrote instructional articles about her sport. Caulkins was inducted into the International Women's Sports Hall of Fame and the Olympic Hall of Fame.

See also Broderick Cup; Sullivan Award
Reference Gildea, "American Swimmer Tracy Caulkins," *Reader's Digest*, July 1984, 128–129.

Chadwick, Florence (b. 1918)

Before Florence Chadwick swam the English Channel from England to France in 1951, people thought the feat was impossible. Chadwick proved them wrong. A native of San Diego, California, Chadwick won her first race at age six, and she became the first child to swim the channel at the mouth of San Diego Bay. As she continued to compete, Chadwick found that she was not as fast in short races as many of her competitors. Her best performance in national competition was a second-place finish, once, at age 14.

Chadwick tried out for the U.S. Olympic team in 1936, the year she graduated from high school, but was not chosen. Yet she had the skills needed for long-distance swimming, a sport that requires stamina and steady effort, sometimes for hours. For 10 years in a row, she won a 2.5-mile race held in nearby La Jolla, California. Chadwick was inspired by the story of long-distance swimmer Gertrude Ederle. In 1926, Ederle had become the first woman to swim across the English Channel, swimming 21 miles from France to England.

During World War II, Chadwick directed and produced aquatic shows for military service groups and veterans' hospitals. She became a professional swimmer in 1945, the year the war ended, and appeared in a motion picture. She then worked as a swim instructor for several years.

At age 32, Chadwick sought to enter a contest to swim across the English Channel, sponsored by the London *Daily Mail*. Her application was rejected, though, because she did not have the required previous record or international recognition in her sport. Undaunted, Chadwick decided to swim across the English Chan-

nel on her own. Only a few other top long-distance swimmers had done so. She practiced by swimming in the Persian Gulf, where she was then employed by an Arabian-American oil company.

During her 1950 channel swim, Chadwick broke all previous records with a time of 13 hours, 20 minutes. When she reached Dover, she said that she felt fine, then announced, "I am quite prepared to swim back," meaning that she would next try to swim the channel in the *opposite* direction, something others had tried and failed. To accomplish her goal, Chadwick knew she must battle strong tides and winds, as well as icy water, even in summer. While training for the swim, she ate a rich diet that increased her body fat.

In September 1951, weather conditions were not optimal for her swim. Nonetheless, Chadwick set out. Powerful waves soon rinsed off the body grease she had applied, and thick fog obscured her view as she swam along. A few hours into the swim, Chadwick suffered from stomach pains. She took seasickness pills, carried by her trainer, who rode alongside her in a boat. During the swim, she often stopped to tread water, her arms and legs too numb from cold to keep swimming. After 16 hours and 22 minutes, she reached the rocky shore of Cap Gris-Nez, France, where local residents waited to see the daring American athlete.

After this triumph, Chadwick completed other challenging long-distance swims, often setting new records for speed. In both 1953 and 1955, she repeated her England-to-France swim, setting new world records for her times (14 hours, 42 minutes; 13 hours, 55 minutes). She also crossed the Bristol Channel, between Wales and England, covering these 14 miles in world-record time—

Florence Chadwick waves to supporters before the start of her swim across the English Channel in 1950. Thirty-two-year-old Chadwick defied authorities who rejected her application to enter a channel-swimming contest by setting a new world record of 13 hours, 20 minutes.

6 hours and 7 minutes. She was the first woman to swim across the Cataline Channel, and her swim across the Straits of Gibraltar in 1953, with a time of 5 hours and 6 minutes, beat previous records attained by both men and women.

Chadwick retired in 1960, becoming a swimming instructor and public speaker. She appeared on radio and television and earned money through commercial endorsements. Elected to the International Swimming Hall of Fame in 1970, Chadwick continued to coach swimmers during the 1970s while working as a stockbroker. Her achievements have inspired young swimmers, especially female athletes, around the world.

See also Ederle, Gertrude
References Campbell, *Marathon* (1977); Hickok, *A Who's Who of Sports Champions* (1995); Hollander, *100 Greatest Women in Sports* (1976).

Chaffee, Suzy (b. 1947)

Olympian Chaffee helped to develop the sport of freestyle skiing. Born in mountainous Rutland, Vermont, Chaffee had learned to ski by age three. During her teens, she excelled at downhill racing and was a member of the Olympic ski team that competed in Grenoble, France, in 1968. After the Olympics, Chaffee worked to perfect new kinds of freestyle movements that were known as "hot-dogging." When freestyle skiing was designated a separate sport in 1971, men were the only competitors. Chaffee skied against them, using short skis and performing athletic routines to music. She mastered the standard moves and invented some of her own. From 1971 to 1973, Chaffee was ranked as the number one freestyle skier in the world. Other women followed her spirited lead, and after the mid-1970s, women had their own professional freestyle contests. Besides skiing, Chaffee appeared as a television sports commen-

tator and spokesperson for several commercial products. In 1976, Chaffee was named to the U.S. Olympic Committee's board of directors. Freestyle skiing became an Olympic sport in 1992.

Cheerleading

Before the 1970s, cheerleading was the major and sometimes only way in which girls participated in organized high school and even college athletics. From the sidelines, they cheered as male players competed in basketball, football, and other sports. The girls' role was to support male players and teams, rather than to compete themselves.

After 1972, more girls' athletics teams were formed in high schools, following the passage of equal access legislation in the form of Title IX. In the early seventies, school officials in some towns and cities sparked controversies by designating cheerleading as a varsity sport. They used athletic funds for these programs rather than to develop sports teams for female students. In recent years, cheerleading has become coeducational, with both boys and girls eligible to try out for the squad. Cheerleading squads also appear at sporting events featuring both boys' and girls' teams, often performing difficult individual and group movements.

Cheeseman, Gwen (b. 1951)

Field hockey player Cheeseman was goalkeeper on the U.S. women's team that won a bronze medal in the 1984 Olympics. A native of Harrisburg, Pennsylvania, Cheeseman was also a member of the U.S. team that competed in World Cup matches in 1975, 1980, and 1983. Named to the Olympic field hockey team for 1980, she was unable to compete when the United States boycotted those Games for political reasons.

Although Cheeseman left the game for a year, she returned in 1982 to play on the national team and at the National Sports Festival in 1983. In March 1984, she played the position of goal-keeper at every match in the Four Nations tournament. There, the U.S. women defeated New Zealand and Australia. They tied with Canada, then beat them in the next match. Despite her petite size (5 feet, 2 inches) Cheeseman allowed only one goal during these four matches.

Ching, Laura Blears (b. 1951)

In 1973, Ching became the first woman to compete against male surfers. The competition took place off the island of Oahu, Hawaii, with 31 amateur and professional surfers taking part. At the time of the contest, Ching had been named the best woman surfer in Hawaii twice. She had also won the women's international surfing contest, held at Makaha Beach, Hawaii, in 1972.

Chunichi Cup

This prestigious gymnastics competition is held each year in Nagoya, Japan. The United States Gymnastics Federation chooses two U.S. women each year to compete for the cup. Competitors from around the world take part in the usual gymnastics events—all around, balance beam, vault, floor exercises, and uneven bars. They also perform an optional routine in each event. A panel of international judges presides over the competition. During the same two-week period, a follow-up invitational competition, also quite prestigious, is held in Tokyo.

In 1973, Mary Lou Retton became the first U.S. gymnast to win the cup.

See also Durham, Dianne; Gymnastics

Civil Rights Legislation (See Title IX)

Clapp, Louise Brough (See Brough, Louise)

Coaching

Women athletes have most often been taught and coached by males rather than by coaches of their own gender. But as more and more women have become top athletes, many have also become coaches after retiring from competition. Universities, colleges, and high schools have been criticized for not hiring more women.

Women have distinguished themselves as coaches in various sports. One of the best-known women's basketball coaches is Cathy Rush, who took a little-known team at Immaculata College in Pennsylvania to several national collegiate championships during the 1970s. Other top women basketball coaches include Mary Lou Johns, who coached at Memphis State University, and Maureen Wendelken, who led a nationally recognized team at Montclair State College in New Jersey in the late 1970s. In 1978, Sue Gunter, a basketball coach at Stephen F. Austin College, was named head coach of the 1980 U.S. Olympic women's team.

In the sport of figure skating, Olympic gold medalist Carol Heiss went on to coach other skaters, including former world champion Jill Trenary and Tanya Kwiatkowsky, who won second place in the 1996 U.S. ladies' competition.

See also Anders, Beth; Betz, Pauline; Heiss, Carol; Jackson, Nell; Karolyi, Bela; Rush, Cathy; Temple, Ed

Coachman, Alice (b. 1923)

In 1948, Alice Coachman became the first African-American woman to win an Olympic gold medal in track and field. She would later tell a reporter for the

Winning the high jump event at the National Women's Track and Field meet in 1939, Alice Coachman would go on to become the first African-American woman to win an Olympic gold medal in track and field in 1948.

Albany *Herald*: "I was sincere about my work. As I look back, I wonder why I worked so hard, put so much time into it—but I guess it's just that I wanted to win. And competition was very tough."

Coachman was born in Albany, Georgia. She showed promise as an athlete as early as elementary school, where she was the highest jumper among all her classmates, girls and boys alike. She later told *Ebony* magazine that she had gone through a "rough time," since she was a tomboy at a time when it was considered unladylike: "I was good at three things: running, jumping, and fighting."

Excited by Coachman's talent, her high school teachers urged her to join the track team. She went on to Tuskegee Institute High School in Tuskegee, Alabama, and competed for them in a national women's track and field championships even before she began taking classes there. Coachman earned her first medal at a high school meet in Waterbury, Connecticut.

During her senior year, in 1943, Coachman won the Amateur Athletic Union (AAU) national title in both the running high jump and the 50-yard dash. From 1943 to 1946, while studying for a trade degree in dressmaking, Coachman played on the basketball team and continued to compete in track and field. She held national titles in four events: the 50- and 100-meter dashes, the 500-meter relay, and the running high jump. By 1948, she had been the national high jump champion for 12 consecutive years, with 25 AAU titles to her credit. Unfortunately, during World War II (1939–1945), Coachman was not able to compete in international events.

Coachman was a nationally known track and field star when she transferred to Albany State College in Georgia in 1947, where she received a degree in home economics two years later. In the meantime, she was asked to compete in the 1948 Olympics, the first time the Games had been held since 1936. Coachman sailed to London with other members of the All-American Women's Team, including Audrey Patterson. Patterson would become the first black woman to win an Olympic medal when she took third place in the 200-meter race.

Competing with an injured hip, Coachman was impressed by the skill of the European women. Nonetheless, she pushed herself hard and won the high jump, attaining 5 feet, 6 ⅛ inches, an Olympic record. Returning home with her gold medal, Coachman met President Harry Truman and was interviewed by the press in her native Georgia, where she received a motorcade from Atlanta to Macon.

After the Olympics, Coachman worked in Albany as a physical education teacher. She married and, as Alice Coachman Davis, reared two children. In 1975, she was elected to the National Track and Field Hall of Fame and the International Women's Sports Hall of Fame.

See also National Track and Field Hall of Fame

References Bernstein, "That Championship Season," *Essence*, July 1984, 124, 128; Leder, *Grace and Glory* (1996); Smith, ed., *Notable Black American Women* (1992).

Cochran, Barbara Ann (b. 1951)

Born into a ski-loving family, Cochran practically grew up on skis, using a rope tow ski lift her father, Mickey Cochran, had built in the family's Vermont backyard. A former international skier, he taught his four children to ski well. They trained by lifting weights, running, and exercising daily. As the Cochran children grew up and entered races, they sometimes competed against one another. Barbara's sister Marilyn won a Giant Slalom during the 1968–1969 European tour and placed second in two World Cup events that same season.

In 1969 Barbara Cochran won the U.S. National Giant Slalom Competition. The next year, she won that competition again and placed second in the world giant slalom championships. She followed up these victories with two World Cup titles. Meanwhile, Marilyn became the first American woman ever to win the French championship. Later, in 1975, Linda Cochran would win a European Cup event, the Giant Slalom, then go on to the 1976 Olympics.

Along with Marilyn and her brother Bobby, Barbara Cochran made the U.S. Olympic team that went to the 1972 Winter Games. The course in Sapporo, Japan, was steep and risky, with shifting winds and fogs that impaired visibility on the slopes. Heavy snow fell the day of the race.

In her first run, Cochran finished ahead of the other skiers by less than 1 second. Skiing efficiently, with sweeping, graceful turns, Cochran completed a second strong run that put her in first place by 0.002 second. When the 41 other skiers had completed their runs, Cochran had the gold medal, the first won by an American in an Alpine skiing event since Andrea Mead Lawrence had captured two golds in the 1952 Olympics. Cochran retired from competition and graduated from the University of Vermont, later working for the *Washington Post* as a writer.

After her marriage, Barbara Cochran Siegle became the mother of three children and a professional ski instructor in Vermont. She regularly worked with the Vermont Special Olympics Summer Games and with the "Kids and Cops" program sponsored by the state police to encourage more children to take part in sports.

See also Lawrence, Andrea Mead
References Moffett, *Great Women Athletes* (1974); Stambler, *Women in Sports: The Long, Hard Climb* (1975); "Olympic Gold," *Good Housekeeping*, 1992.

Cohen, Tiffany (b. 1966)

Cohen achieved international recognition as a swimmer in both short- and long-distance races. Born in Culver City, California, she enjoyed swimming year-round as a child. At age 15, she won her first national title, a gold medal in the 400-meter freestyle and silver medal in the 1,500-meter race at the outdoor national championships. She won the 400-meter national title again the next year, placing third in that event at the world championships. Cohen became known as the top U.S. woman distance swimmer during the early 1980s.

Cohen had a standout year in 1983. She won gold medals at the national indoor championships in freestyle competition at 200 yards, 500 yards, 1,000 yards, and the 800-yard relay. She also set a U.S. record in the 1,650-yard freestyle, with a time of 15 minutes, 46.54 seconds. Competing at the national outdoor events that year, she won the 400-, 800-, and 1,500-meter races. She won gold medals in the 400- and 800-meter races at the 1983 Pan American Games. She was ranked as the world's top 400- and 1,500-meter freestyle swimmer in 1983.

Cohen took part in her first Olympics on her home turf in Los Angeles in 1984. She set a new U.S. record when she won the 400-meter freestyle race with a time of 4 minutes, 07.10 seconds and won a second gold medal in the 800-meter race, in which she set an Olympic record (8 minutes, 24.95 seconds). In 1986 at the national outdoor championships, Cohen won the 400- and 800-meter freestyle races and 200-meter butterfly. She retired from competition in 1987.

Reference Chambliss, *Champions: The Making of Olympic Swimmers* (1988).

Collett Vare, Glenna (1903–1989)

People cheered as 56-year-old Glenna Collett Vare hit her last stroke and won the Rhode Island women's state golf championship. Collett Vare's triumph was all the more amazing because she had won this same tournament 37 years before, at age 19. Once again, she had turned in the kind of performance that had won her the nickname "Wonder Woman of American Golf."

Born in New Haven, Connecticut, in 1903, Glenna Collett became one of the first American woman golf champions. Her father, an expert golfer, encouraged her to begin playing the game at age 6. She entered her first major tournament at age 17. From then on, her strong drives and consistent, nearly error-free play brought her dozens of important golf titles.

In 1921, Collett Vare won the Berthellyn Cup in Philadelphia. She went on to win the British Ladies Championship three times. Collett distinguished herself as the first women's champion to swing vigorously, unlike the daintier swings that often prevailed among women golfers in the early 1900s. Frequently, she hit the ball 200 yards off the tee. The great men's champion Bobby Jones admired her game, especially her long drives and accuracy, saying it was a treat to watch Collett play. She won an amazing 59 of the 60 matches held during the 1924 women's golf season.

Her victories included six National Amateur titles, which set a record. In 1922, she won her first U.S. Ladies Championships, with others following in 1925, 1928, 1929, and 1930. In 1931 and 1932, she placed second at that event. Her sixth and final U.S. crown came in 1935, when she was a 32-year-old mother of two children. She defeated 17-year-old Patty Berg, who would go on to become the top women's player of her day.

Collett Vare also found time to write two books about golf: *Golf for Young Players*, published in 1926, and *Ladies in the Rough*, published in 1928. As both player and captain, she was part of the U.S. Curtis Cup team, which played against other nations. She served as a nonplaying captain in 1950.

She donated the Vare Trophy in 1952, awarded to the player on the Ladies Professional Golf Association (LPGA) tour with the lowest annual per-round score. Her husband Edward Vare, whom she married in 1931, died in 1975. Collett Vare continued to play golf into her eighties. She died in New Haven, Connecticut, in 1989.

See also Curtis Cup; Vare Trophy
References Hollander, *100 Greatest Women in Sports* (1976); Collett Vare, *Golf for Young Players* (1926) and *Ladies in the Rough* (1928).

Colorado Silver Bullets (See Baseball)

Connolly, Maureen (1934–1969)

The San Diego, California, native was the youngest women's national tennis champion and the first American woman ever to win the Grand Slam. A good all-around athlete, Connolly loved horseback riding as a child. Lacking enough money to ride often or buy her own horse, she began playing tennis. Connolly practiced several hours a day, seven days a week for five years, before winning the national junior championship when she was 13. The press quickly nicknamed the young champion "Little Mo" because of her petite build.

Between 1951 and 1954, Connolly played on the Wightman Cup team, never losing a singles match. The year 1952 brought her the crown at Wimbledon, then the Australian, French, and U.S. titles. By winning these four tournaments within a one-year period, she achieved the coveted Grand Slam of tennis. The Associated Press named Connolly Woman Athlete of the Year in 1952, 1953, and 1954. With strong, accurate groundstrokes from the baseline, Connolly was able to outlast opponents on clay, grass, and other surfaces.

She won two more Wimbledon titles and two more at the French Open before 1954 when her career was cut short by a horseback-riding injury. Connolly married and began raising a family while writing a sports column for the *San Diego Union* and promoting tennis rackets and other sports equipment. She coached and worked to promote junior tennis in America through the Maureen Connolly Brinker Foundation. In 1968, Connolly was inducted into the International Tennis Hall of Fame. She died the next year from cancer, survived by her husband and two children.

See also Grand Slam
References Collins and Hollander, *Bud Collins' Modern Encyclopedia of Tennis* (1994); Hickok, *The New Encyclopedia of Sports* (1977).

Copeland, Lillian (See Shot Put)

Costello, Patty (b. 1954)
Left-hander Patty Costello won the U.S. Open bowling tournament in 1972 along with 4 more of 11 major Professional Women's Bowlers Association tournaments held that year.

As a child in Pennsylvania, Costello began bowling early and was averaging 132 as a 16-year-old. In 1972, she was rolling 205. During the early years of her bowling career, Costello could not support herself just with her playing. Among other jobs, she worked in a potato chip factory and sold encyclopedias. As a full-time professional bowler, she spent hours a day practicing, often playing 15 games a day.

In 1974 and 1976, Costello won the All-Star Bowling Proprietors Assocations of America United States Open Championship, with an average of 196.67 for 1974 and 226.27 for 1976—the highest ever recorded as of that date. In 1975, she was the runner-up at the Women's International Bowling Congress Queens Tournament Championship, with an average of 185 points.

Costello hoped she would be allowed to compete with male bowlers on the Professional Bowlers Association (PBA) tour in 1976. But the group steadfastly refused to include women. That year, she was named Woman Bowler of the Year, as she had been in 1972.

In 1973, a poll of 47 bowling sportswriters named Costello one of the ten all-time greatest women players. The *Bowler's Journal* poll of 1976 included Costello in its "all-time greatest" women's team made up of ten players. Four years later, in 1980, Costello was again the top bowler at the All-Star U.S. Women's Open, where she had been runner-up in 1979. She won the

Open with an average score of 206.0. In 1985, the Ladies Professional Bowling Tour named Costello Bowler of the Year. As of 1996, with 25 major titles to her credit, she was second only to Lisa Wagner, winner of 28.

References Ladies Professional Bowlers Tour, *LPBT Guide* (1994).

Costie, Candy (See Ruiz-Conforto, Tracie; Swimming, Synchronized)

Cricket
Centuries old, the game of cricket was played by royalty and the nobility in England. It may have originated with shepherds who used broken off crooks to hit a ball. Played with a stick or bat, and ball, cricket has been called the English baseball. A woman, Christine Willes, has been credited with giving her brother John the idea of using a round-arm or overhand style of slinging the ball. The wide, flounced skirts worn by women of the day kept Christine from being able to bowl underarm when she and her brother played the game in their yard.

During the mid-1700s, cricket reached America and was quite popular until baseball took its place about 100 years later. Cricket clubs from different cities competed against each other, and at the first international match, Americans from New York defeated Canadian players in Toronto. Women play informally but not in organized national and international competitions.

Crockett, Rita (b. 1957)
All-around athlete Crockett was good at basketball and track and field events, as well as volleyball. In junior college, her volleyball team won the national title and she decided to focus on that sport.

She was good enough to be named an All-American. A powerful hitter, spiker, and high jumper, she was one of six women players named to the All-World Cup Team.

In 1978 Crockett became a member of the U.S. women's volleyball team as hitter-blocker. She was named Rookie of the Year, and some commentators called her one of the best women athletes playing any sport. Crockett played on the U.S. team that won the bronze medal at the world tournament in 1982 and the silver medal at the Olympic Games in 1984.

Croquet

The French game known as *paille malle* gave way to modern croquet. During the 1850s, when the game was revived in France, it spread to Ireland and England, where it was called Pall Mall. It was a popular pastime at European country houses and estates, and people took pains to keep their croquet lawns in fine shape. The All-England Croquet Club was formed in 1868 and was later expanded to include lawn tennis. Lawn tennis replaced croquet in popularity and prestige and the word "croquet" was dropped from the name of the club. During the U.S. Civil War, the game quickly became popular in the United States.

Women have played croquet years longer than many other sports, and croquet is the first outdoor sport to become popular with women. From its early days, croquet has been played by both men and women, often at picnics and garden-parties. Yet, the game had its critics. In Boston during the 1890s, a Reverend Skinner called upon people to stop "the immoral practice of Croquet."

But the sport continued to catch on.

A 1903 article in the *Graphic* said, "Croquet . . . is even more popular than golf, and suits equally the active old lady, or the dashing young girl." (Brasch, 93) It requires no physical contact between players, who use mallets to hit balls through raised iron rings or hoops set up on the ground. In the United States, the standard croquet set features ten or nine hoops, arranged in a figure eight. But the international competitive version is for the six hoop game common in Great Britain.

The United States Croquet Association (USCA) governs the sport, setting rules, organizing competitions, and ranking players. Founded in 1977, it is located in Palm Beach Gardens, Florida, where it maintains a Croquet Foundation and Hall of Fame. USCA tournaments use the six-wicket game. During the 1970s, Nelga Young was ranked as the best woman player in America.

References Gipe, *The Great American Sports Book* (1978); Guttman, *Women's Sports: A History* (1991).

Crosson, Marvel (1904–1929)

A pilot, Crosson began flying when her brother rebuilt a plane from surplus airplanes they were able to retrieve after World War I. Later, they operated an air transport company together.

In 1923, she soloed for the first time, after which she became a stunt flyer. Crosson set the record for women's altitude (23,996 feet) while flying a monoplane in California. Crosson entered the Women's Air Derby, the first of the American air derbies for women, which began at Santa Monica, California, on August 18, 1929. Near Wellton, Arizona, her plane became disabled. When Crosson's parachute failed to open, she became the first casualty of the race.

See also Air Derby, Women's

Croteau, Julie (b. 1971)

As a child, Croteau loved to play baseball. While attending high school in Manassas, Virginia, she played for three years on the junior varsity team. Croteau filed a lawsuit when she was dropped from the junior varsity and barred from the all-male varsity baseball team. She lost the suit.

After graduating, Croteau spent the summer playing first base on a semiprofessional baseball team in the Virginia Baseball League, the Fredericksburg Giants. Later, at St. Mary's College in Maryland, she played first base on her college team, in Division III of the National Collegiate Athletic Association (NCAA). She was the first woman to play for an NCAA school.

In 1991, Croteau was a guest speaker at a reunion of about 160 former players of the All-American Girls Professional Baseball League (AAGPBL) held in Clearwater Beach, Florida. Croteau told the former players they were "living proof" that women could play baseball and play it well. Referring to her own struggles to play baseball, Croteau said, "You were not only ahead of your time, but apparently, you were ahead of ours."

Julie Croteau appeared in the feature film made about the AAGPBL, *A League of Their Own*, which was released in 1992. She served as an extra and was a stunt double for actress Anne Elizabeth Ramsay, who portrayed one of the women ballplayers.

References Macy, *A Whole New Ball Game* (1993); Nelson, *Are We Winning Yet?* (1991).

Crump, Diane (b. 1949)

Jockey Diane Crump was the first woman to ride in a pari-mutuel race in North America and in the Kentucky Derby. The Connecticut native had been an exercise groom before becoming a jockey. Crump rode Bridle 'N Bit on February 7, 1969, when she raced at Hialeah Park in Florida as a licensed jockey. The duo finished only tenth out of a field of 12, but six weeks later Crump won a race at Gulfstream Park, also in Florida. That day, she became the first woman jockey ever to win a stakes race.

In May 1970, Diane Crump appeared at the Kentucky Derby riding Fathom. Until that time, women had owned and trained Derby entrants but never competed as jockeys. Not until 1984 would another woman ride in the Derby—Patricia Cooksey, who finished eleventh.

During 17 years as a jockey, in which she entered 1,614 races, Crump won 235, finished second in 204, and came in third in 203. She became a trainer in 1986. Her pioneering efforts paved the way for other women jockeys to compete on equal terms with men.

See also Bacon, Mary; Jockey, Professional; Kentucky Derby; Krone, Julie; Kusner, Kathy
References Thoroughbred Association of North America, *1994 Directory and Record Book* (1994); Moffett, *Great Women Athletes* (1974).

Curling

In this sport, two teams of four players each slide curling stones over a stretch of ice, aiming toward a circle target. The curling stones have gooseneck handles and are ellipsoid in shape. They are sometimes made of iron.

Curling was not an Olympic event as of 1994 but had been a demonstration sport, played by teams of men at some Winter Games. In 1924 Great Britain's team triumphed over Sweden and France. Four Canadian teams vied with four U.S. teams in 1932, with the Canadians winning the four top spots. Eight teams played in 1936. The next demonstration was held in 1964, with Austria winning.

Round-robin championship matches are held each year by the United States Women's Curling Association (USWCA). Between 1949 and 1977, the association sponsored a national curling festival for players, which was changed to a national championship in 1977. During the early years of the national championships, eight teams competed, a number that grew as more clubs formed around the country.

The national event has been held in different northern and midwestern cities, with Duluth and St. Paul, Minnesota, having each twice sponsored the championship. In 1992 and 1995, Lisa Schoeneberg was skip, or captain, for the victorious Madison, Wisconsin, team. In 1993 and 1994, Bev Behnke was skip for the winning team from Denver, Colorado. As of 1995, no American women had won the world curling championship, which has been dominated by curlers from Canada, Germany, and Scandinavian countries.

Curry, Denise (See Basketball)

Curtis, Ann (b. 1926)

People who saw Curtis swim as a child marveled at the ease with which she seemed to glide across the water. Later, after her Olympic triumphs, some sportswriters called her the best freestyler that had yet been developed in the United States and perhaps the world.

The San Franciscan started swimming at age nine but did not start working with a coach until she was 11 years old and had won a freestyle event. Curtis won the city's 1937 Amateur Athletic Union (AAU) freestyle event for girls under 16 when she was only 11. Later that year, she

Ann Curtis, the first woman to win the Sullivan Award, is known for the stroke she invented, called the "Curtis Crawl."

broke a record in the 100-yard event at the Pacific Coast Senior meet.

Curtis trained hard to improve her form and "turnaround" time at the end of the pool. Racing coach Charles Sava helped her improve her arm motion and knee action. By age 17, she was a national champion and had set new records for speed in the 400- and 880-yard freestyle events. During the next two years, Curtis broke various standing U.S. records for women's swimming. In 1944, she became the first woman and first swimmer to win the Sullivan Award, given each year since 1930 to the most outstanding amateur athlete.

During World War II, Curtis worked as a Red Cross volunteer and completed high school. Like other swimmers, she had to take good care of her bathing caps during those years when rubber was scarce and new caps were hard to acquire.

After the war, Curtis took her effective front crawl stroke, named the "Curtis crawl," into international competition. Again she set a new record when she swam the 100-yard race in 59.4 seconds, the first woman to break 1 minute. By 1948, she had set four other world records. She joined four thousand competitors at the Olympic Games and won the 400-meter freestyle event and another gold as part of the winning 4 x 100–meter relay team, which also set a new Olympic speed record. In the 100-meter race, she earned a silver medal. It was a great year for U.S. athletes, who won 35 gold medals, more than any of the 59 countries at the Games.

In 1949, Curtis turned professional and became an instructor and coach. She raised four children, all of whom took up swimming, and started her own swim club.

See also Curtis Crawl; Sullivan Award
Reference Hollander, *100 Greatest Women in Sports* (1976).

Curtis Crawl

This front crawl swimming stroke was named for world champion Ann Curtis. It involves carefully synchronized movements of the arms and legs, with strong shoulder movements. Powerful leg motions create a strong thrust when the swimmer first hits the water. The chin is held forward, with the water line at the forehead, and the shoulder level with the surface of the water. There are eight leg beats to one complete arm cycle.

See also Curtis, Ann

Curtis Cup

This women's international golf trophy is awarded every two years when cup matches are held, alternately in the United States and Great Britain. Two teams vie for the cup: One is made up of amateur women golfers from the United States; the other is composed of amateur golfers from England, Scotland, Wales, Northern Ireland, and the Republic of Ireland. The United States Golf Association chooses those who will play for the United States, while the Ladies' Golf Union selects the British team.

The cup stays in the winning country for two years. If there is a tie, the cup remains with the former winner until there is a new winner. Since 1932, when the Curtis Cup matches were first held, the trophy has changed hands several times, although the U.S. team has triumphed more often than not.

The cup was first donated by two sisters, Margaret and Harriet Curtis, of Boston, Massachusetts. Harriet had won the national women's golf championship in 1906, and Margaret took top honors in 1907, 1911, and 1912.

Cycling

The first bicycle, made in France during the 1700s, had no wheels or pedals. Luckily, new and more efficient bicycles were invented through the years. The sport of bicycling became popular in the 1860s. Riding schools opened, and racing became a Sunday pastime. Women were as involved as men, prompting some feminists to claim that cycling might become a symbol of the movement for equality between the sexes. Since women could not cycle while wearing the accepted long skirts of those times, they had to adopt other garments. Some women caused a commotion by wearing divided skirts or bloomers.

People debated whether it was appropriate for a woman to ride a bicycle. Many women disregarded the controversy, such as 16-year-old Tessie Reynolds of England. In 1893 Reynolds rode about 120 miles in 8.5 hours. In an issue published that year, the English cycling magazine *Northern Wheeler* commented: "Woman has taken her stand, and her seat in the saddle. . . . I am tolerably certain that the net result will be that woman will take her true position as man's equal."

By 1895, many more women had taken up cycling, both for transportation and recreation. Women in France had entered races at Bordeaux in 1868. There were national cycling races in the United States beginning in 1937, with events for women. In 1958, women's events were added to the world cycling championships.

U.S. women competed in national championships for the first time in 1937, and women were admitted to world cycling championships starting in 1958. American women won four world titles between 1969 and 1994.

Top American women sprint cyclists have included Doris Travani (U.S. national road champion in 1947, 1948, 1949, and 1950); Sheila Young (U.S. national champion in 1971, 1973, and 1976); and Sue Novara-Reber, who won the title in 1972, 1974, 1975, 1977, and 1978. American Jean Robinson, a scientist from Seattle, Washington, won the 1974 Women's National Road Championships in Pontiac, Michigan, over a 34.5-mile course.

Robinson had trained by riding between 35 and 50 miles a day.

The number of cycling races has continued to increase both for men and women competitors. Races are held around the world. Cycling clubs are also popular, and women, who tend to excel in sports requiring endurance and tactical skills, are enthusiastic cyclists. Races are held for younger cyclists in midget divisions (ages 8–11); intermediate (12–14); and juniors (15–17). There are also senior races, such as the National Senior Women's Cyclo-Cross Championship for women over age 35. Many of these American contests are sponsored by the United States Cycling Federation.

Road races, held on open roads and highways, have become especially popular. The courses for these races may be flat or hilly and require riders to go from one place to another or from a starting point to a different destination and back again. In the 1986 Race Across America, for example, cyclists rode more than 3,100 miles from Huntington Beach, California, to Atlantic City, New Jersey. The Coors International Classic, which lasts nine or ten days, covers a course that includes both short, flat racing areas and about 40 miles through the Colorado mountains.

The First Women's Tour de France, a 616-mile race, was held in 1984. Two U.S. cyclists won medals: Marianne Martin won the gold with a time of 29 hours, 39 minutes, and 2 seconds, and Deborah Schumway placed third.

In 1995, Seana Hogan, age 34, set a new record in the Race Across America cross country bicycle race. The annual race goes from Irvine, California, to Savannah, Georgia. This was Hogan's third Race Across America title—a record number of wins.

Cycling

Track cycling became the first women's Olympic cycling event, and a 79-kilometer road race was added to the 1984 Games in Los Angeles. Among the top U.S. cyclists were Rebecca Twigg and Janie Quigley (b. 1970). Twigg competed at the 1992 Olympics, and Quigley won five national and two world junior titles. At the senior level, Quigley won the national individual-pursuit race four times. In this event, two cyclists start at opposite ends of the same track and try to overtake each other, or else beat the other's time. Quigley hoped to compete in both the 79-kilometer race and 3,000-meter individual pursuit race at the 1996 Games.

The Olympics also features a 110-kilometer road race for women. U.S. cyclist Jeanne Golay came in sixth at this event in the 1992 Olympic Games and won the event at the 1995 Pan American Games. The Florida-native, a member of the Saturn cycling team, hoped to compete in the 1996 Games.

See also Bloomers; Heiden, Beth; Young, Sheila

Dawes, Dominique (b. 1977)

Dawes, a gymnast, won the gold medal in all four events of the 1994 National Gymnastics Championships, held in Nashville, Tennessee. She topped all other competitors in the vault, uneven parallel bars, balance beam, and floor exercise events. In addition, the 17-year-old native of Gaithersburg, Maryland, won the gold medal as best all-around gymnast. No woman gymnast since Joyce Schroeder, in 1969, had managed to sweep all five gold medals. Watching Dawes, gymnast Mary Lou Retton commented that she "doesn't have a weak event."

Dawes grew up in Silver Spring, Maryland, the middle child of three born to Don and Loretta Dawes. She showed tremendous energy and athletic ability by age four, so her parents enrolled her in gymnastics classes. Her coach Kelli Hill recognized that Dawes had both talent and an ability to pursue her goals diligently. As a nine-year-old, Dawes prepared herself mentally for meets by writing the word "determination" on her bedroom mirror.

At the 1992 Olympics, Dawes was part of the U.S. team that won the third-place bronze medal. She trained for seven hours a day while managing to finish high school as an honor-roll student. In 1993, Dawes won the vault and balance beam events at the U.S. national championships. At the World Gymnastics Championships, held in Birming-ham, England, Dawes became the first African-American gymnast ever to win two silver medals in that competition. She placed second in the uneven parallel bars and balance beam events. In the pommel horse vault event, Dawes came in fourth.

At the 1995 national championships, Dawes won a gold medal in the uneven bars, the floor exercise, and the overall competition. She trained hard that year preparing for the 1996 Olympics, after which she planned to attend Stanford University.

In Atlanta, Dawes was part of the team that made history by winning the first team Olympic medal in gymnastics ever captured by the United States. Her strong performance in all five events made her a top scorer during that evening. Competing the next week in the floor exercise individual event, Dawes won a bronze third-place medal with her well-choreographed routine that featured difficult tumbling passes.

See also Gymnastics
References Cyphers, "Golden Girls," *New York Daily News*, July 24, 1996, 59.

de Varona, Donna (b. 1947)

Swimmer Donna de Varona won two gold medals in the 1968 Olympics. A California native, she learned a great deal about athletics from her father, who had been a member of a championship rowing crew in college. She later said, "He took the principles of rowing and applied them to swimming—angles, pace, knowing when to increase the stroke, like an oarsman in a crew race would do to pick up speed. He also has been very interested in diet and nutrition all his life."

As a child, de Varona pursued tumbling and baseball. She was disturbed to find out there were no Little League teams for girls. The sponsor of her brother's team made her the first bat girl in their local league. Soon she found out that she had a lot of aptitude for swimming. De Varona's parents could not afford private lessons, but she received excellent instruction through a YMCA swimming program. Within months after taking up the sport, de Varona was winning her first races. In 1960, she qualified as an alternate on the U.S. Olympic swim team, becoming the youngest member of the team and one of the youngest athletes ever to go to the Olympics. But since the regular team members were all able to compete, de Varona had to sit on the sidelines that year.

De Varona continued to train and went to the 1964 Olympics in Tokyo, Japan, where she won the 400-meter medley, the first time that event had been held at the Olympics. Her time broke a world record and brought her first gold medal. She won another gold as a member of the 400-meter freestyle team. De Varona retired from competitive swimming that year, at age 17, and became a television commentator for ABC's *Wide World of Sports*. In 1970, she received her college degree from the University of California, Los Angeles.

During the 1970s, de Varona joined other top woman athletes to promote women's sports through the Women's Sports Foundation, which aimed to oppose inequality and sexism in athletics.

Her public appearances and articles raised money and support for women athletes and their training programs. She also wrote a book about water fitness exercises and served on a president's commission on Olympic sports. In the 1990s, she continued to write about sports, serve as a spokesperson for women's athletics, and do television commentary.

Decker, Mary (b. 1958)

Distance runner Mary Theresa Decker was the first woman to run the 1,500-meter race in less than 4 minutes. Born in New Jersey, Decker grew up in Huntington Beach, California, where she entered her first big race at age 11. After winning this local cross country event, she began training to run distances of more than 1 mile.

In 1972, Decker stood 5 feet tall and weighed 86 pounds, making her the smallest runner at a meet she entered in Russia that year. She surprised spectators by winning the 800-meter race, defeating the Russian girl who had won a silver medal in that year's Summer Olympics. Decker later recalled, "I knew I wanted to run in the Olympics." Running indoors at the Los Angeles Forum, she set a new world record of 2 minutes and 6.7 seconds in the 880-yard race.

In 1973, Decker set more new world indoor records, in the 800-meter (2 minutes, 01.8 seconds) and 1,000-meter races. She outdid her previous world record in the 880-yard run, with a new time of 2 minutes, 2.4 seconds. Spectators marveled at Decker's smooth, easy motion, and coaches analyzed her running techniques.

During the mid-1970s, Decker suffered from leg injuries and underwent leg surgery in 1976. Yet she began training again in 1979 and won a gold medal in the Pan American Games that year. In early 1980,

Mary Decker takes the lead in the 3,000-meter run at the 1984 Olympics.

she set a world record for the outdoor mile race, making her the first American woman to lead the world in a race longer than 200 meters. She also set another record that year, running the mile in 4 minutes, 17.6 seconds, the fastest time ever recorded for a woman running the mile either indoors or out.

The United States boycotted the 1980 Olympics, held in the Soviet Union, to protest that country's invasion of Afghanistan, so Decker was not able to compete. But she did set a new American record in the 1,500 meter run: 3 minutes, 59.5 seconds.

For the next few years, Decker continued to win races and set records. At the 1983 world championships, she won both the 1,500- and 3,000-meter races. In the 3,000-meter, she defeated the 1980 Olympic gold medalist. But during the 3,000-meter race at the 1984 Olympics, Decker had a disappointing fall, which hurt her time. That year, Decker was selected by the Woman's Sports Foundation as one of five of the greatest athletes of the years 1960–1984. Illnesses and injuries kept her from the 1988 Olympics. Despite never winning an Olympic medal in years of racing, Mary Decker met records set at the Games by other runners. In all, she broke 36 American and 17 world records.

Decker married Richard Slaney, a businessman, in 1985, and they had a daughter, Ashley. British-born Slaney had been a champion discus thrower. In 1994, at age 36, Mary Decker Slaney was training again and considering a comeback. But the fall she had suffered in 1984 left its mark: some of her heel bone had been trimmed off, and she had ongoing problems in that bone. She had also undergone 20 operations to repair shin splints and treat inflamed Achilles tendons.

Although Decker Slaney said it would be wonderful to run in Atlanta at the 1996 Olympics, her main goal was "being healthy. That's all I need to be."

References Reed and Cernetig, "Going the Distance," *People*, 1995; McCane and Wolf, *The Worst Day I Ever Had* (1991); Stambler, *Women in Sports: The Long, Hard Climb* (1975).

DeFrantz, Anita

As the first American woman and the first black American to sit on the International Olympic Committee (IOC), DeFrantz played a key role in planning the 1996 Summer Olympics in Atlanta. A former Olympian, DeFrantz had won a bronze medal in rowing at the 1976 Olympic Games and was also on the 1980 team. She was awarded the Olympic Order in 1980.

In 1986, when she was appointed to the IOC, DeFrantz was serving as president and member of the board of directors of the Amateur Athletic Foundation in Los Angeles. Her appointment to the IOC will last until the year 2027. In 1992, she was elevated to the IOC executive board and re-elected to a four-year term, from 1993 to 1997. DeFrantz also served on a number of IOC committees and commissions, including the Congress of Unity Study Commission, the Commission for the Olympic Movement, and the Sport and Law Commission.

DeFrantz remained actively involved with the sport of rowing. She was elected vice president of FISA, the International Rowing Federation, in 1993. Finding herself one of the few women of color in the upper echelons of sport governance and management, DeFrantz studied the matter. She found that none of the 50 governing bodies of Olympic sports had an African-American woman at its head. In 106 large college athletic programs, there was only one African-American athletic director as of 1993.

DeFrantz has supported hiring more women in these positions.

During the opening ceremonies at the 1996 Olympics, DeFrantz was one of several Americans to have a key role. She helped to carry the Olympic flag into the stadium.

Del Ferraro, Danielle (b. 1981)

This Akron, Ohio, native made history in 1994 by becoming the first two-time winner of the All-American Soap Box Derby. In 1993, she won the kit division, following that with a victory in the masters division the next year.

Devers, Gail (b. 1966)

Track and field champion Devers won the 100-meter race at the 1992 Olympic Games. During 1990, Devers became ill and doctors were puzzled as to the cause. She had gone from 115 pounds to 139 and had experienced memory and hair loss, headaches, vision problems, convulsions, and other disturbing symptoms. They finally diagnosed her with Graves' Disease, a disorder of the thyroid gland. She began receiving radiation treatments but then experienced other health problems. At one point, Devers was unable to walk and doctors feared they might have to amputate her feet.

After the radiation treatments ended and her disease was brought under control, Devers resumed training with her coach, Bob Kersee. At the 1992 Olympics, she won the 100-meter race in one of the closest sprints in Olympic history. She called the previous three years and her Olympic victory "a miracle." In 1993, she won the 100-meter dash and the 100-meter hurdles, setting a new American record of 12:46 seconds. She also won the 60-meter indoor title that year, with a time of 6.95 seconds.

Devers won the 100-meter hurdles again at the 1995 national championships, retaining her title. At the 1996 Summer Olympics in Atlanta, Georgia, Devers won her second gold medal in the 100-meter dash.

Devlin Cup

Devlin Cup matches are played between women's badminton teams from the United States and Canada every three years. The cup was named for the famous badminton-playing Devlin family. J. F. Devlin of Ireland is regarded as the best player of all time, with six All-England singles titles and others. His daughter, Judith Devlin Hashman, was considered the greatest woman player of all time, while another daughter, Susan Devlin Peard, won numerous titles as well. Both women were elected to the Badminton Hall of Fame.

Devlin, Judy (See Badminton)

Didrikson Zaharias, Babe (1911–1956)

In 1950, Babe Didrikson was named Woman Athlete of the Half Century. Some people have called the versatile Babe the best all-around athlete of all time, male or female.

Growing up in south Beaumont, Texas, all seven Didrikson children liked sports, and Mildred Ella (Babe's given name) seemed to love them most. She even turned housecleaning into a sport, wearing scrub brushes on her feet and "skating" across the floor, spreading soapsuds. Running through her neighborhood, she tried to beat the streetcar and leaped over hedges in the yards.

Her parents had no extra money for sports equipment, so Mr. Didrikson, a carpenter, built a jungle gym and trapeze in the backyard. Old broomsticks became hurdles; homemade barbells were weighted with flatirons. The children also enjoyed swimming and racing in a nearby river.

Whatever sport she played, Mildred wanted to win, to be the best. Her ability to hit homeruns in baseball led the neighborhood boys to call her "Babe" after the famous New York Yankee, Babe Ruth. But Babe Didrikson was sometimes teased for shunning dresses and traditional "girlish" activities, preferring to wear pants and play sports. People criticized her short, straight hair and aggressiveness. Many were also offended when she boasted about her athletic skills or predicted she would win a competition.

In 1930, a scout for a Dallas insurance company saw Babe play in a high school basketball game. He offered her a place on the women's team his company sponsored, which included a job as a secretary. Babe took the job after she finished high school, sending part of her paycheck home. She soon became a star forward on the team, once scoring 210 points in five games.

That same year, Babe Didrikson attended her first track meet. She decided to master all the sports involved in track and field and began practicing at once to reach this goal. In her first meet, Didrikson won five gold medals. She set new world records and impressed onlookers by throwing a baseball a distance of 268 feet at one meet. Didrikson decided she would try her skills in the next Summer Olympic Games. In the meantime, she played on the company softball team, competed in tennis tournaments, and gave exhibitions of springboard and platform diving. She began taking golf lessons, too.

Just before the Olympics, Didrikson went to an American Athletic Union (AAU) track meet in Illinois. For three hours, she competed in every event, making track and field history. She won first place in the long jump, hurdles, javelin throw, baseball throw, and shot put, and tied for first place in the high jump. In the discus throw, she came in fourth. Sportswriters called her "Supergirl."

Babe Didrikson easily made the 1932 Olympic team and went to the Games in Los Angeles. She won two gold medals, one for her javelin throw (a new world record of 143 feet, 4 inches) and in the 80-meter hurdles, again setting a world record (11.7 seconds). In the high jump, she won a second-place medal.

Although Didrikson enjoyed competing, she needed to earn more money than she could as an amateur athlete. So Didrikson began touring America in vaudeville shows, where she exhibited her athletic skills and played the harmonica. She promoted automobiles, rode horses, bowled, and played exhibition basketball and baseball. Her earnings enabled her to save money and help her family.

Eager to return to competition, Didrikson turned to golf. She practiced for hours, often smacking 1,000 balls a day to better her swing and hit longer drives. In 1935, after only a few tournaments, Didrikson won the Texas Women's Amateur tournament but was soon disqualified. The United States Golf Association (USGA) said Didrikson was a professional athlete, not an amateur. She would one day write of that disappointment, "[I had] hit balls until my hands were bloody and sore. Then I'd have tape all over my hands and blood all over the tape." Now she would not be allowed to compete.

In 1938, Didrikson married a champion wrestler and businessman named George Zaharias. He encouraged Babe to regain her amateur golfer status and supported her economically. The USGA agreed to reinstate her after a three-year waiting period. During that time, Didrikson cooked, sewed, tended a garden, and decorated her Los Angeles home. She played tennis and bowled. She and George traveled, went dancing, and entertained friends.

When Didrikson returned to golf tournaments in 1943, she began winning, first in the United States, then in Great Britain. She set a record by winning 17 tournaments in a row. During those years, the Ladies Professional Golf Association (LPGA) was born. It soon organized a tour featuring cash prizes for women golfers. Didrikson later took pride in earning large sums as a professional golfer.

Didrikson's standards of sportsmanship were high. Once while playing in a golf match, she realized she had accidentally hit the wrong ball out of the rough. She told officials, "I've been playing the wrong ball and I have to disqualify myself." When a spectator commented that nobody would have known what happened, Didrikson replied, "I'd have known the difference, and I wouldn't have felt right in my mind. You have to play by the rules of golf just as you have to live by the rules of life. There's no other way."

When Didrikson found out that she had cancer in 1953, well-wishers sent letters, telegrams, and gifts. Surgery did not cure her illness. Nevertheless, she kept playing golf and won the world championship in 1953 and the U.S. Women's Open in 1954. She continued to encourage younger golfers and expressed the hope that she could inspire cancer victims. After winning the All American title that year, Babe Didrikson Zaharias was voted Woman Athlete of 1954. The spunky athlete said, "I'll go on golfing for years." But

two years later, the incomparable Babe was gone.

See also Basketball

References Dailey, "Implausible Is Best," in Vecchione, ed., *The New York Times Book of Sports Legends* (1991); Didrikson Zaharias, with Harry Paxton, *This Life I've Led* (1955); Knudson, *Babe Didrikson, Athlete of the Century* (1985); Smith, *The Babe: Mildred Didrikson Zaharias* (1976).

Discrimination, Gender

Women have been discouraged, banned, and ousted from various sports through the centuries. Opponents have argued that women are too mentally and physically weak for various sports and that they are too easily injured. Some have suggested that blows to the breasts might lead to cancer. But the American Cancer Society has concluded that a blow to the breast does not influence breast cancer. One long-standing argument held that strenuous physical activity and competitive sports would prevent women from being able to conceive and bear children. In more recent decades, researchers have questioned whether the reproductive organs, primarily the uterus, are injured during sports. But most experts agree with Dr. Denis Barrault, of the French National Institute of Sport and Physical Education, who said, "The uterus and ovaries are better protected by nature than are the male sex organs."

Controversies also swirled around the Olympics, as women have struggled to be included in more events at both the Winter and Summer Games. A 1973 article in *Sports Illustrated* stated, "There may be worse forms of prejudice in the United States, but there is no sharper example of discrimination today than that which operates against girls and women who take part in competitive sports, wish to take part, or might wish to if society did not scorn such endeavors."

In 1972, Congress passed Title IX, a statute that required schools either to provide sports teams for girls or let girls try out for the boys' teams. Schools were also required to treat boys' and girls' teams equitably. A number of lawsuits were filed.

In 1978, federal Judge Carl Rubin of Ohio ruled that girls could not be banned from contact sports like football, hockey, or wrestling on the basis of gender alone. In some places, girls have gained places on boys' high school teams, after trying out and being selected to play. At a New York State high school, for example, two girls were place kickers on the football team during the 1992 season. In Michigan, a girl was playing goalie on the boys' ice hockey team.

In 1970, about 300,000 girls were playing competitive high school sports in the United States. By the early 1990s, more than 2 million girls were competing. Changes have occurred, although critics point to many remaining inequities. At some schools, boys' teams are given priority to use the gym or the best athletic facilities. When high school or college budgets are cut, girls' athletic programs are often eliminated or scaled back while boys' programs remain in place. As of 1980, women's athletics budgets had risen from 1 percent of men's to 16 percent.

Surveys conducted by the National Collegiate Athletic Association (NCAA) in 1991 showed that female athletes received only about one-third of the scholarship money available for students. Women coaches' salaries were lower than those of male coaches with similar experience and qualifications.

See also Baseball; Femininity; Fothergill, Dorothy; King, Billie Jean; Little League; Marathon Running; Motherhood; National Collegiate Athletic Association; Olympics; Postema, Pam; Pregnancy; Switzer, Kathrine; Title IX

Discrimination, Racial

For decades, African-Americans, both men and women, were excluded from official competitions or teams in certain sports. Some sports, such as tennis and golf, were typically played at private clubs, which also hosted major tournaments. These clubs had long-standing policies of barring people of color from membership.

Cost was also a discouraging factor, since people of color have had lower average incomes than white Americans and higher rates of poverty. Certain sports are expensive and were thus available only to a small, wealthy segment of the population. Few Americans owned polo ponies or thoroughbreds, for example. Equipment, lessons, travel expenses, and other costs prohibited people of modest means from becoming top athletes in a number of sports. And working class people did not have as much leisure time to pursue amateur sports. Until recent decades, full-time athletes could not earn enough to support themselves.

Black athletes also suffered from inequalities in funding at elementary and secondary schools and at colleges and universities. Often, these institutions lacked the facilities and money needed for sports programs and proper equipment, and white-dominated sports organizations did not give their support. Before the 1960s in southern states, the Amateur Athletic Union (AAU) permitted whites-only events in places where racial segregation was legal. Furthermore, the media often ignored the achievements of black athletes. Besides receiving less coverage in the print media, they had generally much lower salaries as athletes.

Left to their own devices, African-American athletes thrived nonetheless, organizing their own athletic organizations, training, and competitive events. Coaches found ways to improvise when facilities and equipment were lacking. Communities supported their athletes and sports events.

A major breakthrough against racial injustice in sports took place in 1947, when baseball player Jackie Robinson signed a contract with the Brooklyn Dodgers, becoming the first black person to play in the modern major leagues. Robinson's achievement was a major step, not only for athletes but for the American civil rights movement. During the 1950s, tennis player Althea Gibson made breakthroughs in that sport.

By the early 1990s, black players would make up more than 50 percent of the players in both the National Football League and National Basketball League. African-Americans, both male and female, have won top honors in track and field, tennis, golf, and other sports once dominated by whites. African-Americans continue to work toward more positions at the management and ownership levels of athletics.

See also All-American Girls Professional Baseball League; American Tennis Association; Baseball; DeFrantz, Anita; Gibson, Althea; Rudolph, Wilma; Stone, Toni Lyle; Temple, Ed

Discus

The discus, a wooden disk with metal rims, has often been compared to two pie plates joined together. But among the ancient Greek athletes, none were more esteemed than those who threw the discus.

In high school, male and female competitors throw a discus of differing weights: the boys' discus weighs 3 pounds, 9 ounces, while the girls' discus weighs 2 pounds, 3.5 ounces. At collegiate events, both use a discus that weighs about 4.5 pounds. The thrower must take care to stand inside the circle (8 feet, 2.5 inches in diameter) during the complete throwing motion. Speed and efficiency are the key traits for those who would excel at throwing the discus. To some coaches, these traits count for more than sheer strength.

Since Lillian Copeland won a gold medal in this event in 1932, no U.S. woman had won the Olympic discus competition as of 1996. Copeland also set world records in the javelin throw in 1926, 1927, and 1928 and won the silver medal in the discus throw at the 1928 Olympics.

See also Track and Field

Diving

Diving, once known as "plunging," was merely an adjunct to swimming for many centuries. The sport of developing unusual, acrobatic dives evolved during the 1890s. In 1893, a plunging championship was held in England. This contest, which was held annually for 44 years, involved plain or flat dives as well as one called the swan dive.

In Germany and Scandinavian countries, gymnasts began diving from boards placed higher above the water in order to perform fancier dives. They used scaffolds with trapezes and other acrobatic devices. A springboard was developed to give divers more height. From both springboard and platforms, the divers learned dives in which they performed somersaults and twists in the air before entering the water.

In 1905, Great Britain sponsored competitive diving events. Men's platform (called high board) diving was an event in the 1904 Olympics, with men's springboard being added in 1908. Women began competing in the platform (high board) at the 1912 Games, with springboard being added in 1920. At the 1920 Games, Aileen Riggin won the springboard event, the youngest Olympian to win a gold medal (and one of the only Olympians to win both a diving and swimming event). U.S. women would hold onto the gold in springboard diving until 1960, then again from 1968 through 1976. American divers have also won numerous gold, silver, and bronze medals in the platform event.

One of the most successful Olympic divers was Pat McCormick, who achieved a "double-double" at two successive Olympics: in both 1952 and 1956, McCormick won gold medals for both springboard and platform diving. Diver Dorothy Poynton-Hill won medals in three separate Games—1928, 1932, and 1936, earning two golds in platform diving and a silver and bronze in the springboard. Paula Myers-Pope also won medals in three Olympics (1952, 1956, 1960), two silvers and a bronze in the platform event. A couple from the United States, Clarence Pinkston and Elizabeth Becker Pinkston, both competed as Olympic divers, winning three gold, two silver, and two bronze medals between 1920 and 1928.

The sport of diving and diving competitions are sponsored by the Amateur Athletic Union (AAU) and are also part of the Pan American Games. Three categories of fancy dives are recognized in competitions: the layout, in which both the body and the arms are kept straight, with feet together; the pike, in which the body bends at the hips while legs remain straight; the tuck, in which the diver clasps his or her ankles, assuming a tightly compact body position. Jackknife dives are part of the pike category, as are most somersault dives. When divers complete more than one full revolution

before entering the water, they most often use a tuck position at the end. These basic dives are varied in hundreds of ways.

An example of a layout dive is the classic swan dive, in which the diver begins with head bent backward and the back hollowed slightly. The feet stay together, so there is a straight line from hips to toes. As the diver approaches the water, she moves her arms to the side at shoulder height, holding them until she reaches the water at which time she swings them over her head and the hands hit the water before the head and rest of the body.

At the 1996 Summer Olympics in Atlanta, Georgia, U.S. diver Mary Ellen Clark won her second consecutive bronze medal in platform diving. Clark also became the oldest American diver to win an Olympic medal. It was an amazing comeback for the 33 year old, who had been suffering from vertigo, a mental condition that causes severe dizziness and disorientation, during the past year and could not train normally until December 1995, when the condition was brought under control.

In the United States, the governing body for the sport of competitive diving is U.S.A. Diving, Inc. Former Olympic gold medalist Micki King has been part of this organization.

See also King, Micki; McCormick, Pat; Poynton-Hill, Dorothy; Riggin, Aileen

Reference Clary, "Clark Bounces Back for Second Bronze," *New York Times*, July 29, 1996, C4.

Donahue, Margaret (See Management)

Donovan, Anne (b. 1961)

Donovan, from Ridgewood, New Jersey, was part of the U.S. women's team that won the gold medal in basketball at the

1984 Olympics. At 6 feet 8 inches, she was the tallest woman on the U.S. team. Even so, the Soviet center Juliana Semenova, whom she often met in international competition, stood 2.5 inches taller.

At Old Dominion College in Virginia, Donovan played every game scheduled during her four years on the team, for a total of 136. She scored 2,719 points during those years and averaged 14.5 rebounds a game. In 1983, she won the Naismith College Player of the Year award and the Champion Player of the Year Award, given by the Women's Basketball Coaches Association that year for the first time. Also in 1983, Donovan totaled an amazing 504 rebounds. As of 1995, this was the third highest number ever attained by a woman player in NCAA Division I. From 1981 to 1983, Donovan was an All-American. She won both the Wade and Naismith trophies.

Donovan was selected to play on the U.S. women's team in 1980, but President Carter announced that the nation's athletes would boycott those Games for political reasons. She finally did get to play at the 1984 Olympics, where the U.S. women won a gold medal. Donovan went on to become a basketball coach at Old Dominion College.

Drag Racing

Racing in dragsters or hot rods, as they are often called, was a sport dominated by men until the 1960s. The cars reached speeds of more than 200 miles per hour as drivers raced around the track, usually in pairs. Women drivers, such as Shirley Muldowney, Judi Boertman, Paula Murphy, and Della Woods, entered the sport and fought for the right to be officially licensed by the American Hot Rod Association and the National Hot Rod Association. Women faced strong opposition

from those who said they were not physically strong enough to compete safely in the sport and from men who resented the idea of competing against women. After much urging, the official associations finally agreed in the mid-1960s to allow all drivers, whether male or female, to apply for a license, take the same tests, and be judged according to the same standards. Since then, top women drivers have proven their ability to race alongside men and to win.

See also Muldowney, Shirley

Dress Code

Formal rules and social norms about appropriate dress for women have affected their ability to perform and excel in different sports. Objections to women's sports costumes have centered on the style and cut of uniforms as well as how closely they fit the body. Critics complained when outfits were viewed as too revealing or clinging, and therefore not ladylike, or too much like those of men, and therefore not feminine enough.

During the early 1900s, women competing in track and field were criticized or sometimes teased for their attire—shortened bloomers and sleeveless tops. Women in basketball and track were also urged not to wear outfits made with shiny material.

In figure skating, the International Skating Union (ISU) used clothing as one of the main reasons to exclude women from early figure skating competitions. When Madge (Maggie) Syers of Great Britain entered the men's event in 1902, the ISU had no rules in place to refuse her. Syers finished second in the men's skating competition. In response, the ISU formally banned women from the competitions. Among other reasons, the officials said that because a woman must wear ankle-length skirts, judges could not examine the movements of her feet as she skated.

One example of dress codes can be seen in the objections to women's basketball uniforms. During the 1920s, physical education leaders from some schools complained that women playing on industrial and Amateur Athletic Union (AAU) teams sometimes looked "tawdry" or "loud." Women's uniforms featured collars and short sleeves, while men wore low-necked sleeveless shirts.

Informal codes about what is appropriate dress continued to affect athletes into the 1980s and 1990s. In figure skating, where women's costumes can cost thousands of dollars, certain skaters were praised for dressing tastefully while others have been criticized for their choices of colors, designs, and trimmings. In 1984, Olympic gold medalist Katerina Witt of East Germany wore a dress with high-cut legs to the European championships. She was encouraged by officials to cover more of her legs for the Olympics. For her Olympic performance, Witt appeared with feathers sewn to the costume, concealing more of her upper thighs.

See also Bleibtrey, Ethelda; Bloomer, Amelia Jenks; Bloomers; Cycling

Dressage

Both individual and team competitions are held in this equestrian event. Riders and horses are judged on how well they perform various exercises, in which the rider shows the different gaits of the horse and moves the horse in different directions in the show ring. During the exercises, horse and rider must move smoothly from one movement to the next in harmony with each other. Dressage is an Olympic sport and is featured at the Pan American Games and other international competitions.

Three-time Olympian Edith Master was the national dressage champion for several years. In 1968, after the U.S. equestrian team placed eighth at the Olympics, Master decided to polish her skills by studying in Europe. At the 1976 Olympics, riding "Dahlwitz," Master was part of the bronze-medal winning team.

Individual American women and coed U.S. teams have done well in international dressage events. Hilda Gurney led the U.S. equestrian team in points scored at the 1976 Olympic Games held in Montreal. Riding her horse, Keen, she won a bronze medal. At the 1979 Pan American Games, she rode her gray stallion, Chrysos, and won gold medals in both individual and team dressage. At the 1981 Pan American Games, Gurney was part of the U.S. team that won a gold medal. Gurney won the silver in individual dressage.

See also Equestrian Sports

DuPont, Margaret Osburne (b. 1918) DuPont was known as a brilliant tennis player who used a variety of well-planned strokes to defeat opponents. She accumulated 37 titles during her career, 31 of them in doubles and mixed doubles play.

Born in Oregon, DuPont grew up in San Francisco, where tennis was a popular game. She reached the rank of number seven among U.S. women in 1938. Over a period of 20 years, she was in the top ten 14 times, the last time at age 40.

DuPont won her first U.S. women's singles title in 1948, the first of three consecutive wins. In that 1948 final, she outlasted her frequent doubles partner, Louise Brough, in a 48-game match, the longest U.S. women's singles final ever. The score was 4-6, 6-4, 15-13.

Among DuPont's other singles titles were two French championships and one at Wimbledon. She triumphed on various court surfaces to win doubles at the U.S. tournament three times, as well as three French and five Wimbledon doubles titles. With four different men as partners, she held the record for mixed doubles at the U.S. championship, winning it nine times in a row between 1941 and 1950, then winning again in 1955, 1956, and 1957. She also won the mixed doubles crown at Wimbledon once. She was undefeated during her years on the Wightman Cup team, winning ten singles matches and nine doubles. DuPont was captain of the U.S. team nine times, and while she was captain, they lost the cup only once.

Married to William DuPont in 1947, DuPont later became a mother. She returned to tournament play afterwards, winning other major titles. She was inducted into the Tennis Hall of Fame in 1967.

See also Brough, Louise

Dunn, Natalie (b. 1956)

In 1976, Dunn became the first American woman to win the world figure roller skating championship. The San Antonio, Texas, native began skating as a young child and won her first contest at age seven. At 16, she was the U.S. national ladies' champion, the first of nine times she would win that crown.

Dunn won her first world crown in 1976 in Rome, Italy, where she performed two very difficult moves: the triple Salchow jump and the triple Mapes. Only a few women roller skaters have mastered these movements. Dunn held on to her world title in 1977, then won a third title in 1979.

See also Roller Skating

Durham, Dianne (b. 1968)

In 1983 Durham became the first African-American woman to win a national gymnastics championship. She began gymnastics training at a local YMCA in Gary, Indiana, as a four-year-old. Durham also loved dancing and found that gymnastics blended with her interest in jazz. In 1981 and 1982, Durham won the national junior elite gymnastics championship.

At the 1983 senior women's championships, Durham prevailed, winning gold medals in the balance beam, floor exercises, vault, and all-around events. She tied for second place in the uneven bars. At the McDonald's International Championships that same year, Durham won the all-around gold medal and a silver for her performance on the uneven bars. Because of a knee injury, she had to withdraw from the remaining individual events.

After surgery, she returned to competition and came in third in the all-around at the prestigious Chunichi Cup gymnastics competition in Japan. In 1984, Durham suffered from recurring knee problems, which forced her to withdraw from several competitions. She was also not able to compete in that year's Olympic Games.

Earhart, Amelia (1897–1937)

In 1920, during her first trip aloft as the sole passenger in a small airplane, Earhart was struck by the view of Glendale, California, below. She later said, "As soon as we left the ground, I knew I had to fly myself. . . . We were friends, the ocean, the hills, and I."

Amelia Mary Earhart was born in Kansas. After graduating from high school, she moved to Los Angeles. A true pioneer, Earhart studied flying with another pioneer woman pilot, Neta Snook, and earned the first pilot's license ever issued to a woman. When she was 25 years old, she sold personal belongings and used her earnings from working at a telephone company in order to buy a plane called "Lady Lindy." In 1921, Earhart proceeded to break the previous woman's altitude record when she reached 14,000 feet. She did stunt-flying in exhibitions and flew in air races. Taking on new challenges, Earhart became the first woman pilot to cross the Atlantic and the first to cross the Atlantic solo (1932). With other women fliers, she helped to found the Ninety-Nines and served as its president. The group, consisting of 99 women pilots, helped to promote women in aviation.

In 1937, Earhart set out for what was called an around-the-world flight, another first for a solo woman pilot. She was never heard from again after her plane was lost somewhere in the South Pacific. Her death remained an unsolved mystery, with some speculating that Earhart may have been captured by the Japanese while on a secret spying mission for the U.S. government. Historians later concluded that the plane probably ran out of fuel.

References Earhart, *The Fun of It* (1932); Goerner, *The Search for Amelia Earhart* (1968); Randolph, *Amelia Earhart* (1981).

Early, Penny Ann

A jockey, Early had planned to ride in the Kentucky Derby in November 1968, but her horse was eliminated. She was again scheduled to ride two days later but was replaced after male jockeys said they would boycott the race. In 1969, she won the Lady Godiva Handicap race at Suffolk Downs, Massachusetts, a race that was, at that time, the only pari-mutuel thoroughbred race open to women jockeys.

Early was also a pioneer in another sport when she became the first woman to play professional basketball. In 1969, she played in a promotional game with the Kentucky Colonels, a team in the American Basketball Association (ABA). Her brief appearance at the onset of the game was a publicity gimmick.

See also Kentucky Derby

Eating Disorders

During the 1980s, a number of observers and researchers alleged that women athletes suffered from eating disorders at higher rates than women in the general population. It is estimated that around 1 percent of the U.S. female population suffers from anorexia (an avoidance of eating that results in severe malnutrition) or bulimia (the practice of bingeing—overeating—then purging—vomiting). Women also reported using diuretics (medications designed to promote water loss) and over-the-counter preparations, such as laxatives, in unapproved ways in order to lose weight. A 1992 study by the University of Washington of 182 women college athletes found that 32 percent had some kind of eating disorder, whether routine vomiting or using laxatives, water pills, or diet pills in order to lose weight.

In her book *Little Girls in Pretty Boxes*, author Joan Ryan discussed eating disorders among women athletes in the sports of gymnastics and figure skating. Ryan found that in gymnastics, coaches played a large role by insisting that the athletes remain thin and adhere to strict diets.

Some tennis players, including Zina Garrison and Canadian Carling Bassett Saguso, have talked about their struggles with eating disorders. Saguso was once hospitalized when her weight fell to 98 pounds. Writing for *Tennis* magazine, Cindy Hahn quoted Julie Anthony, a tennis player who became a clinical psychologist: "I wouldn't be surprised if around 30 percent of the women on the tour have some form of an eating disorder. I know a number of the women in the top 20 [who do]."

See also Gymnastics; Henrich, Christy; Karolyi, Bela; Rigby, Cathy
References Blue, *Faster, Higher, Further: Women's Triumphs and Disasters at the Olympics* (1988); Ryan, *Little Girls in Pretty Boxes: The Making and Breaking of Elite Gymnasts and Figure Skaters* (1995).

Ederle, Gertrude (b. 1906)

Gertrude Caroline Ederle became the first woman to swim across the English Chan-

nel, making the trip in record time in 1926. An excellent swimmer as a child, she nevertheless had few opportunities to swim. She lived on the lower East Side of Manhattan, where her father was a butcher and owner of a delicatessen. She joined a local swim club at age 13 in order to swim year-round.

Her older sister Margaret, also a swimmer, encouraged "Trudy" to compete, and Ederle won her first long race in 1921. Despite a fierce tide, she defeated other swimmers, many of them older, in the 3-mile race around New York Bay for the J. P. Day Cup. When Ederle swam in a 500-meter race in Brighton Beach, New York, in 1922, she broke seven world records while reaching various distances on route to the finish. That year, she held the national title in 220- and 440-yard races.

By 1924, Ederle held an astonishing 18 world swimming records. She had won the 440-meter National Amateur Athletic Union competition twice. Her specialty was the eight-beat crawl, a stroke that includes eight kicks for each full arm stroke. Ederle was on the U.S. Olympic swim team that competed in Paris that summer. As part of the winning women's 400-meter relay team, she took home a gold medal. She also won bronze medals in both the 100-meter freestyle race and the 400-meter freestyle. During the early 1920s, she set world and U.S. women's records for freestyle competition in distances ranging from 100 to 880 yards.

Ederle decided to turn professional in 1925. At that point, she held world records in three freestyle events: the 100-meter, the 220-meter, and the 400-meter. Commenting on her achievements, the *Saturday Evening Post* stated, "There is every reason to hope and be-

Gertrude Ederle greases up before her 1926 record-breaking swim across the English Channel. Ederle was the first woman to accomplish the feat.

lieve that Miss Ederle's great achievement will intensify interest in distance swimming as a sport for both men and women."

During her 1926 Channel swim, Ederle used the American crawl stroke. Wearing a heavy coat of body grease, she battled cold, rough seas and persistent nausea to swim from Cap Gris-Nez, France, to Dover, England. She was accompanied by a tugboat, which moved alongside her in case of an emergency. At Dover, citizens had lit fires on the shore so that Ederle could find her way. When she returned to America, the famous New Yorker was greeted by a ticker-tape parade and more than a million well-wishers, cheering her accomplishment.

It took Ederle 14 hours and 31 minutes to swim the 35 miles, a time that beat the men's record by 1 hour and 59 minutes. Along with Ederle, five men had swum across the Channel. This record stood until 1964, when another woman, Denmark's Greta Anderson, swam the channel in 13 hours, 14 minutes.

After her channel swim, Ederle had a permanent hearing impairment, due to inner ear damage caused by the cold water. She became a professional swimmer and instructor, as well as a fashion designer, and spent much of her time teaching deaf children to swim. Ederle received several awards for her humanitarian work and was voted into the International Swimming Hall of Fame in 1965 and to the Women's Sports Hall of Fame in 1980.

Elite

Athletes who are considered elite have reached the most accomplished level in a given sport. The term is often used to describe top gymnasts. In gymnastics, competitions are also sometimes called elite, such as the Elite National Qualifying Meet and the Elite National Trials.

Ellis, Betty (See Officiating)

Endestad, Judy Rabinowitz (See Skiing)

Endorsements, Commercial

Male athletes were offered chances to endorse commercial products years before women athletes received such offers. Their images could be seen next to candy, soft drinks, cereals, and various pieces of sports equipment, among other products. But beginning in the 1970s, a boom in women's sports and increasing media attention to female athletes led to more commercial endorsements. Advertising executives began to use women athletes to sell products such as cosmetics and hair-care products, as well as sports equipment, clothing, and shoes. Maureen Connolly was among the players, mostly male, who had a tennis racket named for her. The Wilson "Maureen Connolly" wood racket was popular with female players during the 1950s.

In the late 1900s, women figure skaters, tennis players, and gymnasts tended to receive the most offers, as well as women who did especially well at the

Olympics. Figure-skater Dorothy Hamill, for example, sponsored a line of Clairol hair-care products called "Short and Sassy." Hamill's distinctive wedge haircut started a trend. Another gold medalist, Kristi Yamaguchi, has been featured in ads for watches, contact lenses, and milk. Another popular spokesperson was tennis player Chris Evert. Skier Suzy Chaffee became "Suzy Chapstick" as she swooped downhill in ads promoting a protective lip balm. During the early 1990s, figure skater Nancy Kerrigan, who won a bronze medal at the 1992 Olympics and a silver medal in 1994, later earned millions of dollars endorsing a variety of products, including Reebok shoes, Ray Ban sunglasses, Revlon cosmetics, and Campbells's soup.

In 1995, basketball player Sheryl Swoopes became the first woman to have a signature shoe named after her. Swoopes was 1993 NCAA Female Player of the Year and helped her team at Texas Tech reach the Final Four championships in 1993. She also played on the U.S. women's team that competed in the 1994 World Championships. Along with the black-and-white Air Swoopes high-top shoes, sold by Nike, Swoopes endorsed Kellogg's cereal and Wilson basketballs and promoted her posters and trading cards. Her teammate at the 1996 Olympics, Rebecca Lobo, was featured in Reebok ads, as was young tennis star Venus Williams.

In choosing athletes to represent their products, companies often consult the "popular sports star" ratings found in *Advertising Age* magazine. Some also round up focus groups made up of consumers of different age groups. During the 1990s, top U.S. athletes could make millions each year from endorsements, sometimes two or more times as much as they made from their playing salaries. For example, according to *Forbes* magazine, basketball star Michael Jordan had a salary of $3.9 million for 1995 and an endorsement income of about $40 million. Nancy Kerrigan, perhaps the highest paid woman athlete in 1994, earned about $4 million combined income from skating and endorsements.

Equal Access (See Title IX)

Equestrian Sports

Equestrian events are performed on horseback. In equitation class events, riders show their proficiency in riding at different standard gaits—the walk, trot, and canter. Judges evaluate how well the rider controls and handles the horse and the coordination between horse and rider. More advanced events called performance events allow riders to take part in the hunter division and jumping. The skill of both the horse and rider are tested in the hunter division as the horse rounds a course set up like a fox hunting course. In the jumper division, the horse is judged on its ability to make high and wide jumps.

At one time, women competed in separate equestrian events. The women-only World Championship was held for the last time in 1974. Women and men now compete on equal terms in showjumping.

A number of American women have excelled at equestrian events in the Olympics. Leslie Burr, a native of Westport, Connecticut, was part of the U.S. Olympic equestrian team that won a gold medal in jumping at the 1984 Games in Los Angeles. Burr also won two Grand Prix events in 1979 and three in 1983. Melanie Smith was the world champion in show jumping in 1982. The U.S. team

won a team dressage medal at the 1996 Olympics.

See also Sears, Eleanora

Evans, Janet (b. 1971)

Swimmer Evans won a total of four gold medals in two different Olympic Games. She also set three world records in freestyle swimming—the 400-meters (4 minutes, 03.85 seconds in 1988); the 800-meters (8 minutes, 16.22 seconds in 1989); and the 1,500 meters (15 minutes, 52.10 seconds in 1988). These were still world records in women's swimming as of 1995.

Janet Evans won more individual gold medals at the 1988 Olympics in Seoul, South Korea, than any other athlete—three, for the 400- and 800-meter freestyle races and for the 400-meter individual medley. Evans won the Sullivan Award in 1989, then continued to perform well in world competition, winning the 400-meter freestyle race in 1991 and the 800-meter freestyle in both 1991 and 1994. She won her fourth Olympic gold medal at the 1992 Games, when she finished first in the 800-meter freestyle.

From 1987 to 1994, Evans did not lose the 800-meter freestyle race in national competition. Her winning streak ended in 1995 when she placed fourth in that event at the nationals in Pasadena, California. Fifteen-year-old Brooke Bennett won the 400-, 800-, and 1,500-meter freestyle races at that competition. At the indoor national championships in March 1995, Evans had won those three events.

Evert, Chris (b. 1954)

In a white tennis dress, her hair tied back with ribbons, Chris Evert pleased both spectators and photographers at the 1971 U.S. Open. In the second round, the 16-year-old newcomer defeated the fourth-ranked American woman, Mary Ann

Eisel. She continued winning until the semifinals, where she faced 27-year-old Billie Jean King, who went on to capture the title.

Christine Marie Evert grew up in Fort Lauderdale, Florida, with sisters Jeanne and Clare, and brothers Drew and John. Her father, Jimmy Evert, had won the National Indoor junior title in 1940 and the Canadian singles men's title in 1947. He was captain of the tennis team at Notre Dame University. In Florida, he worked as the manager and a teaching pro at the Holiday Park Tennis Center where Chris began to play at age six. She later said that her whole family played at Holiday Park so they could spend more time together.

Soon, Evert was practicing every day and showed great promise, winning several local junior tournaments. She was a quiet and disciplined player who showed little emotion on the court, though in later years, other players on the women's tour would speak of her great sense of humor off the court.

Groomed on clay courts, she learned to play a patient, baseline game, hitting strong, well-placed groundstrokes. Often, she outlasted her opponents who eventually made a mistake and lost the point. Evert also developed a two-handed backhand, which many tennis players later copied. Her father later explained that she was "too small and weak to swing the backhand with one hand." He had hoped she would eventually use a one-handed stroke, but she stayed with the two-hander, and he remarked, "When she got good at it, why should I change her?" And she was definitely good at it. When she was only 15, Evert astonished spectators by defeating long-time women's champion, Australian Margaret Court. Court had just won the Grand Slam when the

Florida teenager staged an upset on a clay court at a tournament in North Carolina.

Evert entered the women's tennis circuit when she was 16 years old. By the time she played in the U.S. Open in September 1971, she had won 46 straight singles titles. At 17, Evert played in her first Wimbledon and reached the semifinals, where she was defeated by the talented Australian player Evonne Goolagong (Cawley).

During high school, Evert practiced for hours after school, with time for homework and meals but no real extracurricular activities. Her father praised her hard work, saying, "She will work as hard as required to improve." Her school principal also called Evert a hard-worker who "amazed her teachers by how quickly she made up the work."

Chris's younger sister Jeanne was also playing in tournaments, and the two often practiced together. Although competitors, they spoke of each other as best friends. Sportswriters noticed that the Everts seem well-adjusted despite the rigors of being stars so young. Neil Amdur, who wrote for the *New York Times*, said that the Everts "seem to be able to maintain the balance that's necessary for enjoying the sport . . . while still preserving a sense of family commitment."

Chris Evert turned professional in 1973 when she was 18 years old and had finished high school. She chose to play in the United States Lawn Tennis Association (USLTA) circuit, hoping to win some important titles. As a professional, she could keep any money she won in tournaments. Later, she would become the first woman player to earn $1 million. During her career, which lasted 20 years, she would eventually earn nearly $9 million in prizes, making her one of the top earners in her sport.

When she was invited to play Wightman Cup tennis, Evert became one of the youngest ever to play on the team. During her 13 years playing on the Wightman team between 1971 and 1985, the United States was victorious 11 times. Evert won all 26 of her singles matches.

Evert had a stellar year in 1974, winning the Italian, French, and Canadian championships. By June of that year, she had collected 35 consecutive titles. At Wimbledon, she was delighted to win the women's singles title, sharing that joy with her then-fiancé Jimmy Connors, who won the men's singles title. The two later called off their engagement but remained friends.

From 1973 to 1986, Evert won at least one Grand Slam title each year. In 1976, she made the cover of *Sports Illustrated* magazine and was named Sportswoman of the Year. In previous years, that award had gone to men and went under the title Sportsman of the Year. A popular athlete, Evert received many fan letters and offers to endorse hair-care products and other items.

During the late 1970s and early 1980s, Evert often played against the powerful left-handed Czechoslovakian-American Martina Navratilova. At the 1978 Wimbledon, Navratilova defeated Evert in the finals. The two players took turns being ranked number one in the world. Evert had the top ranking in 1975, 1976, 1977, 1980, and 1981. As Evert neared the end of her career, Navratilova dominated the women's game and would eventually win more titles than any other player. Their matches had been among the most exciting ever played on the women's tour. Off the court, they became friends.

When she retired in 1989, Evert had amassed 157 professional singles titles. In her final playing year, she won all five singles matches at the Federation Cup competition, where the U.S. team took the title.

Evert married British tennis player John Lloyd in 1979; the two were divorced in 1987. She later married skier Andy Mill and became the mother of two children. The family divided their time between homes in Aspen, Colorado, and Boca Raton, Florida. After her retirement from professional competition, Evert stayed busy as a television commentator and with charitable work and commercial endorsements.

References Frayne, *Famous Women Tennis Players* (1979); Gutman, *Modern Women Superstars* (1978); Jenkins, "I've Led a Charmed Life," *Sports Illustrated*, May 25, 1992, 60–64; Lichtenstein, *A Long Way, Baby: Behind the Scenes in Women's Pro Tennis* (1974).

Federation Cup

Women's tennis teams from around the world compete in this annual competition, a parallel to the Davis Cup events for men. However, unlike Davis Cup competition, Federation Cup matches are completed within a week at one location. The men play for nine or ten weeks. Four-woman teams play two singles matches and two doubles matches. Two different players must enter the singles matches, but any combination may elect to play the doubles.

The first cup matches were held in 1963, the fiftieth anniversary of the founding of the International Tennis Federation (ITF), and 16 countries sent teams to the first competition. Within 30 years, 32 different teams were entering the qualifying rounds to compete for the cup. Beginning in 1976, prize money became part of the tournament.

The U.S. team has won more often than any other—14 times—followed by the Australian team with seven wins.

Fédération Sportive Féminine Internationale (FSFI)

Founded in 1921 by a French woman, Alice Milliat, the Fédération Sportive Féminine Internationale (FSFI) marked the first time that women's sports were organized at the international level. American women joined with women from Great Britain, Czechoslovakia, France, Italy, and Spain to cofound the FSFI.

The next year, the FSFI sponsored international competition for women athletes. These were the first Women's Olympic Games, held in Paris. The FSFI also urged officials at the International Olympic Committee (IOC) to include track and field events in the Games. They finally agreed, adding five such events in 1928. When the International Amateur Athletic Association was formed in 1936, it took over the role of governing women's sports. The FSFI was then dissolved.

Federation of Women's Field Hockey Associations (See Field Hockey)

Female College Athlete of the Year (See Association for Intercollegiate Athletics for Women)

Femininity

The issue of what is feminine in appearance and behavior has affected views about women and sports for centuries. Athletics were long the domain of men, proving grounds for their masculine skills and traits. At the risk of being ridiculed and criticized, many women avoided taking part in sports, thinking it was unfeminine to compete, behave aggressively, or try hard to win.

But as some women began to take part in sports, new attitudes evolved about which sports were feminine—usually those in which women did not exert

Two Smith College basketball players display the old (left) and new (right) bear-legged uniform in 1929. Critics often rallied against short haircuts, such as the style pictured here (right), but note that her shoes are in keeping with the traditional notion of "feminine" appearance.

themselves greatly, perspire, or have physical contact with other players. For instance, during the early 1900s, croquet and archery were viewed as more feminine than basketball or track and field events. Later, golf, tennis, and figure skating were viewed as appropriately feminine.

Women athletes have often been criticized for adopting what were labeled as masculine traits or for not having a traditionally feminine appearance. Critics once railed against the short haircuts favored by Babe Didrikson Zaharias and other athletes. Those women athletes who fit the socially accepted ideas about feminine appearance tended to be more popular with fans and received more offers to endorse commercial products. During the 1940s, the All-American Girls Professional Baseball League (AAGPBL) based many of its rules on what it called the "femininity principle" and enrolled players in a charm school. The league believed that the public would not accept women professional ballplayers unless they were also carefully groomed and dressed in ways that were not too "masculine."

But attitudes continued to change as more and more women took up various sports. By the late twentieth century, many women felt that definitions of femininity could encompass most any sport and that the large and well-defined muscles of body-builders could also be feminine.

The controversial sex tests during the late 1960s provided ways of physically identifying a person as "male" or "female." At the 1968 Olympics, the International Olympic Committee (IOC) used a mandatory test in which they scraped cells from the inside of the female athletes' cheeks to analyze the chromosomes. In some cases, they found chromosomal abnormalities that were the result of genetic defects. A number of physicians and scientific experts denounced the tests, pointing out that some women have an abnormal genetic makeup but are still not males. Athletes have also called the procedures degrading and some referred to the certification card they received after testing as their "fem card."

Critics of this kind of testing point out that there are no such tests for men. Heptathlete Jane Frederick has said, "I think they are just saying, 'You are so good, we can't believe you're a woman, so prove it.'" Others agree that when success at athletics is defined as masculine or requiring masculine traits, women who do well are seen as less feminine. Volleyball star and coach Mary Jo Peppler addressed this issue in her 1977 book:

As an athlete you will no doubt come to a point in your training where you are going to think twice before you lift weights, sweat, grunt and groan, or beat your boyfriend at tennis. These are not normal "ladylike" activities. Nonetheless, just the fact that you are female should not exclude you from them. Women must shape their own amateur and professional sports so that they are consistent with positive female values. In this way, a woman can become more feminine through her involvement in sports. . . . Positive dynamics of the feminine contribution to sports must be identified and developed.

See also All-American Girls Professional Baseball League; Battle of the Sexes; Baugh, Laura; Discrimination, Gender; Dress Code; King, Billie Jean; Prize Money; Sears, Eleonora; Sex Tests
Reference Peppler, *Inside Volleyball for Women* (1977).

Fencing

Fencing, sometimes grouped with the martial arts, refers to attack and defense maneuvers using a sword or similar weapon. During the Middle Ages, warriors used fencing to break through their opponents' armor in combat. Some men also challenged each other to fencing duels when a matter of honor was at stake. Fencing schools were developed in Italy during the 1500s, and by the 1800s, there were numerous fencing academies in France and other countries. The sport became a leisure pursuit for European men in the higher social classes.

Fencing has been called "the physical game of chess." A fencing bout usually lasts no more than six minutes, and players have to adjust rapidly to changing moves on the part of their opponents. They alternate between attack and defense maneuvers.

Men have long dominated the sport, competing in a fencing event at the first modern Olympics in 1896. Europeans won most international events during the early 1900s. The U.S. men's team won its first Olympic medal at the 1920 Olympics, where it placed third in the team foil competition. The word "foil" refers to a modern version of a particular type of sword. The U.S. men's sabre team came in fourth at those Games. Women's fencing became part of the Olympics in 1924, although as of 1992, men had three times more fencing events than did women.

The Intercollegiate Women's Fencing Association (IWFA), which later became the National Intercollegiate Women's Fencing Association (NIWFA), was formed in 1929. Women from Cornell, Bryn Mawr, New York University, and Hunter College took part in early competitions.

Talented European fencing instructors immigrated to the United States during and after the 1930s, helping to develop better fencing programs. By the late 1940s, U.S. women were reaching the finals and winning recognition in world events. Maria Cerra Tishman, a two-time IWFA champion and member of the fencing team at Hunter College, finished fourth at the 1948 Olympics after a three-way tie for second place. (In 1968, Tishman, an elementary school teacher active in national fencing programs, would become the first woman appointed to the U.S. Olympic Committee.) In 1952, Janice York Romary earned fourth place in women's foil at the Olympics, and Maxine Mitchell was sixth.

At the 1963 Pan American Games, U.S. women fencers came in second (Harriet King), third (Janice York Romary), and seventh (Bonnie Linkmeyer) in the foil competition. The U.S. women's team won first prize at the 1967 Pan American Games. Harriet King repeated her second place finish in 1967, and Ruth White won the silver medal in foil at the Pan American Games of 1971.

In 1972, about 100,000 American women were fencing. During that decade, U.S. Champions included Harriet King (1970 and 1971); Ruth White (1972); Tanya Adamovich (1973); Gaye Jacobsen (1974); Nikki Tomlinson (1975); Ann O'Donnell (1976); Sheila Armstrong (1977); Gay Dasaro (1978).

During the 1980s, Jana Angelakis was the top American woman fencer. From Peabody, Massachusetts, she had won the American junior title six times and at 17 became the youngest winner of the senior women's title. She won the title for three consecutive years, beginning in 1980. In 1980 she placed twelfth at the world fencing competition, the best finish up to that time for any American woman. In 1983, Debra Waples of Portland, Oregon, became the U.S. women's fencing champion.

A women's epee event (an epee is a smaller sword invented in France) became part of the world championships in 1989. Donna Stone of the United States finished fifth. In 1992, the U.S. women's epee team finished seventh, its best finish in that event as of 1995.

Age need not be a barrier for women fencers. In 1991, at age 42, Margo Miller, who had been competing for seventeen years, won the National Championship in Division One women's epee. Julia Jones, a fencing coach at Hunter College in New York and member of the fencing Hall of Fame, was still competing in 1992 at age 84.

During the early 1990s, other top fencers included Caitlin (Katy) Bilodeaux, Rachael McDaniel, Ann Marsh, Sharon Monplaisir, Susan Paxton, and Felicia Zimmerman. At age 17, Zimmerman, from Rochester, New York, won the U.S. women's national foil title in 1995. Zimmerman earned numerous titles, including the 1994-1995 Junior Women's Foil World Cup title and finished thirteenth in the Women's Foil World Cup competition in 1995. Along with Ann Marsh and Susan Paxton, Zimmerman made up the U.S. women's foil team, which was ranked first in the world as they prepared to compete in Atlanta at the 1996 Olympics.

As of 1992, about 200,000 women had taken up fencing, either as professionals or amateurs, with the numbers increasing each year. They were also using heavier swords called the epee and sabre, as well as the lighter foil women had used in the past. During the early 1990s, slightly fewer than one-third of the members in the U.S. Fencing Association were women.

A national women's fencing competition is held in the United States annually. Top women fencers work to develop upper-body strength through weight lifting and tennis, while running and playing sports like soccer to improve their leg strength and balance.

See also York-Romary, Janice Lee.
References Lodge, "Women en garde," *Harper's Bazaar*; U.S. Fencing Association Media Relations Department, "History of American Fencing," 1981, with updates through 1995.

Field Hockey

First played in England during the mid-1800s, field hockey became popular in many countries. It first came to the United States in 1901, when Constance Applebee organized teams and taught girls and young women how to play. At first it was an elite game, played by teams at private schools and colleges. More women than men played the game, and it was First Lady Eleanor Roosevelt's favorite sport.

After the 1920s, the popularity of field hockey spread throughout the country. The United States Field Hockey Association (USFHA) was formed in 1922. Five years later, the Federation of Women's Field Hockey Associations organized with associations from the United States, England, Scotland, and Ireland to promote international competition. In the United States, the game remained especially popular at private eastern women's colleges and private girls' high schools, though midwestern universities also formed more teams during the mid-1900s.

In 1932, men's field hockey became part of the Olympics. A women's event was not added until 1980—almost 50 years later, though most field hockey players around the country were girls and

The Boston Normal School class of 1906 plays field hockey, one of the few socially accepted sports for women at the turn of the century.

women. The first U.S. women's Olympic team went to the 1984 Games, where it won a bronze third-place medal. Women play two 30-minute periods with a brief rest period between. The game requires speed, skill, and endurance.

By the 1990s, field hockey was one of the most popular sports for women in high schools and colleges. The United States Field Hockey Association (USFHA) regulates the sport.

See also Applebee, Constance

Field Hockey Association, United States (USFHA)

The USFHA was organized in 1922 in Philadelphia, spearheaded by coach and educator Constance Applebee. Applebee had promoted field hockey for women in schools, colleges, and clubs throughout America.

As the governing body for the sport, the USFHA set standards and rules of play and began sponsoring a national tournament. It went on to develop sectional tournaments as well and to organize foreign tours. The USFHA also conducts summer developmental camps at various college campuses for young players. It aims to attract more players and encourage sportsmanship and a love of the game.

By 1932, more than 400 field hockey clubs around the United States were taking part in USFHA competitions. There were seven regional districts sending between two to four teams to the annual national championship. Interest in the sport has continued to grow. In 1984 the USFHA sponsored the first American team to compete in the Olympics. The U.S. women won a third-place bronze medal at those Games, held in Los Angeles.

See also Field Hockey

Fields, Crystal (b. 1969)

In 1980 Fields became the first girl ever to win the national Pitch, Hit, and Run Championship. The Maryland native competed in Seattle, Washington, at age 11, against seven boys in the 9–12 age-group division. Prior to winning this title, Fields had played in the Little League in her hometown of Cumberland, Maryland, where she was an all-star shortstop and outfielder with a batting average of .528.

In order to win the annual Pitch, Hit, and Run competition, contestants must compete in three events, hitting a ball for distance, running a base path for speed, and pitching at a target. Local winners go on to the district, then to divisional competitions, and finally to the national playoff.

Figure Skating

Although people had skated for centuries as a form of transportation and recreation, modern artistic skating evolved during the late 1800s. In 1864, Jackson Haines, an American dancer, performed ballet movements on ice skates during an exhibition in Europe. Haines's ice dancing had emotion and rhythm, and he became known as the founder of interpretative skating.

Others also took up this style of skating. The first skating club was founded in Great Britain, also the home of the world's first national skating association (1879). In 1892, the International Skating Union (ISU) was formed, and the ISU and local skating clubs began sponsoring skating competitions.

Until 1906, women were banned from competing in ISU events. In 1902, when Madge (Maggie) Syers of Great Britain applied to enter the men's event, no rules were in place that enabled officials to refuse her. Syers finished second in the men's competition. As a result, in 1903, the ISU passed a rule banning women from skating competitions. Judges cited various reasons for excluding women, including clothing. They explained that because a woman must wear ankle-length skirts, judges could not see her feet during the performance.

During the early 1900s, a kind of skating called the international mode—moving more freely across the ice with fluid movements—became more and more popular. Ice skating became an event in the Winter Olympics for the first time in 1908, the competitors using both the international mode and more athletic movements. There were both singles and pairs events. Mixed pairs, with a male and a female skater, had become popular after 1888. Maggie Syers became the first woman to win a gold medal in figure skating and also won a bronze medal in the pairs event, where she skated with her husband.

During the first Olympic Games, women skaters completed rather routine movements. In 1924, Norwegian champion Sonja Henie startled onlookers with an athletic display of jumps and spins. Until that time, only male skaters had performed such feats. The judges did not approve of Henie's routine or her knee-length skirts and placed her last among the women skaters. Undaunted, Henie went on to win ten world championships and three Olympic gold medals (1928, 1932, and 1936).

The number of women skaters rose from 5 competitors in the 1925 world championships to 13 in 1932. Many young women were inspired by Henie's example and by the skating films she made after moving to America. As a professional, Henie earned around $47 million, a sum that was the highest ever earned by an athlete until boxer Muhammad Ali. Interest in women's skating rose as competitors combined graceful movements with increasingly difficult jumps and spins.

During World War II, European skating suffered. Many coaches moved to Canada and the United States, where they trained talented young skaters. In 1947, Canadian Barbara Ann Scott, known for her remarkable spins, became the first

North American to win a world title. Theresa Weld became the first U.S. women's champion (1914), and Maribel Vinson went on to hold that title from 1928 to 1937. Vinson also won a bronze medal in the 1932 Olympics. In 1956, Tenley Albright became the first American gold medalist. Since that time, a number of other American skaters have won Olympic medals, including gold medalists Carol Heiss (1960), Peggy Fleming (1968), Dorothy Hamill (1976), and Kristi Yamaguchi (1992).

Linda Fratianne won a silver medal in 1980, while Debbi Thomas captured bronze in 1988. Nancy Kerrigan, who won bronze in 1992, narrowly missed a gold medal in 1994, winning the silver.

By the 1990s, interest in figure skating was at an all-time high in the United States. It was one of the most popular events at the Winter Olympics, where competitors had to perform a short program with seven elements of jumps and spins and combinations of footwork, as well as a free-skating routine lasting 4 minutes. Numerous professional skating exhibits and shows achieved high ratings on television, and ice shows attracted thousands of spectators around the country. Enrollment in basic skating courses tripled between January 1994 and January 1995. Television sponsorship revenues increased by $4.3 million during that same year.

See also Albright, Tenley; Babilonia, Tai; Figure Skating Association, U.S.; Fleming, Peggy; Fratianne, Linda; Hamill, Dorothy; Harding, Tonya; Heiss, Carol; Kerrigan, Nancy; Kwan, Michelle; Lynn, Janet; Sumners, Roslyn; Thomas, Debi; Trenary, Jill; Vinson Owen, Maribel; Weld Blanchard, Theresa; Yamaguchi, Kristi; Zayak, Elaine

Figure Skating Association, U.S. (USFSA)

The U.S. Figure Skating Association (USFSA) governs amateur figure skating and aims to maintain high standards in the sport. Throughout the nation, many local rinks belong to the USFSA. To enter competition, a skater must belong to the organization as an individual or be a member of a club that belongs to the USFSA. Member clubs sponsor testing, competitions, and ice carnivals. By passing increasingly difficult USFSA tests, skaters earn the right to compete at the juvenile, intermediate, novice, junior, and senior levels. Women have held a number of leadership positions in the USFSA. Claire Ferguson served as president during the early 1990s.

Fish, Jennifer (See Speed Skating)

Fitzgerald, Benita (b. 1962)

Fitzgerald won the 100-meter hurdles event at the 1984 Olympic Games in Los Angeles, the first American woman and the only one of African descent to win that event. Later, she served in leadership positions with the United States Olympic Committee (USOC).

A native of Dale City, Virginia, Fitzgerald attended the University of Tennessee. She was national champion eight times, and first became a member of the U.S. women's track team in 1980. In 1984, she won a gold medal in the 100-meter hurdles at the Pan American Games, won her Olympic gold medal, and received her degree in industrial engineering. When she won her medal, the people of Dale City named a street in her honor.

In 1992, Fitzgerald worked as regional director of Special Olympics International. She also served as Program Director for the Atlanta Centennial Olympic Properties, which was the marketing division of the Atlanta Committee for the 1996 Games. In 1996, Fitzgerald was named director of the USOC's new ARCO Training Center, located in Chula Vista, California, not far from San Diego. (The ARCO petroleum company funded the facility.) Fitzgerald was chosen from among 75 applicants. A busy executive, she continued to run for exercise and plans to start a foundation that would develop educational and athletic programs for young people living in inner cities.

Fleming, Peggy (b. 1948)

The balletic movements of figure-skater Peggy Gale Fleming impressed audiences throughout the world. She was the only American to win a gold medal at the 1968 Winter Olympics held in Grenoble, France.

Fleming was born in San Jose, California, and began skating at age nine, while the family lived in Cleveland, Ohio. A "natural" on the ice, Fleming soon began taking lessons seriously. She quickly passed the first level of tests given by the United States Figure Skating Association (USFSA). When the Flemings moved back to California, Peggy resumed her lessons and won a local skating competition. She continued to study, practice, and work on her distinctive style, adding ballet lessons to her schedule. Her family pitched in to help. Fleming's mother made her costumes, while her father went with her to the rink in the mornings, smoothing the surface with the ice machine.

In 1962, Fleming placed second at the national championships. People commented on her elegant lines and graceful arm movements. Slender and fragile-looking, she surprised people with her athleticism. Fleming was only 15 when she entered the senior ladies' competition in 1964. She won the first of five national ladies' titles that year, becoming the youngest champion ever.

At the 1964 Olympics, Fleming placed

sixth and joined an international touring group of champion skaters. Fleming then moved to Colorado Springs, Colorado, in order to study with a top coach, Carlo Fassi. Hard work paid off when she won world titles in 1966 and 1967. She developed a special move in which she did a double axel–spread eagle–double axel, a combination that delighted audiences. At the 1968 Olympics, Fleming seemed to float onto the rink, wearing a chiffon dress of chartreuse in honor of the famous green-colored liqueur made in Grenoble, France, the site of the Games. The strains of Tchaikovsky filled the stadium as she began with two double loops and an axel. The rest of the program, also performed to classical music, showed off her smooth, graceful style. She captured the only medal won by the U.S. during the 1968 Olympics.

After the Games, Fleming won her third world crown. As a professional skater, she toured with the Ice Follies and performed in several television specials, some of which she developed herself. Fleming also attended Colorado College and became a television commentator, appearing at the Olympics and other skating events. With Dr. Gregory Jenkins, whom she wed in 1970, she reared two sons, Andrew and Todd. She was active in charities, such as the American Cancer Society.

In her forties, Fleming ran to maintain her fitness, and she continued to skate in exhibitions and competition. In 1991, she took part in a 30-city tour. In November 1995, she performed for the third time with other Olympic gold medalists in the series called "Skates of Gold." During that same year, she skated in a Gershwin show in Florida and a tour of "The Nutcracker."

In a 1995 interview with *New York Times* sports columnist Robert Lipsyte,

Fleming said, "Perfection is still when you love the number, you land all your jumps, and you win."

References Condon, *Great Women Athletes of the Twentieth Century* (1991); Lipsyte, "In This World on Ice, Fleming Still Glides," *New York Times*, September 22, 1995, B11; Litsky, *Winners on the Ice* (1979); Sullivan, *Great Lives: Sports* (1988); Van Steenwyk, *Women in Sports: Figure Skating* (1976).

Football

At a school called Rugby in England, a soccer player who missed a kick picked up the ball and ran with it down the field. This move was against the rules, since only the feet can be used to move the ball in soccer. About 16 years later, a sport that became known as rugby had evolved. It combined the use of both hands and feet to move the ball. In 1871, rugby reached America and evolved into a new game called football.

In 1974, the Women's Professional Football League was formed. Seven teams took part, playing ten games a year. The teams included the Dallas Bluebonnets, Los Angeles Dandelions, Detroit Demons, Columbus Pacesetters, Fort Worth Shamrocks, and California Mustangs. Teams were coached by male staffs, and players received $25 for each game.

A number of women distinguished themselves as football players. Playing for the Toledo Troopers, a team that was part of a women's league formed in the midwest, 5 foot 3 inch Linda Jefferson distinguished herself as a star player. Jefferson played while studying at Toledo University during the day and working the night shift at United Parcel Service. She was named Athlete of the Year in 1975 by *Womensports* magazine. During the early 1990s, Kathy Klope of the University of Louisville was the only woman to play on a National Collegiate Athletic Association (NCAA) Division I-A football team. Klope was a place kicker.

Although boys' football was the most often-joined team sport in U.S. high schools as of 1991, there were no organized leagues for girls. However, a few girls throughout the nation were playing on boys' teams. In 1986, a judge ruled that Beth Balsey of New Jersey had the right to play on her high school football team. The National Federation of State High School Athletic Associations found that as of 1994, 328 of the 955,000 high school football players in the United States were girls. In 1993, Heather Sue Mercer was the place-kicker for Yorktown High, of New York state, when that team won the state Class B championship.

One high school player, Sarah Mergenthaler, a 16-year-old at Marlboro High School in New Jersey, made headlines in 1995 as the first female kicker at the school. A former member of the girls' track team as well as a volleyball and basketball player, Mergenthaler was chosen to play on the 75-member football team. An article in the *New York Times* described Mergenthaler's style: "[She] kicks boomers that sail 50 yards. She kicks end-over-end floaters. She kicks softies that curl over the crossbar like tennis lobs. Her right foot reaches for the sky. Each ball is on target." Her coach said that she was as good a kicker as he had seen in his 24 years of coaching.

References Bloom, "A Show-Stopper Puts Her Best Foot Forward," *New York Times*, September 27, 1995, B9, B14.

Fothergill, Dorothy (b. 1945)

Bowler "Dotty" Fothergill filed a lawsuit against the Professional Bowlers Association in 1970 after being refused membership because she was a woman. She and many others believed that bowling was a sport in which women and men could compete on an equal basis. Fothergill explained that she had not taken legal action to cause trouble but to enable herself and other women bowlers to earn a better living at their sport. She said, "There weren't enough women's tournaments around, so I felt I should give the men's tour a try, if possible." The case was settled out of court, and Fothergill never did get to compete on the men's tour.

That year, she won the Women's International Bowling Congress (WIBC) Open All-Events Championship. She won the WIBC Queens Tournament two years in a row—1972 and 1973. Among her other titles were the All-Star Bowling Proprietors Association of America (BPAA) United States Open Championship in 1968 and 1969. Both years the Bowling Writers Association of America chose her as woman Bowler of the Year. With partner Mildred Martorella, Fothergill won the WIBC Open Doubles Championship in 1971. They repeated this victory two years later.

In 1973, 47 bowling sportswriters were asked to name ten women to an all-time greatest team; the writers placed Fothergill fourth. The *Bowler's Journal* poll of 1976 voted her number five on their list of the all-time women's team of ten players.

References Hickok, *A Who's Who of Sports Champions* (1995); Porter, ed., *A Biographical Dictionary of American Sports: Basketball and Other Sports* (1989).

Frank, Nance

Frank captained the first all-woman crew in an ocean sailboat race. In 1991, in the 50-foot *Ichiban*, the 13 women sailed in a 475-mile race from Annapolis, Maryland, to Newport, Rhode Island. They came in eighth among nine boats.

Fraser, Gretchen Kunigk (1919–1994)

Dubbed "the housewife from America," the 29-year-old, married Gretchen Fraser was the first American woman to win an Olympic gold medal in skiing. She grew up in Tacoma, Washington, where she was inspired by her Norwegian, ski-loving mother's love for the sport. The elder Kunigk had helped develop the public ski area in Mt. Rainier, Washington.

By age 16, Gretchen was racing in competition. She met and married Donald Fraser, a member of the 1936 Olympic ski team. She became the first woman to receive the Silver Belt Trophy in 1940. Both Fraser and her husband were chosen to compete for the United States in the 1940 Olympics, but the Games were canceled after World War II began in Europe in 1939.

During the war, while Donald Fraser served in the navy, he encouraged his wife to continue skiing. In 1940 and 1941, she won the Diamond Sun competition, held in Sun Valley, Idaho. In 1941, she added the National Combined and Downhill titles. The next year, she became National Slalom Champion but quit in order to serve in a veteran's hospital. There she taught men who had lost arms or legs in the war how to swim, ski, and ride horseback. Fraser also learned how to pilot a plane.

When the war ended, the Frasers opened a gas and oil distribution business. Gretchen Fraser began skiing competitively again and was chosen for the U.S. women's team that went to the 1948 Winter Olympics in St. Moritz, Switzerland. She was the first woman skier at that competition to take on the challenging slalom course, where icy patches and bumps posed many hazards. Concentrating carefully, Fraser maneuvered down the course, making sharp turns while moving at speeds close to 60 miles per hour. She reached the finish line in less than 1 minute. Since each skier had to be timed twice, Fraser ascended the slope again for her second run. This time, she did even better. Pigtails flying, she swerved down the course in only 57.7 seconds. She had won America's first gold medal in skiing. "I had no idea I could do it," Fraser said after the race.

After the Games, she retired from competition. With her husband and son, she later bred and trained Labrador retrievers and camped in Alaska. She was also named an officer of the National Ski Association. In 1952, Fraser returned to the Olympics to manage the women's ski team. She was voted into the U.S. National Ski Hall of Fame in 1960. In the years that followed, she continued to ski. She could still be found on the slopes at age 65 when she told reporters that she liked to ski "downhill in the morning and cross country in the afternoon."

Gretchen Fraser helped to found the first U.S. ski club for amputees and was selected as chairperson of the Special Winter Olympics in 1983. She died in Sun Valley, Idaho, at age 75.

Fratianne, Linda (b. 1960)

"She was the very first girl to do triple jumps easily," said coach Frank Carroll of his pupil, figure-skater Linda Fratianne. Fratianne was born in Northridge, California. A quick learner and natural athlete, she passed all the U.S. Figure Skating Association (USFSA) tests—from preliminary to gold— in just three years. At age 15, she won a spot on the U.S. figure skating team and went to the 1976 Olympics.

Fratianne won two world titles, in 1977 and 1979, and was a silver medalist at the 1980 Olympics. She had worked hard to add artistic elements to the ener-

getic, athletic skating that was her trademark. Her free-skating performance at Lake Placid, New York, received the highest marks of any competitor, but she was narrowly defeated by German skater Anett Potzsch, who had taken a strong lead in the compulsory (school) figures. After placing second in the world ladies' championship shortly after the Games, Fratianne became a professional skater.

Linda Fratianne raised the level of jumps in women's figure skating. After 1980, triples became a standard and expected part of women's competition, and young skaters worked hard to master them.

Frederick, Jane (b. 1953)

Frederick, a track and field athlete, was the American champion in the pentathlon competition for several years. As a teenager growing up in California, Frederick joined a local track team and found that she excelled in several events. She trained to compete in the multievent pentathlon and heptathlon.

In 1978, Frederick won the women's world heptathlon title. She jumped a height of 6 feet in the high jump, a distance of 20 feet 7.5 inches in the long jump, put the shot 51 feet 7 inches, completed the 100-meter hurdles in 13.48 seconds, and ran the 800-meter race in 2 minutes 18.6 seconds. Since the United States boycotted the 1980 Olympics for political reasons, Frederick did not compete that year in her sport.

See also Heptathlon; Pentathlon
Reference Kaplan, *Women and Sports: Inspiration and Information about the New Female Athlete* (1979).

Frederick, Marcia (b. 1963)

At age 15, the Springfield, Massachusetts–native became the first U.S. woman to win a gold medal at an international gymnastics championship. Frederick trained in Milford, Connecticut, at the famous gymnastics school run by former U.S. champion Muriel Grossfeld.

Competing at the world gymnastics championships in 1978, in Strasbourg, France, she took top honors in the uneven bars. Frederick performed a Stalder Shoot and full pirouette (circle swing with legs apart, straddling the bar), then a shooting pirouette landing in a handstand. No gymnast had previously completed these movements together in competition. For her scores, Frederick received two perfect 10s, with an overall score of 9.95.

See also Grossfeld, Muriel Davis

French Tennis Championship

The French national tournament, played on a clay court, is one of the four major events that make up the Grand Slam of tennis. To win the slam, players must take all four tournaments within a 12-month period.

The French national championship was open only to French players before 1925. That year, it became an invitational tournament, changing to an open tournament in 1968. Women players with strong, consistent groundstrokes, such as Chris Evert, tend to prefer clay courts and win more often on clay surfaces.

See also Grand Slam

Fry, Shirley (b. 1927)

During her tennis career, Shirley Fry achieved the feat of winning each of the major women's singles tournaments at least once.

Fry was born and raised in Akron, Ohio. At 14, she became the youngest woman ever to play at the U.S. national championship, then held in Forest Hills, New York. The next year, she defeated some top women players to reach the quarterfinals. In 1956, she won several top tournaments. At Wimbledon, she defeated Althea Gibson for the title. Then in her sixteenth attempt, she won the U.S. championships in the fall. Fry was named number one woman player in the world that year. A superb doubles player as well, Fry and her partner Doris Hart won four straight French doubles titles, three at Wimbledon, and four U.S. championships.

In 1957, Fry retired from competitive tennis and married Karl Irvin, settling in Hartford, Connecticut. She was named to the International Tennis Hall of Fame in 1970.

Garrison-Jackson, Zina (b. 1963)

Born in Houston, Texas, Zina Lynna Garrison learned to play on the public tennis courts. From the start, she showed promise. In 1979 she became the youngest player ever to win the American Tennis Association (ATA) championship; the next year, she won again. Garrison-Jackson was also the first African-American woman ever ranked number one in Texas.

In 1981 Garrison-Jackson won the junior titles at both Wimbledon and the U.S. Open. She reached the quarterfinals at the French Open in 1982, her first tournament as a professional. The next year, she was a semifinalist at the Australian Open and came in second at the U.S. Clay Court tournament. In 1988, she upset the world's number one woman player, Martina Navratilova. Garrison-Jackson reached the semifinals of the U.S. Open in 1989, defeating long-time champion Chris Evert in Evert's final professional match. Although she did not win many major singles titles, Garrison-Jackson was a durable player. She reached at least the fourth round in the U.S. Open ten times between 1981 and 1992. She upset top players Monica Seles and Steffi Graf at Wimbledon in 1990.

A strong, aggressive serve-and-volley game made Garrison-Jackson a top doubles player. She won three Grand Slam mixed doubles titles—two at Wimbledon and one Australian. She and Pam Shriver won the Olympic gold medal together in 1988, when Garrison also won the bronze in singles play. As of 1993, she ranked ninth among women players in total prize winnings.

During the 1980s, Garrison-Jackson courageously admitted that she suffered from bulimia, an eating disorder, and struggled to overcome it. An articulate speaker, she helped inform the public and offered encouragement to others suffering from the problem. She also worked with inner-city tennis programs in Houston and several charities.

Although she had considered retiring in 1995, Garrison-Jackson found that she missed playing in tournaments. She competed in the U.S. Open, winning the first round against her teenage opponent. Then she won a major tournament in Birmingham, England, and continued to play well on the grass courts of Eastbourne that June. "I still love the game," she told *New York Times* sportswriter George Vecsey.

See also American Tennis Association
References Collins and Hollander, *Bud Collins' Modern Encyclopedia of Tennis* (1994); Vecsey, *New York Times*, September 1, 1995.

Geer, Charlotte (See Rowing)

Gestring, Marjorie (b. 1922)

At age 13, Gestring won a diving event at the 1936 Olympic Games, making her the youngest competitor ever to win a gold medal in any event. A native of Los

Angeles, California, Gestring had been preceded by Aileen Riggin, who at age 14 had won a gold medal in 1920, also in diving. Sports historians believe Gestring would have won more Olympic medals had the Games not been cancelled during World War II.

Gibson, Althea (b. 1927)

A ticker-tape parade . . . thousands of fans . . . a luncheon in her honor given by the mayor of New York City. These were some of the tributes paid to tennis champion Althea Gibson when she returned from winning the 1957 women's singles title at Wimbledon. "I just can't describe the joy in my heart," she said during one speech. Gibson had overcome incredible obstacles to become a tennis champion at a time when players were predominantly white and wealthy, often members of exclusive clubs.

She was born on August 25, 1927, to South Carolina sharecroppers who moved to a poor neighborhood in Harlem when Gibson was young. As a child, she played stickball, basketball, and paddle tennis on New York City streets. She was mischievous and sometimes unruly. Her strict father punished her for staying out too late or cutting school, something she did often. Gibson later recalled nights when she slept on a subway car because she did not want to face her father by going home late.

Gibson was 13 when a Police Athletic League (PAL) instructor in her neighborhood noticed her outstanding skill in paddle tennis. He got her some second-hand rackets and showed her how to hit balls against a wall. Then he took Gibson to the Cosmopolitan Tennis Club, one of the few clubs of its type open to both blacks and whites.

While she was learning tennis, Gibson left school and took on a series of jobs,

working at a chicken processing plant, as an elevator operator, in a button factory, and in a coffee shop. She had nearly reached her full height of 5 feet 11 inches. In 1942 Gibson won her first tournament, the girls' title of the state American Tennis Association (ATA), an organization for black players. She reached the semifinals of the national tournament later that year. In 1946 she won the ATA national championship, the first of 12 consecutive victories. She won the National Negro Women's Singles title in 1947.

Now recognized as the top black woman player in America, Gibson naturally hoped to play in major tournaments with other top women. Unfortunately, the United States Lawn Tennis Association (USLTA) banned people of color at that time. But members of the USLTA and ATA were working to change the rules so that any talented players could compete in USLTA matches, regardless of color or ethnicity. In 1949 Gibson was accepted to play in the USLTA Eastern Indoor Championship. She played well, reaching the quarterfinals. She reached the quarters of the National Indoor Championships the next week. Gibson was the first and only black player at both events.

While training and competing, Gibson had also been working to complete her high school courses. She graduated in 1949, ranked tenth in her class. With a scholarship, she attended college in Florida, where she worked part-time, played on the basketball team, and studied, while pursuing her tennis career. She managed to defend her ATA title and reach the finals of the USLTA Indoor match. Still, she was not invited to compete at the U.S. national tournament held at the West Side Tennis Club in Forest Hills, New York. Competitors were

Althea Gibson, 1957 Wimbledon champion.

expected to have proven themselves by playing well at other grass court tournaments—Orange, Seabright, Essex, and Hampton. Yet these private clubs banned black players.

The great tennis champion Alice Marble wrote an editorial in *American Lawn Tennis* (July 1950) magazine for Gibson's cause. She said that all top women players, including Gibson, should be able to meet at the same tournaments. With emotion, Marble wrote, "If tennis is a game for ladies and gentlemen, it's also time we acted a little more like gentlepeople and less like sanctimonious hypocrites."

The Orange tournament extended an invitation, which allowed Gibson to compete at the Eastern Grass Courts Championships. She was then invited to try for the U.S. national title. Former champion Sarah Palfrey befriended Gibson and arranged for her to practice at the West Side Tennis Club before the nationals so she would be familiar with the courts. Gibson stayed with family friends in Harlem and rode the subway to and from the club.

In 1950, at age 23, she became the first African-American to play at the Forest Hills tournament. She lost in the second round. During those years, Gibson played inconsistently and had trouble maintaining her momentum throughout a major tournament. She was ranked number seven among women in 1952 and number seven in 1953, the year she finished college. But she was only number 12 the next year, when she was teaching physical education at Lincoln University in Missouri. Although proud of her achievements, she longed to win some of the top tournaments.

Gibson was chosen as one of four tennis players to go on a goodwill tour of Asia starting in 1955. She accumulated a string of victories—the Indian national, the Asian women's title, and the Italian and French crowns in the spring. The French was an important international tournament, one of four Grand Slam events. This experience recharged her interest in the game, which she had considered abandoning in 1954. A new grip helped her to hit stronger groundstrokes. When the tour ended, she won 16 of the 18 tournaments she entered in an eight-month period.

Elated, she entered the prestigious Wimbledon tournament but did not reach the finals. But by playing a smart, aggressive game, she did reach the finals of the U.S. championship, where Shirley Fry defeated her. Gibson began to feel confident that she could win a top tournament within a year or two.

That dream came true at the 1957 Wimbledon championship. All week, Gibson played consistently well and with confidence, choosing the right strategy for each opponent. Battling the 100°F heat, she defeated Darlene Hard 6-3, 6-2. Gibson said of that victory, "All I can remember is running to the net and shaking hands with Darlene [Hard] and saying that she had played very well and that I had been lucky." But journalists said skill, not luck, had brought 30-year-old Gibson this victory. Later that year, she won the U.S. national title. In 1958, she repeated both of these victories and was ranked as the top women's player in both 1957 and 1958.

After Gibson retired from amateur tennis, she played tennis exhibitions at halftime with the Harlem Globetrotters basketball team, then became a professional golfer, playing well enough to earn a living in the sport. She became the first black member of the Ladies Professional Golf Association (LPGA).

During the mid-seventies, Gibson married a businessman and served as state athletic commissioner for New Jersey and a business partner in a sports equipment company. She was also active in state politics. Gibson later became national director of the Pepsi Cola mobile tennis program. She taught tennis and directed programs for a tennis club in North Vale, New Jersey, all the while continuing to enjoy professional tennis and encouraging new players to succeed. She was elected to the Tennis Hall of Fame in 1971. Gibson once said that she hoped to be "a credit to tennis and my country."

See also Marble, Alice

References Ashe, *A Hard Road to Glory* (1988); Bontemps, *Famous Negro Athletes* (1964); Condon, *Great Women Athletes of the 20th Century* (1991); "First Black Wimbledon Champ, Althea Gibson, Recognized in England," *Jet*, July 23, 1984, 46–48; Gibson, *So Much To Live For* (1968).

Gilder, Virginia (b. 1959)

A determined athlete, Gilder continued to train as a rower, even after she was rejected as being too small for a U.S. team touring Europe in 1978 and then failed to make the world team in 1979. After Gilder made the Olympic team in 1980, the United States boycotted the Games for political reasons, another disappointment.

Rowing in quad sculls (boats with a crew of four rowers) in the world championships in 1982, the Yale graduate placed fourth. While working in Boston in the computer business, Gilder switched from team rowing to single sculling. She competed in the 1982 national championships as a member of the Boston Rowing Club and came in second in the elite single race with a time of 3:59.9. Improving her time to 3:55.8, Gilder won that race a year later.

Gilder also competed in the elite double race, winning with a time of 3:39.

With her partner Ann Strayer in the bow, Gilder was at stroke. In 1983 she won a bronze medal in the single scull race, the first time any American woman had won a medal in international sculling competitions since the 1976 Olympics. That same year she narrowly lost to world champion Jutta Hampe of East Germany at an international regatta. Because she broke a rib close to the time of the 1984 Olympics, Gilder was unable to take part in the single scull competition. However, she and Joan Lind, a former silver medalist, rowed with the quad scull crew that won a silver medal at the Games.

See also Rowing

Giovinco, Lucy

In 1976, Giovinco achieved a score of 620 for a three-game final round to win top honors at the Women's Bowling World Cup. She was the first U.S. bowler to win this competition, which was held in Teheran, Iran, that year.

Girl Scouts of the U.S.A.

The Girl Scouts was the first, and is now the largest, voluntary organization for girls. More than 40 million young women, ages 6 to 17, have been members since the organization was founded in 1912 by Juliette Gordon Low. About three million girls are active members during a given year.

Low had become familiar with the Boy Scouts while traveling in England. The Boy Scouts' founder, Sir Robert Baden Powell, asked Low to organize similar groups, called Girl Guides, for girls in Scotland and England. Using the Girl Guide model, Low started the first Girl Guide troop in America in her home state of Georgia. The name was changed to Girl Scouts in 1915.

From the onset, scouts hiked and learned outdoor camping skills and were required to master certain physical activities in order to pass their scouting tests. The out-of-doors was one of the five major interest areas designated for scouting. Merit badges are awarded for achievement in sports, including ice skating, swimming, bicycling, and hiking. A number of girls began taking part in sports through the Girl Scouts.

Girls' Rodeo Association (GRA)
(See Rodeos)

Golden, Diana (b. 1964)
As a child, Massachusetts native Golden preferred individual sports to team sports, so she took up skiing. At age 12, she was diagnosed with cancer in her right leg. The leg had to be amputated, and she learned to use an artificial leg. She resumed skiing with her doctors' approval, learning to balance and manage on the edge of one ski.

When the high-school ski instructor invited Golden to work out with the team, she began training hard, developing more strength and technical skill. She later recalled that it was a wonderful experience to find this strength in her body. Golden became a top athlete with the United States Disabled Ski Team and competed in the World Games for Disabled Athletes in Geilo, Norway. She won the downhill event in the World Handicapped Championships. A sportswriter for the *Boston Globe* wrote that Golden "moved back and forth down the hill with an unbroken motion as graceful as grass waving in a breeze."

Golden continued to compete while attending Dartmouth College. By that time, many people were inspired by her courage and talent. For a while, she gave up competitive skiing to pursue her studies and religious interests. After gradua-tion, she returned to ski competition and was sponsored by the Rossignol ski equipment company.

Then Golden began competing in races with skiers who had no physical disabilities. In 1987, racing with 40 women, she finished tenth, an achievement that meant a great deal to her. A great many gold medals and athletic honors came her way, including the Beck Award for the best American racer on the international circuit in 1986. She was named U.S. Female Alpine Skier of the Year in 1988, a title bestowed by *Ski Racing* magazine. Golden was also named Female Skier of the Year in 1988 by the U.S. Olympic Committee.

That year marked her first time at the arduous Aspen World Cup Downhill Race. By the end, she felt her leg "giving out" but forced herself over the finish line. Later, she would explain that she wished to be known as an athlete first, not someone who overcame handicaps. Golden told one sportswriter, "I wanted to be recognized as a top-notch athlete, as the best in the world."

After retiring from competition in 1991, the 27-year-old Golden became a skiing coach and took up rock-climbing.

References Dupont, "Golden Demonstrates Her Ability," *Boston Globe*, February 22, 1988; Dupont, "Golden Voice," *Boston Globe*, August 20, 1991; Miller, "Golden Girl—That's Diana Golden, U.S. Three-Track Ski Racer Extraordinaire," *Skiing*, November 1987.

Golden Skates Classic
This roller skating event, held annually in Bakersfield, California, includes both a competition and performance put on by the competitors. Amateur skaters vie for prizes, awarded for those who show proficiency in both the technical movements of roller skating and artistic moves.

Golf

Golf evolved from a sport called *paganica* that originated in ancient Rome. Players used a bent stick to hit a ball stuffed with feathers. The game spread to the British Isles, where it was later called "golfie," and became enormously popular. Gradually, the game we know as golf took shape, with players proceeding from one hole on the course to another, trying to hit the ball into each hole with as few strokes as possible. To further challenge players, golf courses were built with various obstacles, including traps and bunkers, as well as ponds, lakes, and trees.

Mary Queen of Scots (1542–1587) was among the first women to pursue the sport. The queen played at the world's oldest golf course, St. Andrew's in Scotland. She enlisted young boys to carry her clubs and look for her lost balls on the course, calling these helpers "cadets," which later developed into the word "caddy." By the 1800s, some golf clubs occasionally featured "ladies days," when women were permitted to play on the course. At first, women's golf clubs were separate from men's. The first women's golf club was established at St. Andrew's in 1867. More clubs sprang up throughout England. The Ladies' Golf Union was formed in 1893 and sponsored the first British Ladies' Championship that year.

Golf spread to the United States during the late 1800s. An American woman is first known to have played the game in 1889. In 1895 a women's tournament became part of the national amateur event sponsored by the United States Golf Association (USGA). Mrs. Charles S. Brown won the title that year with a score of 132 for an 18-hole course. She defeated 12 other women at the Meadow Brook Club in Hempstead, New York, winning a silver pitcher. In 1896, 16-year-old Beatrix Hoyt won the tournament, the first of three straight wins. Hoyt won the championship five times before retiring at age 21. Two sisters, Harriet and Margaret Curtis, dominated women's golf during the early 1900s.

At first, women usually played only 9-hole courses, later moving to 18-hole, or a full, courses. Eventually, the rules for women's golf were no different from those in the men's game. But at the turn of the century, women were still not welcomed on the links with men. The earliest successful woman golfer in America was Glenna Collett Vare, who became known as the "Bobby Jones" of golf, after the top male champion of her day. Other talented women followed, but few played as professionals during those years.

Interest in women's golf increased dramatically after World War II. More talented players emerged to compete both as amateurs and professionals. In 1944 the Women's Professional Golfers' Association (WPGA) was formed, spearheaded by professional golfer Hope Seignious and her father. Seignious also began publishing a short-lived golf magazine to promote women in the sport. The WPGA hoped to gain more tournaments, publicity, and prize money for its members. It sponsored the first Women's Open, held in Spokane, Washington, in 1946. The women's tour expanded after Alvin Handmacher, a clothing manufacturer, agreed to supply a total of $15,000 in prize money for a set of four women's tournaments—in San Francisco, Chicago, Cleveland, and New York City. Helen Lengfled, golf enthusiast and publisher of *National Golfer,* also agreed to sponsor a spring tour, offering a similar amount in prize money.

The WPGA was later supplanted by a stronger rival organization called the

Ladies Professional Golf Association (LPGA), which became the ruling body for the sport in 1948. The LPGA sponsored the Women's Open until 1953, when the United States Golf Association (USGA) took over. The USGA later added a Girls' Junior tournament and Senior Women's tournament.

During these early years, stars like Babe Didrikson Zaharias and Patty Berg drew fans to women's golf tournaments. By the fifties and sixties, new stars emerged to excite spectators and inspire other Americans to take up the sport. Beverly Hanson won the first LPGA championship tournament in 1955 when she defeated Louise Suggs by three strokes.

Women golfers of the fifties had competed for small cash prizes and did not receive much attention. But in 1963, the U.S. Open offered $9,000 in prizes, the largest amount offered at one tournament up to that time. The event was also broadcast on television. Other commercial sponsors joined those that were supporting women's tournaments, and several matches were televised, attracting more spectators. By the 1980s, the LPGA's annual tour of 38 events offered a total purse of $8 million. During the seventies, the popularity of the game continued to increase, as the number of women players around the United States rose from about 500,000 to 5 million in 1982.

Top women golfers receive awards from the LPGA and other organizations. Besides awards offered exclusively to women, female golfers are eligible to receive the Ben Hogan trophy, given each year by the Golf Writers Association of America to a golfer who is active in the sport despite a physical handicap. Among the women who have received this trophy are Babe Didrikson Zaharias (1953) and

Shirley Englehorn (1967). The magazine *Golf Digest* offers an annual award to the man and woman considered by other players to be the most improved golfer of the year, as well as a Rookie of the Year award to both men and women players.

See also Alcott, Amy; Blalock Jane; Carner, Jo-Anne; Collett Vare, Glenna; Curtis Cup; King, Betsy; Lopez, Nancy; Rankin, Judy; Rawls, Betsy; Suggs, Louise; Vare Trophy; Whitworth, Kathy; Wright, Mickey
References Cotton, *A History of Golf, Illustrated* (1975); *LPGA Player's Guide* (1995); Ross, *Golf Magazine's Encyclopedia of Golf* (1979).

Gorman, Micki (See Marathon Running; Ultra Running)

Graff, Sunny (b. 1951)
Martial arts champion Graff grew up in Parma Heights, Ohio, near Cleveland. After entering the Ohio State University in 1969, she became involved in political and social causes, such as the movement to end the Vietnam war. She also joined a group of university women who were concerned about equal rights for women, an experience that shaped her life from then on. She recalls, "I had just accepted the common view of women, the view which said that women weren't worth much. These women were saying that it was all right to be a woman, that we weren't inferior versions of men."

Graff became more involved in women's causes and helped form a group called Women Against Rape (WAR). She spoke publicly about rape and women's liberation, appearing on the "Phil Donahue Show" in April of 1973. After graduation, she became a bond investigator for the Columbus court system. A good friend of hers was murdered that year.

She began studying the martial arts in 1974, and initially encountered opposition from men involved in the sport.

Through a friend, Graff was introduced to tae kwon do, a discipline she believed would help her overcome the anger she felt over her friend's death and the continuing threat of violence against women. Although Graff began studying for self-defense reasons, she later "fell in love with the martial arts—the beauty, philosophy, the sport." She practiced intensively and received some support from her male instructors, who encouraged students of both sexes.

Graff decided that she could best promote social changes she believed in by becoming a lawyer. While attending law school, she earned top grades, worked full-time for WAR, and continued studying the martial arts, which she said gave her "more energy." By 1977, she was entering tae kwon do competitions. The next year, she entered the National Amateur Athletic Union (AAU) Tae Kwon Do Championships and won a gold medal along with her first title: National AAU Champion, Bantam Weight Division. At 5 feet 5 inches, Graff weighed 115 pounds. That same year, the AAU invited her to join the first women's tae kwon do team ever assembled to take part in international competition. At the pre–World Games in Seoul, Korea, Graff won a bronze medal.

After graduating from law school, Graff worked as an attorney with the county defender's office in Columbus, Ohio. She also founded a prominent rape-prevention program and a tae kwon do club for women. Along with skills in the martial arts, her school helped women to develop their self-esteem and believe in their right to defend themselves.

In 1979 Graff won her second gold medal and national title. She also served as captain of the AAU Women's Tae Kwon Do team. July 1979 brought a third gold medal and the world championship, which she won at the World Invitational Tae Kwon Do meet in Taiwan. In both 1980 and 1981, Graff was named Outstanding Female Taekwondoist of the Year.

Graff won her fourth national title in 1982 and represented the United States at the Pan American Games in Puerto Rico. It was the first year those Games included tae kwon do events for women. There, she earned another gold medal. In all, she won six gold medals, four national championships, and the world championship of the Tae Kwon Do Federation.

See also Martial Arts
References Atkinson, *Women in the Martial Arts: A New Spirit Rising* (1983).

Grand Slam

In tennis, the Grand Slam is the feat of winning all four of the major tournaments in the same year. Grand Slam events include the Australian, French, Wimbledon, and U.S. tournaments.

The first player to win the four-championship Grand Slam was Australian Don Budge in 1938. In 1953 American Maureen Connolly was the first woman player to achieve a Grand Slam, followed by Australian Margaret Smith Court (1970) and German Steffi Graf (1988).

Doubles teams have also won the Grand Slam. Martina Navratilova and Pam Shriver accomplished this in 1984. Billie Jean King won it playing mixed doubles, with Owen Davidson, in 1967.

In 1978, Australian Karen Scott Happer became the first woman tournament director of a Grand Slam tournament, the Australian Open.

See also Connolly, Maureen; French Tennis Championship; Wimbledon

Grayson, Betty Evans (1925–1979)

Softball player Grayson starred both as a pitcher and outfielder, beginning at age 13. She started as an outfielder but learned pitching skills playing with her father almost daily until she was 15. Then she took to the mound for her team, Erv Lind Florists.

For 17 years, she played fast-pitch softball as an amateur, with Erv Lind's Florists, a team in the Portland City League. With Grayson pitching, the team won the world softball championship in 1943. In 1944 they won the national title at the championships held that year in Cleveland, Ohio, where her team had fought hard to pull out a victory by scoring the winning run in the eleventh inning. Grayson was named Oregon Woman Athlete of the Year.

Known as "Bullet Betty" for her speed and power, she pitched three perfect games and recorded 465 wins to 91 losses during her career, which included three seasons with the Chicago Queens. In 1945, she hurled an amazing 115 scoreless innings in a row. Grayson was also known for the time she devoted to coaching and developing young softball players.

Grayson retired in 1955 and worked as a license clerk in the Portland City Hall. In 1959, she was inducted into the National Softball Hall of Fame. Grayson died of cancer at age 53. A year later, the Portland Metro Softball Association dedicated the Betty Evans Grayson Memorial Hall of Fame at Erv Lind Stadium in her honor.

Reference "Betty Evans Grayson," a biographical sketch from National Softball Hall of Fame.

Griffith-Joyner, Florence (b. 1959)

Track and field star Joyner won four medals at the 1988 Olympics—gold medals in the 100-meter dash, 200-meter dash, and 400-meter relay, and a silver in the 1,600-meter relay.

Born Delorez Florence Griffith in the Watts section of Los Angeles, she became known as "FloJo," one of the fastest women runners of all time. Griffith-Joyner has recalled a happy childhood. She praised her mother, a divorced woman with 11 children, who worked hard as a seamstress: "We didn't know how poor we were; we were rich as family." Griffith-Joyner began running as a child and competed in races sponsored by the Sugar Ray Robinson Youth Foundation when she was 11.

Griffith won numerous races during her teen years and earned a scholarship to California State University, where she majored in business. Working with top coach Bob Kersee there, and later at the University of California at Los Angeles (UCLA), she became a world-class runner. In 1983 she won the National Collegiate Athletic Association (NCAA) 400-meter race and placed second in the 200 meters. At the 1984 Olympics, she won the silver medal for the 200-meter race. There, the stylish runner caught fans' attention with her fancy running clothes and 6-inch-long fingernails, painted red, white, and blue.

For a while, Griffith left competitive racing and devoted herself to her career as a bank representative and writer. But as the 1988 Olympics approached, she resumed training, losing weight and working to perfect various weaknesses, such as the time she lost getting off the starting blocks. Weight-training strengthened her leg muscles. She also married Al Joyner, the brother of famed track star Jackie Joyner-Kersee, who is married to coach Bob Kersee. During this time, Griffith-Joyner juggled her job with a demanding training schedule. For extra practice, she ran from the bank to the track and then ran home afterwards.

Running the second heat of the 100-meter dash in a time of 10.49 seconds,

Florence Griffith-Joyner receives a congratulatory hug after she set a new world record in the 100-meter dash at the Olympic track and field trials in 1988.

Griffith-Joyner shattered the previous world record by more than a quarter of a second. When she won the race at the Olympics, her time of 10.54 seconds broke the previous Olympic record. She broke the world record for the 200-meter race as well. A third gold medal was hers after the 100-meter relay team raced to victory, and she captured a silver as part of the 400-meter relay team.

After the Olympics, Griffith-Joyner worked as a model and actress, and endorsed commercial products. Her personal style and athletic prowess boosted women's sports. By 1995, her activities included serving as cochair of the President's Council on Physical Fitness, coaching young people as part of Florence Griffith-Joyner Youth Foundation, running a nail-kit company, and designing clothing. The Joyners' daughter Mary was born in 1991.

Although known as a sprinter, Joyner has said she is a "distance runner at heart." During the early nineties, she trained for the marathon harder than for the 400-meter race. She also advocates women's causes, saying, "It's important to see women making strides.... Women need to be in control of their own lives and feel good about themselves."

References "The Best and the Brightest," *Newsweek,* September 19, 1988, 54–57; Biddaugh, "Flo Jo: In for the Long Run," *Women's Sports and Fitness,* May-June 1992, 14; Eller, "Going with the Flo," *Women Sports and Fitness,* September 1995, 44–45; "Great Olympic Moments: Florence Griffith-Joyner" *Ebony,* June 1992, 99.

Grossfeld, Muriel Davis (b. 1941)
The famous American gymnastics champion and coach was All-Around U.S. champion in 1957 and 1963. Starting in 1955, she won 16 national individual events and was national champion 18 times. She took part in three Olympics,

including the 1956 Games, where she competed in the vaulting horse and parallel bar events.

After turning professional, Indiana native Grossfeld appeared in several feature films as a stuntwoman. In Milford, Connecticut, she opened the Grossfeld Gymnastics School, which accepted the most promising students in 1962. Students spent at least 5 hours each day studying gymnastic techniques. From 1967 to 1972, Grossfeld coached the U.S. and Pan American Games women's teams, which included top gymnasts Cathy Rigby, Linda Metheny, and Marcia Frederick.

See also Frederick, Marcia; Metheny, Linda; Rigby, Cathy

Gulick, Charlotte Vetter (See Camp Fire Girls)

Gunter, Nancy Richey (See Richey-Gunter, Nancy)

Gurney, Hilda (See Dressage)

Guthrie, Janet (b. 1938)
A gymkhana (precision) and endurance race-car driver, Guthrie was the first woman to compete at the Indianapolis 500, the most prestigious of all races. Not only had no woman ever qualified to race in the "Indy," women had not even been allowed to enter the pit area (where cars are repaired and refueled) before 1970. Critics said women did not have the physical strength to handle the 1,500-pound, open-cockpit cars with their powerful engines.

Janet Guthrie was the eldest of five children born to a commercial pilot and his wife. At age 13, the Iowa-native could already fly a plane, a small Piper Cub. By 16, she was flying solo and had taken up parachute-jumping. She earned a private pilot's license, then, at age 19, a commercial flying license. She also qualified as an instructor.

Guthrie's favorite courses at the private girls' school she attended were in science. She earned a degree in physics at the University of Michigan, then worked as an engineer for the Republic Aviation Company in Long Island, New York. Guthrie was excited to do work connected with the U.S. space exploration program, then just beginning. She helped to develop vehicles used in space. After six years with Republic, she joined Sperry-Rand Corporation as a technical publications editor. In 1965, she applied to become one of the first women astronauts and passed the first series of tests. However, NASA decided to require doctoral degrees, which Guthrie did not have.

In the meantime, she had begun racing cars, including a used Jaguar XK-120 that she owned. Guthrie belonged to a sports car club and raced in local low-speed competitions, called gymkhanas, for beginners. By 1962, Guthrie was the Long Island women's gymkhana champion. She attended a training program at the well-known track in Lime Rock, Connecticut, and found that racing challenged her in some of the same ways that piloting a plane did. She competed both in endurance races and shorter ones.

In 1971, Guthrie had won nine endurance races in a row. But when she tried for a tenth, her car broke down on the track. She went on to win the North Atlantic Road Racing title in 1973. Two years later, she defeated 27 men drivers to capture the Vanderbilt Cup, then won the Bridgehampton 400.

Her excellent record inspired executive Rolla Vollstedt to ask her to drive one of his cars in the Indianapolis 500. Many people objected to a woman driver at Indy, with some calling it a publicity stunt. Male drivers complained that Guthrie had not driven in enough of the big-car races around America that made up the "Championship Trail." Others complained that another woman driver, Arlene Hiss, had driven too slowly in the Phoenix 150 and her last-place speed had endangered other drivers.

Aware that many people hoped she would fail, Guthrie prepared for the February 1976 test runs that determine whether a driver qualifies for the Indy. At the Trentonian race, the announcer began by saying, "Janet and gentlemen, start your engines." Guthrie later said that she would rather the announcers say simply, "Championship drivers, start your engines."

Driving the *Bryant Special*, Guthrie set out to race at the 1976 Indy. Only the fastest 33 cars would get to compete in the 500-mile race. The 5-foot 9-inch, 135-pound Guthrie wore a helmet with the word "Janet" spelled out on the side. That year, she became the first woman to drive a practice run, take the 500's rookie test, and qualify to compete in the race. But during a practice run, a piston in the car burned out, and she could only complete six laps. During her rookie test, she got her car up to speed, about 160 miles per hour. After six laps, the car had more mechanical problems. After repairs, Guthrie circled 23 times. She passed the test, handling her car at the required speeds.

In the qualifying rounds, cars made unusually high speeds. Guthrie saw that she might need to hit 180 to qualify. But again, her car refused to cooperate and get up to that mark. Defending champion A. J. Foyt then agreed to lend Guthrie his back-up car, the *Coyote,* so that she would have the chance to prove her ability. She held that car steadily in the groove while

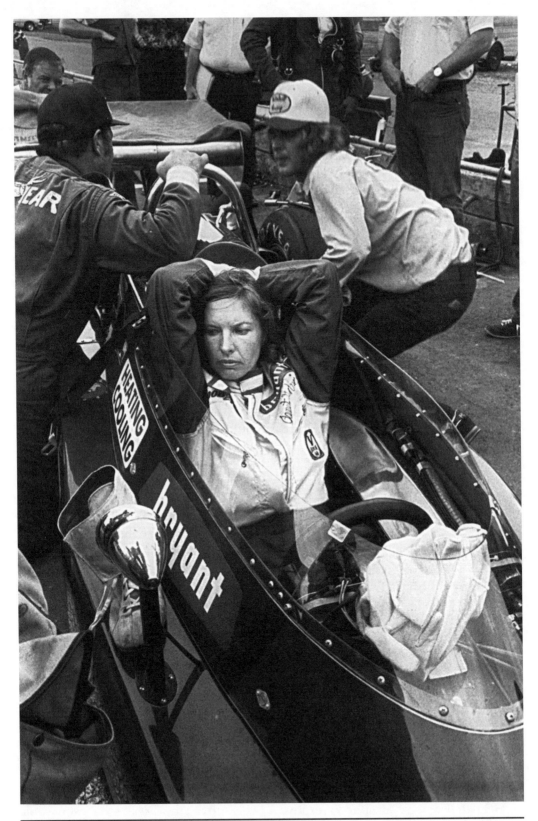

Professional race-car driver Janet Guthrie waits for mechanics to make adjustments to her car before running some test laps at the Trenton, New Jersey, raceway. Guthrie was the first woman to finish the Indy 500 in 1978, completing 200 laps in 3 hours, 5 minutes.

hitting speeds of 181 miles per hour. But she could not use the *Coyote* in the actual race and thus missed her chance to compete at Indy in 1976.

Soon Guthrie was invited to race in a North American Stock Car (NASCAR) competition, the World 600 Stock Car Race. Again, she was criticized, told that a woman could not handle a 3,500-pound stock car. At the Charlotte, North Carolina, track she became the first woman ever to qualify for a major NASCAR event, this one a Grand National Speedway. She placed fifteenth in a field of 27 cars that finished. Twenty-three others failed to complete the race. She went on to other NASCAR events at Daytona Beach and elsewhere.

In 1977, she was ready to try again at Indy. The first day out, she posted the highest speed of any driver—185.6 miles per hour. Within days, she had hit 191 miles per hour. Driving the *Lindsey Hopkins Lightning,* she qualified and went on to compete in the 33-car field on Sunday, May 29. For a few laps, all went well. Suddenly, due to valve problems, fuel leaked into the cockpit and soaked through Guthrie's driving outfit, burning her. After stopping for repairs, she took off again, only to be thwarted by a breakdown in the ignition system. The crew was forced to remove Guthrie's car from the race.

Guthrie returned to Indy in 1978, for a ninth-place finish—the first woman ever to finish the race, completing 200 laps around the track in 3 hours and 5 minutes. Later, it was discovered that she had driven that day with an injury. A small bone in her right wrist had been broken during a fall two days before the race. She had had to use her left hand to shift and do most of the steering.

Guthrie had proven her ability and opened doors for women in the racing world. It could no longer be said that a woman did not have the strength or ability to handle a car at the big races. Off the track, the versatile driver enjoyed cooking, classical music, the ballet, and reading great literature.

References Dolan, *Great Moments at the Indy 500* (1982); Dolan and Lyttle, *Janet Guthrie* (1978); Gutman, *More Modern Woman Superstars* (1979).

Gymnastics

The sport of gymnastics has been popular since ancient times. In Europe, centuries ago, first men, then women took it up. People in the Far East also joined competitive gymnastics events. In the United States, gymnastics developed during the early 1800s, but the women and girls who took up the sport wore body-covering costumes. The first class in women's gymnastics was taught in 1862 at Mount Holyoke College, an all-female school in South Hadley, Massachusetts.

Two different schools and styles of gymnastics evolved. Artistic gymnastics, sometimes called Olympic gymnastics, involves floorwork, vaults, and movements on the balance beam and uneven bars. In rhythmic gymnastics, athletes do floorwork using the rope, ball, hoop, clubs, and ribbon.

In 1928, women first competed in the artistic gymnastics events. World championships began in 1934. Rhythmic gymnastics was part of the 1948 Olympics, at which time competitors were required to complete both artistic and rhythmic routines. The two forms were separate events at the 1952 Games, then rhythmic routines were dropped in 1956. The Soviet Union and Eastern Europe continued to pursue rhythmic gymnastics and held a world championship in Bulgaria in 1963. The U.S. Gymnastics Federation recognized it as an

Shannon Miller performs her floor exercise at the 1992 Barcelona Olympics. At the 1996 Atlanta Olympics Miller earned a gold metal in the balance beam competition and played a major role in the women's gymnastics team taking gold in the team competition.

official sport in 1973, and in 1984, this form of gymnastics returned to the Olympic slate. Among the U.S. women who have excelled in rhythmic gymnastics are Michelle Berube of Rochester, Michigan, who was the 1983 U.S. women's champion and placed fourteenth at the 1984 Olympics. Valerie Zimring of Los Angeles placed eleventh at those Games.

In 1968, the U.S. women's gymnastics team reached sixth place at the Olympic Games in Mexico City. That same year, Cathy Rigby won a silver medal in the balance beam event at the world championships. American women began winning more top prizes in international artistic gymnastics events. In 1978 Marcia Frederick became the first U.S. woman to win a gold medal in international competition when she took top honors in the uneven bars competition.

During the 1970s, the televising of gymnastics events made the sport increasingly popular. The sales of balance beams, uneven parallel bars, and tumbling mats increased by more than 50 percent from 1970 to 1980. In 1970, about 17,000 girls were involved in high school gymnastics programs, a figure that rose to 35,000 by 1973. During those same years, the number of gymnastics clubs rose from about 15 to more than 600. Some top European coaches, including world-famous Romanian coach Bela Karolyi, opened elite gymnastics training centers in the United States. Karolyi coached Mary Lou Retton, who won the All-Around competition in the 1994 Summer Olympics.

At the 1984 Summer Olympics in Los Angeles, the U.S. women's gymnastics team placed second, the first medal the team had won since 1948. During the 1980s and early 1990s, the sport came under close scrutiny as some sportswriters and others criticized the way training was conducted. They publicized the physical and emotional problems suffered by many young female gymnasts as well as gymnasts who had retired from the sport. Some critics also said the competitors were becoming increasingly younger.

At the 1996 Olympics in Atlanta, Georgia, America's women gymnasts made history, winning the team competition to capture the first-ever gold medal in that event for the United States. The team, which comprised Amanda Borden, Amy Chow, Dominique Dawes, Shannon Miller, Dominique Moceanu, Jaycie Phelps, and Kerri Strug, scored the highest total points in the compulsory events and optional round, which included events on the balance beam, parallel bars, floor exercise, and vault. The Russian and Romanian teams won the silver and bronze medals, respectively. The last event of the night brought high drama as Strug, the final gymnast, injured her ankle while doing her first vault. Despite the pain, she completed her second vault, landing on both feet to receive a score of 9.712 out of a possible 10, sealing the U.S. victory.

With her leg heavily bandaged, Strug later joined her teammates on the victory stand, carried by Karolyi. Her injuries kept her out of the remaining individual events. Chow went on to win a silver medal in the uneven bars, while Dawes captured bronze in a close floor exercise competition and Miller won America's first-ever gold medal on the balance beam.

See also Dawes, Dominique; Durham, Dianne; Frederick, Marcia; Grossfeld, Muriel Davis; Karolyi, Bela; Miller, Shannon; Moceanu, Dominique; Retton, Mary Lou; Rigby, Cathy; Strug, Kerri

Gymnastics

References Adler and Starr, "Flying High Now," *Newsweek*, August 10, 1992, 20–21; Gault, *The World of Women's Gymnastics* (1976); Kantrowitz, "Living with Training," *Newsweek*, August 10, 1992, 24–25; Lundgren, *Mary Lou Retton: Gold Medal Gymnast* (1985); Press, "Old Too Soon, Wise Too Late?" *Newsweek*, August 10, 1992, 22–24; Ryan, *Little Girls in Pretty Boxes* (1995); Tarshis, "What It Takes," *Scholastic Update*, May 1, 1992, 6–8.

Hagge, Marlene (b. 1934)

In 1950 Hagge became the youngest woman ever to win a tournament on the Ladies Professional Golf Association (LPGA) tour. She was just 18 when she captured the Sarasota Open title in 1952.

Eight years earlier, Hagge had begun her amateur golfing career by winning the Long Beach Boys' Junior tournament. She added the Western and National Junior championships, the Los Angeles Junior title, and the Northern California Junior to her list of achievements. In 1948 Hagge was the Associated Press's Athlete of the Year, Golfer of the Year, and Teenager of the Year.

On the professional tour, Hagge won the LPGA title in 1956, defeating longtime champion Patty Berg. She collected seven more titles and became the top LPGA money winner in 1956. An enduring athlete, Hagge set a new LPGA record in 1971 by scoring 29 for nine holes. She was still playing pro golf in the 1980s on the senior women's tour.

See also Golf

Hamill Camel

This movement in figure skating was named for 1976 Olympic gold medalist Dorothy Hamill, who first performed it in competition in 1970. It consists of a layover camel-sit spin in which the skater moves from a spin into a sitting spin position.

Hamill, Dorothy (b. 1956)

Olympic gold medalist Hamill's first pair of ice skates were a Christmas present. The eight-year-old immediately asked if she could take lessons because, as she later said, "I wanted to learn to skate backward." Her father later recalled that soon Dorothy also "wanted to spin like someone she saw on television."

By age ten, Hamill had progressed so rapidly that she skipped the Intermediate level of the United States Figure Skating Association (USFSA), moving from Juvenile to Novice. There were few practice rinks near her home in Riverside, Connecticut, but Hamill's mother drove her to various towns and to New York City. After she won the National Novice title in 1969, she began studying in Lake Placid, New York, with Gustave Lussi. Lussi encouraged the athletic jumps and spins that became Hamill's trademark.

Her unique style earned Dorothy Hamill a second-place finish in the 1970 National Junior Ladies' event. Her program included a layover camel-sit spin that became known as the Hamill Camel. In 1971 Hamill began training in Denver, Colorado, with coach Carlo Fassi. The high altitude was considered helpful in increasing the skaters' stamina. Hamill studied ballet and spent hours in fitness training while practicing, taking lessons, and completing high school courses. By 1974, Hamill was National Senior Ladies' champion. She won second place in the

Perhaps the most recognized female ice skater, Dorothy Hamill spins her way to a gold metal at the 1976 Olympics.

world championship that same year. She was discouraged when she fell during the 1975 worlds, coming in second once again.

A more mature and polished Hamill competed in Innsbruck, Austria, at the 1976 Olympics. She received the highest scores in all three events—the compulsory (school) figures, short program, and long free-skating program. Skating in a dark rose dress, Hamill completed an error-free long program with several difficult jumps. She received nearly perfect scores and captured the gold medal. After capping that triumph with a first-place finish at the world championships, Hamill retired from amateur skating and joined the Ice Capades. She also took part in numerous benefits and professional competitions, often winning top honors, while raising a daughter.

Hamill and husband Kenneth Forsythe bought the Ice Capades in 1993. Late in 1994, they sold it to International Entertainment, Inc. After performing with the show for the last time in December 1994, Hamill announced her retirement from professional skating. She continued to appear as a skating commentator on television.

References Dolan, *Dorothy Hamill: Olympic Skating Champion* (1979); Hamill, *Dorothy Hamill On and Off the Ice* (1983); Hilgers, *Great Skates* (1991); Van Steenwyk, *Dorothy Hamill: Olympic Champion* (1976); Van Steenwyk, *Women in Sports: Figure Skating* (1976).

Handball

The game of handball came to America from Ireland in the 1880s. It may date back to the tenth century, when it was called "Fives" for the five fingers of the hand. A tough game requiring stamina, handball has become a popular sport in urban areas because it requires little equipment. Players use a ball and court, which can frequently be found at YMCAs, youth clubs, sports clubs, and professional health clubs. Today, women athletes often play handball in addition to their major sport in order to increase their speed, agility, and eye-hand coordination.

The first amateur handball tournaments were held at the turn of the twentieth century. The Amateur Athletic Union (AAU) sponsored handball competition starting in 1919. People played the standard four-wall game and a variation using one wall. As women took up the sport of handball, they often played the one-wall version.

Founded in 1951, the United States Handball Association standardized rules and court sizes and began organizing competitions for players. National championships, sponsored by the United States Handball Association, are held each year in one-wall, three-wall, and four-wall versions of the game. At the 1994 championships, Barbara Canton of Bronx, New York, won the one-wall women's event, while Anna Engele of St. Paul, Minnesota, won the three-wall and four-wall titles. The world championship is a four-wall event for women, men, and men's doubles teams.

An outdoor handball event was held at the 1936 Olympics but was not part of the Games again until 1976, when it became an indoor event. In women's handball, Soviet and South Korean women athletes have dominated the Olympics.

Hansell, Ellen (1869–1937)

A native of Philadelphia, Ellen Forde Hansell Allerdice became America's first women's tennis champion. As a child, Hansell suffered from anemia but loved to play tennis. The family doctor encouraged the sport saying it might build up her strength.

Hansell later told an interviewer that

when she began playing tennis, women had to "grip our over-draped and voluminous skirts with our left hand to give us a bit more limb freedom when dashing to make a swift, snappy stroke." She wore a corseted tennis dress of red plaid gingham that her mother had made, along with a red felt hat and striped blazer.

Ellen Hansell was not quite 18 years old when she won the U.S. championship in 1887, the first year a women's event was held. This was her only major title. She was inducted into the Tennis Hall of Fame in 1965.

Hantze, Karen (See King, Billie Jean)

Hard, Darlene (b. 1936)
The versatile Darlene Ruth Hard succeeded in winning tennis matches both on the slow surface of clay courts and the faster grass, or lawn, surfaces like those at Wimbledon.

Born in Los Angeles, California, Hard developed a strong serve-and-volley style of play, along with solid groundstrokes. While attending Pomona College, she won the U.S. Intercollegiate women's title in 1958.

A particularly skillful doubles player, Hard won the U.S. doubles title from 1958 to 1962 and again in 1969, playing with four different partners. She also won two French championship doubles titles and four at Wimbledon. In 1957, she teamed with Althea Gibson to win the National Clay Court doubles title, which she captured again in 1960 with Billie Jean King and in 1962 and 1963 with two other partners. Hard won the French mixed doubles seven times, as well as the three mixed doubles crowns at Wimbledon.

In singles play, Hard won three Grand Slam titles, including the French (1960) and two U.S. titles (1960 and 1961). From 1960 to 1963, she was ranked as the number one U.S. women's player. She helped the Wightman Cup and Federation teams to several victories. In 1973, she was inducted into the Tennis Hall of Fame.

References Collins and Hollander, *Bud Collins' Modern Encyclopedia of Tennis* (1994).

Harding, Tonya (b. 1970)
As of 1994, Harding, a native of Oregon, was the first American female figure skater and second woman in the world to land a triple Axel in competition. When she was just ten years old, Harding began landing triple loops. As a novice skater, at age 12, she did a triple Lutz. Harding had also tried to complete a quadruple jump but found the movements placed too much stress on her ankles. In 1991, Harding won the national ladies figure skating title for the first of two times. That year, she also placed second at the world championships, in which U.S. skaters won all three medals, with the gold going to Kristi Yamaguchi and the bronze to Nancy Kerrigan.

At the 1992 world championships, Harding dropped to sixth place, and at the 1993 and 1994 world championships, she did not finish in the top ten. She won the U.S. ladies title again in 1994 when defending champion Nancy Kerrigan was unable to compete. Kerrigan had been clubbed in the knee while leaving a practice session at the U.S. national championships by a man who fled the scene. Appreciation of Harding's skating was overshadowed for several months in 1994 by the discovery that her then-husband, Jeff Gillooly, had plotted with others to assault Kerrigan before the Winter Olympics. Publicity surrounding Harding and Kerrigan dominated American television, newspapers, and tabloid magazines up to and during the Olympics. The controversy made headlines all over the world as well. Allowed to compete at the Winter Games pending a legal investigation, Harding placed eighth among all the skaters at the end of the final program.

After pleading guilty in March 1994 to charges of conspiring to hinder the investigation into the attack on Kerrigan, Harding resigned from the U.S. Figure Skating Association (USFSA) and withdrew from the world competition that was held later that month in Japan. The USFSA stripped Harding of her 1994 national title and banned her from competing in official figure skating events for life.

See also Kerrigan, Nancy

References Longman, "Kerrigan Triumphs in Short Program," *New York Times*, February 24, 1994, 49; Longman, "Baiul Edges Kerrigan in a Narrow Decision to Capture Gold Medal," *New York Times*, February 26, 1994, 1ff; Smith, *Figure Skating: A Celebration* (1994); Starr, "A Five Ring Circus," *Newsweek*, February 28, 1994, 46.

Harlem Globetrotters

This entertainment basketball team was started by Abe Saperstein in 1927 with five black male players. At their first game in Hinckley, Illinois, the Globetrotters amazed spectators by smoothly performing two-hand set shots, spin dribbling, and other tricky moves on the court.

In 1985 the Globetrotters' management decided to update the group and add interest by hiring a talented female basketball player. Twenty-five-year-old Lynette Woodard won the coveted job over 17 other candidates. Woodard remembered that, as a five-year-old, she had been impressed when Globetrotter star Geese Ausbie had come to her house for dinner and twirled a basketball on his finger. When she was a junior in college, Woodard began hoping she could someday join the team. She played with the Globetrotters for a year.

See also Woodard, Lynette

Hart, Doris Jane (b. 1925)

Tennis player Hart won all four major singles titles and numerous doubles events during her career. Born in St. Louis, Missouri, she grew up in Coral Gables, Florida. As a child, Hart suffered from a serious knee infection. Left with a weakened leg, she became a top player anyway, compensating for her lack of full mobility by polishing a strong serve and carefully planned strategies against opponents.

In 1949 Hart won a Grand Slam title, the Australian championship. A year later, she won the French title, which she would repeat in 1952. In 1951 Hart lost to Shirley Fry in the French singles championship but defeated her to win at Wimbledon for another Grand Slam title. At that same Wimbledon, she won the doubles and mixed doubles titles as well for a triple victory.

Hart then lost to Maureen Connolly in two sets in the semifinals of the U.S. national championship at Forest Hills, New York, where the U.S. Championship was held from 1913 to 1978. She finally captured the U.S. singles crown in 1954. That year, she won all three events open to her—singles, doubles, and mixed doubles. She repeated her singles victory in 1955 and was ranked as the top woman player in the world both years. In addition, she won singles titles at the Italian tournament (1951 and 1953) and the South African (1952).

Playing on the Wightman Cup team from 1946 to 1955, Hart lost only one match. She was especially effective on clay courts like that at the French national tournament. She won the women's doubles and mixed doubles there in 1953 but lost to Maureen Connolly in the Wimbledon singles final. London tennis critic Peter Wilson said it was the best women's singles final he had ever seen at

Wimbledon. Hart and her partner Shirley Fry defeated Connolly and Julie Sampson in doubles play. They won 12 games in a row to take the match, a record performance in a Wimbledon final.

In 1969 Hart was voted into the International Tennis Hall of Fame. She had won a total of 35 major singles, doubles, and mixed doubles titles during her career.

Reference Collins and Hollander, *Bud Collins' Modern Encyclopedia of Tennis* (1994).

Heiden, Beth (b. 1959)

The versatile Heiden won an Olympic bronze medal in the 3,000-meter speed skating event at the Olympics and a gold medal in the world championship road race, both in 1980.

A native of Madison, Wisconsin, Heiden grew up in an athletic family. At the 1980 Olympic Games, her brother Eric would win five gold medals in speed skating events. Like Eric, Beth Heiden found that by training in both cycling and speed skating, she enhanced her performance in each sport. In high school, she set a national age group record for the one-mile run. A year before her third-place finish at Lake Placid in the Winter Games, she won the women's overall world cycling title, the first American woman to do so. Her other cycling titles in 1980 included the national road championship and Coors International Classic.

In 1982 Heiden left cycling and entered the University of Vermont, where she became a proficient cross country skier, winning a National Collegiate Athletic Association (NCAA) division title. In 1983, she returned to cycling as part of the 7-Eleven team.

Heiss, Carol (b. 1940)

Figure skater Carol Elizabeth Heiss won the 1960 Olympic gold medal. When Heiss was growing up in Ozone Park, a part of Queens, New York City, her parents saw that she had unusually good balance and coordination. At age four, she roller-skated with ease. At age six, she delighted audiences in an amateur show at the Figure Skating Club of Brooklyn. Famed coaches Andree and Pierre Brunet offered to train her.

For years, the Heiss family made sacrifices to support Carol's skating—paying for the skates, costumes, rink time, lessons, traveling, and music and ballet classes. (During the 1950s, it cost more than $5,000 a year to become a champion skater, a cost that reached $50,000 by the 1990s.) At about 6 a.m. each day, Carol rode the subway to Madison Square Garden where she worked with coaches for about three hours, repeating figures and striving to improve. When Heiss won the National Junior Title at age ten, she became the youngest winner ever. She amazed onlookers again three years later when she placed fourth in the women's world competition.

For several years, Carol Heiss and another American, Tenley Albright, vied for skating's top honors. Albright continued to win first place, with Heiss placing second. In 1956 Albright won the Olympic gold medal, but Heiss captured the world crown shortly thereafter. Intricate footwork and daring leaps enabled her to keep that crown for four years and to win the 1960 Olympics at Squaw Valley, California. Shortly after winning her fifth world championship, Heiss turned professional. She went on to receive her college degree and skate in ice shows as well as a Disney production based on the fairytale of Snow White.

Also in 1960, Heiss married fellow skater and Olympic champion Hayes Allen Jenkins and moved to Akron, Ohio, where Jenkins practiced law. While rearing three children, Heiss also coached promising figure-skaters, including Jill Trenary, who was the 1990 U.S. ladies' champion. Heiss could be seen with her students at skating events during the early 1990s.

References Hilgers, *Great Skates* (1991); Hollander, *100 Greatest Women in Sports* (1976); Van Steenwyk, *Women in Sports: Figure Skating* (1976).

Heldman, Gladys (b. 1922)

A tournament tennis player during the 1940s, Gladys Medalie Heldman became a Houston businesswoman who launched the magazine *World Tennis* in 1953. She was instrumental in promoting women's tennis during the 1960s and 1970s. Heldman was a key force in developing the prestigious Virginia Slims tennis tour for professional women players. Through her magazine, Heldman also provided a forum for women to discuss the inequities in the prize money between the men's and women's tennis tournaments. She worked with Billie Jean King and Rosie Casals, among other players, to address these problems.

Heldman became a tennis lover after marrying her husband Julius, who had won the U.S. junior title in 1936 and later won many senior men's titles. The Heldmans saw daughters Trixie and Julie win junior titles. Julie become a tennis champion during the early 1970s, after winning the Italian Open in 1969, then worked as a sportswriter and television commentator. She had graduated with an honors history degree from Stanford University in 1966 after beginning college at age 16.

A staunch supporter of the game and promoter of opportunities for women players, Heldman was inducted into the Tennis Hall of Fame in 1972.

See also Prize Money; Virginia Slims

Henning, Anne (b. 1955)

Growing up in suburban Northbrook, Illinois, a region known for its world-class skaters, Anne Henning took to the ice at age four, when her parents bought her some double-runner learner's skates. Young Anne proved to be coordinated on the ice and excelled in other sports as well—swimming, baseball, and skiing.

Like fellow Olympian Dianne Holum, Henning studied speed skating with the well-known coach Ed Rudolph, who managed a skating club in Northbrook. Nine-year-old Henning impressed Rudolph, who later called her "a genius on skates." He encouraged her parents to allow her to train for competitive skating. The family agreed that she could pursue her skating, as long as she enjoyed the sport. Henning and other serious speed skaters at the Northbrook club sometimes made the 80-mile round trip to West Allis, Wisconsin. There they could practice in the only Olympic size rink in the United States, an outdoor rink located near the Milwaukee fairgrounds.

In 1971, at the Women's World Championship in Helsinki, Finland, 15-year-old Henning won the 500-meter event, with a time of 43.7 seconds. She competed at the 1972 Winter Olympics in Sapporo, Japan, where she won the same event with a time of 43.3 seconds. For the United States, the performance of Henning and teammate Holum marked the beginning of a new era in speed skating, when the Americans would win medals at the world level.

References Stambler, *Women in Sports: The Long Hard Climb* (1975).

Henrich, Christy (1972–1994)

A native of Independence, Missouri, Henrich, a world-class gymnast, focused attention on the problem of eating disorders among female athletes.

The hardworking Henrich made the U.S. national junior team at age 12. She trained for about 9 hours a day at the Blue Springs, Missouri, gym operated by coach Al Fong, while maintaining an A-average in school. In 1988, she placed tenth in the all-around competition at the U.S. Gymnastics Championships. When the Olympic trials were held that year, Henrich was recovering from both a fractured vertebra in her neck and mononucleosis. She missed making the Olympic gymnastics team by 0.118 of a point, a major disappointment. Returning to training, Henrich hoped to compete in the 1992 Olympics.

At about age 15, Henrich developed a serious eating disorder when she became convinced she must lose weight. She weighed about 90 pounds and stood 4 feet, 11 inches tall. She developed both anorexia, a disorder in which people eat little or nothing, and bulimia, a cycle of bingeing on food followed by purging through induced vomiting. Her weight fell to 80 pounds.

Weakened by a lack of nutrients, Henrich was not able to compete at the 1989 World Championship Trials. She was also pulled from the U.S.A-U.S.S.R. Challenge Meet in Oregon in 1990. Henrich retired from the sport in 1991, at age 18, and still weighing only 80 pounds. Her health problems and retirement prompted more talk of the widespread incidence of eating disorders among female gymnasts. The U.S. Gymnastics Federation (USGF) organized seminars for coaches on eating disorders and published articles on anorexia and bulimia. Gymnasts who had been battling these disorders discussed them more publicly.

Henrich had looked forward to marriage and family life after leaving her sport. However, her health continued to deteriorate as she lost more weight. By 1992, she weighed a shocking 60 pounds.

Her parents had her placed in the hospital for treatment several times during these years. In 1993 she entered the Menninger Clinic in Topeka, Kansas, where specialists tried to halt the progress of the disease. But Henrich weighed only 52 pounds in the summer of 1993.

Hospitalized once again, Henrich received financial help for her illness from a Houston group called the Association for Young Athletes. Some of her gymnastics teammates, including Kim Zmeskal, took part in a fund-raiser to help support her care. For a while after her five-month hospitalization in 1993, her weight increased and slowly surpassed 70 pounds. But by spring 1994, she was again growing thinner and her weight dropped to 52 pounds. Her muscles and internal organs had been so severely damaged from years of inadequate nutrients that she died on July 26, 1994, of multiple organ failure.

Near the end of her life, Henrich expressed a hope that her experiences might enlighten other people and prevent others from suffering a similar fate. Her death focused public attention on eating disorders among female athletes, as well as the methods used in training young women gymnasts.

References Ryan, *Little Girls in Pretty Boxes* (1995).

Heptathlon

This grueling two-day, seven-event competition requires an athlete to excel in speed, strength, and jumping. The events include the 100-meter hurdles, high jump, shot put, 200-meter dash, long jump, javelin throw, and 800-meter run. Points are awarded in each event, depending on the speed of the run, height or length of jumps, and distances of the throws.

The heptathlon replaced the women's pentathlon, a five-event competition, in the 1984 Olympics. Athlete Jackie Joyner-Kersee attained the record in the heptathlon when she scored 7,291 points in the 1988 Olympics. It was the fifth time she had exceeded 7,000 points, a feat only one other woman had accomplished before her.

One of the most inspiring women heptathletes of the 1990s was Marla Runyan, who competed despite a degenerative eye disease that impaired her central vision. Classified as legally blind, Runyan had to rely on her timing and became adept at judging the number of steps she should take between hurdles, for instance. At the 1992 Paralympics, held for athletes with physical disabilities, Runyan won four gold medals—in the 100-, 200-, and 400-meter races and long jump. Competing in national track and field championships in 1995, she hoped to qualify for the 1996 U.S. Olympic team. Besides competing, Runyan, who has a master's degree in elementary education, taught school children with visual and hearing impairments.

See also Joyner-Kersee, Jackie; Track and Field

Herman, Robin (b. 1952)

The *New York Times* sports reporter Herman was covering a hockey game in Montreal, Canada, on January 21, 1975, when coaches of the New York Islanders and Montreal Canadiens invited her and a fellow reporter into the locker rooms for a postgame interview. The players had not been told that female reporters would be present, and they later petitioned to have women barred from their locker rooms. It was said that the players' wives also protested the presence of women in the players' dressing rooms.

See also Sportswriters

Himalayan Expedition

In September 1978, a group of nine women, including seven Americans, became the first all-woman expedition to climb the 26,545-foot high Annapurna mountain in Nepal. Arlene Blum, who had taken part in the first all-woman climb of Alaska's Mount McKinley, also known as Denali, headed the group. Tragically, two British women in the expedition lost their footing on an ice wall en route to the summit of Annapurna. They fell to their deaths. When the survivors reached the peak, the climbers placed U.S. and Nepali flags there, along with a banner that read: "A woman's place is at the top."

Hockey (See Field Hockey; Ice Hockey)

Hockey Association, U.S. Field

Founded in 1922, the U.S. Field Hockey Association established standards of play for women playing hockey in schools, colleges, and other organizations. The league sponsors sectional and national tournaments and foreign tours.

Hogshead, Nancy (b. 1962)

A native of Iowa City, Iowa, Hogshead has won medals in national and world racing competitions using a variety of swimming strokes.

At age 12, Hogshead began to experience symptoms of asthma. Nonetheless, she became a top swimmer. Using the butterfly, she won gold medals in 100-yard and 200-meter events at the national championship events in 1977. The next year, she captured the national championships gold medal for the 200-yard butterfly.

Hogshead was named to the 1980 Olympic swim team, but the United States boycotted the 1980 Games for political reasons. She left competitive swimming for two years, then returned in 1983. At the national indoor championships, Hogshead won a bronze medal in the 200-yard butterfly. She began training in the freestyle as well and finished third in both the 100- and 200-meter events at the U.S. Swimming International meet held in January 1984. She captured a gold medal in 100-meter freestyle swimming at the 1984 national indoor championships.

At age 22, Hogshead competed in her first Olympics, the Summer Games in Los Angeles. She and Carrie Steinseifer, her teammate, tied for first place in the 100-meter freestyle. Hogshead was also part of two gold medal winning relay teams: the 4 x 100–meter medley and the 4 x 100–meter freestyle, in which she achieved the fastest time, 55.18 seconds. Besides those three gold medals, Hogshead took home a silver, for second place, in the 200-meter individual medley.

In 1986, Hogshead graduated from Duke University with honors. To inspire and educate others, she conducted research on the subject of world-class athletes with asthma and wrote a book called *Asthma and Exercise*. She also advanced the cause of women's participation in sports and worked on programs to prevent drug and alcohol abuse among young people.

References Levin, "Making a Splash," *Women's Sports and Fitness*, January-February 1992, 13; "Olympic Gold Still Shining," *Good Housekeeping*, February 1992, 142ff.

Holiday on Ice (See Ice Shows)

Holm, Eleanor (b. 1913)

Swimmer Holm won a gold medal in the backstroke at the 1932 Summer Olympics in Los Angeles. Some sportswriters have called her the best backstroke swimmer of all time.

The daughter of a Swedish-American fire captain and an Irish mother, Holm was raised in Brooklyn. She later said that she was a "water rat as a child." She had no fear of the water and swam so far out into the ocean that a lifeguard kept coming after her, then gave her free swimming lessons. Holm began watching races and diving competitions held in Long Beach by the Women's Swimming Association of New York. When she joined the association, her coaches encouraged her to develop her backstroke.

At age 14, Holm came in fifth in the 100-meter backstroke at the 1928 Olympics. But within a few years, she held the world record in that event (1 minute, 18.2 seconds). Holm competed again in 1932, winning first place in the backstroke at the Los Angeles Games with a time of 1 minute, 19.4 seconds.

During the early thirties, Holm continued her training. En route to Berlin by ship for the 1936 Olympics, she was accused of breaking training by drinking champagne. Avery Brundage, head of the Olympic Committee, banned her from competing in the Games. Although Brundage wanted to send Holm back to the United States, her supporters gave her a press pass so that she could attend the Games while writing a column for the Associated Press.

Holm also became a popular singer and entertainment figure, first as a dancer with the Ziegfeld Follies and later at the 1939–1940 New York World's Fair Aquacade, produced by her husband, theatrical director Billy Rose. As an actress under contract with Warner Brothers, she starred as Jane in the 1938 Hollywood film, *Tarzan's Revenge*, opposite Glenn Morris, an Olympic decathlon champion.

Later in life, Holm became an interior decorator and retired in Florida. She was inducted into the International Swimming Hall of Fame in 1966 and was one of the first six women chosen to enter the International Women's Sports Hall of Fame in 1980. In her seventies, Holm played tennis for exercise. She said that she still had the swimsuit in which she had won her 1932 gold medal.

See also Aquacades
References Carlson and Fogarty, *Tales of Gold* (1987).

Holum, Dianne (b. 1951)

Growing in Northbrook, Illinois, Dianne Holum was lucky to have a fine coach and speed skating facilities available. Former skating champion Ed Rudolph taught young skaters at the local speed skating club he had founded. Through the efforts of "Big Ed" and the achievements of its skaters, Northbrook eventually became known as the Speed Skating Capitol of the World.

Holum competed in her first Winter Olympics in 1968. She was part of a three-way tie for the second-place silver medal when she and two U.S. teammates, Jennifer Fish and Mary Meyers, finished the 500-meter race with exactly the same time—46.3 seconds. In the 1,000-meter race, Holum was third, bringing home a bronze medal. She attained Olympic gold in 1972 at Sapporo, Japan, by winning the 1,500-meter race.

Returning home to Illinois, Holum became a top speed skating coach. Her hometown, Northbrook, continued to send champions to competition and had produced 29 national champions and eight members of the U.S. speed skating team by 1975. One of Holum's students, Eric Heiden of Wisconsin, went on to win five gold medals in speed skating events at the 1980 Olympic Games. Heiden's sister Beth, another world-class skater, was also Holum's student. As of 1995, Heiden's remained the record for the most gold medals ever won by an individual at one Winter Olympics.

References Hollander, *American Women in Sports* (1972); Holum, "Power Legs," *Shape*, November 1992, 55ff.

Hoover, Lou Henry (See National Amateur Athletic Federation)

Horseback Riding (See Equestrian Sports; Jockey, Professional)

Horseshoe Pitching

The American game of horseshoes evolved from a British game called quoits, in which players pitched flat metal rings toward a stake placed in the ground. Early American settlers on the frontier may have improvised with horseshoes, rather than making or purchasing special equipment for this activity. The goal is to score ringers.

In 1921, the National Horseshoe Pitchers Association was formed to develop consistent rules for the game and promote horseshoe pitching as a recreational as well as competitive sport. It began publishing a newsletter and sponsoring an annual world tournament. The game was especially popular in the midwestern plains regions, and the first world championship was held at the Minnesota State Fair.

Measuring 6 feet in width, the length of the pitching court, or playing field, differs for men and women. Men play in a court that measures 40 feet from stake to stake. The women's court measures 30 feet, and children play in a 20-foot court. Competition at the local, national, and world level is available for girls and women. One of the top women horseshoe pitchers in the United States was Ruth Hangen, who won the national title from 1970 through 1973. The percentage of ringers she tossed peaked in 1973 at 79.6 percent. That record was surpassed in 1974, when Lorraine Thomas hit 80.2 percent ringers, then again by Ohioan Opal Reno, who won the 1978 world championship hitting 82.8 percent ringers. As of 1993, an American man, Ted Allen, held the record for consecutive ringers: 72.

Horvath, Kathleen (b. 1965)
Horvath has the distinction of being the only woman to defeat tennis champion Martina Navratilova during the 84 matches Navratilova played in 1983. Born in Chicago, Horvath was a top junior player. In 1979, one month before she turned 14, she became the youngest player to win the U.S. under-21 title. Her titles the next year included the Pepsi Junior, Orange Bowl Junior, and French Open Junior.

It was in the quarterfinals of the French Open in 1983 that the 17-year-old Horvath beat Navratilova. That year, she was ranked fifteenth among women players, reaching the quarterfinals of the U.S. Clay Court tournament and Canadian Open, the semifinals of the Italian Open, and the finals of the German Open. Horvath was runner up for the Avon Cup in 1984 and played with the U.S. Federation Cup team.

Hotchkiss, Hazel (See Wightman, Hazel Hotchkiss)

Houghton, Edith
Houghton grew up playing baseball and at age 13 competed against Japanese players from Nippon College in Japan, where her family was then living. During World War II, Houghton served with the Navy WAVES (Women Accepted for Voluntary Emergency Service).

A top baseball player for the Philadelphia Bobbles (a short-lived women's team), Houghton became the first woman scout hired by a major league ball team. In 1946, the Philadelphia Phillies, a National League team, hired her to scout promising new players. She was then appointed to the All-American Board of the National Baseball Congress, an organization of top major league scouts.

Hurdles
A track and field event, hurdling involves clearing a group of barriers as quickly as possible. There are competitions in both low and high hurdles, and the courses vary in length. The 100-meter hurdles are part of the heptathlon, which comprises seven events, and the pentathlon, a five-event track and field competition. Pentathlete Jane Frederick, who set U.S. records for the indoor and outdoor pentathlons in 1975, and heptathlete Jackie Joyner-Kersee have used their hurdling skills to win multievents.

A women's hurdling event debuted at the 1932 Summer Olympic Games held in Los Angeles. All-around athlete Babe Didrikson Zaharias won the event that year, with another U.S. woman, Evelyne Hall, winning the silver medal. In 1984, Benita Fitzgerald became the first U.S. woman since 1932 to win a gold medal in the 100-meter event.

During the 1970s, two U.S. women set new world records in hurdling. In 1979, 16-year-old Canzetta (Candy) Young completed the 60-yard hurdles in 7.50 seconds. The previous record had been set by Deby LaPlante, who had completed that event with a time of 7.53 seconds. In 1983, Stephanie Hightower set records in the 100-meter hurdles and 60-yard and 60-meter hurdles.

References Sullivan, *Track and Field: Secrets of the Champions* (1980).

Hyman, Flo (1954–1986)

Hyman was a top volleyball player, part of the U.S. Olympic team from 1974 to 1984. The tall (6 feet, 5 inches) athlete starred on both the basketball and volleyball teams at her Inglewood, California, high school. She began playing volleyball in her later teens and was a naturally strong hitter. Hyman worked to develop a strong defensive game as well and teammates regarded her as a strong and enthusiastic leader. She was an All-American at the University of Houston from 1974 through 1976.

In 1979 Hyman was named most valuable player at the North-Central and Caribbean American championship, in which the U.S. team came in second. She was also named best hitter at the 1981 World Cup volleyball games in Tokyo and was chosen to play on the All-World Cup team, one of only six women to be so honored. At the 1984 Olympics the U.S. women won a silver medal and considered it a great achievement in view of strong competition from the Chinese team.

While playing a match in 1986, Hyman collapsed and died. An autopsy performed after her death showed that she suffered from Marfan's syndrome, a rare genetic disease in which there is a dime-sized weak spot in the aorta, a large artery that carries blood away from the heart. Her weakened aorta had ruptured. Hyman was inducted into the International Women's Sports Hall of Fame.

References Demak, "Marfan Syndrome: A Silent Killer," *Sports Illustrated*, February 17, 1986, 30–34.

Ice Capades (See Ice Shows)

Ice Follies (See Ice Shows)

Ice Hockey

During the late 1800s, Canadians developed this fast-moving team sport. It is thought that soldiers who enjoyed skating and field hockey combined these two favorite pursuits so they could continue playing hockey in the wintertime. By 1893, the game had spread south of the Canadian border to those northern states that contained many ponds and lakes. The development of indoor ice rinks eventually enabled people in warmer regions to play ice hockey, too.

Teams of six players include three forwards, or offensive players, whose main job is to score by hitting the puck (a rubber disk) across the opposing team's goal line. The two defensive players help the goalie, the sixth member of the team, keep the puck out of the goal and attempt to regain the puck for their side when the opposing team has control of it.

More women and girls began to play ice hockey after the mid-1900s. (Figure skating champion Nancy Kerrigan is among those who enjoyed playing the game as a child, when she joined her brother and his friends.) Girls' teams are organized into three groups: tyke or pony for those ages 5–10, pee wee for those 10–12, and bantam for players 12–14. While male players are allowed physical contact during play, girls' ice hockey has a "no checking rule," banning players from hitting or bumping each other to gain the puck. Since the sport requires body protection, players of both genders wear helmets and face masks, elbow pads and knee pads, gloves, upper body and arm pads, and leg guards, as well as their skates and uniforms.

The International Federation of Women's Hockey Associations was formed in 1927. It oversees the rules for competition and has developed international matches. As of 1995, women's ice hockey was not yet an Olympic event, though women's teams competed in world tournaments. The U.S. women's hockey team reached the finals of the women's world hockey championship in 1992, but lost to Canada. At the tournament, U.S. forward Cammi Granato was top scorer, with eight goals and two assists. Also playing in that game, on the Canadian team, was Manon Rheaume, who had made sports headlines when she played three games in the men's Quebec Major Junior Hockey League. Collegiate women's hockey teams also compete with one another.

Ice Shows

Women figure skaters are prominently featured in the major touring ice shows. Ice Follies was introduced from Tulsa, Oklahoma, in 1936. Hollywood Ice Revue followed, featuring Olympic gold medalist and world champion Sonja

Henie, who had become a successful film star, earning millions of dollars with her performances. Ice Capades was founded in 1940, and Holiday on Ice began touring in 1944.

In recent decades, Ice Follies and Ice Capades continue to tour North American cities while Holiday on Ice tours in both North America and Europe. Acts vary widely—comedy, drama, romantic duets, scenes featuring characters from popular movies and television shows. All of the ice shows feature elaborate sets and costumes. Among the well-known amateur skaters who have joined ice shows as professionals are Carol Heiss, Peggy Fleming, Dorothy Hamill, and Janet Lynn.

Ice Skating (See Figure Skating; Speed Skating)

Iditarod Trail Sled-Dog Race

This long sled-dog race, which covers about 1,049 miles between Anchorage and Nome, Alaska (the distance varies annually but is always at least 1,000 miles), has been called the most challenging international sled-dog race of all. Drivers, called mushers, must navigate through wilderness, over icy rivers and hilly country, through blinding storms, breaking trail at times. Along the way, they sign in at about 26 checkpoints.

On the trail, racers are required to do all their own chores, such as cooking, caring for their dogs, and repairing their sleds if necessary. Veterinarians at the checkpoints examine the dogs. Mushers are required to take at least one 24-hour rest during the trip, at a stop they choose. Another eight-hour rest must be taken at White Mountain, the second checkpoint from the end. The race can take up to two weeks, and, as of 1992, the record time for

the Iditarod was 10 days, 19 hours, and 17 minutes, set by Martin Buser.

The idea for the race was sparked by sled-dog racer Joe Redington, who wanted to honor the history of sled dogs and his state, Alaska. One inspiration for the race was the famous 1925 Great Race of Mercy, during which a team of 20 sled-dog drivers relayed life-saving diphtheria serum along the Iditarod trail to Nome. Shortly before the 1967 centennial celebration of the United States purchase of Alaska Territory from Russia, Redington met Dorothy Page, who was heading the local centennial committee. She agreed that the race was a superb idea. More than 50 teams entered the first race, in February 1967, which was run in two heats over a 25-mile area.

Women have been entering the Iditarod since its second year, when two women, Lolly Medley and Mary Shields, completed the race. Dee Dee Jonroe became one of the top competitors in the 1980s and early 1990s. In 1991, with Susan Butcher, Jonroe shared the prize for reaching the halfway mark before any other racers. That year, she also received the Seppala Humanitarian Award, given to the racer who has taken the best care of the dog team during the race.

In 1985 Libby Riddles became the first woman to win the race. Butcher then proceeded to win four races, the most recent in 1990, at which time she also set a record for speed.

Indianapolis 500

Sometimes called the most important auto race in the world, the Indy, as it is known, is held each May at the Indianapolis Motor Speedway in Indiana. The track was built in 1909, designed as a rectangle 2.5 miles long. It has four sharp, angled turns; the straightaways are 50 feet wide, the turns 60 feet wide.

Kathy Swenson crosses windswept ice in Unalakleet, Alaska, during the Iditarod Trail Sled-Dog Race in 1993. Begun in 1967, women have competed in the race that covers more than 1,049 miles and can last up to two weeks since 1969.

Since most tracks are designed in the shape of an oval rather than a rectangle, drivers find it more challenging to keep a speeding car on the track at Indy. The surface of the track has been changed more than once since 1909, and race cars have been designed to adapt to its unique characteristics. The annual race attracts thousands of spectators—often 100,000 spectators watch the qualifying rounds.

In 1977 Janet Guthrie became the first woman to qualify for the Indianapolis 500. She completed the race that year and in 1978. In previous years, women had been confined to the role of spectators; until 1974, they were not even allowed to enter the pit area, where the race cars are repaired and refueled.

See also Guthrie, Janet
Reference Dolan, *Great Moments at the Indy 500* (1982).

International Olympic Committee (IOC)

The IOC is made up of 133 nations and 89 members representing various nations that take part in the Olympics. The IOC regulates the Summer and Winter Olympic Games, making the final choice of sites. It sets rules for the competition and guidelines for athletes who wish to compete. In 1972, the IOC described the goals of the Olympics as helping young people to develop "health, strength, and character" through physical training and competition; encouraging sportsmanship in all spheres of life; and promoting the value of sports as "games and distractions" rather than just a means of material gain.

See also DeFrantz, Anita

International Skating Union (ISU)

Formed in 1892 as the International Eislauf Vereinigung, the organization began with six founding nations—Austria, Germany, Britain, Hungary, the Netherlands, and Sweden. Its purpose was to standardize distances for speed skating competitions. The name was later changed.

The ISU established the rules for amateur competition and developed a list of compulsory (school) figures—figure eights and loops that skaters were required to complete successfully in order to demonstrate their technical skill. In order to master these figures, skaters had to learn control of the inside, outside, backward, and forward edges of their skates. School (compulsory) figures became a required segment of amateur figure skating competitions. From 1932 to 1968, they counted for 60 percent of the skater's final score, changed to 50 percent in 1968, then to 30 percent in 1976. Compulsory figures were eliminated completely from singles' competition after the 1990 season.

The ISU rules continue to define who is eligible for amateur skating events, such as the Olympics, and to regulate procedures at these events. The ISU also may add or alter rules from time to time, as when it specified in 1980 that certain movements must be included in pairs skating competition. The rules also specify when and why points will be deducted from a skater's performance and how ties will be broken. The ISU continues to sponsor nonprofessional world championships each year in both figure and speed skating.

International Swimming and Diving Hall of Fame

Located in Fort Lauderdale, Florida, the hall, once called the Swimming Hall of Fame, honors outstanding swimmers and divers as well as synchronized swimmers and water polo players from around the world. Both distance and racing swimmers are eligible and have been inducted into the hall, where there are displays on nearly 300 honorees, including Esther Williams, Ethelda Bleibtrey, Eleanor Holm, Helene Madison, and Dorothy Poynton. The hall is associated with a library and museum devoted to water sports and athletes, and to those who contributed to water sports through the years.

See also Williams, Esther

International Tennis Hall of Fame

Founded in 1953 as the National Tennis Hall of Fame, this institution honors great champions. Memorabilia, photographs, equipment, and various exhibits show the history of the game. The landscaped grounds feature a 5,000-seat lawn tennis stadium and 12 grass courts.

Tennis-lover Jimmy Van Alen was the chief instigator of the hall, originally limited to American tennis and called the Tennis Hall of Fame. It was located at the Newport Casino in Van Alen's hometown of Newport, Rhode Island, which had long been a summer resort for wealthy Americans. Van Alen, a champion player himself, had helped to preserve the casino, which was known as the "cradle of American tournament tennis." He also contributed the idea of a streamlined scoring system, including the tiebreaker, and sponsored the Casino Pro Championships, which began in 1965.

The hall of fame was sanctioned by the United States Tennis Association (USTA) and officially opened in August 1954. The first members, seven men, were voted into the hall in 1955. The next year, May Sutton Bundy became the first woman player chosen. Van Alen was himself inducted in 1965. In 1975 it was decided to include players from around the world, and Fred Perry of Britain was inducted as the first non-American. The name of the hall was changed to the International Tennis Hall of Fame. As of 1995, 42 women tennis players were members, along with Mary Outerbridge, inducted for her contributions to the sport.

International Women's Sports Hall of Fame

Located in East Meadow, New York, the hall was established by the Women's Sports Foundation in 1980 to honor women from around the world who have attained greatness in their sport and/or contributed greatly to women's sports. Both athletes and coaches are eligible in two membership categories: contemporary (after 1960) and pioneer (before 1960). Among the sports included are skiing (alpine and Nordic), auto racing, aviation, baseball, basketball, bowling, cycling, diving, equestrian sports, fencing, figure skating, golf, track and field, gymnastics, shooting, softball, speed skating, swimming, tennis, volleyball, and water skiing. As of 1994, seven women were honored as coaches in the hall: Constance Applebee, Sharron Backus, Muriel Grossfeld, Nell Jackson, Rusty Kanokogi, Pat Head Summit, and Margaret Wade.

See also Applebee, Constance; Grossfeld, Muriel Davis; Jackson, Nell; Kanokogi, Rusty

Italian Open

Held every spring at the *Campo Centrale* (center court) in Rome's *Il Foro Italico*, this is the national tennis tournament of Italy. The clay court event is open to players from all over the world. Between 1935 and 1950, the tournament was canceled because of World War II. In 1971, the tournament became an "open"—a competition in which both amateurs and professionals could enter.

See also Heldman, Gladys

Jackson, Nell (1929–1988)

A native of Tuskegee, Alabama, Jackson excelled as an athlete, a coach, and later in management, supporting athletics and women athletes.

Jackson grew up near an important center of athletics for African-Americans, the Tuskegee Institute. Fast, tall, and thin, Nell Cecelia Jackson excelled in basketball, tennis, swimming, and track. As she grew older and began concentrating on track and field events, Jackson was surprised that some people discouraged girls from sports. She later said, "They thought a girl was masculine if she was athletic. It bothered me for a while, but I was determined to be a successful athlete, so I got over it."

In 1948, Jackson competed with the U.S. Olympic track team in London. Her time in the qualifying rounds was just shy of that needed to compete in the final races. In 1949 and 1950, she reached her peak as a sprinter. In 1949, she won the national 200-meter race with a time of 24.2 seconds, which broke a 14-year-old U.S. record. The next year, she won again with a time of 25 seconds. At the Pan American Games that year, she finished second behind a runner from Tennessee State University, Mae Faggs. The two women worked together to bring the American team a gold medal in the 400-meter relay.

Jackson earned a bachelor's degree in physical education from Tuskegee University, then a master's degree from Springfield College. She spent the summer of 1955 completing a special summer course in Oslo, Norway, after which she became a successful coach and physical education instructor at Tuskegee Institute. In 1956, she was asked to coach the U.S. women's track team at the Olympics in Melbourne, Australia. That year, Mildred McDaniels won a gold medal for the high jump.

Returning to school in 1960, Jackson received a doctoral degree in physical education for the handicapped from the University of Iowa. She returned to Tuskegee as assistant professor, then taught at Illinois State University. She organized the Illinois Track Team for Girls, the first such team at the University of Illinois, and authored many articles and a book, *Track and Field for Girls and Women*. Later in her career, she produced educational filmstrips on track and field for women. By 1968, Jackson was recognized as an expert in her field. She chaired the U.S. Women's Track-and-Field Committee as well as the Amateur Athletic Union's Women's Track-and-Field Committee, and served on the Board of Directors of the U.S. Olympic Committee. Besides her many other duties, Jackson coached the U.S. women who went to the 1972 Olympics.

Moving into another aspect of athletics, in 1964 Jackson became an assistant manager of the U.S. women's national track and field team. From 1965 to 1966 and in 1972 and 1977, she served as team manager. In 1979 and 1982, Jackson managed the Senior National Team. Throughout these years, she was involved in public service, developing sports clubs for girls in various communities. Jackson also served on a number of Olympic committees. She was a member of the board of directors of the U.S. Olympic Committee for three years and later served on its development committee. In 1973, Jackson accepted a position as director of women's athletics at Michigan State University and oversaw the development of new programs for women's competitive athletics, a trend across the nation in the years after the passage of Title IX.

From 1981 to 1988, Jackson was director of physical education and intercollegiate sports for the State University of New York (SUNY) at Binghamton. During her career, Jackson encouraged women to pursue careers as athletes, coaches, and managers and to devote time to public service. Among her many honors were alumni awards from the colleges she had attended and the National Association for Girls and Women in Sports (NAGWS) presidential citation. She was inducted into the Black Athletes Hall of Fame in 1977 and into the National Track and Field Hall of Fame in 1989.

See also Title IX

References Ashe, *A Hard Road to Glory* (1988); Bortstein, *After Olympic Glory: The Lives of Ten Outstanding Medalists* (1987); "Nell Jackson Inducted into Hall of Fame," *NAGWS News*, Winter 1990, 1.

Jacobs, Helen Hull (b. 1908)

A right-handed tennis player born in Globe, Arizona, Jacobs later lived in the San Francisco Bay area and studied with coach Pop Fuller at the Berkeley Tennis Club in California. Jacobs was known for her speed, tenacity, expert net game, and sportsmanship. As a junior, she won two national championships in a row. From age 18 to 30, she played on America's Wightman Cup team. Jacobs was ranked among the top ten women players from 1928 to 1940. During her years of competition, she often reached the finals of major tournaments, only to lose to one of the two greatest champions of the day, Helen Wills or Alice Marble.

Sportswriters called the competition between Jacobs and Wills "The Battle of the Two Helens." Their matches were among the most dramatic ever played in women's tennis. Although it was rumored that Wills and Jacobs were feuding, Jacobs told journalists that this was not true. Jacobs admired Wills's abilities on the court and later wrote about their first match, played when they were teenagers: "As we commenced to rally, I realized for the first time what speed of shot meant. The ball came straight as a die and fast as a bullet. In 7 minutes from the time we started our game, she had beaten me 6-0."

Jacobs had lost to Wills eight times before she finally defeated her at the 1933 U.S. national championships at Forest Hills in New York. But the thrill of that victory was dampened by the fact that Wills defaulted after two sets, claiming she had leg pains. The U.S. title went to Jacobs four times, from 1932 to 1935. In 1936, she finally won the Wimbledon title she had sought for ten years. It was at Wimbledon in 1933 that Jacobs also became the first woman player to dare to wear shorts rather than a skirt. In 1932, 1934, and 1935, Jacobs won the U.S. women's doubles title with partner Sarah Palfrey.

Jacobs was named to the Tennis Hall

of Fame in 1962. She also became an author, publishing an autobiography, tennis stories, and novels for young people.

References Collins and Hollander, *Bud Collins' Complete Encyclopedia of Tennis* (1994); Jacobs, *Beyond the Game* (1948).

Jaeger, Andrea (b. 1953)

Jaeger became a top tennis player at an early age. By 13, she had won seven national tennis titles, including the girls' national 16-and-under clay court singles title, along with the doubles title, which she won with her sister Suzy. Sportswriters called the 4-foot 11-inch, 76-pound Jaeger a "powerhouse."

Growing up in Lincolnshire, Illinois, Jaeger maintained an A-minus average in school while training and competing. She was named Most Impressive Newcomer in 1980 and won the Avon Futures tournament in Las Vegas. A year later, she became U.S. clay court women's champion. In 1983 she faced 39-year-old Billie Jean King in the semifinals at Wimbledon. With strategically placed lobs and passing shots, Jaeger kept King on the move and defeated her. The score for the two-set match was 6-1, 6-1.

Playing in the 1980s, Jaeger was often pitted against the great champion, Martina Navratilova, to whom she lost in the 1982 French Open and at the 1983 Wimbledon finals. An injury forced Jaeger to end her promising competitive career in 1987. In 1990 she started the nonprofit Kids Stuff Foundation, which sponsors a camp for critically ill children. Many of the contributions came from professional tennis players whom Jaeger had known on the tour. She started the Silver Lining Ranch in the summer of 1993. In 1994 Jaeger spoke about her work on television and organized fund-raising events to maintain this year-round camp in Col-

orado. President Bill Clinton honored Jaeger at the White House for her efforts on behalf of children.

References Collins and Hollander, *Bud Collins' Modern Encyclopedia of Tennis* (1994); Markels, "A Kid Champion Champions Kids," *Tennis*, June 1994, 28–29; Min, "Child's Play," *People Weekly*, August 29, 1994, 75–76.

Jameson, Betty (b. 1919)

As a high school student, Jameson, who was born in Norman, Oklahoma, played on the boys golf team—there were no teams for girls. She gained her first victory at age 15, outscoring her competitors at the Southern Amateur Championship in 1934. In 1935 she won the Texas State championships, a title she would hold for four years in a row. The next year, she added the Trans-Mississippi title to her honors, repeating that victory in 1940. As an amateur, she won the Texas Open in 1938, the U.S. Golf Association Amateur Championship in 1939 and 1940, and the Western Amateur in 1940 and 1942. She achieved another first in 1942 by becoming the first woman to win both the Western Amateur and Western Ladies' Open in the same year.

Betty Jameson became a professional golfer in 1945, winning the National Open two years later. Her total score in that event (295) made her the first woman to score lower than 300 strokes for a 72-hole tournament. She added another Texas Open title in 1949, a World Championship in 1952, and a second Western Open title in 1954. A year later, Jameson honored another golf great, Glenna Collett Vare, by presenting a trophy to the Ladies Professional Golf Association (LPGA) to be named the Vare Trophy. Jameson had helped to found the LPGA.

Jameson won the Babe Zaharias Open in 1955, a year in which she won three other major golf tournaments. She was inducted into the LPGA Hall of Fame in 1951.

References Eds. of *Golf Magazine, Golf In America: The First Hundred Years* (1981); LPGA, *LPGA Media Guide* (1995); Scarff, ed., *Golf Magazine's Encyclopedia of Golf* (1970).

Javelin (See Track and Field)

Jockey, Professional

Women struggled for acceptance as jockeys in major horse races. Judy Johnson was permitted to ride in a steeplechase at the Pimlico track in Maryland in 1943, but women were kept out of flat (non-jumping) thoroughbred racing events. During the late 1960s, Penny Ann Early had tried and failed to ride at Churchill Downs and in the Kentucky Derby. Until 1968, women were not granted state licenses as jockeys. That year, Kathy Kusner sued the state of Maryland in order to get a license to ride and won her case. Barbara Jo Rubin had struggled to ride at Tropical Park in Miami, Florida. She was harassed and threatened by people who opposed her efforts, but became the first woman jockey to win a regular pari-mutuel race in 1969, at Hobby House Hall Racetrack in the Bahamas. At New York race tracks, Robyn Smith and some other women were allowed to compete.

See also Bacon, Mary; Crump, Dianne; Kentucky Derby; Krone, Julie; Smith, Robyn

Johnson, Kathy (b. 1959)

A Florida native, Johnson didn't discover that she was a natural at gymnastics until the relatively late age of 12. She trained in Louisiana under Vannie Edwards, who was then an Olympic gymnastics coach. Like several other well-known female gymnasts, Johnson suffered from eating disorders during her teens when she drastically restricted her food intake in order to stay quite thin for competition. She experienced episodes of weakness and dizziness and suffered from injuries as a result of training in a weakened condition. During 1978, Johnson broke an arm and went through months of rehabilitation before she could compete again. After recovering, at age 19, she won a bronze medal for her floor routine at the World Championships in France. At that time, few U.S. women had won medals at world gymnastics competitions.

Johnson overcame another bout of bulimia, and by 1980, after struggling to become mentally and physically fit, she had increased her weight from 90 to 102 pounds. She performed beautifully at the 1980 Olympic trials and was crushed when the United States announced that it was boycotting the Summer Games that year for political reasons. At that point, Johnson faced a difficult decision: whether to retire from her sport or keep training and try for the 1984 Olympics, at which time she would be almost 25—much older than most competitors. She opted to try again and began training hard in Southern California with coach Don Peters. At the 1984 World Championships, Johnson finished in 11th place, higher than any other American gymnast. She continued to train diligently and competed in the 1984 Olympics, where she won a third-place bronze medal for her balance beam routine.

After the Olympics, Johnson retired from competition and once more found herself battling bulimia. Again, she overcame her problems and became a successful television sports commentator for both ABC and ESPN. In an effort to help others, Johnson has spoken publicly about the pressures she experienced during her competitive career and the problems of today's young athletes.

References: Ryan, *Little Girls in Pretty Boxes* (1995).

Jones, Loree Jon (b. 1966)

"Bulletproof concentration" is how George Fels, a columnist for *Billiards Digest*, once described Jones's playing style. Jones began playing billiards at age four in Garwood, New Jersey. Her father, John Ognowski, loved the game. Within three years, Loree Jon was amazing audiences at charity exhibitions with her skill. She won her first national title at age 11. Four years later, she made the *Guinness Book of World Records* as the youngest player ever to win a world billiards championship. The previous record-holder was Willie Mosconi, who had won when he was only 17.

During 1993, Jones compiled a remarkable record, with back-to-back victories in the national and world billiard championships. But in 1994, her ranking fell to number four in the world, as Jones began a slump that left her discouraged. Determined to make a comeback, she practiced for hours in the basement of the home she shared with her husband, Sammy Jones, a former professional billiards player who had become her coach. By late summer 1995, Jones had won four of the five events she entered that year and led the field in prize earnings. With a total of 60 career championships, she seemed poised to reach the top of her sport.

Reference Berkow, "Jones Sinks, Then Soars," *New York Times*, August 12, 1995, 31.

Jonroe, Dee Dee (See Iditarod Trail Sled-Dog Race)

Joyce, Joan (b. 1940)

During an exhibition game, softball pitcher Joan Joyce thrilled fans by striking out baseball legend Ted Williams. Followers of women's softball were not surprised, however. They knew that Joyce was not only a great woman player, but one of the greatest ever. Some of her fastballs had been timed at 116 miles per hour, a speed that exceeded some of the best male pitchers, who threw at speeds closer to 100 miles per hour. The versatile pitcher would later tell author Bill Gutman, "I can throw a screwball, a rise ball, a drop, a curve, and a knuckleball. . . . I challenge [batters] with what I think they can't hit."

Born in Waterbury, Connecticut, Joyce was called a "tomboy" as a child, excelling at baseball, golf, bowling, and other sports. Yet, like other talented women athletes, Joyce could not play varsity sports in high school, since there were no such teams for girls in those days. Those who loved basketball played on an intramural team one afternoon a week. Joyce later recalled that the teacher in charge limited individual players to no more than ten points a game. After Joyce had scored ten points, which she did routinely, she would be switched to a guard position.

A gifted softball player as well, at age 13 Joyce joined the Brakettes, a woman's softball team. Joyce played with the Brakettes for 20 years. She had been playing in the outfield before the 1957 National Fast Pitch Softball playoffs, so when she took over as a relief pitcher and pitched a no-hitter, her team and fans were delighted. The Brakettes won the championship and went on to win 11 national titles, four in a row from 1969 to 1973. Joyce was a key part of those victories, pitching more than 70 no-hitters and achieving a batting average of .400. Some of her pitches came from a distance of 45 feet at speeds of 116 miles per hour. Her team gave her the outstanding player award in 1968. Joyce helped her team capture the Women's World Championship in 1974, the first time a U.S. team had won the title. No team scored a run against the Brakettes in 36 innings during their five consecutive wins at the tournament. Two weeks later in Orlando, Florida, for the national championships, Joyce pitched 45 innings in a 24-hour period, and no team scored a run against the Brakettes.

In 1974, Joyce became a basketball and softball coach and instructor at Brooklyn College. She said that coaching brought her great satisfaction. From 1957 to 1975, Joyce was an Amateur Softball Association All-American. For three seasons, she also pitched for the Orange, California, Lionettes, and in 1965, the Lionettes won the national title. During those years, she played basketball with the Amateur Athletic Union (AAU). She was chosen as an all-American three times. From 1971 to 1975, Joyce chalked up an amazing record both as a hitter and as a pitcher. She had a 36-0 record on the mound in 1975, as well as a batting average of .381. Joyce was named Most Valuable Player in the national playoffs for the eighth time.

In 1976, Joyce worked with tennis star Billie Jean King and others to form the International Women's Professional Softball Association. She turned professional to play with the teams until the league folded in 1979, serving as manager and coach as well as player for the Connecticut Falcons. While she was pitching, the team won the Women's Pro World Series all four years. Joyce achieved a lifetime amateur batting average of .325, batting in 534 runs.

At the same time she was breaking records in softball, Joyce was pursuing another sport she had long loved: golf. In 1977, the year the Falcons won their second softball world series title, she qualified as a member of the Ladies Professional Golf Association (LPGA). She traveled from one sporting event to another, in the meantime working to improve her golfing skills. She played in numerous golf tournaments in 1978, yet helped her softball team win another world series title, their third in a row. Joyce was elected to the National Softball Hall of Fame in 1983. During the 1990s, Joyce was head softball coach at Florida Atlantic University in Boca Raton, Florida.

References Condon, *Great Women Athletes of the Twentieth Century* (1991); Gutman, *More Modern Women Superstars* (1979); "Joan Joyce," profile from the National Softball Hall of Fame.

Joyner-Kersee, Jackie (b. 1962)

Jacqueline (Jackie) Joyner-Kersee has often been called the "greatest woman athlete alive," as well as one of the greatest male or female athletes ever. She was the first woman ever named "Man of the Year" by the *Sporting News,* a national weekly sports newspaper. Of her achievements, Joyner-Kersee has said, "I'm a firm believer in the three Ds—determination, desire, and dedication."

Growing up in East St. Louis, Missouri, Jackie Joyner and her three siblings lived in an impoverished neighborhood. Her father worked in construction and at the railroad, and her mother was a practical nurse. The family was rich in "love and caring," Joyner-Kersee recalled, but sometimes they could not afford heat during the winter or other comforts many Americans take for granted.

Her family encouraged her to do her best at school, both in academics and in sports, at which she excelled. Joyner studied modern dance and track at a recreation center in her neighborhood, and by age 12, she had become a skilled runner and jumper, able to leap more than 17 feet. She succeeded in sports despite asthma, a problem she had since childhood.

Jackie Joyner-Kersee clears a hurdle on the way to an American record in the heptathlon 100-meter hurdles during the Olympic track and field trials in 1988.

Noticing Joyner's skills in several areas, a coach suggested that she compete in the five-event pentathlon. She won the National Junior title from ages 14 through 17, and it was clear she had a bright future in track and field. Meanwhile, Joyner was a star on her high school's basketball and volleyball teams. She was ranked as the best female basketball player in Missouri and also earned such high grades that she graduated tenth in her class.

At the University of California at Los Angeles, where she majored in communications and history, Joyner played basketball and was an all-American her senior year. She competed with the track team, coached by her future husband, Bob Kersee. Jackie's brother, Al Joyner, who won a gold medal in the men's triple jump at the 1984 Olympics, also became a coach and married runner Florence Griffith.

As Jackie Joyner-Kersee, she competed in the heptathlon event in the 1984 Olympics, where she earned a silver medal, losing the gold by a mere 5 points in one race. She resumed training and began setting records in international competition. Her thrilling score of 7,148 points in the heptathlon at the Goodwill Games in Moscow exceeded old records by 200 points. She earned an even higher score—7,158 points—later that year. Joyner-Kersee won the coveted Sullivan Award as the outstanding American amateur athlete of 1986. She went on to a double win at the Pan American Games—the pentathlon and the long jump.

At the 1988 Olympics in Seoul, South Korea, Joyner-Kersee "doubled" again, winning gold medals for the long jump and the heptathlon. Competing with an injured knee, she again topped 7,000 points, scoring 7,291, a new Olympic record. In 1992, once again, she won the gold in the Olympic heptathlon competition, along with a bronze medal in the long jump. No other woman had won multievent titles at two Olympics and no man or woman had done so at three Olympics.

Her fame brought Joyner-Kersee lucrative commercial endorsements and opportunities to appear on television. She told an interviewer that one of her most cherished goals was to "open doors for minority women and for women in general." Besides her incredible athletic achievements, Joyner-Kersee distinguished herself as a philanthropist and role model for young people. Her Jackie Joyner-Kersee Community Foundation sponsored educational and recreational programs in needy communities. When the center she had used as a child was about to close for lack of funds, she worked to reopen it.

By 1993, Joyner-Kersee was also a mother. She competed in the 1993 world heptathlon and was trailing her German rival as she went into the 800-meter race. Yet she managed to win the race and the gold medal for the title. Looking ahead to the 1996 Olympics, when she would be 34 years old, she noted that nobody had ever won a pentathlon or heptathlon at that age. Joyner-Kersee decided to compete, but a recurring leg muscle injury forced her to withdraw during the first week of the Games.

See also Pentathlon
References Condon, *Great Women Athletes of the Twentieth Century* (1991); Levin, "Interview: First Lady," *Women's Sports and Fitness*, January-February 1993, 30ff; McCane and Wolf, *The Worst Day I Ever Had* (1991); "Track and Field: The Olympics," *Sports Illustrated*, August 10, 1992, 17–24.

Judging (**See** Boxing; Shain, Eva)

Judo

A martial art developed by Jigaro Kano of Japan in the late 1800s, judo evolved from the ancient martial art called jujitsu, dating back to the 1500s. This most popular of the martial arts comes from the words *ju,* meaning "yielding," and *do,* meaning "the way." Practitioners learn how to use the laws of gravity to flip an opponent to the ground and use different holds and locks to keep them immobilized. Much time is spent learning how to fall without being hurt. Traditionally, judo was practiced for the benefit of the individual's physical, mental, and spiritual growth, but it is now an organized competitive sport.

Judo was long considered a sport for males only, but women fought for admittance at training schools and competitive judo events. During the 1960s and 1970s, more women studied judo, but they often found themselves the sole female in their classes. They studied to master the sport as well as learn self-defense techniques and become stronger individuals.

Men's judo has been part of the Olympic Games since 1966. For years, women in the martial arts sought to have judo for women added to the Olympics. During the 1980s, led by Rusty Kanokogi and other women, thousands of people signed petitions to the International Olympic Committee (IOC). The petitioners also threatened to sue the television networks for sexual discrimination, since they had contracted with the IOC, an organization they claimed discriminated against women.

At first, the IOC decided to wait until 1992 before women's judo was added to the Games, with a demonstration only in 1988. However, it changed its decision, and judo finally became an Olympic event for women at the 1988 Summer Games. The Amateur Athletic Union (AAU) also added judo to its roster of sports for girls and women, and judo is now a competitive event at the Junior Olympics.

See also Kanokogi, Rusty

Junior Olympics

Sponsored by the Amateur Athletic Union (AAU), these Games are held annually and offer competition for young people in the following sports: in basketball, bobsled, boxing, cross country, decathlon/pentathlon, diving, gymnastics, judo, luge, swimming, synchronized swimming, taekwando, track and field, trampoline and tumbling, volleyball, water polo, weight lifting, and wrestling.

Kanokogi, Rusty (b. 1935)

Born Rena Glickman, the 5-foot, 9-inch native of Brooklyn, New York, became the highest-ranked woman in judo in the United States. Growing up, Rena became "Rusty" to her friends because of her fiery red hair. She was a natural athlete who could not take part in organized sports teams at school because they were not available for girls at that time. With boys in her neighborhood, she played handball and basketball. At home, she endured poverty and other problems, since her father was a chronic gambler and her mother was often ill and had little time for the children. At about age seven, she began working at odd jobs, such as selling candy on the boardwalk at Coney Island.

At age 19, she discovered judo through a male friend who was taking classes. She was then a new mother, divorced, and working as an assistant to the physical education director at the YMCA. Her boss convinced the director at a YMCA offering the judo classes to accept her. One of the barriers against women was a lack of dressing rooms, so Glickman changed her clothing in a broom closet at the YMCA. She flattened her breasts with Ace bandages and was careful not to cry when she broke bones or injured herself during a class. But she later said that her instructor, Mr. Saiganji, was fair-minded and supportive.

Judo did not come easily to Glickman, who worked hard to master the movements and techniques. She suffered from numerous bruises, broken toes, and other injuries, but her work was rewarded when she made the Judo Twins Club team. She competed against men, since there was then no organized competition among women. By her third year in the sport, she was winning many of her matches against men. In one case, a man who lost to her told others that she was not really a woman.

Some athletic directors were upset to see a woman in competition. As a result, judo competition entry forms from the Amateur Athletic Union (AAU) and local organizations began to include the words "males only." At an international meet held in 1961, she won her match against a male competitor. British women, with a longer history of judo training in their country, competed against other women. The AAU, which opposed women in judo, kept the medal Glickman won in the match.

Publicity about Glickman brought more interest in judo from women in the United States and other countries. She met Phyllis Harper, a judo expert and teacher from Chicago who was a pioneer in women's judo, and Glickman decided to begin teaching other women. In 1962, she earned her black belt, signifying her high level of achievement in judo. She studied at the Kodokan, a famous judo center in Japan, and competed in world judo events. While in Japan, she met Ryohei Kanokogi, a champion in judo and karate, and they were married in 1964. The couple had two children together.

Back in the United States, she campaigned for the rights of women in the martial arts and helped to form organizations for women in judo. The AAU finally agreed that women could officially take part in judo events as of 1970, but it established different rules for men and women competitors. The women's rules banned certain movements that involved more body-to-body contact. In 1973, the AAU finally allowed men and women to compete by the same rules.

Kanokogi worked with the AAU to organize a women's judo team, which she helped to coach. The team entered the British Women's Judo Open, at which time Maureen Braziel became the first American to capture the gold medal. Kanokogi was also a leader in the movement to set up a world judo championship for women, held in 1980, with Kanokogi as tournament director. She received congratulations from the White House for her work.

When women were barred from judo events at the 1981 National Sports Festival, Kanokogi filed sex discrimination lawsuits against the U.S. Olympic Committee and U.S. Judo, Inc. (a male-run organization that governed the sport). Newspapers publicized the case and the public sided with the women. More money became available to sponsor women's judo events, but Kanokogi had made enemies during her crusade. U.S. Judo, Inc. replaced her as national coach, hiring men to coach women's judo.

Meanwhile, she had achieved the fourth-degree black belt, one of only a few people in the world to hold that honor. She continued to work for wom-

en's judo, urging that it be included as an Olympic event. By 1986, she had attained her fifth-degree black belt, while still teaching classes throughout New York City. Her goal was achieved when judo events were included at the 1988 Olympic Summer Games. Of her experiences, Kanokogi has said, "There's no end to what judo—and all sports—can do for a person. You discover the best in yourself, the best in your competitors. It isn't fair to withhold that from someone just because she's a woman."

References Atkinson, *Women in the Martial Arts* (1983); Smith, "Rumbling with Rusty," *Sports Illustrated*, March 24, 1986, 60–70.

Karate

This popular martial art originated in Japan during the 1400s, inspired by Chinese systems of hand-to-hand combat. It spread throughout Japan, then to other countries during the 1900s. After World War II, various countries developed karate schools and held competitions where practitioners could display their skills and pit themselves against the records others had set.

In karate, athletes use their hands, arms, feet, and legs both as offensive and defensive weapons. They also develop powers of alertness and concentration, as well as courage in the face of danger. Harmony within oneself and with all of nature is stressed, along with the summoning of essential energy in the body, called *ki*.

Increasing numbers of women sought training in the martial arts during the late 1960s, a time when the feminist movement was catching fire. Women sought equality in education, jobs, and other areas of life, rejecting the more passive, helpless role that had often been assigned to them in the past. Karate training offered a chance to gain physical strength and self-reliance. Founded in 1974, Brooklyn Women's Martial Arts, in Brooklyn, New York, is the oldest karate school in the United States for women.

The women's national championships in karate include events in advanced weapons kata, advanced kata, advanced mandatory kata, advanced kumite, advanced kumite 53k (the "k" stands for "kumite"), advanced kumite 60k, and advanced kumite 60-plus kg. Among the top women in this sport was Karen Shepherd, who attained a black belt and was U.S. kata champion. Her specialty was a form of karate called Won hop kuen do. Christine Bannon-Rodriguez, a women's national champion in 1992, hoped to become the first woman to star in karate films. In 1994, Tracey Day of New York City won the advanced kumite and advanced kumite 60k events at the national championships.

In 1994, a young American, Chanese Hall made news in the world of karate when she achieved a brown belt in the sport at age five. Hall, who began the sport at age three, trained both in Japan and in the United States and was expected to earn her black belt by age seven or eight.

References Atkinson, *Women in the Martial Arts* (1983); Hollan, "Five-year-old Girl Is a Brown-Belt Karate Champion," *Jet*, November 21, 1994, 49ff; Karvonen, "Karate Queen: Christine Bannon-Rodriguez Spars Her Way to Stardom," *Women's Sports and Fitness*, October 1992, 50–51; Solomon, "The Power and the Beauty," *Women's Sports and Fitness*, November-December 1992, p. 52ff.

Karolyi, Bela (b. 1931)

Romanian-born Karolyi, a world-famous gymnastics coach, received much attention in 1972 when his team of female Romanian gymnasts took top honors at the Olympics in Montreal, Canada. Nadia Comaneci thrilled spectators with her performance, for which she earned the first perfect 10.0 score ever awarded in an Olympics gymnastic competition. When she had completed her routines, Comaneci had a total of seven 10.0 scores.

After emigrating to the United States, Karolyi and his wife Marta set up a training center in Houston, Texas, for elite gymnasts. Among his most famous students was Mary Lou Retton, who won the Olympic gold medal in gymnastics in 1984. In 1995, another of his gymnasts, 14-year-old Dominique Moceanu, made headlines by becoming the youngest American gymnast ever to win the national all-around title. Moceanu and another of Karolyi's students, Kerri Strug, were part of the gold medal-winning U.S. team at the 1996 Olympics.

Karolyi has been a controversial figure, applauded for his success but criticized for his methods. Critics have said that Karolyi and other elite coaches have trained gymnasts too hard, promoted eating disorders by harassing them to stay extremely thin, and damaged the athletes' self-esteem by being too demanding and intolerant of any mistakes. Some students, such as Retton, have praised Karolyi while others have criticized him. He has responded by pointing out that athletes need rigorous training to develop their skills and need strong discipline in order to win.

After the 1992 Olympics, Karolyi announced he was retiring as a coach. Yet he resumed his work in 1994, taking on some younger teenage students, such as Moceanu, as well as some former champions who were then in their late teens and early twenties.

See also Moceanu, Dominique; Retton, Mary Lou; Strug, Kerri
References Adler and Starr, "Flying High Now,"

Kayaking

Newsweek, August 10, 1992, 20–21; Kantrowitz, "Living with Training," *Newsweek,* August 10, 1992, 24–25; Lundgren, *Mary Lou Retton: Gold Medal Gymnast* (1985); Press, "Old Too Soon, Wise Too Late?" *Newsweek,* August 10, 1992, 22–24; Ryan, *Little Girls in Pretty Boxes* (1995).

Kayaking

In this sport, athletes sit inside a type of enclosed canoe called a kayak, with legs stretched out under the deck. Kayak paddles have a blade on each end, in contrast to Canadian canoe paddles, which have a single blade.

Kayakers compete in national championships, U.S. team trials, various international events, and world championships. Kayak competitions include flatwater sprint races, from 500 yards or 500 meters, on up to marathons that go for 125 miles (200 kilometers). Most marathon courses are rivers, while sprint races are held on calmer waters. There are also whitewater events, both slalom and wildwater racing. The slalom involves racing on rough water through a series of around 25 to 30 gates through which the kayak must pass both upstream and down.

In Olympic kayak sprints, racers move alongside each other in lanes. The K1 race is a singles kayak, while K2 refers to a kayak for two, and so on. The first races for women were held in 1948, with races for single and double kayaks. A four-person event (K4) was added to the games in 1984. As of 1996, there were twelve Olympic flatwater sprint events, with women competing in three of them: single, double, and four-women kayaks in 500-meter races. There were four whitewater slalom events, though women compete in only one, the women's single kayak race.

Women from the Soviet Union and Europe have dominated kayaking events during the 1960s through the 1980s, both at the Olympics and in other international competitions. However, in 1964, the women's team of Francine Fox and Gloriane Perrier won a silver medal in the K2 500-meters at the Olympics, the first U.S. medal since 1952. Marcia Jones earned a bronze medal in the K1 500-meter event.

American Cathy Marino, the U.S. Singles national champion, placed sixth in the world championships in 1983, and Marino and Leslie Klein won the U.S. pairs title that same year. A four-member U.S. team including Klein earned second place in the 1983 world championships. At the 1984 Games, the women's K4 team placed fourth, and at the 1988 Games, Dana Chladek won a bronze medal in the K1 whitewater slalom event.

Kayaking became increasingly popular with women during the late eighties and early nineties. New clubs formed in the United States, and Outward Bound and various camps and outdoor centers offered more instruction courses. The U.S. Canoe and Kayak Team (USCKT) launched a recruitment program to find women ages 17–25 who would become part of the U.S. women's team and take part in competitive events. The United States sent 25 men and women to compete in the 1996 Summer Olympics in Atlanta.

Kentucky Derby

During the early years of the Derby, women did not ride as jockeys, although they sometimes were owners and trainers. The first woman owner of a winner was Mrs. C. E. Durnell, whose horse "Elwood" won the Derby in 1904. The first woman to train a Derby horse was Mary Hirsch, who worked with her trainer-father while she was growing up. She received a license in 1934 from the state of Illinois to train horses and another from New York

State in 1936. Her horse "No Sir" finished thirteenth at the 1937 Derby.

In 1970, a woman jockey rode in the Derby for the first time. Astride "Fathom," Diane Crump finished fifteenth in a field of 17. Fourteen years later, in 1984, another woman jockey, Patricia Cooksey, came in eleventh. Other women would follow the trail laid by these pioneers.

See also Crump, Diane; Jockey, Professional; Krone, Julie

Kerrigan, Nancy (b. 1969)

In 1994, figure skater Nancy Kerrigan managed to recover from an assault that injured her knee two months before the Olympics, then go on to win a silver medal, barely missing the gold. Applauding her courage, coach Evy Scotvold called it "the gutsiest two months I've ever seen."

Nancy Kerrigan grew up in Stoneham, Massachusetts, the daughter of a welder and homemaker. Growing up, Kerrigan sometimes played ice hockey with her two brothers. When it became clear during figure skating classes that she had talent, the family made sacrifices so that Nancy could take private lessons and compete. Although Brenda Kerrigan, Nancy's mother, was almost completely blind as the result of a viral illness, she attended skating events in order to encourage her daughter.

Kerrigan edged up in the rankings and finished third in the world championships in 1991. The next year, she won a second-place silver medal, with that year's Olympic gold medalist, U.S. skater Kristi Yamaguchi, winning the title. Kerrigan was pleasantly surprised to take home the bronze medal when she finished third at the 1992 Olympics, after Yamaguchi. At the 1993 world championships in Prague, Czechoslovakia, how-ever, Kerrigan did not skate her best and finished a disappointing fifth.

On January 6, 1994, two months before the Lillehammer Olympics in Norway, Kerrigan was assaulted in the hall after a practice session in the Detroit rink where the national figure skating championships were being held. Her knee was seriously injured, and after the swelling subsided, she went through weeks of physical rehabilitation to recover her strength and mobility. As she recuperated from her injury and returned to practicing for the Olympics, Kerrigan was applauded for her courage.

Before the Olympics, it was discovered that her assailant was acquainted with the bodyguard of a rival U.S. skater, Tonya Harding, and that Harding's husband may have plotted to injure Kerrigan. For weeks, this dramatic story unfolded on television and in magazines and newspapers. Kerrigan received thousands of gifts, telegrams, and letters from well-wishers, as well as offers to endorse commercial products.

At Hamar, Norway, in the Olympic Village, Kerrigan had to withstand intense scrutiny and the constant presence of people from the news media. She later said, "Everyone would be looking at me like I was some sort of freak." Nonetheless, Kerrigan focused on her skating and was in first place after the short, or "technical," program. Skating a clean, athletic, and graceful program in the finals, Kerrigan was tied in the total point scores with Russian Oksana Baiul. The tie was broken in Baiul's favor since she had a slightly higher score in the marks for artistic impression. Kerrigan has been praised for the long, elegant lines she creates on the ice and for her graceful spiral movements, called "stars." In this one-foot movement, skaters course from one end of the ice to the other while turning and changing their position to build up speed.

Publicity about the Harding-Kerrigan affair increased interest in women's figure skating. CBS-TV later announced that the women's figure skating event at the Olympics had been the sixth-highest-rated television program ever and the third-ranking sports program of all time, after two Super Bowls.

After the Olympics, Kerrigan performed in Disney ice shows, on television specials, and at professional competitions. It was rumored that she would earn about $9 million through various endorsements and professional skating contracts. Kerrigan took part in a 70-city world tour that included world and Olympic champions. She also made several television appearances and hosted the comedy show "Saturday Night Live." At Emmanuel College near Boston, she earned a two-year associate degree in business studies. In 1995, she married her manager, Jerry Solomon.

See also Harding, Tonya
References Smith, *Figure Skating: A Celebration* (1994); "Getting Her Gold," *People Weekly*, May 3, 1995, 139; Longman, "Kerrigan Triumphs in Short Program," *New York Times*, February 24, 1994, 49; Longman, "Baiul Edges Kerrigan in a Narrow Decision to Capture Gold Medal," *New York Times*, February 26, 1994, 1ff; Starr, "Heartwarmer: Women's Figure Skating Competition, Olympics 1994: Lillehammer," *Newsweek*, March 7, 1994, 58; Swift, "Silver Belle," *Sports Illustrated*, March 7, 1994, 20.

King, Betsy (b. 1955)

In 1992, Elizabeth (Betsy) King became the first woman in the history of the Ladies Professional Golf Association (LPGA) to score under 70 for four rounds of golf in a major tournament.

A resident of Scottsdale, Arizona, King joined the professional golf tour at age 21, but did not win her first tournament until 1984. That year, King won three events and was the top money-winner. She ranked second among women golfers in all-time earnings, with more than $4.5 million in prizes. During her first 15 years on the LPGA tour, she was named Player of the Year twice and won 25 tournaments, including the Dinah Shore (1987, 1990) and the U.S. Open (1989, 1990). She was known for her wide-arcing swing, with a high follow-through, that some said was unattractive. King tried other kinds of swings and grips but found she had less power. She resumed her unique style and, in 1992, at age 36, King shot her four rounds with scores under 70 for a record-breaking win at the LPGA tournament at the Bethesda (Maryland) Country Club. She won by 11 strokes. In 1993, King was again named Player of the Year and was the leading money-earner on the LPGA tour. She won 29 tournaments during that season.

King, Billie Jean (b. 1943)

King once said, "The first day I hit a tennis ball, I knew what I wanted. It has made my life." Born on November 22, 1942, in Long Beach, California, Billie Jean Moffitt was the daughter of a fireman and a homemaker. She enjoyed team sports, especially softball, and sometimes joined her younger brother Randy and his friends. Randy Moffitt later became a professional baseball player who pitched for the San Francisco Giants.

Told that just three sports were suitable for girls—golf, swimming, and tennis—King said she would try tennis. She took lessons at park programs throughout the city, making rapid progress by practicing after school and on weekends. With $8 earned from doing odd jobs around the neighborhood, she bought her first tennis racket. Later, King would say, "Throughout my adolescence, I found a subtle social pressure against being an athlete."

At age 11, she won a tournament, defeating a college junior. She also experienced the sting of rejection and the sense of being different from more affluent players. After a match held at a Los Angeles Country Club, a photographer motioned King out of a group picture because she was not "dressed properly." It was her custom to wear white shorts and a white shirt rather than a tennis dress. In addition, she had less-expensive equipment than her competitors and brought her own brown-bag meals, while they bought the food sold at tournaments.

An aggressive player who liked to come to the net, King had to learn control and patience to improve her game against patient backcourt players. She ranked nineteenth among U.S. women in 1959, and tennis great Alice Marble became her coach. In 1961, Billie Jean went to Wimbledon but lost in the second round. However, she and her partner Karen Hantze became the youngest pair ever to win the women's doubles title at the tournament. When she returned the next year, King upset champion Margaret Smith (later Margaret Court) in the second round. They would meet again the next year, this time in the finals where Smith would win.

In the meantime, Billie Jean had enrolled in college in Los Angeles and was dating law student Larry King. With little time to practice, her tennis suffered. King recommitted herself to the game, spending 1964 in Australia with coach Mervyn Rose. She ran, practiced, and learned to think more about strategy during a game. By the end of 1965, now married, Billie Jean King was ranked the number one woman tennis player in

the United States for the first of seven times. Quick and nimble, King could hit any kind of shot and had a strong will to win. She played a serve-and-volley game, moving in to the net to volley (hit the ball before it bounced) whenever possible.

In 1966, she won the singles, doubles, and mixed doubles events at the United States Lawn Tennis Association (USLTA) indoor competition. She won the South African Open and Wimbledon, as well as leading the U.S. Wightman Cup team to a victory over the British team. In 1967, she won at Wimbledon again and added a U.S. Open title to her credits. That year, she swept all three titles—singles, doubles, and mixed doubles—at both Wimbledon and the U.S. national championships at Forest Hills, New York.

King turned professional in 1968, and gained a new Grand Slam title, the Australian Open. A demonstrative athlete, during the game she could be heard giving herself directions or criticism or exclaiming "Nuts!" when she missed a shot. Although some critics said King had a hard-court rather than a clay-court game, she also won major clay court titles—the Italian Open in 1970 and the German in 1971.

More than anyone else, King brought recognition to women tennis players and to all women athletes. She was the first woman to earn more than $100,000 in prize money in a year (1971). Eventually, her winnings would total close to $2 million. King was instrumental in developing the Virginia Slims tournaments, becoming the first player to sign up on the Slims tour. In 1973, she was named Athlete of the Year by the Associated Press.

That same year, King played in a celebrated tennis match called the Battle of the Sexes against Bobby Riggs, a former men's champion now in his fifties. Riggs had boasted that he could defeat top women players, and he did defeat Grand Slam winner, Australian Margaret Smith Court. But King proved Riggs—and a majority of sportscasters—wrong, in a match that lasted 2 hours and 5 minutes. At the Houston Astrodome, 30,472 spectators saw the match while another 50 million watched on television.

In 1974 King began appearing on television to discuss sports and commentate at tennis events. She and husband Larry King, an attorney who served as her business manager, started a magazine called *WomenSports* and helped to found World Team Tennis (WTT). In 1974 King became the first woman to coach a professional team that included male athletes. She was player-coach for the Philadelphia Freedoms, one of the WTT teams. She also played for the New York Apples, which won the WTT titles in 1976 and 1977. King also took time to coach new players and to give lessons in poor areas of cities and public courts. With swimming champion and gold medalist Donna de Varona, she founded the Women's Sports Foundation, an organization devoted to promoting equal opportunities for women in sports and recognizing women's achievements in sports.

King won 29 Slims titles between 1970 and 1977 and was an All-Star in the World Team Tennis match three times. In 1977, *Harper's Bazaar* placed her on its list of the "10 Most Powerful Women in America." As of 1979, her singles titles included six Wimbledons, four U.S. Opens, and one each of the Australian, Italian, and French opens. At Wimbledon, she had also amassed nine doubles titles and four mixed doubles. She was named Associated Press Woman Athlete of the Year twice (1967 and 1973); Sportsperson of the Year by *Sports Illustrated* in 1972; and *Time* Woman of the Year in 1976.

Recurrent knee problems bothered King during her mid-thirties, making singles play more difficult. Yet she still won the U.S. women's doubles title in 1980 with Martina Navratilova. King played her last professional match in 1983 at Wimbledon, where she lost in the semifinals to Andrea Jaeger. Her career titles included 67 professional and 37 amateur singles championships. She was voted into the International Tennis Hall of Fame in 1987.

See also Battle of the Sexes; Grand Slam; Jaeger, Andrea; Marble, Alice; Virginia Slims; Women's Sports Foundation; World Team Tennis
References Dickey, *Champs and Chumps: An Insider's Look at Today's Sports Heroes* (1976); King, *Billie Jean* (1982); Olsen, *The Lady of the Court* (1974); Stambler, *Women in Sports* (1975); Sullivan, *Great Lives: Sports* (1988); Sullivan, *Queens of the Court* (1974).

King, Micki (b. 1944)

Champion diver King won the gold medal for springboard diving at the 1972 Olympics. A native of Pontiac, Michigan, Maxine Joyce "Micki" King excelled at figure skating and other winter sports. But she also loved to swim and began diving at age 10. She did not study diving much until her mid teens, entering her first springboard competition at age 15.

In the position of goalie, she played water polo at the University of Michigan and was an All American twice, in 1962 and 1963. King also joined the diving team, where a coach noticed her potential. She began to train seriously in both springboard and platform diving, competing against other Big Ten university teams. By her sophomore year, she was the team's leading diver and impressed judges around the country with her technique and ability to perform dives that had never been completed successfully in

Micki King, a 28-year-old captain in the U.S. Air Force, won gold in the women's Olympic spring-board competition, pictured here, in 1972.

competition before. In 1966, her junior year, she won the indoor platform diving title from the Amateur Athletic Union (AAU).

After graduation, King joined the Air Force and became a second lieutenant in 1966. As an officer with the Reserve Officer Training Corps at the University of Michigan, she was able to train with her coach, Don Kimball, during her free time. With her superb form and mastery of various intricate dives, King easily made the U.S. Olympic team in 1968 and was expected to win a medal. In Mexico City, she led the field of mostly younger divers by a good margin until the second-to-the-last dive. As she sprang from the board to do the difficult reverse 1½ layout dive, King struck her left forearm on the board and sensed that it was broken. In great

pain, she completed her final dive but had slipped to fourth place.

Soon King was reassigned to the Los Angeles Air Force Station. She considered retiring from competitive diving but the Air Force asked her to compete in the World Military Games in Pescora, Italy. There King, the only woman competing, won third place in platform diving. She went on to compete in the Pan American Games and in Amateur Athletic Union (AAU) meets, winning the 1970 AAU outdoor diving crown. Promoted to captain, King served in the athletic department at the Air Force Academy in Colorado, becoming the first woman ever to hold an academic position at a U.S. military academy. Once again, in 1972, King earned a place on the Olympic team. In Munich, she completed the required and optional dives of the springboard event without a problem. Her fine performance brought her the gold medal that had eluded her in Mexico City. At age 27, King was older by ten years than the silver medalist. In 1975, King competed with other top women athletes in the Superstar event, cosponsored by the magazines *Ladies Home Journal* and *WomenSports*. The competition, which included ten different sports events, would determine who would have the title Ms. Superstar. King came in third among the competitors, showing her all-around athletic ability.

Married to Jim Hogue, who was also an Air Force officer, she had reached the rank of colonel and commander of the Air Force ROTC at the University of Kentucky by 1992. While pursuing her military career, she served as president of United States Diving, Inc., the governing body of Olympic diving. The mother of two, Micki King Hogue was active with the Boy and Girl Scouts programs and enjoyed playing tennis and other sports with her family.

References: Nelson, *Are We Winning Yet?* (1991); Stambler, *Women in Sports: The Long Hard Climb* (1975); "Olympic Gold Still Shining," *Good Housekeeping*, February 1992, 128ff.

Klein, Kit (See Speed Skating)

Kopsky, Doris

In 1937 Kopsky became the first woman champion of the National Amateur Bicycle Association. The tournament, held that year in Buffalo, New York, covered a distance of 1 mile. New Jersey–native Kopsky finished the race in 4 minutes and 22.4 seconds.

See also Cycling

Krone, Julie (b. 1963)

Krone, born July 24, 1963, in Benton Harbor, Michigan, has won more than 2,000 horse races. Julianne Louise Krone grew up on a horse farm in Eau Claire, Michigan, the daughter of a prize-winning show rider. Young Julie followed in her mother Judi Krone's footsteps, starting to ride at age two and entering shows with her horse Daisy at age five. In her 1995 autobiography, Krone recalled that although people made fun of her small size, she was "as athletic and powerful as the boys." As a teenager, she decided to become a jockey, despite the scornful response of her classmates. Most people thought the only suitable role for girls on a race track was to exercise the horses. By age 15, she had won 20 races at local fairs. She left high school to live with her grandparents in Florida and begin her career.

Krone worked her way from groom to jockey apprentice to professional. She got a job exercising and caring for horses at Churchill Downs, in Kentucky, then at Tampa Bay Downs in Florida. A trainer named Jerry Pace helped her get her first jobs riding in races nearby, and Krone won some of them. Although many male jockeys, trainers, and horse owners harassed her and told her she could never become a top jockey, from 1978 to 1982, Krone continued to pursue that goal. During a 1981 race at a Maryland track, she was thrown and spent two months in bed recuperating from a broken back.

Returning to racing, Krone could not seem to win. She persisted and worked her way back to achieve a ranking of fourth-best jockey in the United States. Still, male jockeys did not accept her, and some tried to hurt her during races by distracting her horse or pulling on her reins, a foul that can disqualify a jockey. As a jockey, Krone did not hesitate to confront men whom she felt were trying to hold her back. She was known as a quick-tempered person and would en-

Jockey Julie Krone gives her horse, "Colonial Affair," a pat after crossing the finish line, winning the Belmont Stakes in 1993.

gage in physical fights, once with a male jockey.

Krone accomplished a remarkable feat in 1987 when she won six races in one day at Monmouth race track and five at the Meadowlands, both in New Jersey. In both cases, she tied track records. In 1987, 1988, and 1989, she won the Meadowlands track riding title. By 1988, Krone had won more races than any woman in history. But 1989 brought another dangerous spill when her horse fell onto the track at the Meadowlands. Her left arm was pulled from its socket, necessitating surgery to place a steel plate and seven screws in her arm and shoulder. For almost nine months, she was unable to race. Nonetheless, her record at the Meadowlands for that fall was 205 races with

58 wins and money prizes 113 times. She was ranked third among all jockeys, male and female, in 1989. On major tracks, she set records, winning four races in one day at Aqueduct, five in one day at the Meadowlands, and six in one day at Monmouth Park.

In June 1993, Krone won the Belmont Stakes on the horse "Colonial Affair." This was another first, since no woman had ever won any of the U.S. Triple Crown races, which include the Belmont, Preakness, and Kentucky Derby. At that point, midyear, she ranked third in victories and sixth in prize money among all jockeys. The year 1993, though, had its upsets, including a near-fatal fall from her horse at a race held in Saratoga, New York. She suffered a shattered ankle and cardiac contusion, the result of being hit in the chest by the 1,200-pound horse.

Early in 1995, the Aqueduct and Gulfstream racetracks opened their joint season with "A Salute to Julie Krone" day. Krone had returned to racing just two months after 13 screws were removed from an injured ankle. That year, Krone again made a trip to the winner's circle at Belmont Park, after her winning ride on "Lite the Fuse," a four-year-old bay colt bred by trainer Richard Dutrow, with whom she had worked for more than ten years. By 1995, Krone had more wins (more than 2,300) and had earned more prize money (more than $30 million) than any female jockey in history.

References Krone, *Riding for My Life* (1995); "Trainer, Krone, Win Together," *New York Times*, June 26, 1995, C4.

Kung Fu

Kung fu, which means task or exercise in Chinese, refers to a group of martial arts. Various skills, such as proper breathing, fitness, nutrition, and care of the body are taught as part of kung fu. It combines physical, mental, and spiritual concepts and is taught by kung fu masters.

One of the best known of the kung fu arts is t'ai chi chuan, which emphasizes smooth, steady movements and slow, deep breathing. T'ai chi artists learn defensive movements based on the ability to sense what is called the "flow of energy" in one's opponent, as well as offensive techniques. Originating in China, kung fu slowly spread from Buddhist communities to selected outsiders, then to other lands.

Until the 1960s, schools of kung fu in the United States were limited to people of Chinese descent. In 1965, LaVerne Bates, an expert practitioner of kung fu, opened the first school for women in the United States, called the LaVerne Bates Women's Kung Fu Studio.

Kusner, Kathy (b. 1940)

Born in Florida and raised in Virginia in horse country, young Kathryn Kusner rode her own pony as a child, taking riding lessons and entering show and ring events. To pay for lessons, she worked in stables and as a groom, then learned to train horses. Kusner became an expert equestrian, able to ride, show, and jump horses. Dealers in Virginia hired teenage Kusner to ride their horses in various shows and display the horses to advantage to potential buyers. At age 18, she set a new women's jumping record at an equestrian event when her horse cleared 7 feet 3 inches. Kusner later said that in order to make a great jump, a rider must "arrange it so that the horse arrives at the fence just right. She has to be on his stride, with the right balance and momentum to jump."

Kusner joined the U.S. Olympic team in 1961 as its leading dressage rider. She placed second in the Women's World Championship of 1965. In 1966, she won numerous European classes, including her second International Grand Prix at Dublin. It was the first time a rider had won the Dublin event twice in a row on the same horse. Kusner won most of the honors at the National Horse Show in Madison Square Garden, competing with top riders from other countries. She won the Women's European Championship in 1967, the first time an American had done so, and was respected as one of the world's finest equestrians.

Since Kusner also loved riding horses fast around local tracks, in 1967, she decided to compete in flat thoroughbred racing events as a jockey. When the Maryland Racing Commission denied her ap-

Perhaps one of the world's best equestriennes, Kathy Kusner won numerous titles, including the Women's European Championship in 1967, an American first.

plication for a jockey's license, Kusner began a legal battle, based primarily on the 1964 Civil Rights Act, which banned discrimination on the basis of sex, race, national origin, or religion. Kusner said, "Horse riding is more a game of technique and skill than strength. It's the same as playing chess with men. . . ." After a year, a court ruled that she had been the victim of sex discrimination. Kusner thus became the first woman to receive a jockey's license. However, an injury kept her from competing as the first woman jockey; that distinction went to Diane Crump.

In 1969, Kusner won a race in Pennsylvania. While pursuing professional racing, she continued to compete in amateur equestrian events. In 1968, 1972, and 1976, she was part of the U.S. Olympic team and won a silver individual medal at the 1972 Munich Games. In the years after 1976, she competed less and devoted herself to teaching others riding and equestrian techniques. Kusner gave riding demonstrations and lectures throughout the United States.

See also Crump, Diane; Dressage; Equestrian Events

References Hollander, *100 Greatest Women in Sports* (1976); McMane and Wolf, eds., *The Worst Day I Ever Had* (1991); Smith, "She Who Laughs," *Sports Illustrated*, March 23, 1989, 88.

Kwan, Michelle (b. 1980)

This gifted figure-skater passed the tests that qualified her as a senior when she was only 12 years old and competed at the world senior ladies' championship the next year. Kwan began skating at age five, taking lessons in a shopping mall rink. She mastered difficult jumps and was able to perform seven triples in the space of 6 minutes. By 1994 she had won the world junior title. She was able to do triple-Lutz combinations at this young age, and hours of ballet training gave her grace on the ice.

In 1994 and 1995, Kwan won silver medals at the U.S. national championships. Moving on to the 1995 world ladies' figure skating contest, she skated a brilliant freestyle program that earned her fourth place among champions from around the world. By the time Kwan was 15 years old, people commented on the increasing ease, maturity, and strength in her skating. Kwan said that she was working "to reach out to the audience more." She appeared at pro-am events (those that include professionals and amateurs) in the United States and abroad, as well as in the Nations Cup competition held in Germany in November 1995. That year, she earned fourth place in the ladies world competition. At the national championships held in San Diego in January 1996, Kwan won her first senior ladies' title then went on to win the world ladies' title that year.

References Longman, "Kwan, in a Rush to Adulthood, Is Given a Makeover at Age 15," *New York Times*, October 27, 1995, B17; Neill, "In the Wings Waits Rising Star Michelle Kwan," *People Weekly*, February 14, 1994, 35

LPGA Hall of Fame

This hall of fame for women golfers was founded at the annual meeting of the Ladies Professional Golf Association (LPGA) in 1967. The hall, once located in Corpus Christi, Texas, now in Daytona Beach, Florida, includes photographs, awards, golf memorabilia, and equipment, along with information about important women players and an exhibit detailing the history of women in golf. Among the outstanding women golfers who have been elected to the hall are Glenna Collett Vare, Patty Berg, Betty Jameson, Louise Suggs, Babe Didrikson Zaharias, and Mickey Wright.

Lacrosse

Perhaps the oldest sport in North America, this field game, played with a ball and special netted stick (or racket), originated with the Iroquois Indians of the St. Lawrence Valley. Their version, called *baggataway* ("little brother of war") involved fierce competition meant to prepare warriors for combat. As many as 1,000 players gathered on the field in the morning and played, nonstop, until one team scored 100 goals or the sun set, whichever came first. Seeing the stick used in the game, a French missionary priest thought it resembled a cross and gave it the name that is still used today.

Until the early 1900s, women did not play organized lacrosse. As women's teams were set up, different rules were developed for female players. They limited body contact and other rough aspects of the men's game. Women were not permitted to hold or block their opponents. In 1926, a women's college in Baltimore, Maryland, sponsored the first official lacrosse game played by women. Many American women and those in other countries took up the sport in the decades that followed.

In modern lacrosse, two teams vie for points, scored when a team sends a ball past the opposing goalkeeper into the opponents' goal or net. The ball, usually made of white rubber, measures about 8 inches around. Fields measure between 60 to 70 yards (55 to 64 meters) wide and 110 yards (100 meters) long. The women's version of lacrosse is still slightly different than that played by men's teams. Each side has 12 players (6 attack and 6 defensive), instead of 10. Women's teams usually play two 25-minute-long halves instead of the 60-minute game divided into quarters played by American men's teams. Substitutions and body-checking are also banned in women's lacrosse.

In 1994, the U.S. women's lacrosse team won the world championship.

References Guard, "Rallied," *Sports Illustrated*, May 25, 1995, 96; Pratt and Benagh, *The Official Encyclopedia of Sports* (1964); Editors of *Sports Illustrated*, *Sports Illustrated 1996 Sports Almanac*.

Ladewig, Marion (b. 1914)

Champion bowler Marion Van Oosten Ladewig grew up in Grand Rapids,

Michigan, where she often played baseball with her brother. Later she was a top player on local girls' and women's softball teams. Shortly after finishing high school, she became interested in bowling, saying that after one game, "I was hooked on the sport." Ladewig analyzed techniques while working as a cashier in a bowling alley. The proprietor at the alley had noticed her strong arm and told her she would probably excel at bowling. He helped to coach her and asked top male bowlers at the center to work with her, so that Ladewig was practicing every day.

With fellow bowlers, Ladewig formed a team called the Fanatoriums. They began to win local championships, then competed in national events. In 1949, Ladewig won the first Bowling Proprietors Association of America (BPAA) Women's All-Star title, which she won again in 1950 (with a 198-point average) and in 1951. She would win this title again in 1955.

At the 1952 BPAA tournament Ladewig won with an excellent average score of 247.5 per game. Between 1949 and 1963, she garnered eight All Star Championships, including one at age 48. She especially enjoyed the 1951 All Star competition, during which she won the women's crown and outscored 160 men as well. Appearing at tournaments all over the world, Ladewig was known for her well-groomed appearance as well as her bowling skill. People said that she brought glamour to the sport.

In newspaper columns, Ladewig shared her bowling tips, also serving as a consultant to a sportswear company and to the Brunswick Corporation, a manufacturer of bowling equipment. At age 50, now a grandmother, Marion Ladewig retired from professional competition. In her farewell appearance, she won the World Invitational Tournament title.

References Hollander, *American Women in Sports* (1976); Berke, *Lincoln Library of Sports Champions*, vol. 10 (1989); Weiskopf, *The Perfect Game: The World of Bowling* (1978).

Ladies Professional Bowlers Tour
(**See** Bowling)

Ladies Professional Golf Association (LPGA)

Established in 1948, the LPGA is the ruling body for women's golf. The LPGA has sponsored numerous tournaments, beginning with the annual Woman's Open (1948 to 1953), now conducted by the United States Golf Association (USGA). It also founded and operates the LPGA Hall of Fame.

In addition, the LPGA honors major women golfers by dispensing several important awards, including its LPGA Player of the Year award (called the Virginia C. Lord award), established in 1966. This cash prize is given to the player with the most outstanding and consistent playing record during the current tour year. A player must finish in the first five positions of official LPGA events in order to be considered for Player of the Year. The LPGA Teacher of the Year award is given to the woman who has best exemplified the profession of golfing during the past year.

See also Gibson, Althea; Golf; Vare Trophy
References LPGA, *LPGA Media Guide (1996)*.

Lahti, Lisa (**See** Triathlon)

Lawrence, Andrea Mead (b. 1932)

The first skier to win two gold medals at the Winter Olympics, Andrea Mead was already skiing by age four at the ski resort her parents operated in Pico Peak, Vermont. She studied skiing with a Swiss instructor her parents had hired to give lessons to their guests. At age 11, Mead was good enough to compete against adults. She won second place in the Women's Eastern Slalom Championship held at Pico Peak in 1944.

Mead was a member of the U.S. Olympic ski team that went to St. Moritz, Switzerland, in 1948 and finished the slalom event in eighth place. In 1952, now married to Olympic skier Dave Lawrence, she went to the Winter Games in Oslo, Norway. Mead Lawrence impressed people with her sheer love for the sport, and though the giant slalom course was patchy on the day of the race, she skied to victory. In the special slalom race, she fell halfway down her first run on the perilous course. The Associated Press later reported that she "quickly picked herself up and continued the run with a wild recklessness that brought cheers from the crowd." On her next run, she got off to a swift start. With quick-poled turns, she navigated 49 gates to reach the end of the course. Her total time for the run was 2 minutes, 10.6 seconds—good enough to win her second gold medal.

Before the 1956 Games, Mead Lawrence had three children. Her best run there was a fourth-place finish. In 1960, her husband coached the U.S. ski team and she managed it. She skated with the Olympic torch to light the flame that year in Squaw Valley, California. After her divorce in 1967, Mead Lawrence supported the family as a ski instructor at resorts near her home in the Mammoth Lakes region of California. Later, she devoted her time to community service projects and environmental projects and served in local government. She also wrote a book about skiing and mountain climbing called *A Practice of Mountains*.

References Condon, *Great Women Athletes of the Twentieth Century* (1991); Hollander, *100 Greatest Women in Sports* (1976); Lawrence, *A Practice of Mountains*.

Lawrence, Janice (b. 1962)

Born in Lucedale, Mississippi, Lawrence attended Louisiana Tech University, where she was a star center-forward on the basketball team. During her senior year (1983–1984), she averaged 20.7 points and 9 rebounds a game, as well as leading the team in steals. She was part of the gold-medal U.S. team at the Pan American Games and the second-place U.S. World University Games team. Her college team, which had reached the finals every year in the nationals, also won that title and Lawrence was named Most Valuable Player at the tournament. That year, she won the Wade Trophy.

Lawrence went on to play with the U.S. women's team at the 1984 Olympics in Los Angeles, helping her team bring home the gold medal. Upon graduation, Lawrence was the first choice of teams in the Women's American Basketball Association and went to play with the New York team.

See also Wade Trophy
Reference Markel and Brooks, *For the Record: Women in Sports* (1985).

Lewis, Carol (b. 1963)

Lewis, born and raised in Willingboro, New Jersey, was part of an athletic family that included brother Carl, later an Olympic gold medalist in track and field. In some of their childhood races, Carol beat Carl to the finish line. Lewis's parents, both high school teachers, had also been successful in track and field during their high school and college years. They encouraged their children to excel both at academics and in sports and to set high standards for themselves as individuals. In 1980, Carol Lewis received the Dial Award, which is given annually by the Dial Corporation to one male and one female national high school athlete-scholar.

Lewis became a champion long-jumper, and in 1984, she set an American indoor long-jump record of 22 feet, 2.25 inches. She was also outdoor long-jump champion in 1982 and 1983, achieving a best outdoor jump of 22 feet, 10.5 inches. She won third place in the 1983 world championships in Helsinki, Finland. Besides the long jump, Lewis excelled in shot put, hurdles, and high jump competition. She missed her chance to compete in the 1980 Olympics, which were boycotted by the United States, but in 1984 she competed in Los Angeles, placing ninth with the long jump that measured 21 feet, 1.25 inches.

References "Bound for Glory," *Newsweek,* July 6, 1992, 19–26; Carlson and Fogarty, *Tales of Gold* (1977); Markel and Brooks, *For the Record: Women in Sports* (1985).

Lieberman, Nancy (b. 1958)

Born on July 1, 1958, Nancy Lieberman grew up playing basketball on the playgrounds of Brooklyn and Harlem in New York City. She went on to play basketball for her public school in Far Rockaway, Queens. At age 16, she became the youngest member of the 1976 Olympic basketball team, which won a silver medal in Montreal, Canada. When Lieberman was a senior in high school, more than 70 colleges and universities offered her athletic scholarships. At Old Dominion University in Norfolk, Virginia, Lieberman played forward and point guard on the women's basketball team. The team won the national collegiate championships in 1979 and 1980, and both years, Lieberman won the Wade Trophy, the second woman to win

that award. In 1979, she also won the Broderick Cup, given to the outstanding woman collegiate basketball player.

At the 1979 Pan American Games, Lieberman helped the U.S. team to a silver medal. After graduating from college in 1980, she became the first draft choice of the Dallas Diamonds and played with them during the final season of the Women's Basketball League. Lieberman became a strong advocate of a professional basketball league for women. The new Women's American Basketball Association was formed in 1984, and Dallas once again made her its first pick. Three years later, Lieberman decided to play with the Washington Generals, a touring men's basketball team that competes against the Harlem Globetrotters. She also played for the Springfield Fame, a Massachusetts men's team, becoming the first woman to play in a men's professional league. In one memorable game, Lieberman scored ten points, helping her team to defeat the Westchester Golden Apples, 135–115.

During the 1980s and 1990s, Lieberman continued as a strong supporter of women athletes in various fields, helping to organize team sports, and providing commentary on television. In 1996, Nancy Lieberman Cline, now married, was inducted into the Basketball Hall of Fame.

See also Harlem Globetrotters; Wade Trophy; Women's Basketball League
References Anderson, *The Story of Basketball* (1988); Guttman, *Women's Sport: A History* (1991); Sullivan, *Better Basketball for Girls* (1978).

Lind, Joan (See Rowing)

Lipinski, Tara (b. 1982)

At age 12, in 1994, Lipinski became the youngest figure skater to win at the Olympic Sports Festival, a competition for developing U.S. athletes. Later that year, in November, she came in fourth at the junior world championships in Budapest, Hungary.

Like other champions, Tara started skating at an early age. At age 11, she began training at the University of Delaware ice arena, an elite American training center. By then, she had quit school and begun working with a tutor in order to skate several hours a day and travel to contests. She took tests at the local public school and was able to maintain an A average while completing five 45-minute practice sessions a day. By age 12, Lipinski was impressing people with her triple jumps, some of which the top women figure skaters had not been able to do at such a young age. In 1994, her goal firmly in mind, Lipinski said, "I want to go to the Olympics and win." The skater was young enough to compete in more than one Olympics: the 1998 Winter Games (in Nagano, Japan) and the 2002 Olympics.

In 1994, Lipinski moved closer toward her goal by placing fourth in the world junior championships. In February 1995, she came in second in the U.S. junior championships, where 15-year-old Sydne Vogel of Alaska was the winner. After watching Lipinski's short program in that competition, her coach, Jeff Di Gregorio, said, "That was the best I've ever seen her skate." Lipinski performed with world class skaters at exhibition matches during 1995.

Competing with the senior ladies' division for the first time at the national championships in January 1996, Lipinski earned third place and a chance to compete at the world figure skating championships later that year.

References Longman, "Prodigy's Dream Has a Price," *New York Times*, October 11, 1994, B-9, B-12;

Longman, "Lipinski, 12, Shows the Form Marking Her As a Rising Star," *New York Times*, February 8, 1995, B12.

Little League

In 1939 Karl Stotz of Williamsport, Pennsylvania, came up with the idea of baseball teams for boys aged 8 to 12, where they would wear uniforms, work with coaches, and compete among themselves. By 1946, there were 12 such organized groups, known as "Little Leagues," as opposed to the Big Leagues of men's professional baseball. Within seven years, there were nearly 3,000 leagues. Little League became so popular that it was granted a congressional charter that was signed into law in 1964.

The Little League charter contained a "no girls" clause, and the words in the charter referred only to boys. During the late 1960s and early 1970s, Maria Pepe and numerous girls around the United States tried to join Little League programs, and some filed lawsuits when they were denied the opportunity to try out for the teams. A number of coaches threatened to quit if girls were permitted on the teams. Experts were asked to study the issue of whether girls were physically capable of taking part.

The first law permitting girls to play on Little League baseball teams was passed in New Jersey in 1974. A national directive, signed by President Gerald R. Ford, made this policy official throughout the United States, and the league's charter was changed to read "young people" rather than "boys." References to boys and men were replaced with gender-neutral words. Girls trying out for the teams were supposed to be judged according to the same standards as the boys.

Since that time, most towns and cities have developed separate programs for boys and girls, with each competing against teams of the same gender. Many girls also participate in the Little League softball program, which was established in 1973. Nearly 200,000 youngsters were playing on these teams by the 1990s, in three divisions: ages 8–12; ages 13–15; ages 16–18. Ten-player girls' teams play in the younger divisions, while the seniors (16–18) play on teams of nine and are allowed to slide, steal bases, and bunt.

The number of teams continued to grow so that by the 1980s, leagues had been added for young people in the 9–12 and 13–15 age groups. There were nearly 2,000 softball leagues for different age groups, too. Women could be found coaching both girls' and boys' teams. By 1990, about 2.5 million young people in 25 countries around the world were playing on Little League teams. The international headquarters for the league is in Williamsport, Pennsylvania, location of the annual Little League World Series games. The grounds also hold a Little League museum, dedicated in 1982.

See also Croteau, Julie; Lotsey, Nancy

Lloyd Vince, Marion (1906–1969)

Fencing champion Lloyd Vince started to fence in 1925 and became nationally ranked in her sport two years later. Lloyd Vince competed with the U.S. team at three Olympics (1928, 1932, 1936) and was U.S. women's champion in 1928 and 1932. In her second appearance at the Olympics, in 1932, Lloyd Vince became the first American woman ever to place high enough (ninth) to compete in the final events.

Lloyd Vince's husband Joseph Vince was also a champion fencer. He directed the prestigious Salle Vince school and Salle Vince fencing team, of which Lloyd

Vince was a member, competing in nine of the ten consecutive national championships won by the club in the 1920s and 1930s. Both Vinces were inducted into the Helms Hall of Fame. The Marion Lloyd Vince Trophy is awarded annually by the Amateur Fencing League of America to the winner of the national under-19 title.

Logan, Karen (b. 1950)

An all-around athlete during the 1970s, basketball star Karen Logan played with the Red Heads, a women's team that performed exhibition games against all-male teams. The Red Heads, which had been formed in 1936 as the All-American World's Champion Girls Basketball Club, reorganized in 1971 under a new name, with new rules. That year, the team won 169 games. Known for their red or red-dyed hair, the players perfected the kind of humorous and acrobatic shots made famous by the Harlem Globetrotters.

Logan succeeded in several sports, becoming the top singles tennis player on her team at Pepperdine College in Malibu, California. She was also a superb runner, but a pulled tendon prevented her from trying out for the U.S. Olympic team in 1968.

In 1975, she came in second in a grueling ten-event sports competition for women called the Superstars. The event took place in Rotonda, Florida, and Logan competed in the bicycling, bowling, hurdling, running, swimming, tennis, throwing, rowing, and two other events. (She was not allowed to compete in the basketball event, since each athlete was excluded from her primary sport.)

After the Superstars, Logan became a professional basketball player in the new Women's Basketball League, joining the Indianapolis-based Pink Panthers. She was among the nation's top players, often playing against men. She scored an average of 23 points a game. This outstanding player inspired many girls across America to take up the sport of basketball.

Reference Hollander, *American Women in Sports* (1972).

Lopez, Nancy (b. 1957)

One of the most popular and successful women ever to play golf, Lopez was born to Mexican-American parents, in Torrance, California, then raised in Roswell, New Mexico. She began to golf at the age of eight, encouraged by her golf-loving parents, and later said that her father had given her one of the best pieces of advice she had ever received: "Come up real slow, come up real high, extend real far and hit the ball right in the sweet spot, and hit it right in the middle of the fairway and then keep hitting it until you hit it into the hole."

Despite her petite size (5 feet 4 inches), Lopez became a forceful hitter. She won the women's amateur championship of New Mexico when she was only 12 years old. Her score of 75 set a record for women players on that course. Starting in 1972, she went on to win the U.S. Junior Girls and Western Junior Girls Championships for three years straight. Lopez added the Mexican Amateur crown in 1975 and attended Tulsa University on a golf scholarship. She won second place in the U.S. Women's Open in 1976 and captured the National Collegiate title that same year.

Turning professional late in 1976, Lopez moved quickly up the rankings. In 1978, she became the first golfer to win both the Rookie Player and Golfer of the Year titles. She won five straight LPGA tournaments that year, the first woman ever to do so. Her 1978 record included 9 wins out of 29 tournaments entered, including the Ladies Professional Golf Association (LPGA) championship. Winning a total of $189,814 made her the top prize-winner on the women's circuit and the first rookie golfer of either sex to win so much prize money. The Associated Press named Lopez "Female Athlete of the Year," and she won the Vare Trophy.

Her 1979 performance was also outstanding, as Lopez won 8 of the 19 tournaments she entered, setting an LPGA stroke-per-round average of 71.20. Again, the LPGA named her "Golfer of the Year." After Lopez married major-league ballplayer Ray Knight in 1982, she juggled family commitments with her golfing career, at times taking her children on the tour with her. By 1983, Lopez, age 26, had exceeded $1 million in earnings. Two years later, she won the LPGA tournament, a victory she repeated in 1988 for a total of four LPGA wins, all on different courses. Sportswriters marveled at her 1985 average of 70.73 for 93 rounds of golf. When she won the Henredon Classic in 1985, her score—268 for 72 holes—was the lowest ever recorded on the tour.

Lopez was inducted into the Ladies Professional Golf Hall of Fame in 1987 and is also in the World Golf Hall of Fame. The next year, she was named LPGA Player of the Year for the fourth time. In 1989, she won her third LPGA title. By 1993, Lopez ranked fourth among women players for career earnings.

See also Vare Trophy

References Gutman, *More Modern Women Superstars* (1979); LPGA, *LPGA 1996 Player Guide.*

Lotsey, Nancy (b. 1955)

In 1963, at age eight, Lotsey became the first girl ever to play organized baseball in competition with boys. A baseball lover,

Nancy Lopez keeps her eye on the ball as she blasts out of a sand trap on the eighth green in 1980.

the Morristown, New Jersey, native had applied to become a batboy for the New York Yankees, using the name "James Lotsey." When baseball officials saw that she was a girl, they told her she was ineligible for the job. Later, after a struggle, Lotsey was permitted to play in the New Jersey Small-Fry League. She served as the winning pitcher during the first game of the 1963 season and hit one home run. The team recorded ten wins and one loss during that season. In high school, Lotsey played on all-girl basketball, softball, and volleyball teams.

Reference Read and Witlieb, *The Book of Women's Firsts* (1992).

Lucas, Lucky (Joy) Piles (b. 1917)

In 1941 Lucas became the first U.S. woman certified as a professional ski instructor. The Spokane, Washington, native grew up skiing and excelling in a number of other sports—diving, ice skating, roller skating, and swimming. In high school, she played intramural baseball and basketball.

Lucas later said that in the Pacific Northwest, women were more accepted as ski instructors, and that she was not barred from entering this field. She attended a national academy and race camp run by the Professional Ski Instructors of America (PSIA). Besides teaching skiing, she wrote numerous articles about the sport and an instructional book called *Teaching Children of All Ages to Ski*, which was published by the PSIA. Still skiing in her seventies, Lucas continued to teach both students and ski instructors.

See also Skiing

Luge

In French, the word *luge* means sled, and sledding is thought to be the oldest winter sport in the world. There were 21 competitors from seven countries at the first international luge competition, held in 1883 in Klosters, Switzerland. Americans became more involved in the sport after 1945, and women skiers were among the first to try racing down the twisting tracks, reaching speeds of 70 to 80 miles per hour.

Luge became an Olympic event in 1964. Women had been competing in singles and mixed doubles (with a male partner) luge events during the previous decade, but they competed in the singles luge at the Olympics. The women's luge track is at least 700 meters long, with some reaching lengths of close to 1,000 meters. European women, especially those from Germany, have dominated international competition. From the 1964 Olympics to the 1984 Games, the medalists included 13 German women, 2 from the Soviet Union, 1 Austrian, and 1 Italian. Italian Gerda Weissensteiner won the gold in 1994 and broke track records with her first two runs. Weissensteiner was known for keeping her head down during her runs in order to reduce wind resistance, while other lugers occasionally lift their heads to see where they are on the track. Silver-medalist Andrea Tagwerker of Austria commented, "It takes some courage to do it this way, but we are all working on it."

One of the best American women in the sport was Erica Terwillegar, who grew up near Lake Placid, New York, and won a silver medal in an international junior event in 1982, a first for Americans. Praised for her smooth runs, Terwillegar finished in fifth place at the 1983 world championship. American Cammy Myler finished fifth at the 1992 Olympics, the best finish ever by a U.S. woman, then went on to win the World Cup early in 1994. At the 1994 Olympics, her third time on the U.S. luge team, she finished in eleventh place, with another American, Bethany Calcaterra-McMahon, coming in twelfth. The 25-year-old Myler planned to continue training in order to compete at the 1998 Games.

The U.S. Olympic Committee has dedicated itself to helping to train American athletes in the luge, with Lake Placid, New York, designated as the training center and headquarters of the U.S. Luge Association.

References Clarey, "No Asterisk Needed: Italian Wins Luge by a Landslide," *New York Times*, February 16, 1994, 22; Editors of *Sports Illustrated*, *Sports Illustrated 1996 Sports Almanac* (1996).

Lynn, Janet (b. 1954)

Figure skater Janet Lynn has been called the best skater never to win a world championship title. Quoted in *Figure Skating: A Celebration*, Canadian champion Toller Cranston said of Lynn, "On the ice, she became ethereal, magical. She wove a spell."

Growing up in Chicago, Janet Lynn Nowicki began skating at age two and a half. The toddler taught herself to skate backwards, and her parents decided she should take lessons. In 1961, the Nowicki family moved to nearby Rockton, Illinois, so that Janet could study with Slavka Kohout, a well-known teaching professional at the Wagon Wheel Ice Palace. Janet Lynn was only eight when she placed first in the novice competition of the midwestern subsectional division. Three years later, she became the youngest skater to pass the United States Figure Skating Association (USFSA) eighth (gold medal)-level test.

In her autobiography *Peace and Love*, Lynn later wrote, "I started really loving the freedom of being on the ice. I'd be practicing and some music would be playing and I would just start skating to music. And soon, I'd be lost in myself." Soon, Lynn became a common sight at national competitions. She won the junior national ladies' title in 1966 with a program that included a triple salchow and two double axels. Competing as Janet Lynn, she earned a spot on the 1968 Olympic team and finished ninth in Grenoble, France.

Despite a heavy practice and travel schedule, Lynn managed to stay on the honor roll at school, spend time with her friends, and take part in church activities. In 1969, she won the senior ladies' title, the first of five, yet she had trouble taking top honors in world competition. Her freestyle routines were outstanding, but she scored lower in the school figures—compulsory movements in which skaters had to trace variations of two- and three-lobed figure-eights on the ice—then required as part of figure skating competitions. There were 70 school figures and a skater did not know in advance which ones she would be asked to perform. For a while in 1971, Lynn considered quitting skating.

After finishing high school the next year, Lynn trained harder than ever and competed in the Olympics, held in Sapporo, Japan. Once again, she lagged behind after the school figures. But her free-skating program brought raves for its buoyancy and enthusiasm. She took home a bronze third-place medal. Soon afterwards, she placed second at the world championships.

Lynn became a professional in 1973, signing a $1.4 million dollar contract with the Ice Follies that made her the highest paid female athlete in America at the time. She also married and had three children. Viewing her talent as a gift to be shared with others, Lynn devoted much time to promoting charitable causes and visiting hospitals and churches throughout America. After recovering from chronic respiratory problems, Lynn returned to skating and won a U.S. pro championship in 1983.

References Lynn, *Peace and Love* (1975); Van Steenwyk, *Women in Sports: Figure Skating* (1976).

Maccabiah Games

An international competition for Jewish athletes, these Games began in 1937. During that time, Jews were barred from the Olympics. The 1936 Summer Games had been held in Munich, Germany, then controlled by the Nazi government. After World War II, the Maccabiah Games were organized and held in Israel, with support from the American Sports for Israel Committee. Athletes compete in a variety of sports, mostly those featured at the Summer Olympics. Among the U.S. women who have won medals at the Games is Lillian Copeland.

See also Shot Put

McCormick, Pat (b. 1930)

During the 1950s, Patricia Keller McCormick was the world's premier women's diver, winning both the platform and springboard events at both the 1952 and 1956 Olympics. Nobody had ever won two titles in two successive Games, and McCormick's record was not equaled until 1988 by the remarkable U.S. male diver Greg Louganis.

Pat Keller grew up in Seal Beach, California, and spent a lot of time at the beach, swimming and diving. She credited this early physical activity with helping her to develop muscular strength. A coach who saw her diving at age 16 asked her to train at the Los Angeles Athletic Club. Although inexperienced and mostly self-trained, she won second place in the 1947 National Platform Championship. She missed qualifying for the 1948 Olympics by less than a point.

In 1949, she married Glen McCormick and won the National Platform title. She won that title the next year, along with the 1-meter and 3-meter springboard national crowns. In 1951, she managed to win all five national titles, the three outdoors and two indoors. By the 1952 Olympics, she had won the highboard (platform) title at the Pan American Games and taken second place in the springboard.

Just five months before the 1956 Olympics, McCormick gave birth to a son. Coached by her husband Glenn, she swam throughout her pregnancy, then resumed training with 100 dives a day a few weeks after the birth. At the Games, McCormick won her third gold medal when she took the springboard event. She was leading in the platform event when she missed her fourth dive, putting her in second place. Rising to the occasion, McCormick completed two outstanding final dives to regain first place by a large margin and gain her fourth gold medal. She won the Sullivan Award that year, the second woman to receive it since it was established in 1930. Numerous other honors came her way, and she became the first woman elected to the International Swimming Hall of Fame. Retiring from competition in 1956, she operated a diving camp for several years.

McCormick attended the 1984 Olympics as a spectator when her daughter Kelly, carrying on the family tradition of excellence, won a silver medal in springboard diving in 1984 and a bronze in 1988. During the 1984 Games, McCormick was a member of the escort for the U.S. flag at the opening ceremonies.

See also Sullivan Award

McCutcheon, Floretta (1888–1967)

Born in Iowa, McCutcheon became a top woman bowler at a time when many women avoided sports for fear of being labeled "unladylike." Bowling alleys were often located in dark basements, and men dominated the game.

Floretta Doty McCutcheon was 35 years old and a housewife in Pueblo, Colorado, when she began to bowl. She wanted to lose weight, and a friend told her that bowling was good exercise. Venturing out to the alleys and throwing the 16-pound ball was a daunting experience for McCutcheon, but she finished her first game. In a few years, she was known as the best bowler in town.

Men's champion Jimmy Smith, whom some sports historians have called the greatest bowler of all time, visited her area in 1926. McCutcheon watched him play with great interest and later said that she tried to copy his techniques in order to improve her game. In 1927, Smith returned to play an exhibition match and was urged to play against the 39-year-old McCutcheon. Their match made sports history, as McCutcheon rolled for a score of 704 to top Smith's 697. Making no excuses, Smith later called her "simply the greatest bowler I have ever seen." The incident was featured in *Ripley's Believe It or Not*, a regular newspaper column.

At the suggestion of Smith's manager, McCutcheon began to tour the United States as a paid teacher and exhibition bowler. Her income enabled her to send her daughter to college. During those ten years, she achieved some amazing scores: 832 for three games in 1931 and a record ten perfect 300 games and nine at near-perfect 299. She established the Mrs. McCutcheon School for Bowling Instructions. With her warm, enthusiastic manner and grandmotherly appearance, McCutcheon inspired many thousands of people to take up recreational bowling. She helped local communities establish teams and leagues and taught in lessons, clinics, and exhibitions. Her students often included children to senior citizens. In polls taken during the late 1970s, bowling experts still ranked McCutcheon as one of the top five or ten bowlers of all time, male or female.

See also Bowling

References Hickok, *Who Was Who in American Sports* (1971); Hollander, *100 Greatest Women in Sports* (1976); Weiskopf, *The Perfect Game* (1978).

McKinney, Tamara (b. 1962)

McKinney, an expert skier and horsewoman, was born in Lexington, Kentucky. She began skiing during her childhood and competed in her first World Cup event at age 15. Competing with the U.S. women's ski team at the 1980 Winter Olympics, McKinney fell during both the slalom and giant slalom competition. The next year, McKinney won the overall World Cup competition, then the giant slalom World Cup, in 1984, when she was also the national slalom champion. In 1982 McKinney became the first American to win the World Cup overall title for Alpine skiing. She won the U.S. slalom title seven times, from 1982 through 1984 and 1986 through 1989.

Reference Hickok, *A Who's Who of Sports Champions* (1995).

In a sport dominated by men, Floretta McCutcheon, pictured here, could beat the best of them. McCutcheon was discovered in her hometown of Pueblo, Colorado, by champion bowler Jimmy Smith, an instructor she would go on to beat in 1927.

McNamara, Julianne (b. 1966)

This hard-working gymnast from Flushing, New York, was known as an expert on the uneven parallel bars, attempting movements few women gymnasts had mastered before her. McNamara made the 1980 Olympic team only five years after she began studying gymnastics but was not able to compete that year, since the U.S. boycotted the Games for political reasons. That year, she won the American Cup All-Around title and was named female gymnast of the year.

In 1981, McNamara placed seventh in the all-around competition at the world gymnastics championships, the highest placement a U.S. woman had ever achieved in international competition. She then won a bronze medal in the vault event at the 1982 World Cup. Once again, in 1982, she won the American Cup title but came in second in 1983 when future Olympic gold medalist Mary Lou Retton won the title. However, McNamara defeated Retton in the 1983 nationals, winning a silver while Retton took the bronze. McNamara competed in the 1984 Olympics where she shared a gold medal for the uneven bars event with a Chinese gymnast. She also placed fourth in the all-around competition, missing a third-place medal by a mere .275 of a point. In the floor exercise, she won a silver medal, while Retton earned third place for a bronze. The U.S. team won a silver medal.

In 1992 McNamara provided commentary for NBC-TV at the Summer Olympics in Barcelona, Spain. Married to Todd Zeile, a third baseman for the St. Louis Cardinals, she has also been actively involved in promoting Special Olympics since her retirement from competitive gymnastics.

References Lundgren, *Mary Lou Retton: Gold Medal Gymnast* (1985); "Olympic Gold Still Shining," *Good Housekeeping*, February 1992, 128ff.

Madison, Helene (1913–1970)

In 1932, at the Summer Olympics held in Los Angeles, swimmer Helene Madison was the only member of the U.S. team to win three gold medals. She took the 100- and 400-meter freestyle events and helped the 400-meter freestyle relay team to victory. Her time in the 400-meter event set a world record. Dubbed "queen of the waters," the 18-year-old Madison had made history. In 1930, when she was just 17, Madison already held 26 world records for freestyle swimming, ranging in distance from 50 yards to 1 mile. In the decade that followed, Madison won 12 world and 30 U.S. championships. She was named female athlete of the year by the Associated Press in 1931. Madison was inducted into the International Swimming Hall of Fame.

Mallory, Molla (1892–1959)

A tennis champion during the 1920s, Molla Bjurstedt Mallory was born in Norway and moved to Brooklyn, New York, in 1914, while on a trip to America to visit relatives. She won the U.S. national women's tennis title four years in a row, from 1915 to 1918. Her strong, relentless groundstrokes inspired other women to play more aggressively. Mallory kept her opponents on the move by hitting the ball into the corners of their side of the court.

In 1919, she married New York businessman Frank I. Mallory. That year, she lost her U.S. title to Hazel Hotchkiss Wightman, but in 1920, she regained the national crown, which she won for the next three years, capturing a record-breaking eighth in 1926. With Eleanora

Sears, Mallory won the women's doubles crown, as well as the mixed doubles, which she played with the legendary American champion, Bill Tilden.

Often, Mallory was pitted against the legendary French champion Suzanne Lenglen. Lenglen defaulted in their U.S. national match in 1921, the first time the Frenchwoman had played on American soil. Lenglen, who was then losing the match, said she was too ill to continue. Mallory, who had been playing superbly, became the only player ever to defeat Lenglen during her seven years of amateur play.

At the 1924 Paris Olympics, Molla Mallory played winning doubles with Helen Wills. Wills was beginning to defeat her steadily in singles play, however, and in the final of the U.S. nationals in 1929, Mallory lost 6-0, 6-0. It was her last tournament, played at age 45. After retiring from tennis, Mallory worked in government service. She was inducted into the Tennis Hall of Fame in 1958.

Reference Collins and Hollander, *Bud Collins' Modern Encyclopedia of Tennis* (1994).

Management

Until the 1900s, few women managed sports teams. A notable exception was Alta Weiss, who managed a baseball team and also played on a men's semiprofessional team in Ohio during the early 1900s.

Margaret Donohue (1893–1978) became the first woman executive in major league baseball. She had begun as a clerk-typist with the Chicago Cubs in 1919. Within seven years, she was a corporate secretary. Donohue was named vice-president of the club in 1950.

Marguerite Norris (1927–1994) became the first chief female executive in the National Hockey League when she served as president of the Detroit Red Wings from 1952 to 1955. As of 1994, Norris was the only woman to have had her name engraved on the Stanley Cup, given to the hockey team that wins the championship in a given year. During her tenure, the Red Wings finished in first place all three years and won the Cup twice.

During the 1970s, several dynamic women athletes organized professional teams and served as managers and coaches as well as players. In tennis, Billie Jean King helped to found World Team Tennis and served as player, coach, and manager. From 1976 to 1979, softball sensation Joan Joyce served as manager and coach, as well as player, for the Connecticut Falcons, a team in the International Women's Softball League.

See also Joyce, Joan; King, Billie Jean; Moore, Ellie; Weiss, Alta; World Team Tennis
Reference Reed and Witlieb, *The Book of Women's Firsts* (1992).

Mann, Carol (b. 1941)

This golfer from Buffalo, New York, stood over 6 feet tall and was known for her stylish clothing as well as her expertly controlled strokes. Mann won both the Western Junior and Chicago Junior titles in 1958. Two years later, she captured the Trans-Mississippi and Chicago Women's Amateur titles and began her professional career.

As a touring pro, Mann won the prestigious U.S. Open in 1965 and a total of 19 tournaments that year and the next. In 1968, her average score on the Ladies Professional Golf Association (LPGA) tour was lower than any other golfer's, and Mann was awarded the Vare Trophy. The next year, she won ten titles and became the first woman golfer to earn more than $50,000 in one year. For ten years, her

Carol Mann shoots out of a sand trap on her way to winning the Bluegrass Invitational Ladies Golf Tournament in 1968. In 1969 she would become the first woman golfer to earn more than $50,000 in a single year.

1968 average score of 72.04 stood as a record in women's golf.

Mann was elected to the LPGA Hall of Fame in 1977 and the Women's Sports Hall of Fame in 1982. Retiring from competition in 1981, Mann served as a television commentator, covering both men's and women's golf tournaments for NBC-TV. She has also been involved in drug-abuse prevention programs for athletes.

Reference Hickok, *A Who's Who of Sports Champions* (1995).

Mann, Shelley (b. 1937)

In 1956, at the Summer Olympics in Melbourne, Australia, Mann became not only the first American woman to win the 100-meter butterfly swimming event, but the first woman in the world, since it became part of the Olympics that same year. She completed the race in 1 minute, 11 seconds.

As a child in Virginia, Mann survived an attack of polio, a disease that strikes the spinal nerves that control muscles, when she was six years old. Left with weakened limbs, she began swimming on the advice of physicians who told her parents that this form of exercise would strengthen her arms and legs. Mann trained at the Walter Reed Swim Club in Washington, D.C., not far from her home in Arlington, Virginia.

At age 12, she began swimming competitively and won her first national championship two years later, in 1952. During her career, this versatile swimmer set records for the backstroke, butterfly, freestyle, and individual medley races. In 1966, Shelley Mann was elected to the Swimming and Diving Hall of Fame and the International Swimming Hall of Fame.

Manning, Madeline (b. 1948)

Middle-distance runner Manning made numerous comebacks during her career. Growing up in a housing project in Cleveland, Ohio, she was often ill as a child. But when a doctor told her mother to keep her in bed, Manning refused to cooperate. She loved to play outdoors, climbing trees and joining team games. By high school, a tall, strong Manning joined the track team and became a star runner, setting a national record in the quarter-mile run. In 1966 she competed against some of the world's best runners and won the half-mile race. This time she set a world record.

Manning received a scholarship to attend Tennessee State University. There she trained with coach Ed Temple as part of the world-famous Tigerbelles track team. Preparing for the 1968 Olympics, Manning hoped to become the first American woman ever to win the 800-meter race. When Manning won the gold medal in Mexico City, setting an Olympic record with her time of 2 minutes, 0.9 seconds, she said it was the happiest day of her life.

Two years later, she decided to retire from her sport. She married and gave birth to a son. But she missed competitive track and rejoined the U.S. Olympic team for the 1972 Games. Afterwards, Manning, now divorced, worked in Cleveland as a recreation director. Again, she missed running and returned to training in 1975. That year, once again, she won the American half-mile championship. Now 28 years old, she returned to the Olympics but did not run well enough to make it to the finals. Although disappointed, Manning decided to try again in 1976. At a special competition between the U.S. and Russian teams, she set an American record for the 880-yard race—1 minute, 57.9 seconds.

Manning resumed training once again in 1980 and won her fifth national women's indoor title for the 880-yard race. At the Olympic trials that year, she won the 800-meters and set a new record for Olympic trials in the event: 1 minute, 58.3 seconds. The United States boycotted the 1980 Games, which were held in Moscow, when President Carter decided to protest the Soviet Union's invasion of Afghanistan. The boycott stirred controversy, and many athletes and others opposed it. Manning was among those who said she could understand the reasons behind the boycott. She said that the political issue involved was "bigger than the Olympics."

Throughout her career as a runner, Madeline Manning's religious faith had become increasingly important to her. After retiring from track, she pursued her new career as a gospel singer.

Madeline Manning sets a new Pan-American Games record in the 800-meter run in 1967.

Happily remarried, she studied for the ministry at Oral Roberts University and became a popular motivational Christian speaker, appearing at churches, prisons, and schools. She was inducted into the International Women's Sports Hall of Fame and the National Track and Field Hall of Fame.

See also Temple, Ed; Tigerbelles
References Manning, *Running for Jesus* (1977); Sullivan, *Superstars of Women's Track* (1981).

Marathon Running

The first known marathon took place in 490 B.C. when a Greek courier ran from a battlefield on the Plains of Marathon to Athens with important military information. After running 24 miles and delivering the message, the courier collapsed and died. When the first modern Olympics were held in Athens in 1896, the marathon race covered a 24-mile course. However, at the next Games, held in London, King Edward VII asked that the race be run from Windsor Castle to White City Stadium, 26 miles and 385 yards apart. This became the official distance for marathon races.

Until recent decades, women were not permitted to run officially in marathons or other long-distance races. It was thought that women were not capable of running long distances and that this also could damage their health, particularly their ability to bear children. Yet, even in ancient times, women dared to break with such customs. In 1896, a Greek girl tried to enter the first marathon race in the modern Olympic Games. Using the pseudonym Melpomene, she completed the race in 4.5 hours but was ruled ineligible. Englishwoman Violet Pearcy ran a marathon in London in 1936. Her time, 3 hours and 40 minutes, set a women's record that stood for almost 40 years.

In 1928 the International Amateur Athletic Federation banned women from races longer than 200 meters. Olympic races for women did not go above that distance until 1964, when a 400-meter event was introduced. The 1,500-meter race was the longest Olympic event for women in 1976. Women who defied the rules were often banned from other competition. When Australian runner Adrienne Bearnes ran a marathon, she was not allowed to try out for the Olympics.

In the United States, during the 1960s, the Amateur Athletic Union (AAU) banned women from running distances longer than 1 mile. Runner Kathrine Switzer was thrown out of the AAU after she entered the Boston Marathon in 1967. It took five more years before women were officially allowed in marathons, and then rules stated that they must begin the race 10 minutes before male competitors. After women runners protested this rule, it was dropped in 1972 during the New York Marathon. That same year, the AAU agreed that women should be allowed to run long-distance races. In 1979, the American College of Sports Medicine issued a recommendation, based on careful consideration of the research studies, that women "be allowed to compete [in long-distance running] at the national and international level in the same distances in which their male counterparts compete."

Among the best-known marathons is the Boston marathon, which began in 1897. Held annually on the third Monday in April, the race is sponsored by the Boston Athletic Association. It begins in Hopkinton, Massachusetts, and finishes in downtown Boston. Thousands of people from all walks of life take part, watched by thousands of spectators. Long banned from the race, women first entered covertly, as when Kathrine Switzer entered under the name "K. Switzer" in 1967. In 1966, another woman, Roberta Gibb Bingay, had hoped to race with her husband. Wearing a hooded sweatsuit, Bingay hid in bushes along the street and rushed to join runners as the race began. Later, people saw that she was a woman when the heat forced her to take off her sweat clothes. Although Bingay finished 124th in a field of 416, she was disqualified and her participation was not recognized.

At the 1972 Boston Marathon, the best time recorded for a woman runner was 3 hours, 10 minutes, 26 seconds. Within a few years, women were completing the race in 2 hours and 30 minutes, with Joan Benoit Samuelson achieving a time just over 2 hours and 22 minutes in the 1982 race. Today, women compete in marathons around the world. Some marathons, such as the New York Marathon, sponsor separate races for men and women competitors, awarding prizes to those who finish on top in both divisions. After the International Olympic Committee (IOC) gave its approval in 1981, marathons for women became part of the Games, starting in 1984 when the Olympics were held in Los Angeles. Benoit Samuelson won the gold medal.

During the early 1990s, long-distance runner Ann Trason broke new ground in ultra marathon racing, sometimes called ultra running. These endurance races can be 50–100 miles long and may last 24 hours or longer. Marathon runner Micki Gorman broke some of her own speed records when she was in her forties. She began running at age 33, taking up the sport at the Los Angeles Athletic Club. Gorman later recalled that after completing her first half-mile run, she collapsed.

Training hard, a few months later Gorman completed 85 miles in a 24-hour endurance race sponsored by the athletic club. Within a year, she was able to run 100 miles in a 21-hour period.

In some long races, women have been able to sustain fast speeds throughout and have even reached higher speeds at the end than in the beginning. Physiologists have theorized that women are better able to use their body fat as fuel during a race, similar to the way both genders use the glycogen formed during the digestion of carbohydrates (sugars and starches). After about two hours of steady running, men tend to suddenly experience severe muscle pain, a phenomenon known as "hitting the wall." Dr. Ernest van Aaken, a German biochemist and running coach, has found that women do not experience this sudden burst of pain.

See also Benoit Samuelson, Joan; Boston Marathon; Switzer, Kathrine; Trason, Ann; Ultra Running
References Higden, *Boston: A Century of Running* (1995); Kaplan, *Women and Sports* (1979); Leder, *Grace and Glory* (1996); Ross, "The Olympics: Unfair to Women," *Reader's Digest*, November 1983, 19–24; Wynne and Wynne, *The Books of Sports Trophies* (1984).

Marble, Alice (1913–1990)

The daughter of ranchers, Marble grew up loving sports. As an eight-year-old, she helped to pick up baseballs used during practice by the San Francisco Seals team, earning a compliment for her "good arm" from star player Joe Di Maggio. Fans watched as Marble caught flyballs in the outfield before games.

Marble began playing tennis as a teenager at public courts in San Francisco's Golden Gate Park. She and her family worked hard to earn extra money so that she could become a junior member at the California Tennis Club. Although fast and agile, Marble lacked formal training in hitting ground strokes, so, in order to end points more quickly and avoid having to hit so many strokes, she rushed up to the net. This serve-and-volley approach to the game was unusual for a woman of her day. Spectators were surprised to see powerful serves and an aggressive style of play from this trim, rather delicate-looking female.

By age 19, Marble was the California women's champion. She was runner-up in the under-18 girls' national championships of 1931. The next year, she was ranked the number seven woman player in the country by the United States Lawn Tennis Association (USLTA).

Playing with the Wightman Cup team, Marble helped to achieve a victory in 1933. During that time, she began to suffer from anemia and other health problems. Obliged to play 108 games in one day at a tournament in East Hampton, New York, where the temperature reached 100°F, she collapsed. Doctors advised her to quit tennis and rest at a convalescent home, but her months at the home left Marble overweight and weaker. With the help of her coach, Eleanor Tennant, she began a diet and exercise program that reduced her weight and built up her strength.

Marble returned to match play in 1935, stronger than ever, and with a different kind of grip. She won the U.S. national title in 1936, defeating Helen Hull Jacobs, who had won the tournament four years in a row. Returning to Wightman Cup competition, she helped her team win in 1937, 1938, and 1939. Marble won the U.S. title again in 1938, 1939, and 1940, years during which she was ranked the top woman player in the United States. Her successes in doubles play included the mixed doubles at

Wimbledon in 1937, 1938, and 1939 and the ladies' doubles title there in 1938 and 1939. In 1939, Marble also won the ladies' singles title at Wimbledon, thus sweeping three events in one tournament. In 1940, she lost only one match in singles and doubles play.

During World War II, tournament play was suspended. Marble became a professional and toured the country with top male players, taking part in numerous exhibition matches at training stations and camps for U.S. service people during the war. In 1946, her autobiography, *The Road to Wimbledon*, was published.

In 1949, Marble used her prestige and popularity to convince tournament officials to invite Althea Gibson, a black player, to compete in USLTA tournaments. In tennis, as in many other sports, people of color had been excluded from major tournaments. Marble wrote to tennis magazines urging that the ban against black players be ended. Some clubs resisted, but the Eastern Grass Courts championship extended an invitation to Gibson, who went on to win several tournaments, including U.S. women's titles and two Wimbledon crowns.

Marble later coached others, and one of her students was the great Billie Jean King, whom she taught for six months during 1959. In 1964, Alice Marble was named to the International Tennis Hall of Fame. She joined former Wimbledon champions to receive a special Centenary medallion in 1977 and was greeted with much enthusiasm. Marble died in Palm Springs, California, in 1990.

See also Gibson, Althea; King, Billie Jean
References Frayne, *Famous Women Tennis Players* (1979); Gibson and Marble, *The Road to Wimbledon* (1946); Sullivan, *Queens of the Court* (1974).

Marino, Cathy (See Kayaking)

Martial Arts

Martial arts are hand-to-hand fighting, self-defense maneuvers that require technique more than sheer muscle strength or equipment. The focus is on training to develop both physical skills and mental disciplines such as concentration and confidence. Hand-to-hand combat training dates back to ancient China and other Asian cultures and may have started in Buddhist monasteries located in the Hunan province. Both men and women lived in these communities and helped to develop the martial arts. Asian folklore includes tales of women who led battles or fought in armies and who seem to have practiced martial arts. One such heroine is Fa Mulan, who substituted for her father in a battle during the sixth century.

A Buddhist nun in China is credited with developing a type of kung fu during the sixth century. During the seventh century, martial arts spread throughout various provinces in China. The arts encompassed spiritual dimensions by seeking to explore human potential and the links between humankind and the rest of the universe. In Japan, women born into the warrior class often learned techniques used in battle. Several folk heroines led their people in battle against the enemy. However, by the 1700s, Japanese women were being discouraged from martial arts, which were moving from the battlefields to training schools indoors, where women were barred.

After World War II, western countries learned more about the martial arts, and schools for judo, karate, and other arts opened in the United States and other countries. In 1964, judo became an event at the Olympics, but for men only. During the 1960s and 1970s, television and motion pictures featured martial artists who fascinated the viewing public. Still, women were discouraged and often banned from taking part in these sports. Although women were making inroads in many other sports, the martial arts were still seen as inappropriate, perhaps because they are associated with fighting and often involve physical contact between practitioners.

Nevertheless, some women found places to study and worked hard to excel in various martial arts. Rusty Kanokogi became the first well-known American judo expert, while Nadia Telsey and Susan Ribner distinguished themselves in karate. The Women's Martial Arts Union was formed in 1972 to spread information about the martial arts and encourage women to participate. By the 1990s, thousands of women across America were involved in different martial arts, as students, teachers, practitioners, and competitors.

See also Graff, Sunny; Judo; Kanokogi, Rusty; Karate; Kung Fu; Ribner, Susan

Martinez, Patty (See Table Tennis)

Martino, Angel Meyers (b. 1965)

In 1988, this Georgia native became the first American woman to break the 55-second barrier in a 100-meter freestyle swimming event. At the 1992 Olympics, she won a bronze medal in the 50-meter freestyle and a gold medal as part of the 400-meter freestyle relay team. Martino has succeeded as a top athlete while suffering from asthma.

At age 29, Martino was the oldest woman on the U.S. swim team at the 1996 Summer Olympics. There, she won gold medals in the 4 x 100–meter freestyle relay and the 4 x 100–meter medley relay. She also won bronze medals in the 100-meter freestyle and 100-meter butterfly races. After the Games, her hometown of Americus, Georgia, held a parade in her honor.

References Gottesman, "Who's in the Swim?" *Women's Sports and Fitness*, September 1995, 95.

Matterhorn (See Peck, Annie Smith)

Matthieu, Susie

In 1977 Matthieu became the public relations director for the St. Louis Blues, a team in the National Hockey League. It was the first time a woman had been hired in this capacity by a team in major league professional hockey. Previously, Matthieu had served as assistant sports information director for St. Louis University in St. Louis, Missouri.

Meagher, Mary T. (b. 1964)

As a 15-year-old, Meagher set her first world swimming record in 1979. She won a gold medal at the Pan American Games for the 200-meter butterfly (2 minutes, 07.01 seconds). Within a year, she had set another record, this time for the 100-meter butterfly (59.26 seconds). Meagher would have competed in five racing events at the 1980 Olympics had the United States not boycotted those Games for political reasons. No swimmer at the 1980 Moscow Games beat either of her record times, and Meagher later swam the 200-meter even faster, with a time of 2 minutes, 06.37 seconds. Later, she bettered that with a lower time of 2 minutes, 05.96 seconds. In 1991 competitions, she improved her time in the 100-meter butterfly race to 57.43 seconds.

As the 1984 Olympics drew near, Meagher had won the 100-meter and 200-meter races at the U.S. Swimming International Meet and won national titles that year in the 100- and 200-meter butterfly and 200-meter freestyle. At the Olympics in Los Angeles, she won three gold medals—in the 100- and 200-meter butterfly events and as a member of the women's 4 x 100–meter relay team. After the 1988 Olympics, where she won a bronze medal in the 200-meter butterfly, Meagher retired from competitive swimming.

Meany, Helen (1904–1970)

Diver Meany competed in her first Olympics at age 15, traveling by boat to Antwerp, Belgium, along with her teammates. Since World War I had just ended, there was no Olympic Village with its comfortable facilities for athletes. Meany later recalled, "We swam and dove in a moat around Antwerp. Some of the women swimmers fainted when they got in that cold water, which was about 60 degrees. . . . Between dives it was unbearably cold. There was a nurse there who gave massages with wintergreen oil to help keep your muscles from tightening up."

Meany did not win a medal at those Games or in the 1924 Games in Paris. She competed for the third time in 1928 in Amsterdam. Unlike the male divers, who competed separately, all of the women dove at the same time. After what Meany later called the longest afternoon in her life, she found that she had won the gold medal in the springboard competition. In addition, she captured 14 Amateur Athletic Union (AAU) titles in platform and springboard diving between 1921 and 1927.

Retiring from competition in 1928, Meany swam in exhibitions and taught swimming. She later said that the most valuable part of her Olympic experiences was the friends she had made for a lifetime.

Reference Carlson and Fogarty, *Tales of Gold* (1977).

Meno, Jenni (b. 1971)

A native of Westlake, Ohio (near Cleveland), Meno became a champion pairs figure skater. After skating with Scott Wendland, she changed partners in 1992, pairing with Todd Sand, who became her husband in 1995. Both skaters had taken part in the 1992 Olympics in Albertville, France.

In 1994 and 1995, Meno and Sand won the gold medal for pairs skating at the national championships. Sportswriter Johnette Howard called theirs "the most stunning performance of the [1995] championships." They then went on to the 1995 world competition, where they took third place. The pair was notable for their clean-lined elegance on the ice and classical style. Meno received high praise for her balletic grace and beautiful "death spiral"—a movement in which the female member of the pair holds her partner's hand and bends backward with arched back so that her head may touch the ice, while still skating forward.

At the 1996 World Figure Skating Championships, Meno and Sand repeated their bronze-medal winning performance, becoming the first U.S. pairs team to win consecutive medals in world competition since Tai Babilonia and Randy Gardner (1977–1979).

References Howard, "Queen for a Day," *Sports Illustrated*, February 1995, 26–31.

Metheny, Linda (b. 1947)

A five-time winner of the U.S. All-Around gymnastics championship, Illinois native Linda Jo Metheny helped raise the level of women's gymnastics in the United States during a time when the sport was just gaining interest here. Metheny was the U.S. national women's All-Around champion in 1966, 1968, 1970, 1971, and 1972. She won a record five gold medals at the 1967 Pan American Games and competed in three Olympic Games, placing fourth in balance-beam competition in 1968 at the Games held in Mexico City. Metheny thus became the first American woman to qualify for the finals of any Olympics gymnastic event. Metheny often found herself pitted against Olympic teammate Cathy Rigby, whom she defeated in the 1971 and 1972 Amateur Athletic Union (AAU) competitions. At the 1972 Olympics, Metheny helped the U.S. women's team to a fourth-place finish—its best to that date. After the Games, Metheny retired from competition and married her coach, Dick Mulvihill, with whom she opened a gymnastics academy in 1973. Among their well-known students was Olympian Julianne McNamara.

See also McNamara, Julianne

Meyer, Deborah (b. 1952)

While only 16 years old, Meyer held the 1968 world records for her swims in the 400-, 800-, and 1,500-meter events and the 880-yard race. She was known for her elegant freestyle stroke.

Meyer was born in Annapolis, Maryland, and later moved to California, where she learned to swim at age five and trained at a swim club in Sacramento. Growing up, Meyer gave up many other activities, going to bed early so that she could practice swimming before school the next day. She also suffered from asthma but became a top athlete nonetheless. At age 14, Meyer set her first world record. Between 1967 and 1969, she set 15 freestyle swimming records and remained world champion in the 400- and 1,500-meter freestyle events, as well as the 400-meter medley. Some of her times in these races were better than those by attained by men who had won Olympic medals during the 1950s. Her achievements were noted all over the world, and the Soviet Union's news agency, TASS, named her 1967's Woman Athlete of the Year. She was chosen World Swimmer of the Year from 1967 to 1969.

Meyer won the 400- and 800-meter events at the 1967 Pan American Games. At the 1968 Olympics, she won three individual gold medals in the 800-meter, 200-meter, and 400-meter freestyle events. That year was the first time the 800-meter and 200-meter freestyle events for women were featured at the Games. Meyers swam the 800-meter race in 9 minutes, 24 seconds—more than 11 seconds faster than her closest competitor. Her time in the 200-meter race was 2 minutes and 10.5 seconds; she finished the 400-meter freestyle in 4 minutes and 31.8 seconds. By winning three individual gold medals, Meyer achieved an Olympic first.

In her amateur career, Meyer set 24 U.S. swim racing records and won 19 Amateur Athletic Union (AAU) championships. For her remarkable achievements, Meyer received the Sullivan Award as the best amateur athlete of 1968. She retired from competitive swimming at age 20 and did occasional sports commentary for CBS television's "Sports Spectacular" show. In 1972, Meyer left northern California to attend the University of California at Los Angeles (UCLA). She later became a swim coach at Stanford University in Palo Alto, then worked as a full-time representative for Speedo swimsuits. In 1977, she was elected to the International Swimming Hall of Fame.

See also Sullivan Award

References Greenberg, *The Guinness Book of Olympic Facts and Feats* (1983); Litsky, *Superstars* (1975).

Meyers, Anne (b. 1955)
Meyers was the first woman to become a four-time All American in collegiate basketball. She pursued track and field in high school and expected to compete in the Olympics some day as a high jumper. But her talent for basketball earned her a spot on the U.S. women's basketball team that won a gold medal at the Pan American Games. Meyers then competed at the Olympic Games in Montreal in 1976. There the U.S. women defeated Czechoslovakia, Canada, and Bulgaria, taking home a silver medal. Meyers scored 17 points in the final game, making her top scorer among the U.S. women.

Her standout talent enabled Meyers to become the first woman ever to attend the University of California at Los Angeles (UCLA) on a full athletic scholarship. An outstanding passer and shooter, she was also known as a team leader who could boost morale. A four-time All American, Meyers was selected Female College Athlete of the Year in 1978 by the Association for Intercollegiate Athletics for Women (AIAW), winning the Broderick Cup.

In 1979 Meyers signed a one-year contract with the Indiana Pacers, a National Basketball Association (NBA) team—another first for women. She did not make the team, but did TV commentary on their games. A year later, she joined the New Jersey Gems in the Women's Professional Basketball League. Meyers tied for Most Valuable Player during 1979–1980. From 1980 to 1982, Meyers won the TV special "Women Superstars Competition." She then became a full-time sports commentator. She was inducted into the Basketball Hall of Fame and the International Women's Sports Hall of Fame.

Reference Hickok, *A Who's Who of Sports Champions* (1995).

Meyers, Mary (b. 1948)

Meyers made history as one of three U.S. women speed skaters who tied for the silver medal in the 1968 Olympics 500-meter race. At Grenoble, Meyers and her teammates Jennifer Fish and Dianne Holum all achieved the same time: 46.3 seconds. Their performance was also the first time U.S. women speed skaters had done so well at the Olympics.

See also Holum, Dianne

Mighty Mary (See *America³*)

Miller, Cheryl (b. 1964)

Some sportswriters have called Miller the best female basketball player in history. At 6 feet, 2 inches, she was also one of the tallest women to play the game. In world competition, she averaged 20 points and 10 rebounds per game.

An athletic child, Miller grew up in Riverside, California. Her father, an Air Force officer and computer systems superintendent at a hospital, encouraged all five children to pursue sports. At Riverside Polytechnic High School, Miller played 90 games and scored a total of 3,026 points, a California high school record. She also set records for scoring in one season (1,156 points), scoring in a game (105), and for a season average (32.8 points a game). Over four seasons, her team won 132 games and lost only four. During those years, Miller idolized women's basketball star Lynette Woodard, whose number 31 she would later adopt as her own in college.

During the 1970s, women's basketball was receiving more publicity and interest. Colleges were seeking top players for their teams, and Miller received 250 offers from around the country. Miller was particularly in demand, since she excelled in both sports and academics. In 1981, she received the Dial Award, given each year by the Dial Corporation to the two high school students, one male and one female, selected as athlete-scholar of the year. Playing the forward position at the University of Southern California, Miller helped lead her team to two National Collegiate Athletic Association (NCAA) titles, including an exciting final game against Louisiana Tech in 1983, when Miller's team won by two points. A four-time All American, Miller was frequently praised for her great all-around game and the variety of shots she could make from various angles on the court. She was nicknamed "Silk" for her smooth movements on the court.

Miller was the top scorer at the 1983 Pan American Games, where the U.S. finished first, and at the 1984 Olympics, where the U.S. women's team won the gold medal. That year, she was awarded the Broderick Cup from the Women's Intercollegiate Athletic Directors as the outstanding woman college athlete of the year. Her team reached the NCAA finals in 1985, losing to the University of Texas. That year, Miller won her third consecutive Naismith Award as top female collegiate basketball player in the United States. In 128 games during her college career, Miller scored 3,018 points. She had 1,534 rebounds and 462 steals.

Although the Soviet Union had dominated women's basketball in world competition, the U.S. women's team defeated them in 1986 at the Goodwill Games, with Miller scoring 18 points and 10 rebounds. The score in the final game showed an impressive victory, 83–60. At that year's world championship, held in Moscow, the U.S. women again defeated the Soviets in the final. Knee injuries kept Miller out of the 1988 Olympic Games.

After finishing her playing career,

Miller became a popular commentator for ABC-TV, covering college basketball and football. She was inducted into the International Women's Sports Hall of Fame.

See also Woodard, Lynette
References Anderson, *The Story of Basketball* (1988); Editors of *Sports Illustrated, Sports Illustrated 1996 Sports Almanac.*

Miller, Shannon (b. 1977)

Between 1991 and 1995, gymnast Shannon Miller amassed eight world championships and earned five medals at the 1992 Olympic Games in Barcelona, Spain (two silver and three bronze). Driven to excel, Miller told journalist Joan Ryan, "Unless you get a ten [a perfect score in gymnastics competition], [the performance] is not perfect. So you always need to keep looking at what you did wrong."

Born in Edmond, Oklahoma, Miller began her gymnastics training at Nunno's Dynamos Gym, then continued to train with coach Steve Nunno at his Oklahoma City center for elite gymnasts. She developed impressive power, combined with great control.

At the 1992 Olympics in Barcelona, Spain, Miller stood about 4 feet, 8 inches tall and weighed about 70 pounds. She displayed a strong will and ability to perform under pressure. Her best event was the balance beam, her performance on which earned her a silver medal. In the vault, usually her weakest event, Miller performed a near perfect routine, then captured a silver medal in the overall. It was the first all-around medal ever won by an American gymnast competing in Games that included the Soviet Union, which had withdrawn from the 1984 Games for political reasons.

While training, Miller managed to maintain an A average when she graduated from North High School in Edmond, Oklahoma, in spring 1995. She won gold medals in the all-around, floor exercise, and uneven bars at the 1993 world championships. Her dual achievements as both a scholar and athlete earned Miller an award from the Amateur Athletic Association (AAU).

In 1994, Miller lost her national title but retained the world all-around title. She had grown 4 inches and gained about 20 pounds by 1995, evolving into a more muscular athlete. At the American Classic held early in 1995, Miller seemed to be in top form, her experience and talent earning first place. Tough competition from younger gymnasts kept her from reaching the final rounds of the American Cup in 1995. She suffered from shinsplints and back problems. After her defeat, Miller continued to train for the 1996 Olympics, after which she planned to attend college. In March 1995, at the Pan-American Games, the U.S. team gained the lead, after Miller won all four events heading into the finals. She lost the national title that year to 13-year-old Dominique Moceanu. At the 1996 Olympics in Atlanta, Georgia, Miller's strong performance helped the U.S. gymnastics team win its first-ever team gold medal. She also won the balance beam individual event—another first for a U.S. gymnast in Olympic competition.

See also Gymnastics; Moceanu, Dominique
References Clary, "Miller Adds Maturity and Difficulty to Her Repertory," *New York Times,* July 18, 1996, B9, B13; Clary, "U.S. Gymnasts Take Back Seat in All-Around," *New York Times,* July 26, 1996, B9, B16; "Miller Faces a Fight for Title," *New York Times,* August 16, 1995, B12; Ryan, *Little Girls in Pretty Boxes* (1995); Swift, "Growing Pains," *Sports Illustrated,* August 17, 1995, 38, 41.

Miss (Ms.) Olympia (See Bodybuilding)

Moceanu, Dominique (b. 1981)

In 1995, at the age 14, Moceanu became the youngest gymnast ever to win the all-around U.S. national title. During that competition, held in New Orleans, her lowest score was a 9.725 for the uneven bars routine. Moceanu's total score of 78.45 points placed her ahead of former world champion Shannon Miller, who finished second with 78.25. Miller had overcome injuries sustained earlier that year, which had prevented her from competing at the American Cup competition.

Moceanu's parents, both gymnasts, immigrated from Romania in 1980, and Dominique was born and raised in the United States. In 1991, she trained under coaches Martha and Bela Karolyi at their world-famous Houston gym for elite gymnasts. By 1992, Moceanu had earned a spot on the U.S. national junior team, the youngest woman ever selected. In 1994, Moceanu won the national junior women's gymnastic competition.

At the world championships held in 1995, Moceanu defeated a number of more experienced gymnasts to finish in fifth place and help the U.S. women's team win a bronze medal. She also won a silver medal in the balance beam event. Moceanu maintained that she was enjoying her achievements and the positive response of the crowd. She said, "It's very exciting to be working with coach [Bela] Karolyi. He's always telling me, 'Go strong. Be tough.' He's always supportive and I want to work hard for him." In response, Karolyi said of Moceanu, "She has established herself as a real contender for 1996. Now is the time for some quieter, smoother development." At the 1996 Olympics in Atlanta, Moceanu was a member of the women's team that made history by winning America's first-ever team gold medal. She did not win any medals in individual events.

While training hard in her sport, Moceanu earned straight-As in school and enjoyed basketball and country music. She looked forward to pursuing a career in sports medicine as an adult. Former Olympic champion gymnast Nadia Comaneci has said of Moceanu, "People haven't seen someone like her for a long time."

See also Gymnastics; Karolyi, Bela; Miller, Shannon
References "Miller Faces a Fight for Title," *New York Times*, August 16, 1995, B12; Pitts, "Other Dominique to Next Nadia," *Olympian*, January-February 1996, 10–12; Swift, "Growing Pains," *Sports Illustrated*, August 17, 1995, 38, 41; Ryan, *Little Girls in Pretty Boxes* (1995).

Modification (See Perrin, Ethel)

Moe Thornton, Karen (See Swimming)

Moore, Ellie (b. 1940)

Born Eleanor Durall, in Central City, Kentucky, Moore became the first woman to head an all-woman governors board of a professional basketball team in 1973. That year, she purchased more than $1 million worth of stock in the Kentucky Colonels, a team in the American Basketball Association. This made Moore the majority shareholder, and she headed the five-woman board.

A sport-lover, as a teenager, Moore had played on her high school girls' basketball team. Later she graduated from the University of Kentucky at Lexington and taught English. Married twice (to John Y. Brown, Jr., former governor of Kentucky, then to Robert Moore), Moore became the mother of three children. In 1973, she was named Kentucky Woman of the Year, and she was listed in *Who's Who in America* in 1976.

Motherhood

A number of female athletes have distinguished themselves in their sports after giving birth and while raising children. Among the mothers who have won Olympic gold medals in their sport are diver Pat McCormick and runners Wilma Rudolph, Florence Griffith-Joyner, Valerie-Brisco Hooks, and Evelyn Ashford. Gold medalists Wyomia Tyus Simberg and Jackie Joyner-Kersee won medals at many professional track events after becoming mothers, as did Madeline Manning, who set an American record for the 880-yard race—1 minute 57.9 seconds.

Top bowler Marion Ladewig and golfer Nancy Lopez also continued to win tournaments while juggling motherhood and their sport. Australian tennis champions Margaret Smith Court and Evonne Goolagong both were known to take their children with them while on tour, and another tennis champion, Hazel Hotchkiss Wightman, won numerous tournaments during the years she was giving birth to and rearing five children. At age 86, Wightman told journalist Janice Kaplan, "I never thought of my children as handicaps. I enjoyed them and kept them with me. Being a mother doesn't have to limit you."

Pregnancy and motherhood have been addressed in different ways in high school and college athletics programs. In 1976, in Colorado, a married high school senior with a baby was denied permission to play on the basketball team. She had been a star player during her freshman year. A district court refused to overturn the school's decision. However, in Iowa, Ohio, and Oklahoma, as well as other states, school officials have not prohibited mothers from taking part in organized athletic events.

See also Ashford, Evelyn; Brisco-Hooks, Valerie; Griffith-Joyner, Florence; Ladewig, Marion; Lopez, Nancy; McCormick, Pat; Manning, Madeline; Rudolph, Wilma; Tyus Simberg, Wyomia; Wightman, Hazel Hotchkiss

Motoring Club, Women's

Based in New York City, the Women's Motoring Club began holding meetings early in 1908 at the Plaza Hotel. In January 1909, the club sponsored the first all-woman auto race. Twelve women entered the race, driving cars that were powered either with gasoline, steam, or electricity. All drivers and passengers were women, although they were permitted to be followed by a chase car bearing a male mechanic. The cars traveled from New York to Philadelphia.

The winner of the race was Mrs. John R. Ramsay of Hackensack, New Jersey, driving a Maxwell Runabout. She received the Benjamin Briscoe Trophy. Alice DiHeyes of Brielle, New Jersey, drove a Cadillac with four passengers and was awarded the Woman's Motoring Club Cup.

Motorsports Hall of Fame of America

Established in 1989, the hall honors America's best athletes in various motorsports: open wheel stock car, dragster, sports car, motorcycle, off road, power boat, air racing, and land speed racing. A nominee must either have been retired for at least three years or engaged in his or her area of the sport for at least 20 years. The hall is located in Novi, Missouri. As of 1995, three women were members: drag racer Shirley Muldowney and pilots Amelia Earhart and Jacqueline Cochran.

See also Earhart, Amelia; Muldowney, Shirley

Mountain Climbing

During the 1700s, men in Europe climbed mountains as a sport, first approaching such peaks as Mont Blanc in France, the Matterhorn in the Swiss Alps, and various peaks in Austria, Norway, and elsewhere. A British expedition climbed

Pioneer Peak in the Himalayas in 1892, while others tackled the tallest peak in the Andes in 1897.

During the 1800s, more women became involved. A Frenchwoman was part of a group that climbed Mont Blanc in 1838, and Lucy Walker ascended the Matterhorn in 1866. Others from different countries tried the sport. An American woman named Miss Brevoort joined her nephew on several climbs between 1870 and 1876, including a climb to the top of the Matterhorn. Most famous of the American women climbers was Annie Smith Peck, a teacher from Providence, Rhode Island. During the early 1900s, Peck conquered various peaks on five continents, some of which had never been climbed before.

The first all-women mountain climbing expedition took place in Nepal in 1978, when nine women and their six guides scaled Annapurna, the tenth-highest mountain in the world. Sadly, two members of the Himalayan Expedition died when they lost their footing on an ice wall, though two others did reach the summit. The group, led by Arlene Blum, a scientist at the University of California, was the fifth of 14 groups to reach the top of this peak. In October of the same year, Wyoming native Beverly Johnson became the first woman to climb El Capitan, in Yosemite National Park in California, alone. She climbed the 3,600-foot sheer granite peak in ten days. American Stacy Allison was the first woman to climb Mount Everest.

At the 1994 Banff Festival of Mountain Films, the predominantly male group chose as its theme "Women in Adventure." Among the women who made presentations to the group was Canadian Sharon Wood, the first North American woman to scale Mount Everest.

See also Himalayan Expedition; Peck, Annie Smith
References "Climbing Women," *Women's Sports and Fitness,* March 1995, 33–34; Styles, *On Top of the World: An Illustrated History of Mountain Climbing* (1967).

Muldowney, Shirley (b. 1940)

Called the best female drag racer in history, Shirley ("Cha Cha") Roque Muldowney set records for both men and women in drag racing, in which two cars race each other over a quarter-mile course.

Muldowney grew up in Schenectady, New York. By age 17, Muldowney was married and the mother of a son. She had never learned to drive a car but became interested in them through her husband Jack, a drag-racing enthusiast who could build and repair cars. Finding that she enjoyed operating fast cars, Muldowney began watching races, then driving in them. In her first races, she operated a 1940 Ford with a Cadillac V-8 engine. When she craved the chance to race at higher speeds, her husband built Muldowney a dragster that could hit speeds of 170 and 180 miles per hour.

Muldowney became one of the first women to compete in drag racing. But officials of the National Hot Rod Association and the American Hot Rod Association were reluctant to license women drivers. They expressed concern about the adverse publicity that might result if women were seriously injured on the track. Other opponents of women in drag racing claimed that men alone were mentally and physically strong enough to compete in the sport.

In the mid-sixties, women were allowed to try for their professional racing licenses on the same basis as men did. After receiving her license, Muldowney gained respect through her

As the only woman accepted into the Motorsports Hall of Fame, Shirley "Cha Cha" Muldowney had won more races than all other female racers combined.

Hot Rod Association's Nationals meet, Muldowney reached the finals with an outstanding performance in her Mustang racer. By covering a quarter-mile in 6.76 seconds, she established herself as a top driver. For two years, she consistently finished in the top five in the funny car races she entered.

In 1974, Muldowney reached the top level of drag racing, called Top Fuel. Such racing takes a great deal of strength, as the drivers handle long, low-slung roadsters that reach speeds of nearly 300 miles per hour within a few seconds. She went on to win 18 races at the national level, more than all other women drivers combined. She won the National Hot Rod Association National title in 1976 and 1977. Also in 1977, Muldowney won the National Hot Rod Association's Top Fuel world championship and became the first woman to win the Winston World Championship, considered by many to be the most prestigious drag race of all. The next year, she became the first two-time winner of the Top Fuel world title, which she won for the third time in 1982. A five-time All-America race winner, Muldowney was also the first woman to exceed a speed of 250 miles per hour. In 1983 she recorded a speed of 257.87 miles per hour—the fastest speed in drag-racing history for men or women.

In 1984 Muldowney survived a serious accident when a tire blew out on her car. Besides numerous injuries, her leg bones were shattered, numerous other bones were broken, and a thumb was almost severed. She endured several surgeries, and for four months after the accident, she could not move below the waist. She was bedridden and then in a wheelchair for more than a year. Following 18 months of physical therapy, she returned

performance at raceways around the country. She showed courage and quick thinking in critical situations, such as when her brakes failed during a 1967 race and on another occasion when her car burst into flames.

During the early seventies, Muldowney took part in racing a new and popular kind of car called a funny car. The cars were covered with plastic shells and painted in vivid, intricate designs. She won numerous funny car races. In 1971, she reached the last pairings in the International Hot Rod Association's Summernationals in a male-dominated field of top drivers. That fall, at the National to racing and won her eighteenth Nationals race in 1989, at age 49.

Muldowney's amazing career was the subject of a full-length feature film called *Heart Like a Wheel,* made in 1983. As of 1995, she was the only woman driver ever to be inducted into the Motorsports Hall of Fame of America (1990).

References Barrett, *Dragsters* (1987); Olney, *Modern Drag Racing Superstars* (1981).

National Amateur Athletic Federation (NAAF)

The first women's division of the NAAF was organized in 1923. Its motto was, "A sport for every girl and every girl for a sport." The founder of the women's division was Lou Henry Hoover, wife of Herbert C. Hoover, who became the thirty-first U.S. president in 1928. Born in Iowa in 1874, Lou Hoover was an avid athlete who enjoyed camping, horseback riding, and hunting. During her years in Washington, she was actively involved in the Girl Scouts and served as the organization's national president.

See also Amateur Athletic Union; Girl Scouts of the U.S.A.

National Association for Girls and Women in Sports (NAGWS)

A government agency, the NAGWS is a branch of the American Alliance for Health, Physical Education, Recreation, and Dance. It publishes informational and educational materials about sports programs for women as well as guidelines for setting up programs for training and programs for rating officials. Rulebooks, scorebooks, and articles on sports are among the many publications available from NAGWS.

National Baseball Hall of Fame

The Baseball Hall of Fame is located in Cooperstown, New York, on what is thought to be the site where baseball was first played. Local lore held that the game was developed by a Cooperstown man named Abner Doubleday in 1839.

Businessmen in Cooperstown decided to organize a display of baseball artifacts for the hundredth anniversary of the game in 1939. The idea grew as baseball officials discussed building a permanent exhibit, and planned to honor top players by voting them each year into a hall of fame. The first such election was held in 1936. Five players were selected: Ty Cobb, Babe Ruth, Honus Wagner, Christy Mathewson, and Walter Johnson. By 1939, when the building was officially opened to the public, 25 people had been inducted into the hall. The practice continues to this day, and all the players honored are men. Millions of visitors have toured the museum.

In 1988, a new exhibition called Women in Baseball opened, after years of discussion about including women athletes in the museum. The exhibit honored the 550 women from the United States, Canada, and Cuba who played with the All-American Girls Professional Baseball League (AAGPBL), which operated from 1943 to 1954. Included in the women's exhibit are individual and team photographs as well as biographical sketches of the players, action photos, uniforms, equipment, and press clippings.

See also All-American Girls Professional Baseball League

References Helmer, *Belles of the Ballpark* (1993); Macy, *A Whole New Ball Game* (1993)

National Collegiate Athletic Association (NCAA)

Founded in 1905 with 62 colleges and universities as the Intercollegiate Athletic Association, the NCAA was assembled to develop rules and standards for university football. The organization grew in size and authority to form a governing body for men's collegiate sports. Soon it was sponsoring programs and competitions in football, lacrosse, rowing, baseball, basketball, cross country, fencing, golf, gymnastics, ice hockey, soccer, swimming, tennis, track and field, and wrestling, among others.

The NCAA did not admit women until 1974. A different governing body for women's sports had emerged in the form of the Association for Intercollegiate Athletics for Women (AIAW). The AIAW, with 300 member schools, was the first organization with the power to enforce standards and regulations in regard to women's college athletic programs and competitions. Membership in the AIAW continued to grow until the NCAA decided to take charge of women's collegiate sports in 1974.

In 1972, the NCAA lobbied strenuously against the passage of Title IX, civil rights legislation that required girls and women to receive equitable treatment in school and college sports programs, as well as other educational programs. After Title IX became law, the NCAA decided to try to govern women's collegiate sports as well as men's, thus placing authority for all collegiate athletics under one roof. The NCAA challenged the position of the AIAW, setting up a competition between the two organizations. The AIAW fought to maintain control, but the NCAA, with more power and economic resources, prevailed and became the ruling body for most women's collegiate sports programs.

The NCAA sets eligibility rules and sponsors championship tournaments in a variety of sports. It also sets rules about scholarships, specifying the number that will be given to athletes in each sport and determining the process by which they are offered and accepted.

See also Association for Intercollegiate Athletics for Women (AIAW); Title IX
Reference Nelson, *Are We Winning Yet?* (1991).

National Organization for Women (NOW)

The National Organization for Women (NOW), founded in October 1966, played a key role in defining issues in the women's rights movement and worked to end gender discrimination. By the 1960s, women had become increasingly vocal in demanding equal access to educational, professional, legal, and economic opportunities. Betty Goldstein Friedan, author of *The Feminine Mystique*, became the first president of NOW. Many of those involved in the struggle for equal rights for women called themselves "feminists."

Women's sports was one of the areas in which NOW became involved. It advocated equal pay for women athletes and filed lawsuits alleging discrimination in amateur and professional athletics. NOW began providing legal help or advice to girls who had been denied the chance to play in local Little League teams, and to high school and college women who did not have access to sports programs comparable to those provided for male students. NOW also set up a lobbying group to influence members of Congress on these and other issues. A number of prominent women's athletes, such as Billie Jean King, have identified themselves as feminists and members of NOW.

National Softball Hall of Fame and Museum

Founded in 1957 by the Amateur Softball Association (ASA), the hall and museum were officially dedicated on May 26, 1973, in Oklahoma City, Oklahoma. Among the exhibits in the museum are photos of national champions, slow pitch and fast pitch records, uniforms and equipment used throughout history, photographs of players in action, trophies and other awards, and historical narratives. The ASA Research Center and Library contains numerous publications about the game and its players. Players are eligible to be considered for election after they have stopped playing for at least three years.

Since both fast-pitch and slow-pitch softball have long been popular sports for American women, the museum and hall has honored women players and teams since the 1950s. In 1957, the first two women were voted into the hall of fame: fast-pitch players Amy Peralta Shelton and Marie Wadlow. The forty-third woman to be inducted was Kathy Arendson, a pitcher from Zeeland, Michigan, named to the hall in 1996.

See also Grayson, Betty Evans; Joyce, Joan; Tickey, Bertha Reagan; Wadlow, Marie
Reference "Hall of Fame Museum," fact sheet from the Amateur Softball Association

National Sports Festival (See Olympic Festival)

National Tennis League (NTL) (See Tennis)

National Track and Field Hall of Fame

The hall was originally founded by the Athletics Congress (now USA Track and Field) and was located in Charleston, West Virginia. In 1983 it moved to Indianapolis, Indiana, reopening at the Hoosier Dome three years later. The idea for the hall came from an optometrist, Don Cohen, who thought that athletes, coaches, and contributors to track and field sports should be honored. It opened in 1984.

In order to be nominated, athletes must have been retired from their sport at least three years; coaches must have coached for at least 20 years (if retired) or for 35 years (if still coaching). An 800-member panel votes on nominees. It is made up of Hall of Fame and USA Track and Field officials, Hall of Fame members, current U.S. champions, and members of the Track and Field Writers of America.

Memorabilia in the hall, much of it donated by the athletes or their families, includes items from Babe Didrikson Zaharias, who, as of 1994, was one of 19 women athletes in the hall. No women track and field coaches had yet been elected to membership in the hall as of that year.

See also Didrikson Zaharias, Babe

National Women's Football League (NWFL)

The most prominent of the latter-day women's football leagues, it had three divisions: Western, Southern, and Northern. Teams included the Cleveland Brewers, Columbus Pacesetters, Middletown Mavericks, Toledo Troopers, Dallas–Fort Worth Shamrocks, Houston Hurricanes, Lawton Tornadoes, and Oklahoma City

Dolls. The league operated from 1974 to 1987.

Navratilova, Martina (b. 1956)

Growing up in Revnice, Czechoslovakia, Martina Navratilova skied and played soccer and ice hockey at an early age. She began playing tennis at age six, encouraged by her athletic mother and stepfather, both excellent players. Navratilova practiced for hours on local clay courts to improve her game and was inspired by idols such as Australian champion Rod Laver, also a left-handed player, and American Billie Jean King, who played the aggressive serve-and-volley game Martina favored. At age eight, she reached the semifinals of a tournament for children up to age 12.

Starting in 1965, former champion George Parma began coaching her, enabling her to play year-round at the only indoor public courts in Czechoslovakia. Each week, when she went to Prague for lessons, she stayed overnight at her grandmother's. The whole family helped Martina succeed, saving money for her rackets, clothes, and transportation to matches.

In 1965, troops from the Soviet Union invaded Czechoslovakia. Tanks rolled through the country as Martina was playing in a tournament. She later called this a depressing time for herself and many fellow Czechs. Her coach, out of the country at the time, decided not to return. But Martina persisted without him to become the national 14-and-under champion. By age 16, she was the top woman player in Czechoslovakia.

During the early 1970s, as she played tennis in different nations, Navratilova became known for strong strokes, a powerful serve, and an aggressive net game. In 1973, she won the Junior Girls title at Wimbledon (the All-England tournament). Sports commentator Bud Collins praised Navratilova as "bold, determined, and agile." As she reached the finals in top tournaments, she charmed players and spectators with her cheerful manner and quick mastery of languages. But by 1975, Navratilova was worried about increasing government restrictions in Czechoslovakia. She heard that the government planned to limit her travel so that she would be unable to compete in many tournaments. At the U.S. Open, Navratilova decided to ask for asylum in the United States.

Away from her family and old friends, Navratilova had to make many adjustments. A taste for rich foods—pizza, cheesecake, milk shakes, and fast-food hamburgers—led to a weight gain and slump in her game, and she appeared moody and upset when she erred on the court. Still, teaming up with Chris Evert, her arch-rival, she won the 1975 women's doubles match at Wimbledon. This victory as well as Navratilova's other achievements were not reported in her homeland, where she was considered a "nonperson."

During 1977, Navratilova worked hard and adopted a healthy diet and a training program that included weight-lifting. Her serve became even more powerful and was clocked at 93 miles per hour. As her concentration and performance improved, so did Navratilova's confidence. She swept seven tournaments in a row, including the women's title at Wimbledon, a title she had desired for years. She defeated Evert in the third set to win what was to be the first of nine singles' titles there, surpassing the record of eight held by Helen Wills Moody.

In 1979, Navratilova won the women's doubles at Wimbledon with Billie Jean King. Another dream came true that year

Martina Navratilova reaches for a shot at the Virginia Slims tournament in 1993. Between 1982 and 1987, Navratilova was ranked number one in all but 22 weeks of the 282-week time span.

when her mother, stepfather, and sister moved into a home she had bought for them in Dallas, Texas. Yet the family missed their homeland and jobs in Czechoslovakia. When they returned, Martina insisted that they accept a generous gift of money that would enable them to buy a lovely home in the country. During this trying year, Navratilova lost her number one ranking and worked hard to regain it. During 1984, as a doubles player, she won the four events—the Australian Open, French Open, Wimbledon, and U.S. Open—that make up a Grand Slam in tennis. Only one other men's team and one other women's team had done so. During this same period,

Navratilova won 74 professional matches in a row and set a record for the longest winning streak in tennis history. In 1983, she won 16 of 17 matches. From 1981 through 1984, she won the Wimbledon doubles title with Pam Shriver. She was named the Women's Sports Foundation Sportswoman of the Year in 1982, 1983, and 1984 and was inducted into the Women's Sports Hall of Fame in 1984.

During the early 1980s, Navratilova contributed prize money and time to the Martina Youth Foundation, which was organized to help economically disadvantaged children learn to play tennis. Sometimes, Navratilova taught lessons on inner-city courts herself. Nearing the end of her professional singles career in 1987, Navratilova snagged both the U.S. Open and Wimbledon women's titles.

Between 1982 and 1987, she was ranked number one in all but 22 weeks of this 282-week time span. From time to time, she lost to a promising new player or talented veteran, but she remained the number one women's singles player longer than any of her predecessors. She continued to challenge new players in the early 1990s. In 1992, she won her 158th professional title, the Virginia Slims tournament in Chicago, breaking all previous records of total tennis titles won. A year later, she broke another record, becoming the oldest player ever to defeat a number one–ranked player in professional tennis when she defeated Monica Seles in the French Open. As of 1993, she was the top prize-winner in women's tennis, with a total of $19,052,570.

Although Navratilova retired from singles play in 1994, she remained a force in both mixed doubles and women's doubles, winning those two events at Wimbledon in 1995.

See also Evert, Chris; Grand Slam; King, Billie Jean
References Doherty, "Martina Remembers Her Nine Wins," *Tennis*, July 1994, 124–138; Frayne, *Famous Women Tennis Players* (1979); Knudsen, *Martina Navratilova: Tennis Power* (1986); Preston, "Hail and Farewell," *Tennis*, September 1994, 49–53; Vecsey and Navratilova, *Martina* (1985).

Nelson, Cynthia (b. 1956)

One of the best women downhill racers in American skiing history, Cindy Nelson first became part of the U.S. World Cup team at age 15. She won five national skiing titles: the downhill in 1973 and 1978, the slalom in 1975 and 1976, and the Alpine combined in 1978. A hip injury kept Nelson out of the 1972 Olympics, but she won a bronze medal in the downhill event at the 1976 Games, held in Innsbruck, Austria. Nelson also won four World Cup events during the 1970s.

At the 1980 world championships, Nelson won a silver medal in the combined event. She was back competing at the 1980 Games, in Lake Placid, New York. Her best event there was the downhill, in which she tied for seventh place. She was ranked as the seventh woman in the World Cup in 1983, a year in which she won a silver medal in the giant slalom competition.

One of the most experienced skiers at the 1984 Games, Nelson impressed spectators when she competed with a brace on a badly injured knee. Unable to race in the downhill, she nevertheless completed the slalom and came in nineteenth. After recovering from another injury, Nelson continued to compete during the 1990s. In 1995, at the MCI downhill slalom competition at Telluride, Colorado, Nelson and her partner, Phil Mahre, came in third.

Neuberger, Leah Thall
(**See** Table Tennis)

New York City Marathon (**See** Marathon Running)

Nord, Gloria (**See** Roller Skating)

Norelius, Martha (1908–1955)

Born in Sweden, Norelius, whose father had won a gold medal in gymnastics, was raised in the United States. She is thought to be the first woman swimmer to use a high head and elbow position with arched back and a six-beat leg kick in world-class competition, techniques that had traditionally been used only by men.

Norelius was the first woman to win gold medals at two consecutive Olympic Games. In 1924, she won the 400-meter freestyle swimming event, defeating long-distance swimmer Gertrude Ederle. Norelius, at 16½, was the youngest female medalist at those Games. She repeated her victory in the 400-meters at the 1928 Olympics, where she also won a gold medal as part of the women's 4 x 100–meter freestyle relay team. Between 1926 and 1928, she set nearly 30 world records in swimming events, ranging from 50-meter races to marathons.

After turning professional in 1929, Norelius competed in marathon events as well as short races. She won a $10,000 prize in 1920 when she finished first in the 10-mile William Wrigley Marathon in Toronto, Canada. Norelius later married a fellow athlete, Canadian Joseph Wright, an oarsman who had won a silver medal. She was elected to the International Swimming Hall of Fame in 1967.

Novara-Reber, Sue (b. 1955)

In 1975, bicycling champion Novara-Reber became the youngest woman ever to win the world sprint championship, a victory she repeated the next year. A native of Flint, Michigan, Novara-Reber was already known as a national champion in cycling track races. In 1972, she had won the Match Sprint event, a short-distance race, and took the National Track Racing Championship. In 1972, from 1974 to 1976, and in 1977 and 1978, she won the U.S. National Amateur Bicycling Sprint Race Championships. In 1974 and 1975 and from 1977 through 1980, she was national match sprint champion again.

Concentrating on road racing, Novara-Reber won the national title in that sport in 1982. That same year, she won the Eastern Division of the *Self* Magazine Cycling Circuit. She repeated that victory in 1983, also placing second in the Ruffles Tour of Texas and winning two stages of the French road-racing tour. She finished her racing career in 1984, when she won the 24-mile Central Park Grand Prix held in New York City. In 1986, Novara-Reber coached the U.S. women's cycling team, which won four medals, including one gold, at the 1987 world championships.

Nyad, Diana (b. 1952)

Born in New York City, distance swimmer Diana Nyad and her family moved to Florida when she was three. She later said, "I was thrown into the middle of the pool at six months and swam to the edge." At age 11, she joined the swim team at her Fort Lauderdale junior high school. She worked hard and became the state champion in her age group for both the 100-meter and 200-meter backstroke. Her coach, the renowned Jack Nelson, saw the makings of a champion in this slender, strong teenager and later called her the hardest worker he had ever seen. She rose between 4:30 and 5:30 each morning to practice and train and endured stinging eyes from hours of swimming in heavily chlorinated water. Nyad had hoped to compete in the 1968 Olympics in the backstroke competition, but a long viral illness dashed her hopes and left her unable to return to sprint races. In 1970, she took up marathon swimming and finished tenth of 20 competitors and first among all women racers in a 10-mile marathon swim across Lake Ontario, setting a woman's record with her time of 4 hours and 23 minutes. That same year, she was one of only three swimmers to complete the arduous 28-mile race in Chicoutimi, Quebec, one of the toughest in the world.

Entering Emory University as a pre-med student, she continued to train, swimming as well as running, while she attended classes and studied. As a result of some student pranks and disagreements with the dean at Emory, Nyad was expelled and left to travel and work as a lifeguard. Determined to finish college, she applied to Lake Forest College in Illinois and maintained an A-average as well as playing on the varsity tennis team and taking drama classes. She again entered the Chicoutimi race and was among the ten who finished. She set a new women's record in a team race called the 24-Hour La Tuque Swim, held a week after Chicoutimi. She and her partner Guston Pare came in third, but an unconscious Nyad was rushed to the hospital at the end, suffering from a hemorrhaging eye. Her fellow swimmers were impressed by her courage.

Later, in her autobiography, Nyad would describe the difficulties of long-distance swimming and the sensory deprivation swimmers suffer: "Dark goggles cover the eyes; the head turns some 60 times a minute toward the boat so that eye focus is almost never achieved. Tight rubber caps inhibit hearing to the point that a shrill police whistle often can't be heard from a 20-foot distance. Both tactile sense and balance are seriously distorted so that your body feels only an uncontrolled, floaty sensation. . . . You must concentrate on keeping your will strong enough to resist the various bombarding pains while occupying your mind with something other than the pain itself."

In 1973, Nyad entered a Ph.D. program in comparative literature. Between 1970 and 1975, she completed several swims of up to 50 miles, in the Suez Canal, the Nile, and other places. She had swum 20 hours in Lake Ontario, 24 hours in the surf around Australia (swimming inside a cage near the Great Barrier Reef where sharks are common), and 40 hours in the cold North Sea.

In fall 1975, Nyad decided to swim the 28 miles around Manhattan Island. On October 6, she swam the difficult course in dirty waters containing dead rats, trash, and numerous boats in 7 hours and 57 minutes, a new record for both men and women. Her swim around Manhattan Island brought Nyad and the sport of marathon swimming more recognition from the general public. She made television appearances, including one in which she rode a killer whale, and worked on a documentary film.

Nyad coached the swim team at Barnard College in 1975–1976 and 1976–1977 while attending New York University. In 1976, she decided to make the English Channel swim and proceeded to train vigorously and gain weight by eating spaghetti, baked potatoes, toast with honey, and desserts. But severe nausea during the trip forced her to quit before the end. During another trip, extreme cold forced her to stop after four hours, when she had reached the middle of the Channel.

One of her most ambitious long-distance attempts was the 130 miles from Havana, Cuba, to Marathon Key, Florida. In 1978, she completed 70 miles of this distance, leaving the water after 42 hours. Poor weather forecasting information and a motorized cage that hampered her in the water ended this trip sooner than expected. She had also hoped to swim in July, when weather conditions were optimal, but the Cuban government did not issue permission in time, and she had to set out later, on August 13. While in the water, Nyad became quite seasick. Her lips and tongue swelled badly from long exposure to salt water as she fought against waves 6 and 7 feet high. Her trainers convinced her she must stop before reaching Florida. Later, Nyad said she had put the "greatest human effort of my lifetime into that swim."

In 1978, after two attempts, Nyad swam the 89 miles between the Bahamas and Florida in less than 28 hours. During her career, she swam thousands of miles, crossing lakes, rivers, and seas. She also enjoyed playing squash (as of 1978, she was the second-ranked women's player in the New York City area), listening to music, and reading. A swim analyst for ABC Sports, she also promoted skin lotion and other products and became a motivational speaker and the author of articles and a book. In 1975, she competed in the ABC Superstars event with Althea Gibson, Martina Navratilova, and Wyomia Tyus.

References Campbell, *Marathon: The World of the Long Distance Athlete* (1977); Gutman, *More Modern Women Superstars* (1979); Nyad, *Other Shores* (1978).

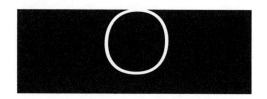

Oakley, Annie (1860–1926)

A sharp-shooter and riflery champion, Oakley was born Phoebe June Mosee, or Mozes, in a log cabin in Darke County, Ohio. She learned to shoot a rifle at about age 12, using her skills to hunt food for her family and to kill rabbits and quail, which she sold at a local market in Cincinnati.

Oakley won a shooting contest at age 15, then toured the country with a vaudeville show, taking the stage name "Annie Oakley," after a town in Ohio. In sharpshooting contests, she competed against the top men shooters of her day. A Quaker, Oakley followed pacifist beliefs by not using her shooting ability for any violence against people. In her spare time, she spent hours reading the Bible.

In 1876, Oakley married champion shooter Frank Butler, the owner of a traveling show. She had defeated Butler in a shooting contest. They worked in the Sells Brothers Circus, then toured America and Europe with Buffalo Bill's Wild West Show. Audiences around the world were thrilled by her feats, as she shot glass balls and dimes tossed in the air and performed stunts on horseback. Oakley met many famous people and was honored by royalty. The Sioux chief, Sitting Bull, called her "Little Sure Shot." Even at age 62, Oakley could break 100 targets in a row.

Oakley was injured in a train wreck in 1901 and stopped performing. She taught shooting and portrayed western women on stage, entertaining soldiers during World War I with marksmanship exhibitions at military camps. Another accident in 1922 left her in frail health. She returned to Ohio where she died at age 66. A famous Broadway musical, later a movie, called *Annie Get Your Gun* was based on her life.

References Guttman, *Women's Sport: A History* (1991); Havighurst, *Annie Oakley of the Wild West* (1992); Hickok, *A Who's Who of Sports Champions* (1995).

Officiating

Once women were rarely officials at professional sports events. But that situation began to change during the late 1900s as women were hired or enlisted to officiate at various amateur and professional sports events. In 1975, Christine Wren became an umpire and worked in minor league training camps, the only woman chosen from among 15 eligible umpires to do so. The next year, in Arizona, Carol Levine officiated at two high school football games, another first. In 1981 Betty Ellis became the first woman to officiate at a soccer match. She served as a linesman during a contest between the San Jose (California) Earthquakes and the Edmonton (Canada) Drillers. Ellis was then the only woman among the 163 officials in the North American Soccer League. She had begun officiating at local

Sharp-shooting Annie Oakley won a shooting contests at the age of 15, competed against champion men shooters, and toured America and Europe with Buffalo Bill's "Wild West Show."

matches ten years earlier, moving up to college then to semiprofessional games.

See also Postema, Pam

Olympic Festival, U.S.

This multisport event, which began in 1978 under the name National Sports Festival, is held in different American cities every summer, except during Olympic Games years. The festival allows athletes to gain more experience competing and thus be better prepared for the Olympics. The events featured include those in the Summer Olympics—for example, archery, diving, swimming, tennis, track and field—as well as speed skating.

At the first festival, about 1,900 athletes competed in 25 sports over a period of four days. By 1993, 37 sports were featured, and more than 3,000 athletes were taking part. The number of women athletes grew from 611 (fewer than one-third of all participants) at the first festival to 1,242 (of a total 1,664 participants) at the 1994 festival. In 1995, the United States Olympic Committee (USOC), which sponsors the event, planned to hold it every two years, between the Winter and Summer Games.

See also Primrose-Smith, Elizabeth
Reference *1995 Fact Book: United States Olympic Committee* (1995).

Olympic Hall of Fame, U.S.

Located in Colorado Springs, Colorado, the hall was established in 1983 by the United States Olympic Committee (USOC). A group consisting of USOC board members, Hall of Fame members, and the National Sportscasters and Sportswriters Association votes on new members. To be eligible, athletes must have been retired from active competition for at least five years. As of 1995, the following women were members: divers Pat McCormick (1985) and Micki King (1992); figure skaters Peggy Fleming (1983), Dorothy Hamill (1991), and Tenley Albright (1988); gymnast Mary Lou Retton (1985); swimmers Debbie Meyer (1986), Donna de Varona (1987), Shirley Babashoff (1987), Tracy Caulkins (1990), and Helene Madison (1992); and in track and field, Babe Didrikson (1983), Wilma Rudolph (1983), and Wyomia Tyus (1985).

Olympic Medal

One of the most coveted awards for athletes around the world is an Olympic medal. Gold, silver, and bronze awards are given to those athletes in each event who finish first, second, and third at the Winter or Summer Olympics. The front of the medal shows the Olympic torch and five interlocking rings, the symbol of the Games. The five rings symbolize the five major world regions sending athletes—Europe, Asia, Africa, Australia, and North and South America. On the back is engraved the date and site of the particular Games. The medals are viewed as having been won by the athlete's nation as well as the individual. During the presentation of medals, the national anthem of the gold-medalist's homeland is played as the medalists stand on a three-tiered podium before the spectators.

The first American Olympic medalists were men. The United States did not officially enter the first modern Games, held in 1896 in Athens, Greece. But a group of male track and field athletes went to Athens as an unofficial team and competed. They won 9 of the 12 track and field events and two shooting events, amassing more golds than any other country.

American women first competed in 1920, at the Olympics held in Antwerp,

Belgium, and captured several medals. Ethelda Bleibtrey won a gold medal in the 100-meter freestyle swim event, while Aileen Riggin became the first U.S. woman to win a gold medal in diving. In 1948 skier Gretchen Kunigk Fraser became the first American woman to win a medal in an Olympic skiing event. Andrea Mead Lawrence became the first skier, male or female, to win two skiing events (1952).

American women have won numerous medals for figure skating at the Winter Olympics. In 1956 Tenley Albright became the first American to capture the gold. Since then, Carol Heiss, Peggy Fleming, Dorothy Hamill, and Kristi Yamaguchi have won gold medals, and several U.S. women have taken second and third place. Fleming was the only U.S. athlete to win a gold medal during the 1968 Winter Games. American women have also done well in swimming and diving events at the Summer Olympics.

Among the women who have set records for the number of Olympic medals won is speed skater Bonnie Blair, who won a record five gold medals in speed skating at the 1994 Games. Diver Pat McCormick won gold medals in both the springboard and platform events at two successive Games, 1952 and 1956, to win a remarkable "double-double." At the 1996 Summer Olympics in Atlanta, U.S. women won more medals than did the U.S. men.

See also Albright, Tenley; Blair, Bonnie Kathleen; Bleibtrey, Ethelda; Evans, Janet; Fleming, Peggy; Fraser, Gretchen Kunigk; Gymnastics; Hamill, Dorothy; Heiss, Carol; Lawrence, Andrea Mead; McCormick, Pat; Meyer, Deborah; Miller, Shannon; Retton, Mary Lou; Riggin, Aileen; Rudolph, Wilma; Yamaguchi, Kristi

References *1995 Fact Book: United States Olympic Committee* (1995); Kierens et al., *The Story of the Olympic Games: 776 B.C. to 1976* (1977); Pratt and Benagh, *The Official Encyclopedia of Sports* (1964).

Olympics

The first Games were held in 776 B.C. in Olympia, near the west coast of Greece, with events for men only. The purpose of the competition was to allow contestants to demonstrate their manly skills and to unite the regions of Greece despite periodic wars and unrest. Women were banned by law, under penalty of death, from even watching the Olympics. Historians have speculated that this might have been because the men competed naked or because athletics was not deemed appropriate for women. Greek women proceeded to organize athletic Games for themselves, called the *Heraea*, after a goddess. They ran foot races every four years, and winners received wreaths fashioned from wild olive branches.

A foot race down the length of the stadium was the one and only event at the first Olympics. In later years, other running events and sports were added, including the prestigious discus, and more athletes joined the competition. In the fourth century A.D., under Roman rule, the Games were abolished for a time. People lost interest, especially after A.D. 67, when Emperor Nero brought thousands of supporters with him to the competition and entered some events himself. Regardless of the outcome, the judges were ordered to give Nero first place. In A.D. 390, the Games were officially banned by Christian rulers, who called them a pagan festival.

The Olympics were not revived until 1896 when Frenchman Pierre de Coubertin arranged for Games to be held that year in Athens. Summer Games were then scheduled every four years and grew to include 20 sports, with the number growing through the years. Olympics have been held every four years since, with the exception of wartime (1916,

1940, and 1944). In 1980, President Jimmy Carter announced that the United States would boycott the Summer Olympics, held that year in Moscow. This action was intended as a protest to the Soviet Union's invasion of Afghanistan. The Soviets then boycotted the 1984 Summer Olympics held four years later in Los Angeles.

Women's events were not included in the first modern Games, at which Baron de Coubertin announced, "Let women practice all the sports if they wish, but let them not show off." However, six women convinced officials to allow them to compete in lawn tennis during the 1900 Olympics. Thirteen others competed in golf and yachting events. In 1904, women's archery became an Olympic event, and a total of six women took part. Women's swimming was added in 1912. There were 136 women athletes at the 1924 Olympics, a number that rose to 290 by 1928. That year, track and field events for women were added. Women's participation continued to expand, so that by 1984, there were 1,500 women competing in 76 athletic events, a number that continued to grow during the 1990s. In 1988, more than one-fourth of the competitors were women. Their number rose to 3,000 by 1992. After 1984, new sports were added for women, such as basketball (1976), judo (1988), and softball and soccer (1996).

To begin the ceremonies, an Olympic flame is lit in Olympia, Greece, then brought to the country where the Games are taking place. The torch is carried to the stadium, where the Olympic flame burns until the end of the Games. As women have become more involved in all aspects of the Games, some have been chosen to carry the Olympic torch. Others have been flag-bearers, leading their

national team into the stadium for opening ceremonies. Women have also become more involved in planning and running the Games.

Throughout the era of the Olympics, there has been an ongoing debate over which events should be open to women. Several sports categories (including bobsledding, boxing, riflery, weight-lifting, wrestling) have been closed to women. As of 1983, women could not participate in 9 of the 27 Olympic sports categories: boxing, soccer, judo, wrestling, modern pentathlon, weight-lifting, biathlon, bobsledding, and ice hockey. By 1996, there were women's events in judo, biathlon, and soccer, as well as softball.

The International Olympic Committee (IOC) developed regulations that determined which events were held and who could compete. The IOC's Rule 44 states that in order to be considered for the Games, a sporting event must be "widely practiced by women in at least 35 countries on 3 continents." In some parts of the world, such as Arab countries, women are discouraged from competing in many sports because of Muslim dress laws requiring women to cover their legs and arms. Thus Rule 44 kept a number of women's events out of the Olympics for decades. In addition, new events could not be added to the Olympics except on request by an international sports federation, most of which are male-dominated. Until 1981, the IOC was composed entirely of men. By 1990, only a few of the nearly 90 members were women. In 1995, the USOC announced a plan to recruit more women into leadership positions.

Olympics, Summer

Trials for Summer Olympic Games are held in April of the year in which the Games are scheduled. The United States

Olympic Committee (USOC) relies on input from various official sports organizations, such as the United States Gymnastics Federation, to govern the qualifying systems, standards, and training programs for each sport. Each of the Summer Olympic sports is supervised by a specific sports organization, which is a member of the USOC.

At Summer Games, women Olympians compete in archery, badminton, basketball, canoeing and kayaking, cycling, diving, fencing, field hockey, gymnastics, judo, rowing, soccer, softball, swimming, team handball, tennis, track and field, and volleyball. They also team up with men to participate in yachting, equestrian events, and shooting.

Olympics, Winter

Winter Games did not become part of the Olympics until 1925, by a vote of the International Olympics Committee. Indoor winter sports, such as figure skating (1908) and ice hockey (1920), had been gradually added to the Summer Olympics. Yet some nations opposed a separate Winter Olympics, especially in Scandinavia, where some people feared that Winter Games would overshadow the Nordic Games.

The French organized an International Winter Sports Week in Paris in 1924, a year in which Summer Olympics were also held. Sixteen nations sent athletes to Chamonix, in the French Alps, for the competition. Women competed only in figure skating events, one of seven sports that were included that year. The festival was so successful that Olympic committee members decided to continue the competitions on a regular basis, and Games were held every four years, except in 1940 and 1944 (during World War II). They were held in both 1992 and 1994;

after that, the Summer and Winter Games would then alternate with each other every two years with Winter Games scheduled in 1998 and every four years thereafter.

The Winter Olympics take place in late January or February of the scheduled year. Not all of the countries who belong to the IOC take part in winter sports. About 37 countries usually compete in these Games, and only three—Great Britain, Sweden, and the United States—have participated in every Winter Olympics.

Sports in the Winter Olympics include skiing, speed skating, figure skating, ice hockey, bobsledding, luge, and biathlon (an event that combines cross country skiing with rifle marksmanship in three events). The skiing events include Alpine, which began in 1936 and now includes three events: special slalom (skiers race downhill while zigzagging through gates made of two poles), giant slalom, and downhill. Nordic skiing became part of the Olympics in 1924, but women did not take part in these events until 1964. Men have seven events: four cross country races, two jumping events, and the Nordic combined—a cross country race and ski jump. Women compete in three cross country races.

Women compete in a biathlon, figure skating, luge, skiing (both Alpine and Nordic), and speed skating. There are four speed skating races for women, held since 1960, although events for men speed skaters have been included since 1924. Figure skating became an official event in 1920, with events for both male and female skaters as well as pairs' and ice dancing events that include male and female couples. There are two luge events for men and one for women, in which the athletes lying on their backs race downhill in small sleds steered with ropes.

Speed skater Bonnie Blair on her way to winning the women's 1,000 meter at the 1992 Olympics in France. Blair set a world record when she won her fifth gold metal at the 1994 Olympics.

O'Neil, Kitty

See also Pan American Games
References *1995 Fact Book: United States Olympic Committee* (1995); Greenberg, *The Guinness Book of Olympics Facts and Feats* (1983); Kieren et al., *The Story of the Olympic Games: 776 B.C. 1976* (1977); Leder, *Grace and Glory* (1996); Pratt and Benagh, *The Official Encyclopedia of Sports* (1964).

O'Neil, Kitty (b. 1948)

Although deaf since birth, O'Neil became a top platform diver, water-speed skier, and land-speed racer. She has often said that being deaf may have been an asset in her pursuits, since it helped her to focus more completely on what she was doing.

Born in Corpus Christi, Texas, O'Neil's ancestors were Irish and Cherokee Indian. She grew up in Wichita Falls, Texas, and mastered lip-reading well enough to attend regular schools. While in her teens, O'Neil excelled as a swimmer and diver, winning the diving competition at the Junior Olympics sponsored by the Amateur Athletic Union (AAU). A broken wrist and serious illness kept her from trying out for the 1968 U.S. Olympic diving team.

O'Neil then took up water-skiing and, in 1970, set a speed-skiing record for women—104.85 miles per hour. After marrying stuntman and motorcyclist Duffy Hambleton, she began learning stunts herself and joined Stunts Unlimited, where she learned to perform daring feats.

In 1976 she set out to break the world land-speed record in a rocket car. In December she achieved her goal when she became the first woman to reach a speed of 618.340 miles per hour in the Alvord Desert in Oregon. Her average speed during this attempt was 514.120 miles per hour. After this achievement, O'Neil set other world speed and acceleration records using jet-powered vehicles and worked as a stuntwoman in feature films.

Reference *Lincoln Library of Sports Champions*, vol. 13 (1989).

Osteoporosis

This is a disease that causes loss of bone mass, making one susceptible to bone fractures, even of large bone masses such as the hip. Women are particularly prone to osteoporosis after menopause. A decline in estrogen production at that time can increase bone loss.

Research has shown that exercise begun early in life and continuing into old age can reduce the amount of bone loss in women as well as men. Studies during the 1990s also showed that athletes tend to have greater bone mass in the limbs they use most often—for example, right-handed tennis players have greater bone mass in their right arms.

Reference Appleton, *Healthy Bones* (1991).

Outerbridge, Mary Ewing (1852–1886)

Outerbridge is known as the "Mother of Tennis." She reputedly brought the game to the United States from Bermuda, where she had been vacationing in 1874. Returning home with a set of rackets and balls, she and her brother and some friends set up a court at the Staten Island Cricket and Baseball Club in New York, where the Outerbridge family were members.

However, historians have debated whether the Philadelphia-born Outerbridge was the first to bring tennis to the United States. People may have also been playing it in Arizona that year, and tennis was also being played in Boston, Philadelphia, and some other cities by 1874. At any rate, Outerbridge was instrumental in helping to spread the game and make it popular. She lived to see the first U.S. championships held in New

York before she died in 1886. For her contributions to the sport, Outerbridge was inducted into the Tennis Hall of Fame in 1981.

References Collins and Hollander, *Modern Encyclopedia of Tennis* (1994); Pratt and Benagh, *The Official Encyclopedia of Sports* (1964).

Outward Bound

A survival training program for people over age 16, Outward Bound offers wilderness experiences to male, female, or coed groups. Participants may canoe, climb rocks or mountains, sail, hike, travel by kayak or canoe, or bicycle as part of their experience, depending on the terrain and goals of the trip. Individuals sometimes engage in a three-day solo experience, left alone with a sleeping bag and minimal supplies. The physical challenges of Outward Bound are intended to build courage, self-confidence, and physical stamina.

Paddle Tennis (See Platform Tennis)

Palfrey, Sarah (b. 1912)
A women's tennis champion from 1930 to the mid-1940s, Sarah Hammond Palfrey Fabyan Cooke Danzig was one of five tennis-playing sisters who won U.S. junior titles. During her amateur career, Palfrey won 13 singles titles and 11 major doubles titles.

As a child, Palfrey studied with Hazel Hotchkiss Wightman, and in 1933, she won the Seabright tournament. Palfrey also became a top-notch doubles player who won six titles with her sister Joanna (Joey). With Alice Marble, Palfrey won the Wimbledon doubles in 1938 and 1939 and the U.S. national doubles event. With several different partners, she captured other U.S. doubles crowns from 1930 to 1941, and she and Marble swept the doubles in Wightman Cup play in 1941. Palfrey went on to win the U.S. women's singles title in 1941 and in 1945.

In 1945, while she was married to Elwood Cooke, Palfrey was allowed to enter a men's doubles tournament with her husband in Ohio, due to the shortage of male players during World War II. In 1947 she played for a while as a professional, performing in some exhibition matches.

When African-American player Althea Gibson was working to gain acceptance in major tournaments, Palfrey supported her cause and befriended Gibson in 1950. The women practiced together at the West Side Tennis Club where Gibson would be competing in the national championships for the first time. Later, Palfrey became a successful businesswoman and devoted a great deal of time to charitable organizations. She served on several tennis committees, including one for the International Tennis Hall of Fame. She also authored a number of articles about tennis. In 1963 she was inducted into the Tennis Hall of Fame.

See also Gibson, Althea; Marble, Alice; Wightman, Hazel Hotchkiss
References Collins and Hollander, *Bud Collins' Modern Encyclopedia of Tennis* (1994); Hickok, *A Who's Who of Sports Champions* (1995)

Pan-American Games
Similar to the Olympics, the Pan-American Games bring together athletes from different countries in North and South America. The sports at these annual Games include archery, badminton, baseball, basketball, boxing, bowling, canoe-kayak, cycling, diving, equestrian, fencing, field hockey, judo, modern pentathlon, racquetball, roller skating, rowing, sailing, shooting, soccer, softball, speed skating, swimming, synchronized swimming, table tennis, taekwando, team handball, tennis, track and field, volleyball, water polo, weight lifting, and wrestling. The top three winners in each event win gold, silver, and bronze medals.

Paralympics

Paralympic Games, which are recognized by the International Olympic Committee (IOC) and governed by the International Paralympic Committee (IPC), feature competitive events for elite athletes with physical disabilities or visual impairments. In order to qualify to represent their nation, the athletes compete in strenuous training programs and meet strict standards. Athletes come from four international federations: the blind, paraplegics and quadriplegics, people with cerebral palsy, and amputees and others, including dwarfs.

The first Paralympics were held in 1960, after which they were held every four years, usually following the Olympic Games in the same location. More than 1.5 million spectators watched the Paralympics in Barcelona in 1992. At the 1996 Summer Games in Atlanta, Georgia, Paralympics were held in conjunction with the Olympic Games for the first time in the United States. The theme of the Games was "The Triumph of the Human Spirit," and the Games also included a Paralympic Congress, where experts from around the world discussed ways to enhance business, social, and recreational opportunities for people with physical disabilities. More than 100 nations sent athletes to the Paralympic Games in Atlanta in 1996, where they competed in 17 sports, including 14 Olympic sports and two demonstration sports.

Peck, Annie Smith (1850–1935)

A daring mountain climber, Peck set out to reach peaks that nobody else, man or woman, had scaled before her. Born in Providence, Rhode Island, Peck was a scholar and teacher as well as a world-class mountain climber. Her interest in the sport was aroused when she saw the Matterhorn while touring Switzerland with classmates studying classic Greek and German literature. (Peck went on to earn a master's degree in Greek studies in 1881 and also became the first woman admitted to the American School of Classical Studies in Athens, Greece, in 1885.)

Her first climbing triumph was Mount Shasta in California, which rises to an altitude of 14,380 feet. In 1895, she achieved a major goal by climbing the Matterhorn in Switzerland, which stands 14,780 feet. Two years later, she tackled two mountains in Mexico—Mount Popocatepetl (17,887 feet) and Mount Orizaba (18,314). In 1904, Peck became the first person to climb the 21,300 feet of Mount Sorata in Bolivia, completing this feat at a time before oxygen could be brought along on a trip.

Four years later, at age 58, Peck tackled Peru's Mount Huascaran, whose twin peaks rise 21,812 feet in the air. This was the highest altitude ever reached in the Western Hemisphere. Along the way, Peck and her two guides endured many difficulties. At one point, she found that her fingers had turned black from the cold. Harsh winds, numbing cold, and slippery surfaces made the descent difficult. Nonetheless, Peck was able to measure the altitude with an instrument called a hypsometer. In a 1910 interview for *Harper's Magazine,* Peck described her observations as she neared the top: "We had now passed the faces of the mountain and were between two peaks, surrounded on all sides by yawning crevasses, ice-falls, great hollows, perpendicular walls of snow, a heterogeneous collection of everything that could be fabricated out of ice and snow by the presiding genius of the upper world." A journalist reporting on Peck's triumph said, "The conquering of Mount Huascaran will stand as one of the most

Feminist and renowned mountain climber Annie Peck set a new record in 1904 for the highest peak reached in the Western Hemisphere when she climbed Mount Huascaran in Peru.

remarkable feats in the history of mountain-climbing." In 1927, the Lima Geographical Society named the north peak of Mount Huascaran in the Andes Cumbre Ana Peck in her honor.

During her later years, Peck continued in her sport, climbing Mount Coropuna in Peru (21,250 feet) at age 69. Upon reaching the top, Peck, who was also an ardent suffragist, placed a pennant that read: Votes for Women. She was 82 when she made her last climb, up the 5,380 feet of Mount Madison in New Hampshire.

During her years of mountain climbing, Peck took time out to promote the sport, helping to found the American Alpine Club in 1902. She represented the United States at international conferences on climbing. A devoted educator, she taught at colleges and universities in several different states. Peck also wrote several guidebooks for mountain climbers, including *The South American Tour* (1913).

See also Mountain Climbing

References *The Grolier Encyclopedia of North American Biographies*, vol. 4 (1994); Styles, *On Top of the World: An Illustrated History of Mountain Climbing* (1967).

Pentathlon

The pentathlon is a five-event track and field competition held indoors as well as outdoors. It evolved from the triathlon, first held in the 1920s, which included a 100-meter dash, high jump, and javelin throw. The first pentathlons added a shot put and long jump to these three events. In 1964, the pentathlon officially became part of the Summer Olympic Games and the pentathlon grew to include 100-meter hurdles, a 4-kilogram shot put, high jump, running long jump, and 200-meter dash or 800-meter run.

Pentathlon competitions are sponsored by the Amateur Athletic Union both locally and at the national level. The competition is usually held over a two-day period, with hurdles, the shot, and high jump on the first day and the long jump and running event on the second. Competitors receive points for their performance in each event, based on a scoring table. The person with the highest point total wins the pentathlon.

Among the top women to compete in the pentathlon is Jane Frederick, who set U.S. records for the indoor and outdoor pentathlons in 1975. Her outdoor total was 4,676 points, and her indoor score was 4,502.

Peppler, Mary Jo (b. 1944)

Born in Rockford, Illinois, volleyball champion Peppler became a woman athlete in what she later called "an exciting time." Peppler lived in different states as a child, attending high school in the San Fernando Valley of California. She enjoyed several sports, including football, which her parents discouraged.

Turning her attention to volleyball, Peppler became a top player. In 1962, as a senior in high school, Peppler was invited to play for the women's national championship team, the Long Beach Shamrocks. She also played for the Los Angeles Spartans, which finished in second place at the national Amateur Athletic Union (AAU) women's volleyball finals. The 6-foot-tall Peppler made the U.S. women's Olympic volleyball team in 1964 while at Los Angeles State University, but at that time the Olympic team had few players of Peppler's caliber and did not win a medal.

After the Games, Peppler helped to form a new women's team, the Los Angeles Renegades. They won the amateur national title in 1965. Peppler was named top woman volleyball player in the world in 1970. Moving to Houston,

Texas, she again helped to start a new team, called the E Pluribus Unum. She coached and played so well that the team won the AAU title in both 1972 and 1973.

Peppler became the first woman to win the televised Superstars, also called "Women's Supersports," competition, held in Rotunda, Florida, in 1974. The women athletes had to compete in ten events outside their specialty, and Peppler won the softball throwing, basketball free-throw shooting, and rowing competitions. She did extremely well in the bicycling (second place), running (fourth and fifth in two races), and swimming events. In the end, Peppler accumulated three points more than her nearest competitor and won the first prize of $49,600.

By the mid-seventies, volleyball was becoming more popular in America, with young women playing seriously on teams at schools. Peppler turned professional in 1975 and competed on the El Paso–Juarez team, part of the newly formed International Volleyball Association (IVA), which brought men and women players together on the same teams. Peppler coached and played with the Phoenix Heat team in 1976.

In 1978 she moved into the ranks of professional basketball, joining one of the newly formed teams in the national women's basketball league. After the league folded, Peppler returned to volleyball and became player-coach of the New York Liberties in 1987. This was one of several teams in major league volleyball, the first professional league for U.S. women players.

Peppler continued to coach and to promote women in her sport. In her 1977 book, *Inside Volleyball for Women,* Peppler said, "by far the most important thing for you to learn is TO TRY. . . . nobody reaches the top without trying hard."

References *Lincoln Library of Sports Champions,* vol. 14 (1989); Peppler, *Inside Volleyball for Women* (1977).

Perrin, Ethel (1871–1962)

Born in Needham, Massachusetts, Perrin became an advocate of physical education and gymnastics training for women. After graduating from Howard Collegiate Institute in 1890, she enrolled at the newly formed Boston Normal School of Gymnastics. There she worked with Senda Berenson, one of America's most prominent physical educators, studying ways women benefited from physical exercise, particularly as a preparation for pregnancy and motherhood.

Perrin focused on Swedish gymnastics, which she later taught. She attended the 1899 Conference on Physical Training organized by the National Education Association (NEA). Like others at the conference, Perrin agreed with the idea that men's sports should be modified for women, a principle that came to be known as "modification."

Along with several classmates, Perrin wrote *One Hundred and Fifty Gymnastic Games,* published in 1902. She and Mary Seely Starks wrote *A Handbook of Rhythmical Balance Exercises,* published in 1906. That same year, she became director of physical education at Smith College. In 1907, she took a similar position at the University of Michigan, where she implemented a more individualized and informal approach to teaching gymnastics. Perrin then served as director of physical education for girls at Detroit Central High School, where she was in charge of the first girls' gymnasium in the Detroit schools. In 1909, she was appointed head of physical education programs in the city's schools. She taught that sports were useful in and of themselves and that women's sports should emphasize moderation and de-emphasize competitiveness.

With her colleagues, she designed the State of Michigan Course of Study in Physical Education, a program that became a model for public schools throughout the United States. She was a leader in the American Physical Education Association (APEA), the National Education Association (NEA), the Amateur Athletic Union (AAU), and other organizations that shaped the field of physical education during the early 1900s. By 1923, Perrin was recognized as a national leader in her field. She became associate director of the Health Education Division of the American Child Health Association (ACHA) and delivered numerous talks on this subject around the country. Among the causes she promoted was more opportunity for women to take part in the Olympics.

After retiring in 1936, Perrin operated a dairy farm in upstate New York. In 1946, she was the second woman and eleventh person to receive the Luther Halsey Gulick Award for outstanding contributions to the field of physical education. Perrin died on her farm at age 91.

See also Camp Fire Girls
References "Ethel Perrin," a biographical sketch from Wellesley College Archives; Sicherman and Green, *Notable American Women of the Modern Period* (1980).

Physical Education

The idea of physical education—that is, the belief that physical activity promotes strength, health, and well-being—is centuries old. Gymnastics and calisthenics were the first elements in physical education, which was practiced in ancient Greece. The concept expanded to include sports and dance.

To promote physical education and health, the U.S. government set up the American Alliance for Health, Physical Education, Recreation, and Dance in 1885. The AAHPERD has continued to promote physical education in the curriculum of elementary and secondary schools. By 1991, it had grown to include 50,000 members.

Since the 1800s, physical education for American school children has sometimes meant coeducational programs, as well as programs that separated boys and girls, teaching them different exercises and sports. Girls' physical education classes, drawing from European exercise routines, often featured milder types of exercise and might exclude team sports. But the idea of physical education for girls and women met with less resistance than the idea of seeing them involved in competitive athletic activities.

In large measure, women's sports and competition evolved from physical education programs based at schools and colleges. Among the leaders in the girls' physical education movements were the athletic directors and educators at all-female schools, such as Constance Applebee, who promoted women's field hockey, and Senda Berenson, who organized competitive basketball games for college students.

Frances Kellor, a social reformer and advocate for black Americans immigrating from the South to northern cities, conducted several studies on physical education during the early 1900s. Her ideas were published in articles in *Education* magazine and in a book, *Athletic Games in the Education of Women*, coauthored with Gertrude Dudley. Physical educator Ethel Perrin (1871–1962) wrote and lectured on the use of gymnastics and other programs for women and described ways to implement these programs in schools.

During the 1930s, negative attitudes about female athletes led physical education departments to focus on traditional attributes, such as posture and grooming. Some schools instigated a process of photographing female students in their underwear as a way of evaluating their posture.

Women's physical education programs were hampered by negative attitudes toward women and athletics, which, in turn, resulted in meager funding for girls' and women's' programs. The passage of federal civil rights legislation in 1972, in the form of Title IX, required schools, colleges, and universities to provide equal opportunities to girls and women in sports and other educational programs. Funding and other resources were to be distributed equally to women's and men's programs, and institutions began expanding physical education and sports programs for female students.

Since the 1970s, more career opportunities in physical education have opened to women. Besides teaching in schools and colleges, they organize and supervise competitive sports and instructional programs in private and public sports clubs and for professional sports organizations, as well as in business and industry. Some women hold administrative positions, directing physical education staffs, developing curricula, and writing grant proposals.

See also Applebee, Constance; Berenson, Senda; Perrin, Ethel; President's Council on Physical Fitness and Sports
References Anderson, *A World of Sports for Girls* (1981); Cahn, *Coming on Strong* (1994).

Physical Fitness

Physical fitness became a national priority during the early 1900s as it was found that many Americans were overweight and lacked some form of regular exercise.

In 1943, the Amateur Athletic Union (AAU) began its Physical Fitness Program, testing young people in different fitness areas and setting standards so that people could set goals and become more fit. By 1995, that program was being conducted in more than 46,000 schools every year.

American women became involved in the "fitness boom" of the late 1960s and early 1970s and have continued to pursue fitness activities in increasingly large numbers. Membership in sports and fitness clubs rose by millions, and more women took up sports and began programs of individual exercise, such as walking, jogging, running, weight-training, swimming, bicycling, and aerobics.

A number of women created exercise videos and became known as fitness experts. One of the most successful series of exercise videos was produced by actress Jane Fonda, who developed several best-selling exercise tapes featuring aerobics and low-impact aerobics routines. Other celebrities lent their names to exercise videos, demonstrating their routines, sometimes in conjunction with a trainer or instructor. Figure-skater Nancy Kerrigan was among the athletes who appeared in such tapes.

During the 1990s, women trained in physical education, such as Denise Austin, Kathy Smith, and Tamilee Webb, were featured on videotape and on television exercise programs. Actresses and other well-known public figures, such as television talk-show host Oprah Winfrey, described the benefits of their exercise and fitness programs. Reflecting this continuing interest in women's fitness was the success of magazines devoted to the subject. The eighties and nineties saw the debut of new health and fitness magazines, including *Longevity, Health,* and *Prevention*, with several, such as *Shape, Living Fit,* and *Women's Sports and Fitness,* directed at female audiences.

See also Aerobics; President's Council on Physical Fitness and Sports

Ping-Pong (See Table Tennis)

Pitch, Hit, and Run Competition (See Fields, Crystal)

Platform Tennis

Tennis lovers who wanted to play a version of tennis year-round invented platform tennis in 1928. James Cogswell and Fessenden Blanchard built a raised wooden platform about half the size of a tennis court, surrounded by a chicken wire fence. The new game was played with paddles and a slow-bouncing ball. People across America began playing the game, which is sometimes called "paddle" but should not be confused with paddle ball or table tennis. Today, platforms are often made of aluminum as well as wood.

Girls and women can compete in regional and national platform tennis events, such as the American Platform Tennis National Championship, with divisions for different age groups. Most events are for doubles competition, with two teams of two players each vying for points. In 1994, the team of Sue Avery and Jerri Vlant won the women's national platform tennis title. As of 1995, platform tennis was not an Olympic sport.

Pollard, LaTaunya (See Wade Trophy)

Postema, Pam

In 1977, Postema became the third woman to work as an umpire for organized baseball. She was initially hired by the Florida Gulf Coast League and served as an umpire until 1989 in the minor leagues.

The Ohio native loved baseball as a child and played hardball with other members of her family. She was visiting Florida in 1976 when she applied to the Al Somers Umpiring School in Daytona Beach. Refusing her application, Somers pointed out that there were no restrooms or other facilities for women at the school. She convinced him that she should be admitted and passed the six-week course. She began working as an umpire for $550 a month.

Working in a male-dominated job, Postema was harassed and insulted. Once she came onto the playing field to find a frying pan on home plate. She persevered despite the problems and moved to a higher level, Triple A. She was invited to umpire the Hall of Fame game at Cooperstown, New York, in 1987 and also worked at spring training games for the National League in both 1988 and 1989. Yet in 1989, Postema was passed over for a promotion to the major leagues and let go from her job. During an evaluation earlier that year, Postema had been rated "better than average." In December 1991, she filed a sex discrimination lawsuit and wrote a book about her experiences called *You've Got to Have Balls to Make It in This League.*

References Postema, "Baseball Treating Women as Equals? Fat Chance," *Sporting News,* May 4, 1992, 8; Postema, *You've Got to Have Balls to Make It in This League* (1992); Richer, "Kiss the Ump!" *Gentleman's Quarterly,* June 1992, 88.

Potter, Cynthia (b. 1950)

Diving champion and coach Potter won 28 national indoor and outdoor diving titles and competed at four Olympic Games. She first became part of the U.S. diving team at age 18. From 1967 to 1979, Potter won at least one national title a year; in world competition, she won more than 20 gold medals.

Potter specialized in the springboard

event but also excelled in platform diving. At the 1970 World University Games, she won a silver medal in the platform event, along with a gold in springboard diving. In 1976, her second Olympics, she won a bronze medal for the springboard.

Starting in 1972, Potter served as a member of the U.S. Olympic Diving Committee. She coached diving at Southern Methodist University in Texas and at the University of Arizona, Tucson. After retiring from competition, she also provided television commentary on women's diving events. Among Potter's many honors is being named World Diver of the Year three times (1970, 1971, 1977).

Powder Puff Derby (See
Air Derby, Women's)

Powerboating
In 1910, Mabel Bacon became the first woman known to take part in a power boat race. She and her husband placed second in the race, having taken their 46.5-foot cabin cruiser a distance of 670 miles, from the Kennebec Yacht Club in Maine south to Hamilton, Bermuda. During the four days at sea, Bacon alternated steering the craft with her husband and one other crew member. In 1971, 28-year-old Sharon Chambers became the first woman in the history of the American Power Boat Association to win a national high-point championship in outboard pleasure craft racing.

In 1977 and 1979, 58-year-old Betty Cook won the World Off-shore Racing title for powerboating, the only woman taking part in this competition.

Poynton-Hill, Dorothy (b. 1915)
At age 13, Poynton-Hill became the youngest American ever to win an Olympic medal, taking the bronze in

springboard diving in 1928. Growing up in Portland, Oregon, then in Los Angeles, Dorothy Poynton was a talented dancer, performing on the stage during her early school years. She studied both platform and springboard diving, winning several national championships in her teens. As a 12-year-old, she caught the attention of coaches at the prestigious Hollywood Athletic Club, who asked Poynton to represent them in competition. At her first meet, she lost the title by one-tenth of one point.

Poynton competed in the first of three Olympics in 1928, when she celebrated her thirteenth birthday on board the ship that carried the U.S. athletes to Amsterdam. By 1932, she was competing in the platform event as well as the springboard. She won the gold medal in the platform and remained national champion until she became a professional diver in 1936. At her third Olympics, as Dorothy Poynton-Hill, she won a gold medal in the platform event and a bronze for her performance in springboard diving. After the 1936 Games, she did commercial endorsements, swam with various swimming shows, and ran the successful Dorothy Poynton Swim Club, built in 1952 by her husband, in West Los Angeles, California. During 18 years as an instructor, Poynton maintained that she could teach anyone to swim in ten lessons. She worked with the children of many motion picture celebrities.

Interviewed in 1986, Poynton-Hill attributed much of her success to the fact that she "can't do anything half-way." She said, "There are so many millions of people out there, so you're lucky if you make a name for yourself in anything. It's great having been the world's best in something."

Reference Carlson and Fogarty, *Tales of Gold* (1987).

Seen flying through the air at a 1932 diving exhibition in Santa Barbara, California, Dorothy Poynton-Hill was the youngest American to win a gold medal when she competed at the 1928 Olympics at the age of 13.

Pregnancy

For centuries, critics who opposed the idea of women taking part in sports argued that it would harm their reproductive functions in various ways and they would not be as physically able to conceive and bear children. Among Native American cultures, however, young women were often encouraged to take part in sports because it was believed that this would strengthen their bodies for childbearing. Research has disproved the idea that physical activity hinders pregnancy. Scientists concluded that athletic women usually had an easier time during pregnancy and childbirth and that, as a group, they had fewer Caesarean sections (surgical deliveries) than women who were not athletic.

Since the 1950s, physicians have generally advised women not to take up new, strenuous sports during pregnancy. They do, however, encourage mild to moderate exercise for women who are experiencing an uncomplicated pregnancy. Women are also advised to continue sports or activities they are accustomed to doing during the early months of a normal pregnancy.

In many instances, women have performed great athletic events and won athletic events while pregnant. At the 1956 Olympics, ten medal winners were pregnant, according to British Olympian Dr. Elizabeth Ferris. Jockey Mary Bacon gave birth on the same day after she rode in a major horse race. Women have also won major athletic competitions and broken records at all stages of the monthly cycle.

See also Bacon, Mary; Discrimination, Gender; Physical Education
References Kahn, *Coming On Strong* (1994); Kaplan, *Women and Sports* (1979)

Presidential Sports Award (PSA)

The Presidential Sports Award, created in 1972, rewards Americans for taking part in one of 58 sports and fitness programs over an extended period of time. Since 1987, it has been directed by the Amateur Athletic Union (AAU). In 1994, 21,800 people earned the PSA.

President's Challenge (See

President's Council on Physical Fitness and Sports

President's Council on Physical Fitness and Sports (PCPFS)

Within its parent government agency, the American Alliance for Health, Physical Education, Recreation, and Dance (AAHPERD), the PCPFS was established during the administration of President Dwight D. Eisenhower in 1956. By executive order of the president, the PCPFS is directed to "promote, encourage, and motivate the development of physical fitness and sports programs for all Americans." The council encourages the public to become aware of the health and other benefits that result from physical fitness. It urges schools, businesses, industry, and organizations run by government recreation agencies and youth organizations to develop such programs. Twenty private citizens are appointed by the president to serve on the council and to propose ways to carry out the 10-point program outlined in Executive Order 12345 and its amendments.

In 1966 an awards program called the President's Challenge Youth Physical Fitness Awards Program was set up. Young people ages 6 to 17 may win the President's Challenge by scoring at or above the 85th percentile mark in these events: the 1-mile run, curl-ups, pull-ups, V-sit reach flexibility test, and shuttle run. Those who reach the goal receive a certificate and special red, white, and blue emblem. The program is administered by the Amateur Athletic Union (AAU).

See also Physical Education

President's Council on Youth Fitness (See President's Council on Physical Fitness and Sports)

Primrose-Smith, Elizabeth (b. 1948)

In 1991, Primrose-Smith became the first woman to head the U.S. Olympic Festival. As president and executive director, she was responsible for running what has become the nation's largest multisport competition, held that year in Los Angeles.

During her teens, Primrose-Smith had competed as a swimmer, nearly making the 1964 U.S. Olympic swim team. She won a gold medal for a 4 x 100–meter freestyle event at the Pan American Games. Before directing the Olympic Festival, she worked as a consultant with the Los Angeles branch of McKinsey and Company, a business consulting firm. She also helped to organize the 1984 Summer Games, which were held in Los Angeles.

Prize Money

One of the most heated debates in sports in recent decades has surrounded the inequities in prize money between men and women. Women involved in various sports have complained about these differences through the years, in some cases trying to compete in all-male tournaments in order to earn a better living. The movement to improve prize money for women caught fire during the late 1960s, led by tennis player Billie Jean King. Women tennis players criticized the inequities publicly, and Gladys Heldman, publisher of *World Tennis* magazine, lent her support. Women tennis players started a tour of their own with sponsors.

Statistics show that prize money for women athletes increased worldwide during the 1970s. The total amount worldwide was $1.5 million in 1973; it increased to $5.5 million in 1975, $7.5 million in 1979, and $9.1 million in 1980. In 1979, for the first time, women received prize money equal to that of male winners at the U.S. Open tennis tournament. From 1970 to 1980, prizes for the women's singles players at the U.S. Open went from $15,425 to $225,304. The winner's share rose from $7,500 to $46,000. Prizes for the women's doubles team winner went from $2,000 to $18,500.

In other sports, such as bowling, figure skating, and golf, women experienced similar gains. In 1975, the total prize money on the women's golf tour was about $1.2 million. By 1982, it had reached $6.4 million, a figure that continued to rise during the late eighties and early nineties.

See also Carner, JoAnne Gunderson; Evert, Chris; King, Betsy; King, Billie Jean; Rankin, Judy; Sheehan, Patty; Virginia Slims

Racine Belles

One of the first four teams in the All-American Girls Professional Baseball League (AAGPBL), the Belles were based in Racine, Wisconsin, from 1943 to 1950. In 1950, the team moved to Battle Creek, Michigan, where it was based until 1951.

Sophie "Flint Flash" Kurys, a Battle Creek native, was one of their top players from 1943 to 1950. Playing second base for the Belles, she made four all-star teams and was named Player of the Year in 1946. Kurys managed to steal 201 bases in 203 attempts in the 1946 season. Throughout her 11-year career, she stole at least one base 80 percent of the time she got on base. In 1943 and 1946, the Belles won the league championship, taking the pennant. They won the play-offs in 1943, 1946, and 1947.

Racing, Auto

The first auto race was probably a 201-mile event held in Green Bay, Wisconsin, in 1878. Other races soon sprang up in France, England, Italy, and other countries, as people yearned to test their speed and skills against other drivers.

During the 1940s, a group of Bostonian men founded the Sports Car Club of America (SCCA) to promote racing and organize races throughout America. Races were often held in city streets and on country roads, but accidents soon led organizers to move the races to tracks away from heavily populated areas. Often

they were held at tracks on airport fields that had been built for World War II.

In its early years, the sport was dominated by male drivers and racing officials. But by the 1960s, some women had proven they could excel at auto racing. The Macmillan Ring-Free Oil Company sponsored a team of women drivers. Called the Macmillan Ring-Free Motor Maids, it first included Smokey Drolet of Florida, Suzy Dietrich of Ohio, Donna Mae Mims of Pennsylvania, and Janet Guthrie, who would later become the first woman to race at the prestigious Indianapolis 500. Besides racing, the team made appearances on television and in public on behalf of the company. In the 1967 Daytona 500 auto race, one of the Maids teams won a trophy for the best performance by an all-women team. In 1965, Maid team member Lee Broadlove, of Bonneville Flats, Utah, set a woman's speed record on a 1-kilometer course by reaching 335.07 miles per hour in her jet-propelled car.

In 1992, more than two decades after Guthrie raced at the Indianapolis 500, driver Lyn St. James became the first woman to be voted the Indy 500 Rookie of the Year. Eager to help more women drivers succeed, St. James started her Lyn St. James Driver Development Program in 1994, open to both men and women. Twenty-one of the 23 people who took her course that year were women. Besides teaching driving skills, St. James also covered topics such as ways of dealing with sponsors and the media, since she believed women drivers could benefit from her experience in these areas.

See also Guthrie, Janet; Indianapolis 500; Muldowney, Shirley

Racing, Endurance (See Marathon Running; Raid Gauloises)

Racing, Hurdle (See Heptathlon; Hurdles; Pentathlon; Track and Field)

Racing, Relay

At track and field and swimming events, relays have been part of the Olympics for decades. At one time, runners had to touch each other as they exchanged places, but it was often hard to observe whether or not they had done so. An exchange of a stick called a baton was substituted. If a runner drops the baton during the exchange, the team is out of the race. Relay racers must also develop great skill in exchanging the baton without losing speed. In 4 x 100–meter races, four runners cover a distance of 100 meters each. Four participants also compete on each team of the 4 x 400–meter race.

Many of the women who have won individual racing events in track and field were also fine relay team members. They include sprinters Wilma Rudolph, Wyomia Tyus, Gail Devers, and Gwen Torrence. Katherine Rawls, a swimming racer, also took part in relays.

See also Devers, Gail; Rawls, Katherine; Roller Skating; Rudolph, Wilma; Torrence, Gwen; Tyus Simberg, Wyomia;

Racquetball

A fast, demanding game that promotes fitness, racquetball evolved from racket sports and court tennis games that have been played for centuries. In London's debtors' prisons, a ball game played against several walls may have taken shape when inmates were let out for brief periods during the day. They apparently used the high courtyard walls surrounding them and paddles they made of wood. The various games spread outside the prison, where they were altered over time.

The game of racquetball resembles both squash and paddleball and was at first called paddle racquets. The variation of racquetball played today emerged during the late 1960s and became a popular leisure sport in the United States. Players use racquets that resemble shortened tennis rackets inside a four-walled court with a wood or cement floor. The balls used measure about 2.5 inches in diameter.

The United States Racquetball Association (USRA) developed during the late 1960s to oversee amateur competition in America, and the International Racquetball Association (IRA) was formed in 1969. In 1970, a women's division of the IRA was formed, and Fran Cohen of St. Louis, Missouri, won the women's national title. More local and regional tournaments developed in the years that followed.

The National Racquetball Club (NRC) has been instrumental in building up the professional sport, organizing professional tournaments and publishing a monthly magazine on racquetball. The Woman's Professional Racquetball Association (WPRA) was founded to support women in the sport, bring more sponsors to tournaments, and improve the existing competitive events. The development of glass-walled courts made the game more accessible to and popular with spectators.

The first prominent women's player was Peggy Steding, who won the national singles title every year from 1973 through

1976. Steding, who began playing at age 35, was still playing championship racquetball during her forties. Some call Shannon Wright of San Diego, California, the best woman player ever to compete in the sport. In 1977 and 1978, Wright won the U.S. singles championships. As a professional on the NRC tour, she became the all-time top female money winner. Karin Walton became the women's national pro champion in 1979. Another top women's player, Kathy Williams, became the first woman manager–teaching pro at a racquetball club, located in Livonia, Michigan. In 1994, U.S. women won both the world amateur team championship and women's individual title (Michelle Gould, of Boise, Idaho). Robin Levine of Sacramento, California, was the women's national champion.

References Keeley, *The Complete Book of Racquetball* (1976); Wright with Keeley, *The Women's Book of Racquetball* (1980); "The Year 1994 in Review," *New York Times*, January 1, 1995, 10.

Raid Gauloises

This rigorous endurance race, first held in 1989, requires participants to hike, paddle canoes, scale rocks, raft, and bike as they make their way through the jungles of Borneo. In 1995, a five-woman team consisting of Robyn Benincasa, Angelika Castaneda, Sarah Odell, Nancy Pistole, and Gail Verwey became the second group of American women to finish the course.

Rankin, Judy (b. 1945)

A child golfing prodigy, Rankin hit a hole-in-one when she was only seven years old. Her golf-loving father taught her to play while she was growing up in St. Louis, Missouri. She won four St. Louis Pee Wee titles and two National Pee Wee golf titles. By age 14, she had won the Missouri Amateur tournament, the youngest woman ever to do so. That same year, Rankin competed in the U.S. Open but never won that major tournament. As a 16-year-old golfer, she was featured on a *Sports Illustrated* cover in 1961.

Rankin turned professional in 1962. In 1965, she won three tournaments, the first of 26 Ladies Professional Golf Association (LPGA) wins. Rankin was known for her strong, consistent game and calm demeanor during a match. She won numerous national and world events and, by 1977, had earned more than $500,000, a huge sum for women golfers in that era. Rankin won the Vare Trophy in 1973, 1976, and 1977 and was named LPGA Player of the Year in 1976 and 1977. Back injuries hampered her progress after 1979, the year she won her last LPGA title.

References Cotton, *A History of Golf, Illustrated* (1975); Gutman, *Modern Women Superstars* (1978); Sparhawk, *American Women in Sport: 1887–1987* (1989).

Rathgeber, Lisa (See Bowling)

Rawls, Betsy (b. 1928)

Unlike many professional golfers, Elizabeth E. (Betsy) Rawls started playing at the relatively late age of 17, yet became one of the top players in history. Born in Spartanburg, South Carolina, and raised in Texas, Rawls had played for only four years when she won the Trans-Mississippi and Texas Women's Amateur tournaments. In 1950, while attending the University of Texas as a physics major, she finished second at the U.S. Open. She graduated from college the next year with high honors.

Rawls turned professional in 1951 and began playing on the women's tour. For 20 years she was a tough competitor with an excellent ability to make shots and putt. She won more than 50 tournaments, including four U.S. Open titles and two

Ladies Professional Golf Association (LPGA) championships. She became the first woman player ever to win ten golf events in one year. A consistent player, Rawls won the Vare Trophy in 1959 for her low scoring average during tournament play that year. During the 1959 season, she earned ten LPGA titles. That year, she was the top money winner on the women's tour, as she had been in 1951.

Known as an expert on the rules of golf, Rawls was the first woman chosen to serve on the Rules Committee at the men's U.S. Open tournament. She was elected to the LPGA Hall of Fame in 1960 while still an active player on the tour, then inducted into the Professional Golfers Association World Golf Hall of Fame in 1987. Rawls was also the second woman to receive the prestigious Patty Berg Award.

See also LPGA Hall of Fame
References Cotton, *A History of Golf, Illustrated* (1975); Sparhawk, *American Women in Sport: 1887–1987* (1989).

Rawls, Katherine (1918–1982)

A top swimmer and diver during the 1930s, Rawls was the only U.S. woman to compete in both swimming and diving events at the 1936 Olympics. The Fort Lauderdale, Florida, native was U.S. springboard women's champion in 1932, 1933, and 1934. Between 1932 and 1938, Rawls won 28 national diving championships and three in swimming. She won a silver medal in the springboard event at both the 1932 Olympic Games in Los Angeles and again at the 1936 Games in Berlin. Also in 1936, Rawls swam the first leg of the 4 x 100–meter relay, in which the U.S. women won a third-place bronze medal. She finished seventh in the 100-meter freestyle race. In 1937, Rawls became the first woman to win four na-

tional titles at one meet. That year, she was named Athlete of the Year by the Associated Press. She was inducted into the International Swimming and Diving Hall of Fame.

References Hickok, *A Who's Who of Sports Champions* (1995); Mandell, *The Nazi Olympics* (1971).

Reinalda, Barbara (See Softball)

Reporter (See Sportscasting; Sportswriters)

Retton, Mary Lou (b. 1968)

The pressure was on gymnast Mary Lou Retton as she prepared for her final round of gymnastics competition in the 1984 Summer Olympics in Los Angeles. In order to win the women's all-around event, the vault, and the gold medal as the world's best all-around women's gymnast, she needed a perfect score of 10. Poised to begin, Retton pictured herself performing the move just as she wished, with a perfect upright landing. She ran down the runway and onto the springboard, then sprang 14 feet into the air. After a back somersault and double twist in the air, Retton landed smoothly on the mat in excellent position. The judges gave her the 10 she needed, and Mary Lou Retton had won her gold medal.

Born in Fairmont, West Virginia, Retton began studying acrobatics, swimming, and dancing at an early age. By age eight, she was doing acrobatic stunts during half-time at West Virginia basketball games with her sister, Shari. Seeing Retton's natural agility, her parents enrolled her in gymnastics classes. (All five Retton children were involved in athletics.) Within a few years, she was the state junior champion.

Watching the 1976 Olympics on television, Retton was inspired by Romanian

Gold medalist Mary Lou Retton performs her floor exercise at the 1984 Summer Olympics.

gold medalist Nadia Comaneci. In contrast to many women gymnasts, though, Retton was muscular, not thin and delicate-looking. Her trademarks became speed and power, used to advantage in the uneven bar routines. Retton developed high jumps and won the U.S. junior's title for the vault at age 12. Her dynamic moves made her a favorite of photographers and fans.

In 1981, Retton won the all-around title at the world competition. She moved to Texas to follow a serious training schedule under world-famous coach Bela Karolyi. Karolyi was impressed with her physical strength and said, "She has the most potential of anyone." In the 1983 American Cup competition, Retton won the all-around, the vault (setting a new world record), and floor exercise events and tied for the gold in uneven parallel bars. She became the first American woman to win the Japanese Chunichi Cup. Just before the Olympic Games, she won the American Cup again.

Mary Lou Retton and Romanian Katerina Szabo were favorites as the 1984 Olympics approached. Along with her strength, Retton had worked hard to develop new and impressive combinations of movements. But a few months before the Olympics, she tore the cartilage in her right knee, and a piece lodged in the joint. Retton later said, "I thought it was all over for me." But a surgeon performed an arthroscopy, using a small scope to locate the cartilage and remove it from her joint. She resumed training the week of her operation. Her coach was amazed but commented, "She is very determined."

At the Olympics, Retton and Szabo vied for the top position. After the balance beam, uneven parallel bars, and floor exercises, Szabo led by .05 points.

Retton's vault propelled her into first place. Another vault earned her a second score of 10. Rather than rest on her success, Retton went on to compete in the individual events. The only female gymnast ever to qualify to compete in all four, she won three more medals—a silver and two bronze.

Retton's Olympic victory was heralded with letters, gifts, parades, and an invitation to the White House. One of her routines on the uneven bars was named the Retton Salto, or Retton Flip. It involved swinging from the high bar in the uneven parallel bars, then hitting the lower bar and flipping to a sitting position on the high bar.

Retton became a spokesperson for Wheaties cereal and other products. After winning the American Cup all-around title in 1985, she retired from competition. In the years that followed, she became a motivational speaker and corporate spokesperson. Retton married Shannon Kelley in 1990. The couple settled in Houston and had their first child, Shayla, in 1995. In 1996, Retton was in Atlanta to witness the U.S. women gymnasts win their first-ever team gold medal. She told a reporter for the New York *Daily News* (August 24, 1996), "The U.S. is no longer a follower in the world of gymnastics. After so many generations, the U.S. is a leader."

See also Chunichi Cup; Gymnastics; Karolyi, Bela; McNamara, Julianne

References Lundgren, *Mary Lou Retton: Gold Medal Gymnast* (1985); Reed, "Golden Girl," *People*, May 22, 1995, 96–97; Ryan, *Little Girls in Pretty Boxes* (1995).

Ribner, Susan (b. 1948)

Karate expert Susan Ribner was one of the first women to study and teach in the field of martial arts, which was, during the 1960s, still dominated by men. Ribner recalled that her instructors typically ended classes consisting of both men and women by saying, "We are proud to be karate men." Women were also banned from certain movements and exercises during the classes. Push-ups were among the moves considered "dangerous" for a woman's body.

As a result, women had to be resourceful in finding schools and instructors. In many cases, they trained themselves. They also began to set their own standards, since men expected women to achieve very little. In an article for *The Sportswoman*, Ribner wrote, "Our sights must be set at the highest level. Otherwise, our true ability may never be discovered." Ribner was one of the founders of the Women's Martial Arts Union in New York City, a pioneer training center.

Reference Atkinson, *Women in the Martial Arts* (1983).

Richardson, Dot (b. 1961)

Softball player Dorothy (Dot) Richardson, called one of the best shortstops of all time, grew up in Florida, where she enjoyed playing catch and baseball with her father and brother. When she was 10, a man who saw her playing invited Richardson to play on a Little League team but told her she would have to cut her hair very short and go by the name of Bob—in other words, pretend to be a boy.

Disappointed at being rejected by a baseball team for her gender—something she could not change—Richardson continued to play outside the league. When she caught the attention of a softball coach at an Orlando park, 10-year-old Richardson was asked to join the Union Park Jets women's class A team. She became a starting player on third base and was named a league all-star that season. At age 11, she attended an instructional camp sponsored by the Orlando

Rebels and earned a spot as bat girl for that major league team, with whom she practiced three times a week. By age 13, Richardson had become the youngest regular player on a women's major league softball team.

Richardson played on the U.S. women's softball team that won a gold medal in the Pan American Games in 1979, 1980, and 1981. In 1981, her team, the Rebels, won the national championship. She also graduated from medical school and went on to specialize in orthopedic surgery. At the 1995 Olympic Festival, Richardson was the torchbearer at the Opening Ceremonies. She was in top form, hitting several homeruns for the U.S. team in Atlanta at the 1996 Summer Olympics. The team won a gold medal in this the first Olympics softball event for women.

References Araton, "The Doctor Steps Up for Her At-Bats, Too," *New York Times*, July 31, 1996, B10; Babb, "Past, Present, and Future," *Olympian*, January-February 1996, 20–23.

Richey-Gunter, Nancy (b. 1942)

Known for her excellent baseline game and dynamite forehand shot, Richey-Gunter ranked among the top ten women tennis players in the world 11 times between 1963 and 1975.

Richey grew up in San Angelo, Texas, part of a tennis-loving family. She and her brother Cliff have the distinction of being the only family pair to have been ranked as number one American tennis players. The two also both won their respective U.S. Clay Court singles events in 1966.

Starting in 1963, Richey dominated the U.S. Clay Court championship, where she won six straight titles comprised of 33 straight matches. Richey was first ranked number one in 1964 and 1965. She rose to the top again in 1968 and 1969. In 1966 she helped the U.S. Wightman Cup team to victory, something she would do eight times in all. That year, she was ranked second in the nation, after Billie Jean King. She won her first National Clay Court championships in 1966, as well as the women's doubles at Wimbledon, the U.S. national (which she also had won the year before), and the Australian national tournaments. She won the singles event at the latter tournament the next year.

Richey was ranked number two in 1972, behind Billie Jean King and ahead of an up-and-coming player named Chris Evert. In 1973, she won second place in the Family Circle Cup tennis tournament, when Rosie Casals defeated her in a close and exciting three-set final.

References Collins and Hollander, *Bud Collins Modern Encyclopedia of Tennis* (1994).

Riddles, Libby (b. 1957)

In 1985, Riddles became the first woman ever to win the 1,100-mile Iditarod Trail Sled-Dog Race. It was the thirteenth time the race had been held, and there were more storms and snow than in past races. Born in Minnesota, Riddles moved to the town of Teller, Alaska, in the Seward Peninsula, just northwest of Nome. She competed in the Iditarod twice before winning the race.

Riddles's team consisted of 13 dogs, led by brothers Axel and Dugan. During the race, she stopped every 60 miles to give her team a hot meal. Meanwhile, she snacked on dried moose meat and "Eskimo ice cream"—grated reindeer fat mixed with seal oil, salmonberries, and sugar. The dogs' feet needed a great deal of care, including fresh booties and regular applications of ointment. In a chronicle of her winning race, Riddles later wrote under March 3: "You rest your dogs during the heat of the day and save

them for the cool night. I feed them, then visit friends and ask to lie down for 1½ hours, but I can't sleep because my sinuses are stuffed up and I can hardly breathe." Later that day when she resumed racing, Riddles said she was "very sleepy and keep dozing off as we move along. In the 1979 race, Patty Friend of Chugiak had a rope tied around her so she couldn't fall off the sled when she slept. But I'm really good at dozing while standing on the back of the sled runners with a good grip on the handlebars."

By March 7, Riddles was ready to go over the top of Ptarmigan Pass "in the heat of the day, into direct sunlight. The snow in the pass is six to eight feet deep, and the trail doesn't have a solid bottom. . . . Coming down, the trail passes through Hell's Gate, a narrow canyon with the South Fork of the Kuskokwim River rushing through it."

On March 20, when Riddles arrived at the finish line in Nome, a fire siren blared to let people know the winner had arrived. A crowd of about 3,000 people welcomed her and her winning team. Along with the silver bowl and $50,000 awarded to the Iditarod winner, she received the glass urn (a humanitarian award that goes to the musher who has taken the best care of his or her team during the race). In 1985, she was named Professional Sportswoman of the Year by the Women's Sports Foundation.

That same year, musher Susan Butcher had hoped to be the first woman winner of the race but had to withdraw on the first day after a moose attacked her team, killing two dogs and injuring others.

See also Butcher, Susan; Iditarod Trail Sled-Dog Race

References Cooper, *Racing Sled Dogs* (1988); Riddles with Verschoth, "Valiant Lady," *Sports Illustrated*, February 17, 1986, 90.

Rigby, Cathy (b. 1952)

Born in Long Beach, California, gymnast Cathy Rigby was a premature infant who weighed just four pounds at birth. She overcame numerous childhood illnesses to become a healthy, athletic young person and began gymnastics training at age 8, showing a natural coordination, flexibility, and great energy. Her parents were encouraged to enroll her in the highly regarded Southern California Acrobatic Team (SCATS) program located in Long Beach. Rigby worked out in the gym there each day after school and practiced at home on equipment her parents set up for her. Despite the rigorous schedule she followed, Rigby later told author Irwin Stambler, "I never felt I was giving up anything. So many kids just long for a chance to get involved in something like this."

In 1967, at her first major gymnastics meet, Rigby took second place for her age group. She continued to compete in national meets and seemed sure to make the Olympic team in 1968. During the years Rigby was training, women from other countries, namely the Soviet Union, Eastern Europe, and Asia, won the top prizes in international competition. When Rigby qualified for the 1968 Olympic team, she was tiny (four feet, ten inches and 89 pounds) and, at 15, less experienced than many of the competitors. She finished sixteenth—the best showing an American woman gymnast had ever achieved. Thanks to Rigby and her teammates, the U.S. group won sixth place overall. At the 1970 world championships, Rigby won the silver medal for the balance beam event. Two years later, at the 1972 Olympics, she raised her placement to tenth, and the U.S. team placed fourth. Rigby's marks were high nines, out of a possible ten points.

Although she had not won an Olympic medal, Rigby's appealing personality and success during the Games made her a popular athlete. Her performances often earned standing ovations from the crowd, and young American girls were inspired to pursue gymnastics after watching her on television. They imitated her pig-tailed hairdo as they worked out in the gym.

In 1974, Rigby was featured in the title role of an NBC Entertainment production of *Peter Pan*. She became a professional sports commentator and made personal appearances to promote gymnastics. During the 1980s, she courageously admitted that for years she had suffered from an eating disorder called bulimia. Recognizing the seriousness of her problem, Rigby sought professional help from a psychiatrist who specialized in eating disorders, and she recovered.

Married, Cathy Rigby-McCoy became a mother. She continued as a public speaker, encouraging people to stay healthy and become physically fit. Her achievements had contributed greatly to the development of women's gymnastics in the United States.

References Ryan, *Little Girls in Pretty Boxes* (1995); Stambler, *Women in Sports* (1975).

Riggin, Aileen (b. 1906)

A native of Newport, Rhode Island, swimmer and diver Aileen Riggin was just 4 feet 7 inches tall and 65 pounds in 1920, making her the smallest Olympian at the Antwerp Games. Because she was just 14 years old, she had been barred from the Olympics, but officials relented. When the springboard diving event was over, she had won—receiving a gold medal in this event the first time it was held for women at the Olympics. It was a great day for U.S. women swimmers and divers, celebrating their first time at the Olympics. It was also a great day for Riggin, who became the youngest person to win a gold medal in any event up to that time. (In 1936, Marjorie Gestring would become the youngest by winning a diving event at age 13.)

Growing up, Riggin practiced diving in New Jersey, where there was an indoor pool with a 3-meter springboard available for women's use. In warm weather, she practiced at Manhattan Beach on Long Island. As an amateur, Riggin won one indoor and three outdoor titles in U.S. springboard championships. She also swam and was a member of the national swim team.

In 1922, Riggin made slow-motion films of swimming and underwater diving for sports columnist Grantland Rice. In 1924, she again competed at the Olympics, held that year in Paris. Although Riggin had been away at school and had not been training as much as before, she won the silver medal in platform diving and the bronze in the 100-meter backstroke.

After winning the U.S. 3-meter springboard title in 1925, Riggin became a professional and performed in many exhibitions, some at the famous New York City arena, the Hippodrome. With marathon swimmer Gertrude Ederle, Riggin toured the country and also appeared in feature films, besides teaching swimming and writing books and articles about the sport. In 1967, she was voted into the Swimming Hall of Fame.

Riggin continued to swim in later years. In November 1986, the 80-year-old athlete won the 75-and-over race at the 13th Annual Castle Swim contest, sponsored by the Outrigger Canoe Club in Honolulu. To win, she completed a 1.5 mile surf course along Waikiki Beach.

References Carlson and Fogarty, *Tales of Gold* (1987).

Riley, Dawn (b. 1964)

Riley skippered the first all-women's crew racing a 74-foot yacht in the qualifying rounds of the America's Cup competition. The Detroit native came from a family that loved sailing and spent her twelfth year on a boat, traveling from the Great Lakes to the Caribbean and back again. After launching her career in advertising, Riley became a crew member of the *Maiden*. This British boat competed in 1988–1989 as the first women's team in the Whitbread Round the World Race. Riley served as engineer and watch captain during the nine-month, 33,0000-mile race.

She was helmsman of the *America*[3] (America Cubed) which won the 1992 America's Cup defender series. In November 1993, she was asked to take over as captain of the U.S. Women's Challenge in the Whitbread race. Riley led an 11-member crew during that 32,000-mile competition. In 1994, she was captain of the 64-foot yacht *Heineken* in the Whitbread Round the World Race.

During 1994 and 1995, Riley trained in San Diego, preparing to race against male teams with the first all-women America's Cup crew. On January 13, 1995, the *America*[3], with its all-women crew, won a race in San Diego, California, against a champion men's team aboard the *Stars and Stripes*. This was a first in the 144-year history of the race.

See also *America*[3]

References Gyure, "Maiden Voyage (Interview with Dawn Riley)," *Women's Sports and Fitness*, May-June 1992, 106–107; Nutt, "Dawn Riley Favored to Become First Female Helmsman in America's Cup," *Sports Illustrated*, May 9, 1994, 72–73; Rudeen, "Steel Dawn," *Motor Boating and Sailing*, April 1994, 46–49ff; Whiteside, "A Whole New Tack," *Sports Illustrated*, February 1995, 40–43.

Ritter, Louise (See Track and Field)

Road Runners Club of America

The club honors outstanding athletes with special awards, including a Runner of the Year award for the best male and female runners. A Runner of the Decade is also chosen each ten years. Among the women who have won these awards is U.S. marathon runner Kathrine Switzer, named Runner of the Decade in 1976.

See also Switzer, Kathrine

Robinson, Elizabeth (Betty) (b. 1911)

In 1928, Robinson became the first woman to win the 100-meter dash at the Olympic Games at what was only the fourth formal track meet of her life.

Robinson was born in Riverdale, Illinois, and entered running events while in high school. She worked out with the boys' track team, since there was none at that time for girls, then began training with the Illinois Women's Athletic Club. At age 16, she became a member of the U.S. women's Olympic track and field team, and at the 1928 Games in Amsterdam, track and field events for women were featured for the first time. Robinson's winning time in the 100-meter race was 12.2 seconds, and she ran with the 4 x 100 relay team that won a silver medal. The next year, she set a world record of 5.8 seconds for the 50-yard race.

While a student at Northwestern University in 1931, Robinson captained the university's rifle team. Three years after her Olympic victory, she barely survived a plane crash that left her badly injured and in a coma for two months. She spent two years recovering the strength in her legs. Robinson had trained hard in order to compete in the 1936 Olympics, but she could not compete in individual events. However, she was a member of the U.S. women's 4 x 100 relay team that captured the gold medal that year in Berlin. Inter-

viewed in the 1980s, Robinson said, "As time goes on, that victory means more and more to me—being the first woman to win a gold medal for this country in track and field."

References Carlson and Fogarty, *Tales of Gold* (1987).

Robinson, Jean (See Cycling)

Rockford Peaches

One of the first four teams in the All-American Girls Professional Baseball League (AAGPBL), the Peaches won the league championship in 1945, 1949, and 1950, as well as the play-offs in 1945, 1948, 1949, and 1950.

One of the top pitchers for the team was Carolyn Morris, a league all-star. Morris pitched in the dramatic 1946 national championship game against the Racine Belles. More than 5,600 fans watched the game that major league veteran Max Carey would later call the greatest baseball game he had ever seen. Morris hurled a no-hit game that went into extra innings. Despite Morris's outstanding performance, after a replacement pitcher took over in the twelfth inning, the Belles scored a run and won the title.

From 1948 to 1954, Ruth "Richie" Richard, a native of Argus, Pennsylvania, was catcher for the Peaches. During her eight years in the league, Richard had a batting average of .241 and was on six all-star teams. At first base, Dorothy "Kammie" Kamenshek, from Cincinnati, Ohio, was a top hitter, winning the batting title for the league in 1946 and 1947. Her averages for the two years were .316 and .306.

Rodeos

Rodeos were taking place in the United States by the 1870s, as cowboys at different ranches in the West vied in shooting, roping, riding, and other events. Cowgirls during the 1800s, like Annie Oakley, were also skilled at riding horses, roping, and shooting but were not allowed to compete in organized rodeos.

During the 1900s, while accompanying male rodeo competitors, women convinced rodeo directors to let them take part in the barrel racing event. This requires horse and rider to race around three empty barrels set up in a cloverleaf pattern. If they knock down a barrel, they are penalized. Some rodeos also had women's pole bending and goat roping events. In the 1990s, barrel racing continued to attract more female competitors than males at both junior and senior rodeos.

The Girls Rodeo Association was formed during the 1960s, and women began to hold rodeos of their own. All-girl rodeos are now often held in California, Wyoming, Oklahoma, Utah, and Texas. They usually include these events: calf roping, bull riding, bareback bronc riding, and barrel racing. There is also an international competition for women rodeo riders, but the women have not received the pay or publicity of male rodeo stars.

The youngest person to win a world title at a rodeo was Metha Brorsen, who, at age 11, won the barrel racing event at the 1975 International Rodeo Association Cowgirls competition.

References *Guiness Book of World Records: 1988*; Kircksmith, *Ride Western Style* (1991).

Roffe-Steinrotter, Diann (b. 1967)

At the 1994 Winter Olympic Games, Alpine skier Roffe-Steinrotter became the surprise winner in the women's super-giant slalom, called the Super G. The Potsdam, New York, native completed the race in 1 minute, 22.15 seconds, 0.29 seconds faster than her nearest competitor. The difficult course on Norway's Kvietfjell Mountain felled several skiers, and 11 of the 57 who started the course did not finish. Skiers had trouble maintaining control on this slope while making the tricky turns.

During the early 1990s, Roffe-Steinrotter returned to an early love, horseback riding, and became a world-class equestrian, competing in international tournaments. She excelled in dressage and endurance events and hoped to compete in international equestrian events. Her mastery of two different sports put her in a special class of athletes.

References Araton, "Once Again, a U.S. Stunner on the Slopes," *New York Times*, February 16, 1994, 15; Araton, "Devil of a Turn," *New York Times*, February 15, 1994, 16.

Roller Derby

A type of endurance skating, roller derby has been called a rough-and-tough sport. The first roller derby was developed by Leo Seltzer of Chicago. Teams included one male and one female skater who alternated on the track. So that spectators could see all the action, the track was small, with 18 laps equaling about 1 mile. Those who skated the longest would win this marathon-type event. Later, the derby included sprint races between two teams of five skaters each, competing on the same track at once. They devised ways to block the competition, sometimes even throwing one another over the sides of the rink. During the early derbies, in the 1950s, teams of five men and five women competed against teams of the same sex. The rules and scoring were the same for both men and women, though, and the men who practiced and skated with the women's team called them tough competitors.

A scene from the early days of roller derby—Jean Porter's ill-fated attempt to hold on before crashing during the 1951 derby between the New Jersey Jolters and the New York Chiefs.

Competitors in this professional game need speed, strength, and agility as they move around a circular course. They may skate while performing movements from other sports, such as hockey, football, or wrestling, or even using a bicycle. Often, they skate at speeds of 25 to 35 miles per hour. Skaters also wear padded clothing and helmets to reduce the severity of injuries.

Among the athletes who have starred in the derby are Earlene Brown, a track and field champion who competed in three Olympic Games, winning third place in the shot put in 1960. The original roller derby ended during the early 1970s, though similar events are still held and attract paying crowds.

See also Brown, Earlene
References Olney and Bush, *Roller Skating* (1979).

Roller Hockey

A sport that evolved from roller polo during the late 1800s, roller hockey was first dominated by men. It became an organized competitive sport, usually in large cities, where there are large, flat areas of concrete. Ball roller hockey is played throughout the world. In 1959, the Roller Skating Rink Owners of America (RSROA) organized rink roller hockey in the United States. A ladies' roller hockey division for both ball and puck competition was introduced in 1977.

In August 1995, the Chicago Cross-Checkers team won the women's title at the first North American Roller Hockey Championships. Four teams from around the country came to St. Louis, Missouri, to take part in the six-day event, which was expected to be held annually.

Roller Skating

The first roller skates apparently originated in the Netherlands, where ice skating was a beloved pastime and an important method of transportation. Someone had the idea of putting wheels on skates in order to enjoy skating during months when there was no ice on the canals, and large wooden spools were attached to stirrups that fit a skater's shoes. Later, a Belgian named Joseph Merlin invented skates with metal wheels, but his version did not allow skaters to turn or stop. In 1863, American inventor J. L. Plimpton devised the "rocking skate," which could be guided by the skater.

Artistic roller skating emerged gradually, as it had in the sport of figure skating on ice. Jackson Haines, a ballet master who performed graceful moves on the ice, also took up roller skating. Spins, jumps, and figures became part of roller skating, often called "rinking." The sport gained popularity as people realized that it could be enjoyed with little expense or equipment. In Great Britain, roller skating enthusiasts joined with ice skaters to form the National Skating Association.

When ball-bearing wheels were patented in 1884 in the United States, the improved roller skates gained many new devotees to the sport around the world. Rinks sprang up in cities across America. The United States Federation of American Roller Skaters became the national governing body, independent of other countries. The world governing body became the Fédération Internationale de Patinàge Roulettes (FIPR).

Some took up roller skating as a marathon sport. In 1933, Gerane Withington skated from Oregon to Florida, a trip that took her over numerous bumpy and unpaved roads. Withington averaged 12 to 13 miles a day and became the first person, male or female, ever to cross the country on roller skates. A six-day race at

Madison Square Garden was held. The winner skated 1,091 miles.

In 1937 skating rink operators joined to form the Roller Skating Rink Operator Association of America (RSROA). The RSROA set rules for roller skating competition in the United States and established national championships for different age groups in three categories: speed skating, figure skating, and dance skating. Working with the RSROA, the United States Amateur Confederation of Roller Skating manages competition in the sport, under a charter from the Amateur Athletic Union (AAU). The RSROA also sponsors proficiency tests for skaters. The tests are based on national standards and evaluate skills in the following areas: dance, figure, freestyle , and speed. Gold, silver, and bronze medals are awarded.

As with ice skating, competition in roller skating encompasses both speed events and figures, or artistic skating. Artistic events include dance, figure, and freestyle skating. There are two styles of dance skating, American and international, with the latter emphasizing ballet-like movements and the American style emphasizing formal elegance. Specific figures, spins, glides, and jumps are involved, as in ice skating. The United States Amateur Federation of Roller Skaters sponsors an annual competition to select national champions in both speed events and artistic skating. Skaters are grouped by age and sex and on the basis of their achievements in local and regional competition. There are speed skating events, including relays, for individuals and teams. Exhibition events include slaloms and marathons.

National figures roller skating champions have come from all over the United States. They include Donna Kiker of Decatur, Georgia, who won the U.S. ladies roller skating championship in 1976; Jean O'Laughlin of Waltham, Massachusetts (1977); and Patti Mashalewski of Concordville, Pennsylvania (1978). In 1976 the American dance team of Karen Mejia and Ray Chappatta won second place at the World Championships. One of the top skaters was world champion Natalie Dunn of Bakersfield, California, who won in 1976 in Rome, in 1977 in Montreal, and again in 1978 at the competition in Lisbon, Portugal. Dunn began skating at age 2 and had won the regional competition in Tiny Tot Division at age 7. In 1973, she also won the national women's speed roller skating title.

Between 1970 and 1980, the number of speed roller skaters in the United States doubled. Women who became national speed champions were Colleen Giacomo (1970 and 1971), April Allen (1972), Robin Wilcock (1974), Marcia Yager (1975, 1976, 1977), and Linda Dorso (1978). In both 1981 and 1982, Sandra Dulaney won the world title in speed skating. Dulaney, age 17, also won five gold medals at America's National Outdoor Sports Festival.

Winners of the senior division of the U.S. National Dance and Figure Roller Skating Championships go on to the World Roller Skating competition. The United States sends teams, as do Canada, Great Britain, Australia, New Zealand, Germany, India, and Japan. The United States did well in artistic roller skating competition in 1994, winning five events out of six at the world championships. Dezera Salas of Goleta, California, won the women's freestyle title, while April Dayney of Maumee, Ohio, took the gold medal in figures. Lisa Friday and her partner Tim Patten, both from Taunton, Massachusetts, won the dance competition.

In 1979, speed roller skating was

included in the Pan American Games for the first time. There are separate races for men and women in roller skating contests, with some mixed relay races. Skaters start about three feet behind the starting line and move when a gunshot sounds to begin the race.

Roller skating continues to be popular during the late twentieth century as new ways of skating emerged in the forms of skateboards and in-line skates.

See also Roller Derby

Rowing

Since ancient times, when canoes, rafts, and other boats were used for transportation, people have devised ways to row them across the water. Sticks and branches were probably the first means by which such crafts were propelled. As far back as 19 B.C., races were held so that men could display their skill in the team sport of rowing. Different Greek states sent crews to compete against each other in contests called regattas. Races were part of many countries' annual fairs and festivals, and talented rowers entertained royalty during special occasions.

Rowing matches were especially popular in England, where intercollegiate competition began in the early 1800s. In America, races among professional rowers and college teams became popular during the 1800s. The first intercollegiate race was held between Harvard and Yale in 1852, making rowing the oldest intercollegiate sport in America.

Women became involved in rowing as a team sport somewhat earlier than in other sports. In 1875, a rowing program was developed at the all-woman Wellesley College in Massachusetts. As other eastern colleges assembled crews, there were women's intercollegiate races. On the West Coast, rowing clubs developed and raced against each other during the late 1800s.

In 1936, Sally Stearns served as the first woman coxswain on an otherwise all-male racing crew from Rollins College, located in Winter Park, Florida. In May of that year, her team defeated Manhattan College in New York City but lost to Marietta College (Marietta, Ohio). In 1938, the Philadelphia Girls' Rowing Club brought together women whose husbands rowed in competition at the local Boat House. The members raced against each other.

In 1962, the National Women's Rowing Association was formed in California, and it sponsored the first national title event in 1966. Forty-five crews competed in that first race. World contests for women rowers began in 1974. Two years later, at the Montreal Games, women rowed for the first time in Olympic events, which took place on a 1,000-meter course. That year, American Joan Lind, who had won the U.S. national singles rowing title five times, won a medal in the single scull competition. She returned to racing eight years later and rowed with the silver medal–winning U.S. quad scull team in Los Angeles.

A team of eight U.S. women set a world record in 1984 when they clocked 2 minutes 54.05 seconds for the standard women's distance of 1,000 meters (1,093.6 yards), an average of 12.85 miles per hour. This race took place on nontidal water, in the Rootsee in Lucerne, Switzerland. At the Olympics that year, there were six rowing events for women, the same number as for men. They included the eight-oar sweep with coxswain (the person who steers); the four-oar sweep, the four-oar sweep with coxswain, the double sculls (two rowers with two oars each), two-man pair oars (two rowers

Rowing

Wellesley College students from the class of 1897 crew propel themselves across the water. The all-woman college in Massachusetts was one of the first institutions to begin a rowing program for women.

with one oar each), and the single sculls. In sweep races, each rower has one oar, while scullers have two oars each. Although Russian and Eastern European rowers had dominated international competition, a U.S. team of eight defeated East Germany at the International Rowing Regatta held in Switzerland in 1984. That same team rowed to victory in the eight-oar shell event at the 1984 Summer Olympics, topping second-place Romania and the third-place winners, the Netherlands.

At the 1994 world rowing championships, the U.S. women's team won the Ladies Challenge Plate, but no Americans won individual events. Since rowing can help to develop strength and a high level of fitness, women rowers were among those chosen in 1995 as members of the first all-women crew to vie for a spot in the America's Cup yacht race. Olympic rower Amy Baltzell and another competitive rower, Sarah Bergeron, became crew members.

Women rowers have proven themselves in marathon rowing as well. In 1981, Kathleen Saville became the first woman to row across the Atlantic Ocean. Saville and her husband, Curtis, residents of Providence, Rhode Island, rowed from the Canary Islands off the western coast of Africa to Antigua in the West Indies. Their journey took 84 days, from March 18 to June 10.

See also America's Cup

Rubin, Barbara Jo (b. 1949)

Jockey Rubin was the first woman to win a flat race against male jockeys. During her racing career, Rubin rode in 89 races, winning 22 times and placing second and third ten times each.

Born in Highland, Illinois, Rubin passed the first test required to qualify for a jockey's license when she was 19 years old. But on January 15, 1969, the day she was scheduled to compete, male jockeys announced that they would boycott the race at Tropical Park in Coral Gables, Florida. Fines were later imposed on the men, but for that race, Rubin was replaced by a male jockey.

On January 28 of the same year, Rubin rode to victory on Fly Away at the Hobby Horse Hall racetrack in the Bahamas. She was the only woman jockey in the race. On February 22, she achieved her historic win at the Charlestown, West Virginia, track, the first time a woman jockey had finished first in a thoroughbred parimutuel race. Impressed by her skill, several male jockeys congratulated Rubin after the race. Problems with torn knee cartilage forced Rubin to retire from the sport in 1970.

Rudolph, Wilma (1940–1994)

Wilma Glodean Rudolph overcame childhood poverty, illnesses, and racial discrimination to become the fastest woman runner in the world. Born on June 23, 1940, in Clarksville, Tennessee, she was the twentieth of 22 children born to Ed Rudolph, a railroad porter, and Blanche Rudolph, a domestic worker. Rudolph was born prematurely and weighed only

4½ pounds. A sickly child, she battled pneumonia, scarlet fever, and other illnesses, then survived a bout of polio at age four.

Afterwards, her left leg was weak and crooked, and she could only walk with the support of a heavy metal brace. Seeking treatment for Wilma, Blanche Rudolph took her on weekly trips, riding 50 miles each way, to an all-black hospital in Nashville. At home, she massaged Wilma's leg and urged her to exercise her leg and foot. Rudolph dreamed of walking someday and later said, "The only thing I ever really wanted when I was a child was to be normal . . . to be able to run, jump, play, and do all the things the other kids did in my neighborhood."

At age 12, Rudolph was walking without a brace. She had often sat and watched others play basketball; now, she was ready to play herself. With her long legs and great speed she became a top player in high school, where she also joined the track team. While serving as a referee at a high school game, Coach Ed Temple of Tennessee State University saw Rudolph playing and invited her to spend the summer at the university, training in track and field with other top athletes. In 1956, Rudolph tried out for the Olympic team and became its youngest member. The 6-foot, 89-pound runner did not win any individual medals at her first Olympics but resolved to do better next time. She earned a third-place bronze medal as part of the 4 x 100–meter relay team.

Rudolph received a scholarship to attend Tennessee State University, where she trained hard and studied to maintain the B average that Coach Temple expected from his Tigerbelles team. Several Tigerbelles, including Rudolph, competed in the 1960 Olympics, held in Rome. Just before her first qualifying race, Rudolph injured her ankle but still managed to win the 100-meter dash with a time of 11 seconds. She won a second gold medal in the 200-meter race, then pushed herself hard in the relay race, where the U.S. team won by three tenths of a second, setting a new record of 44.5 seconds.

"The Tennessee Tornado" was now the most famous woman athlete in the world, praised both for her athletic skill and charming manners. The people of Clarksville held a victory parade for her, the first integrated event in the town's history. Rudolph visited the White House, received numerous awards, and became a popular public speaker. Returning to college, she continued to compete in amateur races, retiring in 1962. The next year she finished college and became a teacher, then married, eventually raising four children.

During the 1960s, Rudolph took part in the black rights movement and helped to develop and lead programs for young people. She worked as a television commentator, a model, and in the field of public relations. In 1977, her autobiography was published, and a television movie about her life was made. In 1980, she was named to the Women's Sports Hall of Fame. The next year, she started her nonprofit Wilma Rudolph Foundation to help young people succeed in school and in sports by providing books, tutors, free coaching, and help with travel expenses. Later, Rudolph called the foundation "my legacy."

In 1988, Rudolph was voted into the National Track and Field Hall of Fame, and the Black Athletes Hall of Fame, now called the Afro-American Hall of Fame. She is also honored in the Olympic Hall of Fame and was the first woman to receive the National Collegiate Athletic Association's Silver Anniversary Award.

In 1994, Wilma Rudolph died at age 54 of a brain tumor.

See also Temple, Ed; Tigerbelles
References Biracree, *Wilma Rudolph* (1988); Jacobs, *Wilma Rudolph: Run for Glory* (1975); Rudolph, *Wilma* (1977); Berkow, "Forever the Regal Champion," *New York Times*, November 13, 1994, 9; Litsky, "Wilma Rudolph, Star of the 1960 Olympics, Dies at 54," *New York Times*, November 13, 1994, 53.

Rugby

In the United States, the sport of rugby, sometimes called British football, was first played by men's college teams. There are now organized rugby teams for women at schools, colleges, and in communities around the United States. By 1980, there were 250 women's rugby clubs around the nation.

National and world rugby competitions are held each year. In 1994, a team from Berkeley, California, won the national Women's Club competition, while the team from the Air Force Academy won the College division crown. No U.S. women's teams won in the world rugby competitive events that year.

Ruiz-Conforto, Tracie (b. 1963)

A native of Honolulu, Hawaii, Ruiz was the first person to win a gold medal in the Olympic synchronized swimming competition. That event, which debuted at the Olympics in 1984, was still held only for women as of 1996.

Two years before the Olympics, Ruiz had won the world solo synchronized swimming title, and with Candy Costie, her partner in duet synchronized swimming since 1975, she had won second place as well. The next year, she won the solo event at the Pan American Games and America Cup. She and Costie won the duet event at both of these competitions, impressing judges with their strong, well-defined, and graceful movements. At the World Cup, swimming legend Esther Williams presented them with their gold medals.

During the 1984 Olympics, Ruiz received a score of 99.467 in the compulsory movements, the highest score ever recorded for that part of the event. For her final solo routine, which began with a 50-second underwater sequence, she scored 99 out of a possible 100 points. She and Costie again won first place during the duet competition, making Ruiz a double gold medalist that year.

Ruiz-Conforto, now married, returned to the Olympics in 1988. She won the second-place silver medal in the solo synchronized event. After she retired from competitive swimming, Ruiz-Conforto became a mother and contributed time to a variety of charitable causes, particularly those that fight child abuse and fund cancer research. She also participated in the Leukemia Society of America's "Super Swim" fund-raiser. Ruiz-Conforto provided commentary for NBC-TV during the 1992 Olympic Games and in Atlanta during the 1996 Games. In that year a new eight-person synchronized event was added to the competition.

See also Swimming, Synchronized
References Guttman, *Women's Sport: A History* (1991); "Olympic Gold," *Good Housekeeping,* August 1992; Markel et al., *For the Record* (1985).

Runner of the Decade (See Road Runners Club of America)

Running (**See** Benoit Samuelson, Joan; Decker, Mary; Devers, Gail; Griffith-Joyner, Florence; Marathon Running; Rudolph, Wilma; Torrence, Gwen; Track and Field; Trason, Ann; Ultra Running)

Rush, Cathy (b. 1941)
Top basketball coach Rush led her women's team at Immaculata College near Philadelphia to national titles during the 1970s. In 1975 her team, playing against Maryland, was the first woman's basketball team to appear on national television. With Queens College of New York, the "Mighty Macs" became the first women's teams to play at Madison Square Garden.

A high school basketball coach at Cardinal O'Hara High School in Glenolden, Pennsylvania, Rush was recruited to head the women's program at Immaculata. Under her direction, the Macs became a top-ranked team. During Rush's first year, Immaculata had a winning season (10-2). In 1971–1972, they won 19 games and lost only one, going on to win the Association for Intercollegiate Athletics for Women (AIAW) title. They had not been expected to finish in the top ten.

The next season, the Macs were the team to beat in the East. With high-scoring freshman Marianne Crawford, defensive and offensive star Theresa Shank, and other strong players, Rush led her team to another national title in 1973 and in 1974. Sportswriters raved about the team, calling them the "UCLA of the East." The Macs' exciting performance also aroused greater interest in women's basketball on the east coast and brought more fans to collegiate games. Throughout the East, fans followed the team's progress, and newspapers chronicled their matches.

As a coach, Rush emphasized basic skills and conditioning. Describing her methods to writer Irwin Stambler, Rush said, "I'll have to say I'm a demanding coach. Our practice lasts for 90 minutes to 2 hours and I stress defense. We practice defense until it comes out our ears."

In 1977, Rush resigned, expressing satisfaction at the progress that had been made in women's basketball in the previous decade. Interviewed during the 1980s, she commented on the heightened interest in women's basketball: "I knew we'd win acceptance one day, but I didn't expect anything like this."

See also Shank, Theresa
References Anderson, *The Story of Basketball* (1988); Stambler, *Women in Sports* (1975).

Russo, Leslie (b. 1964)

Leslie Russo, from Durham, Connecticut, was the first American female gymnast to do a double back flip, called a "doubleback," which consists of two flips in succession. Russo performed this revolutionary movement at a world gymnastics meet in Japan in 1978 when she was 14 years old. Later that same year, Russo competed in Philadelphia at the national gymnastics championships, where she won first place in all four gymnastics events—the balance beam, the uneven parallel bars, the side horse vault, and floor exercises. Russo was not able to compete in the 1980 Summer Olympics, held in Moscow, because President Jimmy Carter asked U.S. Olympians to boycott the Games in protest of the Soviet Union's invasion of Afghanistan.

Ryan, Elizabeth (1892–1979)

Tennis star "Bunny" Ryan won the first of 19 Wimbledon titles in 1914, a record for women until Billie Jean King won her twentieth title in 1979. Although Ryan acknowledges that she hated seeing her record broken, she preferred King to be the one. "Billie Jean's got guts," she said.

A top-ranked doubles player, Ryan won her Wimbledon ladies' doubles titles paired with the great French champion Suzanne Lenglen. The two also met as opponents in the singles final of Wimbledon in 1921 and in the quarterfinals in 1923, with Lenglen winning both matches. Ryan also won a U.S. national doubles title with partner Eleanor Goss and played winning doubles at the same tournament with Americans Mary K. Browne and Helen Wills. Playing with Lenglen in 1925, she won the French and Wimbledon titles. Ryan was inducted into the International Tennis Hall of Fame in 1972. Ryan died in 1979 the day before Bille Jean King won her record-breaking twentieth Wimbledon title.

S

Sailing

Sailing began as transportation and became a sport in which people demonstrated their skills and competed with others. It is not known exactly how the first sails were designed or attached to boats thousands of years ago, but they may have been crafted from papyrus, cloth, or animal skins. People experimented with various shapes—rectangles, triangles, and others.

Eventually, sailing and yacht racing became sports of royalty and the wealthy classes. In 1732, the world's first yacht club was established in Cork, Ireland. It enabled yacht lovers to socialize as well as enjoy their sport with an exclusive group of only 25 members. Englishmen began to hold competitive races during the mid-1700s, and the first yacht club in England, the Royal Thames Yacht Club, was created in 1775.

Dutch settlers introduced sailing to North America, so the earliest American yachts were modeled after Dutch sloops and schooners. In 1844, the first permanent yacht club in the United States was established in New York City. An international yacht racing competition developed in 1851, when the club's founder, John C. Stevens, was invited to race his ship *America* against the yacht owned by the Earl of Witton, of the Royal Yacht Club Squadron in England. The *America* defeated 15 competitors to win the race and an ornate silver trophy, which became known as the America's Cup.

Yachting has been dominated by men through the years, but a few women proved their skill. In the late 1930s, Marion Rice Hart sailed a ketch around the world. (Later, at age 54 in 1947, Rice also took up flying and logged more than 5,000 hours in the air.) Women became more involved in yachting during the mid-1900s. In 1994, a crew of women sailors was assembled to race in the America's Cup competition.

See also *America*[3]; America's Cup; Riley, Dawn

Sanders, Summer (b. 1973)

Olympic medalist Summer Sanders began swimming when she was a baby. Her father had built a backyard pool and insisted that all of the Sanders children take lessons. At first, Summer did not seem to enjoy the lessons or pay much attention to the instructor. Then one day, she removed the flotation devices from her arms and jumped into the pool. Her father later said, "She jumped in the water and swam like she had been swimming all her life." By age three, Sanders could swim 25 yards, and she joined the Roseville (California) Bears Swim Team. At four, she was competing against children as old as seven. Her family also took part in competitive swimming, her mother as a part-time coach and her father as a swim-meet official.

The all-female crew of the America³ maneuver themselves around the second mark in the 1995 America's Cup competition on February 24, 1995.

At age 15, Sanders tried out for the 1988 Olympic Swim Team but missed qualifying by 0.27 of a second. Encouraged by her performance during the trials, Sanders trained hard in order to make the team next time. At Stanford University, she became a leading member of the swim team, which won the National Collegiate Athletic Association (NCAA) championship. At the 1992 NCAA competition, she earned 60 points, more than any other contender, and was named Swimmer of the Year. In Barcelona, Spain, at the 1992 Summer Olympics, 19-year-old Sanders won the gold medal for the 200-meter butterfly event. She earned another gold for the 4 x 100–meter relay, a silver medal in the 200-meter individual medley race, and a bronze in the 400-meters.

Sanders decided to retire from competition, but two years later, she returned to training. With a specially selected group of 12 talented swimmers, she trained in Florida. At the 1996 Summer Olympics in Atlanta, Sanders provided television commentary for NBC-TV.

Schileru, Dacie (b. 1954)
Romanian-American Schileru became the first woman to compete in an event run by the National Collegiate Athletic Association (NCAA). Only men had competed in NCAA events before Congress passed Title IX legislation in 1972. In 1973, when she was a student at Wayne State University in Detroit, Michigan, Schileru qualified for the NCAA diving competition.

Scholarships, Athletic

Athletic scholarships give talented women athletes financial assistance for higher education at a college or university. Men had been receiving such aid throughout the 1900s, but the concept is relatively new for women. It paralleled the idea that women were equally entitled to an education and to other opportunities.

As of 1973, many colleges did not officially offer athletic scholarships to women. The Association for Intercollegiate Athletics for Women (AIAW) had expressly criticized these scholarships, saying that its policy aimed to prevent high-pressure recruitment, commercialism, and exploitation in women's collegiate sports. Schools that offered athletic scholarships were not permitted to participate in AIAW tournaments. But pushed by the women's liberation movement and Title IX federal legislation, the AIAW ended this ban in 1974 and actually encouraged athletic scholarships. Within five years, 450 colleges were offering athletic scholarships for women. That number had nearly doubled by 1980. These changes greatly affected collegiate sports, since the best players often chose to attend schools that offered the most scholarship money. Many small schools could not compete with the higher offers and did not attract the same quality of players that had gone there in the past.

By the 1990s, tens of thousands of women were receiving athletic scholarships each year, for a total of more than $10 million. Athletes could receive scholarships for numerous sports, including archery, badminton, basketball, fencing, field hockey, golf, gymnastics, ice hockey, lacrosse, riflery, sailing and crew racing, softball, squash, swimming and diving, tennis, track and field, and volleyball. As of 1990, the sports offering the most scholarships to woman athletes were, in order, basketball, volleyball, tennis, track and field, swimming and diving, and softball. The fewest scholarships were being offered in the sports of archery, ice hockey, sailing, and squash.

To provide information about scholarships, the Women's Sports Foundation published its annual *Women's Sports Annual Scholarship Guide,* which detailed the sports programs available at various colleges and universities. The National Collegiate Athletic Association (NCAA) had taken over the regulation of recruitment and scholarship policies for both men and women athletes.

See also Association for Intercollegiate Athletics for Women (AIAW); Title IX
References Guttman, *Women's Sport: A History* (1991); Litsky, "When Small Schools Ruled the Women's Game," *New York Times,* March 12, 1995, 6.

Schwam, Marcy (See Annual Empire State Building Run-Up)

Scout, Baseball (See Houghton, Edith)

Sculling (See Rowing)

Sears, Eleonora (1881–1968)
When sportswoman Eleonora Sears was growing up, women were not encouraged to be athletic. Yet she went on to make her mark as a golfer, horsewoman, tennis player, swimmer, squash champion, and race car driver. An all-around athlete, Sears paved the way for other women, withstanding strong disapproval to pursue the sports she loved.

Eleonora Sears grew up in an upper-class Boston family that descended from Thomas Jefferson on her mother's side. The family spent their summers at a luxurious home in Newport, Rhode Island. Like other prominent young ladies of her day, Sears was a debutante, wearing gowns and attending balls, lectures, and tea parties. But she also craved adventure, and by age 19, had shown such skill in long-distance swimming, canoeing, sailing, fishing, and hunting that a magazine called her "the best all-around athlete in American society." To these athletic accomplishments, she added golf and polo.

Urged on by friends, Sears competed in national tennis events. In 1911, paired with Hazel Hotchkiss Wightman, Sears won the women's doubles' title at the U.S. national tournament. The pair won again in 1915, and Sears won with Molla Mallory in 1916 and 1917. With male partner Willis Davis, she won the mixed doubles' title in 1916.

Sears refused to conform when it did not suit her. People stared, astonished, as blond "Eleo" Sears rode horseback astride, instead of sidesaddle (the approved manner for ladies). They were further shocked by the breeches—loose-fitting trousers—that she substituted for a riding skirt. As captain of the International Squash Racquets Team, Sears again chose comfortable rather than socially acceptable clothing. She had taken up squash in 1918, at a time when few women played. Sears used the squash courts at Harvard University during years when women were not even allowed to enter the building. In 1928, at age 47, she won the first national squash title. Sears continued to play this demanding sport into her seventies.

Also an avid horsewoman, Sears entered horse meets and rode in fox hunts. She won numerous first-place awards for horses she had raised and let the U.S. Equestrian Team use her top horses at international events. The team also received financial assistance from Sears,

who donated money to the Boston Skating Club and other sports programs as well.

Keeping fit in her forties, Sears walked long distances, sometimes more than 40 miles, at a rapid pace of about 12-minutes-per-mile. One of her annual walks took her from Providence, Rhode Island, to Boston; she also covered 43 miles between two points in France and 103 miles on one walk in California. She popularized marathon walking as a way for people to keep physically healthy. When Sears died in Florida at age 87, newspapers praised the amazing achievements of this pioneer who paved the way for other women in sports.

References "Bostonian Unique—Miss Sears," *Vogue*, February 13, 1963, 80–83; Condon, *Great Women Athletes of the Twentieth Century* (1991); Scherman and Green, eds., *Notable American Women: The Modern Period* (1980); Obituary, *New York Times*, March 27, 1968.

Segregation

This practice of separating the races, black and white, persisted after the Civil War, particularly in the southern United States. Separate facilities were designated for blacks and whites in education, transportation, housing, employment, hotels, and restaurants until the Civil Rights movement of the 1950s and 1960s prompted changes in the laws. Throughout America, custom and unspoken "rules" barred African-Americans from certain private schools, colleges, and jobs, and from social, professional, and athletic clubs. Segregation deprived people of color of many opportunities in all areas of life. It diminished educational and sports programs for young people, since funding was often low and students did not have enough equipment, facilities, travel money, uniforms, or other resources.

Black athletes were barred from certain sports facilities and organized athletic competitions until the 1950s and 1960s. One result of these inequities was that African-Americans pursued sports in which talent and perseverance, rather than outside resources, could lead to success. Large numbers of young people took up basketball and track and field. Coaches developed strong teams and individual champions, many of whom went on to win medals in world and Olympic competition. Women excelled at track and field programs run by Tuskegee Institute and Tennessee State University, home of the famous Tiger-belles team.

Althea Gibson, the first black tennis player to compete in national lawn tennis events, broke the color barrier in that sport and was followed by the great men's champion, Arthur Ashe. Gibson was the first African-American tennis player to win at the U.S. national women's championship and Wimbledon.

Although there were many talented black women playing baseball, none was offered a place in the All-American Girls Professional Baseball League (AAGPBL), which began during World War II and lasted until the early fifties. Officials considered the possibility of recruiting black women but worried that the public, which had mixed feelings about women athletes in general, might not support integrated teams.

In men's major league baseball, top African-American male players had been confined to their own leagues, where talent was plentiful but pay and recognition were much less than that earned by top white players. Jackie Robinson became the first black man to play in the modern major leagues when he joined the Brooklyn Dodgers in 1947.

The achievements of black men and women athletes gradually opened doors for others in various sports, challenging the centuries-old idea of segregation in American life. In many ways, sports provided a common ground for Americans and brought them together, as in 1960, when Clarksville, Tennessee, held the first integrated event in the town's history to welcome back three-time Olympic gold medalist Wilma Rudolph.

See also All-American Girls Professional Baseball League; Discrimination, Racial; Gibson, Althea; Jackson, Nell; Rudolph, Wilma; Temple, Ed; Tiger-belles; Tuskegee Institute

References Ashe, *A Hard Road to Glory* (1988); Biracree, *Wilma Rudolph* (1988); Bontemps, *Famous Negro Athletes* (1964); Davis, *American Women in Olympic Track and Field* (1992); Smith, ed., *Notable Black American Women* (1992).

Sex Tests

Sex tests conducted on women athletes competing at world events were first developed after an incident in 1955 in which a German who won the women's high jump at the world championship later admitted he was a man. There had been rumors at other competitions about certain athletes who appeared to be men posing as women. When the first tests were conducted in 1966, certain Russian athletes did not show up for the test or the Games that followed, arousing suspicion.

At first, a panel of doctors examined the women's nude bodies to determine that they were, in fact, female. After those tests were abandoned, a standardized sex test, conducted at the Olympics and other international competitions, involved a chromosomal evaluation. Lab technicians scraped cells from the inside of the athlete's cheek. The cells were then analyzed under a microscope to verify the chromosome count indicating the genetic gender identity of the athlete.

Sex tests have been criticized, both for the humiliation the early tests caused and for the implications of current tests.

Athletes said that the tests reflected old attitudes that anyone who could become an outstanding athlete must not be a woman. In addition, they challenged the practice of conducting the test at each sports event, since there would not be a change in a person's chromosomes from one event to the next. In one startling case, a Polish athlete was barred from competition because her test showed one extra male chromosome, yet a few years later, she gave birth to a baby.

In professional sports, there has been no standard way to determine gender. This topic received wide press coverage in the 1970s, when a transsexual tennis player named Renee Richards joined the women's tour. Born Richard Raskind, the 6-foot 2-inch Richards had once played football, as well as other sports, and was now practicing medicine. After a sex change operation, he changed his name and entered women's tennis tournaments. When Richards qualified to play in the Tennis Week Open in New Jersey, several top players boycotted the tournament. A 17-year-old junior player defeated Richards in the semifinals.

References Cahn, *Coming On Strong* (1994).

Sexism

For centuries, women who wished to pursue athletics have been hindered by legal and social barriers that declared certain behavior appropriate for men but not women. Much opposition to the idea of women in sports or in certain sports came from men, but some came from other women. Women who showed too much competitive spirit or athletic ability were often criticized as "unfeminine" or "too masculine" in their behavior. Athletic, competitive women were seen as a threat to a social order in which women were quiet, submissive, and relegated to hearth and home. They were perceived as usurping the male role in society, traditionally one of dominance and strength. A blurring of these roles was deemed quite unacceptable by many people. Some people found it unacceptable for women to display their physical abilities in public in contests of skill against others. Baron de Coubertin, organizer of the first modern Olympic Games, spoke for many when he said in 1896, "Let women practice all the sports if they wish, but let them not show off."

Since men dominated the Olympic committees and other sports organizations, as well as the news media, they could keep women out of what they defined as their arena. Author George H. Sage described these attitudes in his 1981 book, *The World and I:* "Sport has been, and continues to be, an arena that actively and contemptuously excludes females, celebrates 'masculinity,' and reinforces partriarchy. We need only consider how vigorously and persistently some males have fought female inroads into the world of sport [since the late 1960s]." Even so, women slowly gained acceptance into the Olympics, making progress despite arguments about why they should not take part in various sports, especially those that involved strenuous activity or physical contact with others.

Although critics had long insisted that sports would harm women's health and reproductive functions and make them "masculine," research conducted during and after the 1920s did not bear out these theories. According to Dr. Dorothy Harris, who headed the Center for Women and Sport at Pennsylvania State University, "There is no significant difference in injury statistics between men and women athletes when proper conditioning, training, and medical services are available to both." As to arguments about the vulnerability of female breasts, sports physicians conclude that knees and elbows of both sexes are far more susceptible to injury than are women's breasts.

As women made gains in the mid-1900s, they still received less media coverage and less public attention than male athletes. They also had fewer opportunities for competition and lower incomes. The rise of the feminist movement, spurred by groups such as the National Organization for Women (NOW) and disgruntled women athletes, pushed for change. The feminist movement benefited from the modern Civil Rights movement that African-Americans had started during the 1950s. New legislation banned discrimination against people on the basis of color, sex, religion, or national origins. In 1972, Title IX required that publicly funded schools, colleges, and universities equalize opportunities for women and men students in sports and other areas.

Critics say that sexism continues to affect women's athletics, sometimes in subtle ways. Sometimes, the women's sports that become popular are those that feature revealing costumes. Television shows like "American Gladiators" show women in stretch tights fighting each other. Women wrestlers and roller derby events are also popular on television, while women playing traditional team sports have had difficulty reaching wide audiences. According to author Kate Rounds, "Beach volleyball, which is played in the sand by bikini-clad women, rates network coverage while traditional court volleyball can't marshal any of the forces that would make a women's pro league succeed."

See also Croteau, Julie; Kanokogi, Rusty; King, Billie Jean; National Organization for Women; Richardson, Dot; Title IX

References Conniff, "Awesome Women in Sports," *Progressive,* May 1993; Defrantz, "We've Got to Be Strong," *Sports Illustrated,* August 12, 1991; (Editorial) *Glamour,* "Are Men Taking Over Women's Sports?" September 1991; Guttman, *Women's Sport: A History (1991);* Rounds, "Why Men Fear Women's Teams," *Ms.* January-February 1991.

Shain, Eva (b. 1929)

In 1977, Shain became the first woman to judge a world heavyweight boxing match. During her career, Shain officiated at almost 3,000 amateur boxing events.

An accountant who worked as a bookkeeper in New Jersey, Shain attended her first fight in 1963. After years of watching and studying boxing matches, she became one of the first women ever licensed as a boxing judge in 1975. She was one of the judges at the fight between Muhammad Ali and Ernie Shavers held at New York City's Madison Square Garden on September 29, 1977. Ali was unanimously judged the victor in the fifteenth round.

See also Officiating

Shane, Mary Driscoll (See Sportscasting)

Shank, Theresa (b. 1952)

Shank gained acclaim during the 1970s as the best center in women's basketball. Growing up in Glenolden, Pennsylvania, she played the game with the boys in the neighborhood, who found her to be a tough, skillful competitor. As a junior high student, Shank played on a team in the Catholic Youth Organization League.

Like many girls, Shank was discouraged by the rules that applied to the women's game at the time, which allowed players to use only half the court and limited them to three dribbles at a time. Still, Shank shone on the court, with strong leaping ability. She grew to a height of 5 feet 11 inches, which also gave her advantages over many female players.

In high school, Shank became a star basketball player. During her sophomore, junior, and senior years, her team won its league title and lost only nine of the 91 games played. In Shank's senior year, her coach, Cathy Rush, decided to take a coaching position at Immaculata, a college for girls near Philadelphia. Shank and some of her teammates also applied to the college, where they became part of one of the most successful women's college basketball teams in history. Immaculata's team had never won the title in its league, but in the 1970–1971 season, it won 10 games out of 12. Pitted against tougher competitors in the 1971–1972 season, Immaculata posted a 19-1 record. Shank was a mainstay of the team's offense and defense.

Immaculata was invited to play in the Association for Intercollegiate Athletics for Women (AIAW) tournament. There, the "Macs" won all four games and took the national title. Shank used her speed and quick thinking to capture the ball from opponents and get it to her teammates. Her defensive blocks prevented opponents from scoring, and she assisted her teammates in scoring their own points.

Fans and newspaper articles raved as the Macs went undefeated in their next season. However, they faced stiff opposition in that year's AIAW tournament. They struggled to defeat Southern Connecticut in the semifinals, where they were behind 29 to 37 with only 8 minutes left to play. Shank played a key role in turning the game around, accumulating 25 rebounds. Shank's jump shots and the inspired play of her teammates enabled Immaculata to win by two points in the final seconds of the game. The last point

was a dramatic one, as Marianne Crawford threw a shot that just missed, and Shank moved in to tip the ball into the basket for a victory. The Macs went on to win their last game and the national title. Shank received a standing ovation, having scored 22 points. She was voted Most Valuable Player of the tournament and was chosen to play with the U.S. team at the 1973 World University Games, where the Americans won second place.

Theresa Shank's senior year at Immaculata was capped with another regional championship and national title. During the semifinal match in 1974, she scored 18 points and was again top rebounder. She averaged 18.2 rebounds a game during the 1974 AIAW tournament. After graduating, Shank married and, as Theresa Shank Grentz, became a highly regarded basketball coach at Rutgers University in New Jersey.

See also Rush, Cathy
References Anderson, *The Story of Basketball* (1988); Stambler, *Women in Sports* (1975).

Shea, Julie (b. 1959)

Long-distance runner Shea grew up in Raleigh, North Carolina, the daughter of a champion cross country runner and physical education professor. Her father encouraged all seven of his children to take part in sports. Julie Shea's first interest was swimming, and she won the state championship in her age group when she was nine years old. As a teenager, she found that she also loved running and chose to train in that sport over swimming. In her teens, she set a high school record by running the mile in 4 minutes and 43 seconds and competed with a team of Americans in a track meet held in Russia.

In 1977 Shea entered North Carolina State University and went to the world cross country championships in Scotland as part of the track team. She ended the race in fourth place, the best finish of any American woman that day. She improved her position to second place the next year. In 1980 she hoped to win the race, but a knee injury impaired her performance. Preparing carefully for the college track championships that year, she won the 10,000-meter race and set a new college record—33 minutes, 2.32 seconds. The next day, she won the 5,000-meter event as well, running in a cold rain. The 3,000-meter race was held that same day, and Shea had entered that event as well. Although worn out from the 5,000-meter race, Shea also managed to win this third race, the first time any competitor had done so. Her achievement brought several new honors, including the Broderick Cup, an annual award given to the most outstanding female college athlete of the year.

Sheehan, Patty (b. 1956)
In June 1984, golfer Sheehan earned the largest award ever received by a professional golfer. For capturing two of the previous three events sponsored by the Ladies Professional Golf Association (LPGA), Sheehan received a $500,000 bonus in addition to her prize money for the two matches.

A native of Middlebury, Vermont, Sheehan grew up in ski country, the daughter of a skiing coach. She became a champion junior skier, winning the national title for her age group. After the family moved to the Southwest in 1967, Sheehan took up golf and won the Nevada State Amateur title from 1975 through 1978. In 1978 and 1979, she won the California Amateur title, followed by the national collegiate women's title the next year. Despite bouts with illness and

arthritis, Sheehan was Player of the Year in 1983, when she had a string of victories—the LPGA championship, the Corning Classic, the Henredon Classic, and the Inamori Classic, which she had also won in 1982. Wins at the LPGA championship and McDonald's Kids Classic brought Sheehan her record-setting prize winnings in 1983.

Besides playing championship golf, the versatile Sheehan sang with a musical group and devoted time to her favorite charities, including a home for troubled teenage girls in California. In 1987, in recognition of her humanitarian efforts, Sheehan received a Sports Illustrated Sportsman of the Year award as part of a group called Athletes Who Care. In 1994 Sheehan won her second U.S. Open, was tenth on the all-time winners list with 33 tournament victories, and had earned $4,442,299.

References *LPGA Media Guide* (1996); Markel et al., *For the Record* (1985); *Sports Illustrated 1996 Sports Almanac.*

Shetter, Liz Allan (b. 1950)
Water-skiing champion Elizabeth Christine Allan was born in South Carolina and raised in Florida. By age 11, she was taking part in water-skiing competitions and won her first national title two years later. In 1964, Allan won the girls' division title, making two jumps of 98 feet. She would jump 100 feet for the first time later that same year, at the Southern Regional competition. She took top honors in the slalom and tricks events and second in jumping at the All-American tournament.

Fourteen-year-old Allan joined the U.S. water-skiing team in 1965, helping them to retain their world title and winning the overall world title herself. That year, she entered the jump competition at the Dixie Water Ski Championships at

Cypress Gardens, Florida, and leaped 94 feet off the ramp. She placed second in the slalom and third in the tricks competition. One of her great achievements was setting a new jumping record of 110 feet during a tournament in 1968.

After she married William Shetter in 1971, the couple opened a water-skiing school and training camp near Groveland, Florida, where she taught part-time when not traveling to competitive events. She won the U.S. national slalom water-skiing title in 1970, 1973, and 1974. From 1970 through 1975, she won the U.S. National Overall Water Skiing Championship. Her score in 1973 was 3,701, the highest she reached in that competition. In 1975, at age 25, she captured both the national women's title and the Masters Cup. Her score in winning the Overall World Championship in 1975 was an amazing 4,296 points. In all, she won 12 women's national titles, 9 Masters Cups, and 3 world titles in her career. That year, Shetter announced her retirement from competition, after which she devoted herself to teaching at the Florida school and camp.

References *The Lincoln Library of Sports Heroes*, vol. 17 (1989).

Shiley, Jean (b. 1911)

In 1932, track and field star Shiley became the first American woman to win an Olympic gold medal for the high jump. She defeated the remarkable American champion, Babe Didrikson Zaharias, with a jump that measured 5 feet, 5.25 inches.

Born in Harrisburg, Pennsylvania, Shiley grew up with three brothers and often played sports with them. She later praised her high school for its outstanding girls' sports program, which was comparable to that offered to male students—highly unusual during the 1920s. An all-around athlete, Shiley excelled in basketball, field hockey, and swimming, as well as several track and field events. She later said, "We girls had the same money, opportunities, schedule, transportation, uniforms, and support of the principal and community that the boys had. For instance, the boys had 12 football games, and we had 12 hockey games. . . . We had competition in hockey, basketball, track and field, tennis, swimming, golf, and some minor sports in which we didn't have a full schedule."

A female sportswriter for the *Philadelphia Inquirer* saw Shiley jump at a basketball game and arranged for her to try out for the Olympics. She was just 17 years old when she competed in 1928 and barely missed winning a medal when she placed fourth in the high jump event. From 1929 to 1932, she was the Amateur Athletic Union (AAU) national women's high jump champion. Her winning jump at the 1932 Olympics set a new world record. After the Games, Shiley earned her college degree with a major in physical education and a minor in history from Temple University. She worked as a lifeguard and swimming instructor and as a typist with the Work Projects Administration in 1935.

Since she had been paid for an athletic activity—swimming instructor—the AAU said she was a professional and could not try out for the 1936 Olympics. She married and raised three children, living in several cities around the United States. Interviewed in 1986, Shiley said that while winning a gold medal at the Olympics was wonderful, "the biggest benefit comes from the fringe things that happen: the camaraderie of the participants, your increased knowledge of the world, and your greater appreciation of the various cultures and their people."

References Carlson and Fogarty, *Tales of Gold* (1987).

Shooting

Even after they saw sharpshooter Annie Oakley display her skills in the late 1800s, women did not take up the shooting sports in large numbers. But both men and women did attend the shooting matches in large numbers, sometimes as many as 100,000. Trapshooting events, in which shooters had once hit birds, later clay pigeons or glass balls, were especially popular.

After the turn of the century, several women began to publicly display their skills and compete in this sport. In 1930, 33-year-old Marjorie Foster of Great Britain won a shooting championship called the King's Prize, defeating 99 military men in the contest. In the United States, Mrs. Leon Mandel of Chicago broke three world target-shooting records during a competition in 1956. She scored an average of 96.9 percent for 1,000 targets.

Other women, too, have defeated both male and female competitors, as when Sheila Egan won the annual trapshooting title in 1963. In 1970, Captain Margaret T. Murdock of Topeka, Kansas, won the 1970 world rifle-shooting championship. Six years later, Murdock became the first woman to win an Olympic medal in rifle shooting. She won the silver, but nearly captured the gold in a contest that lasted for more than five hours. The gold medalist invited Murdock, a 33-year-old mother and nursing student, to join him on the winner's platform as the national anthem was played during the awards ceremony. Murdock won seven individual world championships, 14 world team championships, and five Pan American Games gold medals during her career.

In 1950, an 18-year-old Floridean, Joan Pflueger, won the Grand American trap-shoot competition. At the event, held that year in Vandalia, Ohio, she hit 100 clay pigeons in a row. The only woman, she defeated men from all the other states and Cuba. Pflueger was the first woman to win the event in its 51-year history. Betty Swarthout won the U.S. high power rifle championship in 1972, 1974, and 1975.

During the late 1900s, more women learned shooting, both as a sport and means of self-defense. Women and men competed together at international meets, since the same rules applied. Shooters in competition are challenged to shoot from various distances and positions at different types of targets. U.S. National Indoor Rifle Champions include Margaret T. Murdock, who scored 795 in 1972; Tricia Foster who scored 796 in 1973; Karen E. Monez who won in 1974 (798), 1975 (797), 1976 (800), and 1978 (scored 798); and Elaine S. Proffitt, who scored 798 in 1977. Among the All-Round U.S. National Skeet Shooting Champions since 1970 are Karla Roberts (1970, 1971, 1973, 1974); Claudia Butler (1972); Jackie Ramsey (1975); Valerie Johnson (1976); Connie Place (1977); and Ila Hill (1978).

The National Rifleman's Association (NRA), the organization that governs shooting competitions, changed its name to the National Rifle Association (NRA) to recognize the fact that many members were women. A few women have won the NRA's national championship. Mary Stidworthy, a member of the U.S. Army, won the small-bore prone rifle championship in 1977. She scored 6,397 points out of a possible 6,400. Some 500 sharpshooters took part in that event.

See also Biathlon; Oakley, Annie

References Durant and Bettman, *Pictorial History of American Sport* (1965); Krout, *Annals of American Sport* (1929); Leder, *Grace and Glory* (1996).

Deena Wigger practices her shot with a .22-caliber rifle at the Pan-American Games in 1983.

Shore, Dinah (1917–1994)

A popular singer, actress, television hostess, and author, Shore was the first person ever named as an Honorary Member of the Ladies Professional Golf Association (LPGA). An avid player, Shore supported women golfers and annually sponsored the Nabisco Dinah Shore tournament, later the Colgate–Dinah Shore Winner's Circle of Golf, one of the major events on the women's golf tour. Shore was also a fine tennis player, frequently seen at professional-celebrity matches for charity. The winner of ten Emmy awards, Shore was named one of the most admired women in the world four times during her life.

Shot Put

A track and field throwing event using the shot (an iron or brass ball, filled with lead, about 4 inches in diameter). The athlete must "put the shot" from within a 7-foot circle, starting with her toes against a 4-inch-high toeboard. No part of the body may touch the toeboard during the throw. The women's shot weighs about 8 pounds, 13.8 ounces, slightly more than half the weight of that used by male competitors. A women's shot put event became part of the Olympics in 1948.

One of the most remarkable American competitors was Maren Seidler, who, at age 13, took part in the shot put event at a South Carolina track meet. She broke the age-group national record by putting the 6-pound shot 6 feet farther than her competitors. Seidler trained vigorously in this event and set a new American record in 1974: 56 feet, 7 inches. A staunch advocate for women in sports once considered appropriate only for men, Seidler once said, "With proper training and dedication, a woman can do anything she sets out to achieve."

See also Track and Field

Show Jumping (See Equestrian Sports)

Shriver, Eunice Kennedy (b. 1922) Shriver founded the Special Olympics, an organization that sponsors athletic training and competitive events on the local, national, and international level for people with mental and physical handicaps.

Shriver grew up in Massachusetts and New York amid wealth and privilege. She was the fifth child of Rose and Joseph Kennedy, born into one of the most prominent and accomplished families in America. Her brother John later became president of the United States, while brothers Robert and Edward (Ted) became senators, exerting a strong impact on American politics. The family later recalled that as a child, Eunice showed strong humanitarian qualities and often looked after her older sister Rosemary, who was mentally retarded. The Kennedy family became involved in raising funds for research into mental retardation and developed the Joseph P. Kennedy, Jr. Foundation to help people like Rosemary. It was dedicated to the memory of Shriver's eldest brother, Joe, Jr., who had died during World War II.

Shriver attended Sacred Heart Academy, Manhattanville College, and Stanford University. During her twenties, she worked in Washington, D.C., in a government bureau conducting a national conference on juvenile delinquency. She impressed people with her energy, optimism, and concern about social problems, such as prison reform and civil

Special Olympics founder Eunice Kennedy Shriver.

rights. In 1953 she married Sargent Shriver, who later helped to organize the Peace Corps and served as its first director under President Kennedy. The mother of four, Shriver continued to promote various charitable causes, becoming director of the Joseph P. Kennedy, Jr. Foundation in 1957.

During the 1960s, Shriver organized a backyard camp at her home in Maryland for mentally retarded children after discovering that there were no other programs of that kind available. Shriver realized that with proper guidance, these children could develop athletic skills and compete in organized sports. In 1968 she worked with people in Chicago who had asked the Kennedy Foundation to help fund a national Olympic event for children with mental and physical disabilities. The first Summer Games were held that July. Nearly 1,000 athletes from 26 states and Canada competed, mainly in track and field and swimming events. The program continued to grow in size and importance.

Shriver has said, "In Special Olympics it is not the strongest body or the most dazzling mind that counts. It is the invincible spirit which overcomes all handicaps. For without this spirit, winning medals is empty. But with it, there are no defeats."

See also Special Olympics
References Grandjean, "Hearts of Fire," *Connecticut*, June 1995, 63–68; Kaylin, "Special Olympics: Hope—and Concern—Grow in New Haven," *Connecticut*, December 1994, 15; Brochures, Special Olympics International; Leamer, *The Kennedy Women* (1994).

Shriver, Pam (b. 1962)

Tennis player Shriver was named Rookie of the Year by *Tennis Digest* magazine in 1978. She had reached the finals of the U.S. Open Tennis Championship at the age of 16, at that time the youngest player ever to have reached the finals. On the way to the final match, in which she lost to Chris Evert, Shriver had to defeat the number one–ranked women's player in the world, Martina Navratilova. Starting in 1981, Shriver and Navratilova teamed up to become one of the top women's doubles combinations of all time, winning 18 Grand Slam titles.

A native of Lutherville, Maryland, the 6 foot 1 inch Shriver played a powerful game with an especially strong serve and overhead smash. After the 1978 championship match, she went on to play tennis for twelve years, as both a singles and doubles player, sometimes serving as a tennis commentator during television sports events. Recurring tendinitis in her shoulder hampered her singles career through the years. Shriver wrote a book about the women's tennis tour and numerous magazine articles.

See also Grand Slam

References Lupica, "Tracy Awesome and the Legend of Lutherville," *World Tennis*, August 1978, 34–38.

Sierens, Gayle (See Sportscasting)

Six-beat Kick

A style of swimming in which the swimmer kicks six times per each armstroke. American swimmers adopted this technique around 1918 and Olympic athletes used it to their advantage, winning several medals at the 1924 and 1928 Games and in subsequent competitions.

Skating, Figure (See Figure Skating)

Ski Patrol, National

Formed in 1938, this group gives emergency aid to victims of skiing accidents and those who suffer a medical emergency, such as a heart attack, on the slopes. Most members are volunteers, while a small percentage are paid professional members. Patrollers must first be 18 years old or older, with a current certification in first aid from the American Red Cross or credentials as an emergency medical technician, then pass certain skiing tests.

Women have become members of ski patrols, although they remained in the minority into the 1980s. A small percentage have joined the ranks of certified and paid professional ski patrollers. The National Ski Patrol System has no special requirements based on gender; both men and women have to pass the same tests to qualify as a patroller. Women may not be required to carry certain heavy equipment but do pull sleds and may patrol any slopes male members patrol.

Skiing

People have skied since prehistoric times when hunters moved down snow-covered hills in search of prey, possibly on pieces of splintered logs. One pair of ancient skis (now in a museum in Stockholm) is thought to date back to about 3000 B.C., and in Russia, a rock carving depicting a skier dates back to around 6000 B.C. Ancient Northern Europeans believed in a goddess called Skadi, who hunted game animals with a bow and arrows while gliding down hills on skis.

The first skiing competitions were held by the Norwegian military. Jumping competition began in 1879, also in Norway, and a famous annual skiing derby was initiated by the Norwegian royal family in 1892. British skiers helped to develop slalom skiing, in which skiers speed downhill, navigating between pairs of gates.

Skiing may have first reached the United States with explorers like Leif Ericson in A.D. 1000. But it was not widely known until immigrants from Scandinavia settled in the United States during the 1800s. American College women began taking part in organized competition when the Lake Placid Club was formed during the 1920s. The three sponsored events were the country trace, slalom, and downhill race.

The International Ski Federation (ISF) was founded in February 1924, about one week after the first Winter Olympic Games had been held. The ISF officially recognizes both the Olympics and the World Ski Championships as world championships.

Today's alpine skiing competitions include three events: the downhill (high-speed run down a course), the slalom (skier must pass through a series of gates marked by two flags), and the giant slalom (skiers must pass between wider gates placed further apart). Nordic skiing events include cross country and jumping, and a Nordic combined score is tab-ulated by adding both together. Cross country skiers glide over a specific distance, in sprints or in marathons. Jumpers wear long skis and take off from a ramp at the end of a hill.

In 1948, Gretchen Kunigk Fraser won the first Olympic medals in skiing for the United States, capturing the gold in the slalom and the silver medal in the alpine combined event. In 1952, Andrea Mead Lawrence became the first American of either sex to win two gold medals in alpine skiing at one Olympics, a distinction she still held as of 1996.

Skiing, Freestyle

In this sport, nicknamed "hot-dogging," skiers perform flips, leaps, and dance-like movements while speeding downhill. The moves have colorful names, like outrigger, kickout, worm turn, and spread-eagle. Three major areas of competitive freestyle skiing are stunt-ballet, in which the skier spins and performs gymnastic moves to music; freestyle-mogul, a type of downhill racing; and aerial-acrobatic, made up of tricky stunts, including dives performed in midair.

Freestyle skiing was designated as a separate sport in 1971, with men as the chief competitors. Olympian Suzy Chaffee, one of the first women to compete in the sport, defeated male competitors to become the top-ranked freestyle skier during the early 1970s. There are also group stunts, in which skiers perform a stunt like a backflip simultaneously.
See also Chaffee, Suzy

Sky-Diving

Although sky-diving—parachuting from a plane—is viewed as one of the most risky and intimidating sports, women already made up about 20 percent of all American participants as early as the

1960s. Training schools could be found throughout the United States, and dozens of colleges had formed sky-diving clubs.

At sky-diving competitions, jumpers are judged in terms of the accuracy and style of their jumps. They may also perform other feats in the air, such as passing a baton and may jump in the daytime or at night. U.S. women first entered the world sky-diving championships in 1960. In 1962, the next time the events were held, the U.S. women's skydiving team won the world championships. Muriel Simbro, a 35-year-old homemaker from California who had already made more than 500 jumps, was the outstanding member of the team.

See also Aerial Sports; Broadwick, Georgia "Tiny"; Stearns, Cheryl
Reference *Guinness Book of World Records: 1988*; Saunders, *Parachuting Complete* (1966).

Sled-Dog Racing

Called an original North American sport, sled-dog races were held first in Alaska and Canada during the 1800s. Teams of dogs worked with men prospecting for gold, carrying mail and supplies over the snowy and icy terrain. It wasn't long before men began racing their dog teams against others.

The Nome Kennel Club in Alaska sponsored the All Alaska Sweepstakes Race in 1908 and offered a first-prize of $10,000, which amounted to several years salary for most people of that era. The winner of the race covered the 408 miles from the towns of Nome to Candle and back in five days. The race continued on an annual basis, and the kennel club devised rules for competition. Many of those rules strictly regulated the care of dog teams used in the race. In 1916 Esther Birdsall Darling, president of the club, said, "The dogs are considered first."

Organized sled-dog racing began in Alaska in 1927 with a 58-mile race from Fairbanks to the town of Summit and back. The first competition for women was held in 1929, a 17-mile event called the Ladies' Fromm Trophy Race. In 1936 the first North American Championship Sled Dog Race was held in Fairbanks and became an important race. By the late 1930s, Anchorage was sponsoring the World Championship Sled Dog races, with sprint events.

Both sprint and long races were held in western states and in eastern states, such as New Hampshire. The New England Sled Dog Club sponsored the Eastern International Dog Sled Derby, starting in 1922. These were open to both men and women drivers. The three most important sprint races of the late twentieth century were: the ALPO International Sled Dog Races at Saranac Lake, New York, held in January; the World Championships Sled Dog Race in Anchorage, Alaska, held in February; and the Open North American Championship in Fairbanks, Alaska, held in March. The Laconia (New Hampshire) World Championship in February is another old and prestigious race.

On March 26, 1936, the *Fairbanks (Alaska) Daily News–Miner* reported an amazing achievement by a 27-year-old referred to only as "Miss Joyce." She and her five-dog team had survived a three-month, 1,000-mile trip as they traveled from Fairbanks, Alaska, to Taku, Alaska. The terrain included dangerous mountain passes, bitter winds, and temperatures ranging between 34 and 60 degrees below zero. Mushers who have distinguished themselves in sled-dog races during the 1980s and 1990s are Jean Bryer, Libby Riddles, Susan Butcher, and Cindy Molberg Bicknell.

See also Butcher, Susan; Iditarod Trail Sled-Dog Race; Riddles, Libby

Sledding (See Luge; Iditarod Trail Sled-Dog Race)

Smith, Caroline

In 1924, this Illinois native became the first woman to win the Olympic platform diving event. Smith narrowly defeated her American teammate Elizabeth Becker, who won the silver medal in the platform event and the gold medal in springboard diving. The U.S. women competed in the first women's diving events ever held at a Summer Games, which took place that year in Paris.

Smith, Melanie (b. 1953)

Champion show jumping rider Smith won numerous national and world titles during the 1970s and 1980s. Growing up in Litchfield, Connecticut, Smith rode bareback until she was 12 years old.

Smith won five major Grand Prix awards in 1978 and was named the 1978 Grand Prix Rider-of-the-Year as well as Leading Lady Rider. Her horse "Val de Loire," whom she had trained herself, was named Horse of the Year. In 1979 she was part of the U.S. equestrian team that won the gold medal at the Pan American Games in Puerto Rico. Three years later, Smith won the World Cup in Sweden. Smith later became a television commentator and helped to cover equestrian events at the 1996 Olympics in Atlanta.

Smith, Robyn (b. 1944)

Jockey Robyn Smith came to her profession in her early twenties, later than most jockeys, who begin riding during childhood. While studying at Columbia Studio's acting workshop, Smith became interested in horses. She began riding at a nearby stable early in the morning and attending classes during the day. It took hours of practice to develop the reflexes and skills she needed to be an expert rider, which had become her goal.

Smith burst onto the racing scene in 1968, determined to become a jockey. Although some horse owners, trainers, and jockeys acknowledged that Smith was a good rider, few believed that she—or any woman—had the courage and physical strength to succeed in this male-dominated world. The next year, 1969, she became one of the first American women to get a jockey's license. Officials at Golden Gate Park near San Francisco thought a woman jockey might attract new spectators to the track and they granted Smith a license, an event that attracted much attention from the press.

Smith competed in her first official race on April 5 and finished, although she won no money. But she faced many obstacles in building her career. At 5 feet 7 inches and about 125 pounds, she was taller and heavier than most jockeys, who are usually about 5 feet tall, so she had to follow a strict diet to keep her weight low. As a woman, she also had trouble finding horse owners who would let her race their horses. But Smith persisted, reading voraciously about racing and horses, practicing hours every day, and competing whenever she could. She moved to the New York area, hoping trainers there would give her a chance. At last, on December 5, 1969, an owner agreed to let her race his horse at Aqueduct, a prestigious track. Although the horse, Exotic Bird, had not been finishing among the top contenders, Smith managed to come in fourth, losing only by a nose. Robyn Smith had proven herself among top professionals.

Even so, during the early seventies,

she still had to convince trainers and owners to let her ride. She raced fewer than 100 times, compared to the thousands of times that experienced male jockeys ride in a year. Despite riding on less accomplished horses, she managed to win 18–20 percent of her races between 1970 and 1974. Her expertise won admiration from many, including Alfred Gwynne Vanderbilt, who owned a first-rate stable. Smith became a regular rider for Vanderbilt and won numerous races at Aqueduct in 1972. By 1975, Smith was riding more often at prestigious tracks throughout America and had proven that women could hold their own in this rigorous sport, opening doors for others who wished to try.

Smith retired from racing and later married movie legend Fred Astaire, a devoted horse lover who owned champions. They lived together in Beverly Hills until Astaire's death in 1990.

References Hollander, *100 Greatest Women in Sports* (1976); Stambler, *Women in Sports* (1975).

Soccer

Ball-kicking games appear to date back to humans' early days. Historians have traced a game resembling soccer to China around the year 1697 B.C. In a game called *tsu chu,* players used only their feet to propel a leather ball stuffed with cork and hair. Similar foot-and-ball games were played throughout the Roman Empire, as well as in the British Isles and North Africa. English rugby and American football developed from these earlier sports, as did the version of soccer that is played today.

During the 1970s, women showed an increased interest in soccer, both as spectators and players. Statistics showed that about 40 percent of spectators at soccer matches were women. As recreational, industrial, and school-based soccer teams sprouted across the United States, women began playing together against other women's teams or against men's or coed teams when no same-sex teams were available. Local leagues grew in size. For example, in Dallas, Texas, there was one women's team in 1973, but within two years, that number had grown to 44.

In high schools, girls began asking for their own soccer teams. In Colorado in 1977, a federal district court justice ruled that girls could not be kept off boys' soccer teams if no teams were available for the girls. The legal basis for this decision was Title IX, passed by Congress in 1972. Some high school girls did play on boys' teams. In Chappaqua, New York, freshman Valerie Robin joined an all-boys squad at her school in 1977, since there was no parallel team for girls there.

Eager to develop more opportunities for women to play, six soccer players joined together in 1977 to form the National Women's Soccer Association (NWSA). Alaina Jones became its first president and executive director. The charter of the organization stated that the NWSA hoped to provide quality opportunities for women in soccer and promote tournaments at the local, state, regional, national, and international levels. In addition, the NWSA planned to foster more college scholarships for women soccer players and develop more chances for professionals in the sport. That year, the Florida Suncoast Soccer League opened a women's professional division.

In addition to women's teams, soccer teams for young people and college teams, both intramural and intercollegiate, have also grown in number. The number of girls playing in American Youth Soccer Organization (AYSO) leagues has grown steadily since the 1970s. During the early 1990s, more than one-fourth of the players were girls. About 3.5 million teenagers were playing soccer at least six times a year as of 1991, and 121,700 were playing on high school teams. At the 1996 Summer Olympics in Atlanta, Georgia, the U.S. women's soccer team won the gold medal, defeating China 2-1 in the finals.

See also Soccer World Championship, Women's; Title IX

References Myers, *A World of Sports for Girls* (1981); Yannis, *Inside Soccer* (1980).

Soccer Hall of Fame, United States

Established in 1950, the hall was an all-male institution until 1951, when Alfreda Iglehart was inducted. A coach in Baltimore, Maryland, Iglehart had taught soccer to 1,200 boys during the 1920s and 1930s.

Soccer World Championship, Women's

Long a popular sport for men in Asia, Africa, Europe, and Latin America, soccer has spread across the United States and become popular with players of both sexes.

For many years, men had a number of competitive soccer events to choose from, the most coveted of which was the World Cup. But girls' and women's soccer teams gained ground after the 1960s. By the 1990s, thousands of teams had sprung up in the United States, affiliated with city recreation programs, elementary and secondary schools, and colleges. There were 65 national women's soccer teams as of 1992.

American women won their first world title in November 1991. Playing in Guangzhov, China, the U.S. women won six matches and lost none. Their total score was 25, and they gave up only five

goals during the tournament. In the final match, against the Norwegians, the U.S. women won with a score of 2-1. U.S. player Carin Jennings was named most valuable player at the tournament. Top scorer was Michelle Akers-Stahl, who kicked ten of the 25 goals earned by the U.S. team.

References Myers, *A World of Sports for Girls* (1981); Yannis, *Inside Soccer* (1980).

Softball

At the turn of the twentieth century, the game of softball evolved as an alternative to baseball. The game was also called Ladies' Baseball and Soft Baseball. It suited people who wanted to develop indoor baseball, since it used lighter bats and softer balls, which would travel shorter distances. The base paths were also shorter. By 1910, most people had given up the idea of indoor baseball and had moved the game outdoors, but softball was popular with both men and women during the Great Depression, since it provided an inexpensive means of recreation.

The first women's softball tournament in America was held in 1933 at the Chicago World's Fair, with championships for both men's and women's teams. The Great Northerns, a Chicago team, won the women's title. That year, a group of leaders in the sport formed the Amateur Softball Association to standardize softball rules and to organize annual national tournaments. These rules were published in 1934, and the sport was officially named "softball."

Time magazine estimated in 1943 that there were about 40,000 semiprofessional women's softball teams in America. By this time, a number of women athletes had achieved fame in the United States—golfers Patty Berg and Babe Didrikson

Kathy Arendsen of the Raybestos Brakettes displays the intensity behind one of the best pitchers in women's fast-pitch softball.

Zaharias, swimmers Eleanor Holm and Gertrude Ederle, tennis player Helen Wills—and, in the process, boosted softball and other women's sports. American servicemen and women played softball during World War II, and the game spread to other countries. During the early 1950s, the International Federation of Softball was formed to organize the various national softball associations. The federation worked for more national and international softball events, including recognition of softball as an Olympic sport.

In 1949, for the first time, the women's national championship was held separately from the men's, and after the 1950s, women were more involved in softball than men. Three teams stood out at the national championships, winning 25 titles from 1942 to 1973: the Jax Maids of New Orleans, the Lionettes of Orange, California, and the Raybestos Brakettes of Stratford, Connecticut. A National Slow Pitch Championship for women was held for the first time in 1962, in Cincinnati, Ohio, and that same year, the National Softball Hall of Fame was established.

By 1965, there were five teams from around the world competing at a Women's World Fast Pitch Tournament, located that year in Melbourne, Australia. Although the U.S. team had been favored, the Australians defeated them 1-0 in the final game of that tournament. At the second world tournament, held in Japan in 1970, ten countries competed. The Japanese women emerged victorious. The final game, between Japan and the United States, drew about 30,000 spectators. A third championship took place in 1974 in Stratford, Connecticut. Fifteen teams competed in two different divisions, and the U.S. team claimed the world title for the first time, winning nine games and losing none.

The first College Women's World Series was held in 1979 in Omaha, Nebraska. It was organized as a joint effort between the Association for Intercollegiate Athletics for Women (AIAW) and the Amateur Softball Association.

Fast-pitch softball became an Olympic event at the 1996 Games in Atlanta, having been officially recognized by the International Olympic Committee as a sport since 1977. The U.S. women won the Olympic gold medal. Women's softball teams had held a demonstration at the Asian Games and Pan American Games in 1966. In 1979, softball became a medal event at the latter Games.

Women's recreational softball has continued to grow, with teams and competitions in communities across the United States as part of the Little League organization, which sponsors baseball and softball teams and games. There are also high school and college softball teams for women. Fast-pitch softball ranked as the fourth most popular sport for high school girls, with 219,400 participating as of 1991, according to the National Federation of State High School Associations. It was ranked tenth among the top sports activities for young people ages 12 to 17, with 4.1 million playing the game at least six times a year.

Many women have become softball stars through the years, and a number of them have been recognized in the National Softball Hall of Fame. Amy Peralta, who pitched for the Phoenix Ramblers, hurled 300 shutouts during her years on the mound. She also pitched 50 no-hitters. Peralta was inducted into the Amateur Softball Association Hall of Fame. In 1984, Raybestos Brakettes Kathy Arendsen and Barbara Reinalda provided the strong pitching that enabled the United States to win its first world title, the Women's International Cup. Reinalda pitched at the 1983 championships, where the Brakette team captured its eighteenth national title. During 22 innings, the opposition scored only one earned run.

See also Amateur Softball Association; Joyce, Joan; Richardson, Dot; Tickey, Bertha Reagan; Wadlow, M. Marie
References Meyer, *Softball for Girls and Women*; Walsh, *Inside Softball* (1977).

Special Olympics

Special Olympics, Inc., is a nonprofit organization headquartered in Washington, D.C. Through Special Olympics, athletes with mental retardation have the chance to take part in organized athletics and compete with others from around the world. A mentally retarded person who is eight years old or older—regardless of race, color, gender, or type of physical or mental handicap—is eligible to join a program so long as a doctor has approved.

Like athletes everywhere, Special Olympians train hard, practice skills, build up their bodies, and prepare mentally for competition. They take part in training and frequent local competitions throughout the year, with local winners going on to state and international games. Gold, silver, and bronze medals go to the individual athletes, rather than being awarded to their country. Other competitors receive ribbons for their participation, and winning is emphasized less than participating to the best of one's ability in the events.

The program began during the 1960s, evolving from a backyard camp for children with mental retardation started by Eunice Kennedy Shriver and her husband, Sargent Shriver. They had established the camp at their Maryland home after they found out that there were no camps for mentally retarded children. Since 1957, Eunice Shriver had been director of the Joseph P. Kennedy, Jr.

Foundation, dedicated to the memory of her oldest brother. Its major activities involved research into mental retardation and helping people with the condition, which afflicted Eunice's older sister Rosemary. In 1963, the foundation developed a physical fitness program for people with mental retardation.

Shriver realized that the children had much potential and could compete in organized sports if they received proper training and encouragement. In 1968, some Chicagoans asked the Kennedy Foundation to help fund a national Olympic event for children with retardation. The first Summer Games, held in July 1968, welcomed nearly 1,000 athletes from 26 states and Canada. The main events were track and field and swimming.

Within three years, the Special Olympics was an official nonprofit corporation, and every state, as well as the District of Columbia, had a chapter. By 1974, there were about 400,000 participants. When the fourth international Games took place the next year in Michigan, 3,200 athletes joined the competition. One highlight of those Games was seeing the oldest participant, 70-year-old Corinne Scruggs of Florida, win the bronze medal in the 25-yard wheelchair race. By 1977, there were 7,000 competitors representing 19 nations.

The first Winter Games, with competition in skiing and skating, were held in Colorado in 1977. Annual Special Olympics were also initiated in Europe. In 1988, Special Olympics had programs in all 50 states, 4 U.S. territories, and 73 countries.

Programs continued to expand during the 1980s. By 1983, athletes from 50 nations were joining those from every state in the Union. Athletes competed in track and field, swimming, diving, gymnastics, bowling, basketball, soccer, volleyball, and several wheelchair events. Television covered the Games as part of ABC's "Wide World of Sports." The 1995 Games in New Haven, Connecticut, drew 7,000 athletes, 2,000 coaches, 15,000 friends and family members, 45,000 volunteers, and 500,000 spectators. Sports for Summer Games include: aquatics, basketball, bowling, gymnastics, horseback riding, roller skating, sailing, soccer, softball, tennis, and volleyball. At the Winter Games, events include alpine skiing, cross country skiing, floor hockey, figure skating, speed skating, and poly hockey, a game played indoors with a plastic stick and puck.

The International Olympic Committee (IOC) officially endorses the Special Olympics and allows for the adaptations that are made in order for people with various disabilities to compete in the different sports—for example, flotation devices for swimmers who are partially paralyzed or angled ramps for bowlers. Donations come from individuals, corporations, and philanthropic foundations. As of 1991, there were about 500,000 volunteers working in programs around the world, including some 100,000 coaches.

Women athletes have been among the Special Olympians since the beginning. Among them are Mandy Meder of Winnetka, Illinois. Weighing just 82 pounds, she could lift weights up to 120 pounds. Meder, also a top basketball player, won a silver medal at the 1990 Summer Games, in addition to a bronze in softball. Swimmer Connie Roll overcame her cerebral palsy to win medals in the 50-meter freestyle race. By the 1994 Games, versatile Kathy Ledwidge of Mystic, Connecticut, had won medals in bowling, basketball, soccer, softball, and volleyball. In 1994, she also qualified for the Special Olympics sailing team. Kim Musitano, a Special Olympics Featured Athlete in 1984, won medals in tennis, bowling, and cross country skiing. A graduate of Darien High School in Darien, Connecticut, Musitano played on the U.S. Special Olympics tennis team at the 1995 Games.

The inscription on the back of Special Olympic medals describes the philosophy that underlies the Games: "In a close 400-meter race one Special Olympian was about to cross the finish line. At the very moment of victory she saw that a friend, also in the race, had fallen. Without hesitation, she turned, ran back, and helped up her fallen friend. Hand in hand, they crossed the finish line together."

This is the spirit of the Special Olympics.

See also Paralympics; Shriver, Eunice Kennedy; Unified Sports

Speed Skating

Ice skating was a form of transportation for centuries in Holland, where the first race for women was held in 1805. Skates became faster as bone blades were replaced by waxed wooden ones, then by the even faster metal ones. Throughout the 1800s, speed skating remained a popular sport for people in the lower economic classes, while figure skating was more popular among the upper classes.

During the 1932 Winter Olympics, women took part in speed skating exhibitions. Two Americans won these events: Elizabeth Dubois (500 meters) and Kit Klein (1,000 meters). Sweden hosted the first international speed skating competition for women in 1936, and women's speed skating finally became a medal event at the Winter Olympics in 1960, at Squaw Valley, California. Jeanne Ashworth, a Tufts University student from Wilmington, Massachusetts, won a bronze medal, placing third in the 500-meter race. In recent years, American women have demonstrated their considerable skill in speed skating events, as shown by the success of Anne Henning, Beth Heiden, Dianne Holum, Sheila Young, and five-time-gold-medalist Bonnie Blair.

As of 1994, the Olympic Games offered eight speed skating events for women, which included seven individual races and one team race: 500-meters, 1,000-meters, 1,500 meters, 3,000-meters, and 5,000-meters and in short track racing: 500-meters, 1,000-meters, and a 3,000-meter relay. Men also compete in a 10,000-meter event. No U.S. woman had won the 3,000- or 5,000-meter events as of the 1994 Games. In both 1992 and 1994, American Cathy Turner of Hilton, New York, won the 500-meter short track race.

During competition, skaters race two at a time, called the European-style race, and the skater with the best time of all the competitors wins the race. In mass-start races, once more commonly used in American competitions, all skaters begin together, and the first one across the finish line is the winner. In all races, any skater who pushes, bumps, or trips another skater is disqualified. While racing, skaters move counterclockwise; during turns, the lead skater takes the inside lane. Speed skaters can exceed speeds of 30 miles per hour, making them the fastest humans to move over level ground without any mechanical aids. Speed skaters combat wind resistance by wearing streamlined, tight-fitting clothing and hoods and by moving their arms carefully or keeping them behind their backs as they skate along straight parts of the rink. In order to practice their sport, speed skaters must live near outdoor rinks of the right size or move to these kinds of locations to train for several months each year.

Divisions of speed skating competition include pee wee for ages 7 and under (100- and 200-meter events); pony, ages 8 and 9 (200- and 300-meter events); midget, ages 10 and 11 (400- and 500-meter events); juvenile, ages 12 and 13 (600- and 800-meter events); junior, ages 14 and 15 (1-mile event).

Among the U.S. National Outdoor Speed Skating Champions are Sheila Young, 1970 and 1971; Nancy Thorne, 1972; Nancy Class, 1973; Kris Garbe, 1974; Nancy Swider, 1975; Connie Carpenter-Phinney, 1976; Liz Crowe, 1988; Paula Class, 1978; and Betsy Davis, 1978. During the late 1980s and early 1990s, Bonnie Blair dominated U.S. and world competition in the 500- and 1,000-meter races.

See also Blair, Bonnie Kathleen; Carpenter-Phinney, Connie; Heiden, Beth; Henning, Anne; Holum, Dianne; Young, Sheila

Sports Illustrated

A major source of news about sports and athletes, this weekly magazine has been praised for increasing coverage of women and their athletic achievements and events since the 1970s. The magazine has also been sharply criticized for having a male slant and for the way in which it has portrayed some women athletes. Women have also scoffed at the popular annual "Swimsuit Issue," which some view as sexist and outside the realm of serious coverage of sports.

Several women have been featured on the cover of the magazine, including golfer Judy Rankin, who appeared in 1961. Tennis players Billie Jean King and Chris Evert made the cover during the 1970s, and others have appeared since.

The magazine also bestows an annual Sportsman of the Year Award, which began in 1954 when track star Roger Bannister was the first recipient. In 1972, Billie Jean King became the first woman to receive the award, sharing it with basketball star John Wooden. King was followed by fellow tennis player Chris Evert (1976), Mary Decker (1983), Mary Lou Retton (1984), and Bonnie Blair (1994). Two other women were honored for their humanitarian work in 1987 as part of a group called Athletes Who Care: golfer Patty Sheehan and track star Judi Brown King.

An examination of the magazine through the years does show more coverage of women's sports, as well as more material written by women journalists. However, when author Madeleine Blais looked at the 50 issues published from February 1993 to February 1994, she found that women appeared on only six covers and each appeared for what Blais viewed as dubious reasons. Blais summed up the six cover subjects this way: "Nancy Kerrigan, because she was clubbed in the knee; Tennis star Mary Pierce, because she was having personal problems with her father; the widows of baseball players; tennis champ Monica Seles, because she was stabbed in the back; and one woman because she was modeling a bathing suit."

See also Blair, Bonnie; Decker, Mary; Evert, Chris; King, Billie Jean; Rankin, Judy; Retton, Mary Lou; Sheehan, Patty
Reference Blais, *In These Girls, Hope Is a Muscle* (1995).

Sportscar Racing (See Racing, Auto)

Sportscasting

As radio and then television assumed large roles in American life, women have tried to break into the field of sportscasting both on- and off-camera. Progress was slow, as one woman at a time broke ground. Many Americans became accustomed to receiving sports news from male sportscasters, assuming that women had neither the background nor the interest to take up this field. But many did, and as more women athletes became visible, coverage of women's events increased, too. In prominent women's sports events, such as figure skating or gymnastics, a former champion sometimes shared commentating duties with a regular network sportscaster.

By the 1990s, with cable stations covering more and more sports events, some women had become the sole commentators or producers of such broadcasts. Women could be seen hosting or cohosting local and national television, on major networks and various cable stations, and many successful athletes have gone on to provide sports commentary on television. Among them are Tracy Austin, Evelyn Ashford, Peggy Fleming, Mary Lou Retton, and Billie Jean King, to name only a few. Among the pioneers was Elaine Perkins, who became Seattle's first woman sportscaster in 1977. While in high school, Perkins had asked to cover sports stories for her high school newspaper, but the editor had told her, "Girls don't write about sports—only boys do." An avid sports-page reader, Perkins was not dissuaded and studied journalism at Ohio State University, writing several freelance articles about sports.

That same year, Mary Driscoll Shane became the first woman to do play-by-play broadcasting for baseball games. Shane had joined WMAQ radio in Chicago in 1975 as a sportscaster and later was the station's announcer for White Sox games. A graduate of the University of Wisconsin at Madison, Shane had previously worked as a history teacher. She had also served as a representative of the Women's Political Caucus from Milwaukee to the 1972 Democratic National Convention. As anchor of the weekend sports segments for KING-TV in Seattle, she produced, wrote, and edited her shows and conducted interviews. Perkins also traveled with the Seattle SuperSonics basketball team and Washington State football team.

A controversy swelled in 1977 during the World Series over whether female reporters should be permitted in the locker rooms after the games to interview players, as male reporters had traditionally done. The Great Locker-Room Controversy, as it was called, had been brewing since women began covering male-dominated sports for television and the print media. One woman magazine reporter filed a sex discrimination lawsuit against the baseball commissioner, who had banned women. He claimed that women reporters in locker rooms invaded the privacy of male players; female reporters said that being barred from the locker rooms prevented them from doing their jobs as well as male reporters. The Los Angeles Dodgers were among the teams that voted to allow women inside the locker rooms for interviews.

In November 1987, Gayle Sierens, a news anchor and sportscaster for WXFL in Tampa, Florida, became the first woman to provide play-by-play coverage of a National Football League (NFL) game. The game, broadcast on NBC, pitted the Seattle Seahawks against the Kansas City Chiefs. Sierens had previously covered equestrian sports and games in the North American Soccer League.

At the 1996 Wimbledon tennis championships, an all-woman team of commentators covered the women's matches.

See also Ashford, Evelyn; Austin, Tracy; Fleming, Peggy; Retton, Mary Lou; Television

Sportsman of the Year (See Evert, Chris; Sports Illustrated)

Sportswoman of the Year Award
This award is one of several given by the Women's Sports Foundation each year. The foundation gives this award to both the top professional woman athlete and the top amateur. The awards are presented at a special annual ceremony.

Sportswriters
Before the 1970s, only a few women had written sports columns or articles on a regular basis. Often, they were well known athletes writing about their sport. Among them were figure skater Theresa Weld Blanchard and tennis champion Alice Marble. During the 1970s, Gladys Heldman published *World Tennis* magazine. Heldman supported the efforts of women athletes to gain equal prize money and recognition.

Since the 1970s, the bylines of numerous women can be seen in sports magazines or sports-related articles in general magazines and newspapers. Sally Jenkins distinguished herself as a writer on tennis and tennis players and has been regularly featured in *Tennis* magazine. Former tennis players Julie Heldman and Pam Shriver also became authors of numerous articles about their sport and about women's athletics. Major newspapers such as the *New York Times* have both men and women on staff writing about sports. A number of sports and fitness magazines are headed by women and also have predominantly female staffs.

See also Heldman, Gladys; King, Billie Jean; Marble, Alice; Shriver, Pam; Weld Blanchard, Theresa

Squash Racquets
The sport of squash racquets, commonly called squash, is played with a soft ball in

a four-sided court. The game reached the United States during the 1880s, with private schools for boys and men taking the lead in developing intramural and intercollegiate squash programs.

Few women played squash during the early 1900s. A pioneer woman in the sport was Eleanora Sears, a versatile athlete who opened doors for women in numerous sports. Sears won the first women's national squash tournament held in America. In January 1928, in Greenwich, Connecticut, Sears was one of 40 women vying for the title. Tennis champion Hazel Hotchkiss Wightman was also among them. Sears won the final match three sets to one, against A. Boyden of Boston.

By the 1970s, there were squash courts in cities and towns throughout America, and both men and women played the game. In 1980, the U.S. girls' squash team won the First International Squash Racquets Federation (FISRF) World Junior Squash Championship, held in Sweden.

See also Sears, Eleonora; Wightman, Hazel Hotchkiss

Stearns, Cheryl (b. 1955)

In 1990, skydiver Cheryl Stearns, of Raeford, North Carolina, received the Diplome Leonardo da Vinci, the world's top award for achievement in airsports. By 1996, Stearns, a full-time pilot for U.S. Air, had been skydiving for 24 years. She had set 29 world records in her sport and held four different world records at the same time, something no other man or woman had yet achieved.

The winner of 17 U.S. women's titles for combined style and accuracy, Stearns won her first national title in 1977. She then joined the U.S. Army and became the first woman of the Golden Knights. Stearns then became the only woman to win the world championship in her sport twice, capturing that title both in 1978 and 1994.

On July 15, 1995, she completed her 10,000th jump, becoming the first woman to win the United States Parachute Association (USPA) Nona Diamond award. By spring 1996, Stearns had broken three more world records when she completed the highest number of jumps in a 24-hour period, the highest number of dead-center jumps in a 24-hour period, and the highest number of jumps in a 24-hour period for women. In a 1995 interview, Stearns said, "I still get butterflies during competition." She claimed, "It makes me feel great when I can share my years of experience with someone. . . . The challenge is what keeps me going."

References United States Parachute Association, "Press Release: Skydiver Targets Five New World Records," October 1995; United States Parachute Association "Women in the News," July 1995.

Stephens, Helen Herring (1918–1994)

Known as the "Fulton Flash" and "The Missouri Express," track and field champion Stephens was a native of Fulton, Missouri. While still in high school, she equaled the world record time (5.8 seconds) in the 50-yard dash and tied the world record for the standing broad jump. Competing at national track meets in 1935 and 1936, she won the 50-yard dash, standing (broad) long jump, and shot put. At the 1935 Amateur Athletic Union (AAU) meet, Stephens defeated champion runner Stella Walsh when she ran the 50-meter dash in 6.6 seconds.

Stephens took part in the notorious 1936 Summer Olympics held in Berlin, Germany, where Nazi leader Adolf Hitler presided. The Nazis were spreading hateful propaganda and denigrating Jews, people of color, and others who did not fit their ideal of a "superior" race. They hoped white athletes would sweep the 1936 Olympics, thus proving their theories of superiority. However, several outstanding African-American athletes, including Ohio State University student Jesse Owens, proved Hitler wrong. Owens won four gold medals for track and field events that day.

During the Olympic trials, Stephens qualified for the shot put and discus throw, as well as two races. At the Games, Stephens was allowed to enter three events and won two gold medals—in the 100-meter dash (in which she set a world record that held until 1960) and as part of the 4 x 100 women's relay team. When Hitler greeted her with a Fascist salute, Stephens responded with a simple midwestern handshake and declined further contact with the German leader. She later told an interviewer that Hitler "pinched me and invited me to spend a weekend with him."

At an event later in 1936, Stephens ran the 100-yard dash in 10.5 seconds, setting a new world record. The next year, she won national titles in the 50-meter dash, the shot put, and 200-meter dash. At indoor events, she set U.S. records for the 50-meter race, the shot put, and the standing broad jump. (When she retired from competition, she was still undefeated in these events.) As a professional athlete, Stephens competed in exhibition races and excelled in basketball, bowling, softball, and swimming. During World War II, she served with the Women's Marine Corps. Later, she became a librarian and a track coach and track consultant at her alma mater, William Woods College in Missouri.

Stephens was inducted in the National Track and Field Hall of Fame (U.S.) and the National Women's Hall of Fame.

The indomitable athlete later competed in track and field events in the Senior Olympics, where she again won many titles during the late 1970s and early 1980s. She won seven gold medals in 1980 and seven golds and one bronze in 1981.

References Carlson and Fogarty, *Tales of Gold* (1977); Condon, *Great Women Athletes of the Twentieth Century* (1991).

Steroids, Anabolic-Androgenic (AAS)

These synthetic chemical substances derive from the hormone testosterone normally found in much higher quantities in males than in females. Some athletes have used AAS to build muscle mass and enhance strength, power, and performance. It is thought that athletes may have been using such substances since the 1950s, and they are sometimes used in doses 100 times higher than that found naturally in a male body. Steroids may be administered as pills, salves, or by patch or injection. The use of AAS has been banned by the International Olympic Committee (IOC) as well as by many other amateur and professional athletic organizations. Athletes with signs of AAS in their urine samples may be banned from competition and subject to other penalties. In the 1988 at the Olympics, for example, Ben Johnson of Canada was stripped of the gold medal he had won in the men's 100-meter dash when traces of AAS were detected.

A number of scientists have addressed the health hazards that may result from the use of AAS. In his book *Drugs, Sport, and Politics*, Robert O. Voy says, "With the female athlete, anabolic-androgenic steroid use may mean liver cancer, menstrual irregularity, hypertension, depression, and irreversible masculinizing changes such as a deepened voice and even abnormal genitalia." Emotional symptoms, such as mood swings and even rages, can also occur. Long-term use might cause heart diseases, joint diseases, and premature hardening of the arteries that leads to brain and kidney damage. Certain psychological effects and stunted growth may be permanent, Voy believes. The long-term impact of AAS use on reproductive function is not completely known.

Although men were more commonly found to take steroids, an estimated 1 to 3 million women athletes in the United States may have used them, too. According to Charles Yesalis, a professor at Pennsylvania State University, steroid use is more common among women who compete in swimming, body building, cycling, weight lifting, and track and field. Athlete Cindy Olavarri, a member of the 1984 U.S. Olympic cycling team, spoke publicly about her use of AAS after suffering from liver inflammation and other lingering problems. She lost her chance to compete in the Games when routine test results showed traces of steroids, but she credits the experience with saving her from the health problems that might have occurred, had she continued taking steroids.

As of the 1990s, testing could not yet detect all types of drugs in a person's system. Tests were particularly sensitive to synthetic steroids such as anadrol and dianabol, substances that are quite different from chemicals humans produce on their own. However, tests were not able to distinguish synthetic testosterone from natural testosterone. Also, people vary in the amount of testosterone they naturally produce in their bodies, so a high testosterone reading alone does not necessarily prove an athlete has used such drugs.

While new and more sophisticated tests were being devised, people were also finding ways to foil them. In a 1996 article, Craig Kemmerer, a research chemist at Bristol Meyer Squibb, said that a person could "take a good moderate dose of testosterone and still not be found positive."

The controversy continued into the 1990s as Chinese women athletes gave exceptional performances in swimming, weight lifting, and rowing, among other events, at the 1992 Summer Olympics. Of a total possible 337 gold medals, the Chinese women's teams won 137. There was speculation that these athletes may have used drugs to enhance their performance. To support this theory, people pointed out that before 1988, none of the Chinese swimmers had ranked among the top ten swimmers in the world and that the athletes seemed to fade out quickly, competing at only one Olympics. They also pointed out that the Chinese men had not achieved the same level of success and that AAS has a much stronger effect on women's bodies than on men's. In response, the Chinese said that rigorous training and special diets were responsible for their success.

This debate raged on during 1996 as the next Olympiad was unfolding. At world competitions and the Olympics, athletes were still being tested for these drugs and a few were disqualified as a result of positive tests. In other cases, athletes who were accused of having used drugs had negative tests and were cleared. Some medal-winning U.S. female athletes endured such charges and were later found to be "clean."

References Brennan, "The China Syndrome," in Meserole, ed., *Information Please, Sports Almanac* (1995), 23; Brooks, "No Place for Steroids," *Current Health*, September 1992; "The Devil's Juice," *Scholastic Update*, May 1, 1992; Monagle, Cowley, and Brand, "Doped to Perfection," *Newsweek*, July

22, 1996, 31–34; Telander, "Mail-Order Muscles," *Sports Illustrated,* November 22, 1993; Voy with Deeter, *Drugs, Sport, and Politics* (1991); Yesalis et al., "Anabolic-Androgenic Steroid Use in the United States," *Journal of the American Medical Association,* September 8, 1993.

Stidworthy, Mary (See Shooting)

Stives, Karen (b. 1950)

In 1984, Stives became the first woman to win an individual Olympic medal in an equestrian event. Riding "Ben Arthur," Stives captured the silver medal after an excellent performance in the cross country, or three-day event.

In previous competitions, she had competed in both dressage and eventing, but decided to focus on eventing in 1978. In 1982, she had been seriously injured at the Kentucky Three-Day Event, when her horse fell on her. But she resumed her sport and made it to the world championships that year. With her new horse, "Ben Arthur," she was able to place third in the Kentucky Three-Day Event in 1983. As part of a five-person team that won the gold medal in eventing at the Los Angeles Games, Stives left that Olympiad with two cherished medals.

Stone, Toni Lyle (b. 1921)

In 1953, Mareena "Toni" Lyle Stone became the first black woman to play professional baseball on a major-league team when she joined the Indianapolis Clowns, part of the Negro American League. The 22-year-old from St. Paul, Minnesota, was known for her accurate throwing and her fielding skills. During her year on the team, she usually played second base.

Stone was accustomed to competing with and against the opposite sex, having played on boys' teams in high school, where she enjoyed baseball and other sports. She was the only girl to attend a baseball school for young people run by Gabby Street, who had been a major-league catcher. Stone began her playing career with a San Francisco team, then joined a well-known black barnstorming team called the San Francisco Sea Lions. She then played for the New Orleans Black Pelicans and the New Orleans Creoles before joining the Clowns in 1953.

See also All-American Girls Professional Baseball League; Discrimination, Racial
Reference Hickok, *A Who's Who of Sports Champions* (1995).

Stouder, Sharon (b. 1948)

At age 15, swimming champion Stouder set a 100-meter butterfly record at the 1964 Olympics in Tokyo, Japan. She came home from the Games with three gold medals (one individual and two relay team victories) and a silver. With her gold medal finish in the 100-meter butterfly, the Glendora, California, native set a new world record and became the first American woman to break 1 minute in the 100-meter freestyle race, where she came in second.

Stouder had been swimming since age three and competing since age eight. Her best competitive year was 1964. Besides her Olympic medals, she won the Amateur Athletic Union (AAU) outdoor 100-meter freestyle, 100- and 200-meter butterfly, and indoor 100-yard titles.

Olympic spectators marveled at the talented U.S. swimming team made up of teenagers the press called "Water Babies." The team won seven of the ten women's swimming and diving events, and Stouder was part of the four-woman team that won the 400-meter relay. A strong competitor, Stouder said that even when she was ahead in a race, she strove to get even further ahead of her nearest opponent. Injuries forced Stouder to retire from competition in 1965.

References Durant and Bettman, *Pictorial History of American Sport* (1965); Laklan, *Competition Swimming* (1965).

Strug, Kerri (b. 1978)

Gymnast Kerri Strug became an American heroine at the 1996 Olympics, where she displayed not only outstanding skill in her sport but great courage. Strug, a native of Tucson, began her gymnastics training at age four. Her talent earned her a place at the elite training school in Houston, Texas, run by Bela Karolyi. She became known as a tough competitor who could perform under pressure. At the 1996 Olympics, Strug was part of a strong U.S. team that included Amanda Borden, Amy Chow, Dominique Dawes, Shannon Miller, Dominique Moceanu, and Jaycie Phelps. During the final rounds of the women's team competition, the U.S. group had moved into first place ahead of the Russian and Romanian teams and hoped to win a gold medal. Two of Strug's teammates faltered in the last event, the vault. On the first of her two vaults, Strug slipped, seriously injuring her left ankle. Although in obvious distress, she managed to complete a second Yurchenko vault, landing on both feet before collapsing in pain on the mat. For that second try, she earned a 9.712 out of a possible 10 points.

Karolyi carried the 88-pound, 4-feet, 9-inch Strug up to the podium so that she could join her teammates for the medal ceremony, the first women's gymnastics team in history to win an Olympic gold medal for the United States. Afterward, she was taken to a hospital for treatment, having been diagnosed with a third degree lateral sprain of the ankle with two torn ligaments. Of Kerri Strug's courageous second vault, Karolyi said, "That was a high-performance, great athletics and great drama. That was sport."

As a result of her injury in the team competition, Strug was not able to compete in the individual women's gymnastics events at the Olympics. However, her gutsy performance earned her a permanent place in sports history, along with praise and good wishes from fans throughout the world. Strug was also barraged with offers to promote commercial products. She and her teammates were chosen to appear together on the Wheaties cereal box. After the Olympics, Strug planned to attend the University of California at Los Angeles (UCLA).

References Bondy, "Kerri Stands Tall on Sprained Ankle," *New York Daily News,* July 24, 1996, p. 7; Cyphers, "Golden Girls: In Pain, Kerri Vaults U.S. to Crown," *New York Daily News,* July 24, 1996, p. 59.

Stunt-flying (See Aerobatics; Earhart, Amelia)

Suggs, Louise (b. 1923)

A native of Atlanta, Georgia, Suggs learned to play golf from her father when she was ten. She developed her trademark smooth swing early on as she practiced and competed in junior tournaments. As an amateur golfer, Suggs won the U.S. Women's Amateur crown and both the U.S. Women's Open and British Open.

In 1948, at age 25, Suggs turned professional and won the first of 50 tournaments on the Ladies Professional Golf Association (LPGA) tour. Among her important victories were two U.S. Opens and the LPGA title. Suggs won her 1952 U.S. Open with a score of 284. In 1953, she won eight tournaments, amassing nearly $20,000 in prize money, a large sum for a woman golfer of that era. The next year, she won the first of three Title-holders, earning the others in 1956 and 1959. In 1957, Suggs was LPGA champion and won the Vare Trophy with her low scoring average of 74.64 for that year. She was inducted into the LPGA Golf Hall of Fame in 1951, the first member chosen, and later, to the World Golf Hall of Fame. In both 1953 and 1960, Suggs was the leading money winner on the LPGA tour.

References *LPGA Media Guide, 1996;* Markel et al., *For the Record* (1985).

Sullivan Award

The James E. Sullivan Memorial Award, or Sullivan Trophy, was established in 1930. Each year, the Amateur Athletic Union (AAU) bestows the Sullivan Award on the amateur athlete who "by his or her performance, example, and influence as an amateur, has done the most during the year to advance the cause of sportsmanship." The AAU looks for qualities of leadership and character as well as athletic achievement.

Most of the winners have been male athletes. Among the women who have won the award are swimmer Ann Curtis (1944), diver Patricia (Pat) McCormick (1956), runner Wilma Rudolph (1961), swimmer Debbie Meyer (1968), swimmer Tracy Caulkins (1978), track and field star Jackie Joyner-Kersee (1986), swimmer Janet Evans (1989), and speed skater Bonnie Blair (1992).

See also Amateur Athletic Union; Blair, Bonnie; Caulkins, Tracy; Curtis, Ann; Evans, Janet; Joyner-Kersee, Jackie; McCormick, Pat; Meyer, Deborah; Rudolph, Wilma

Sumners, Roslyn (b. 1968)

Known for her consistency and graceful movements, figure skater Sumners, a native of Edmunds, Washington, won the U.S. novice title in 1979. A year later, she became the world junior ladies' champion. From 1982 to 1984, the stylish skater was the U.S. senior ladies' champion, and she captured her one world title in 1983.

At the 1984 Olympics held in Sarajevo, in the former Yugoslavia, Sumners narrowly lost the gold medal to Katarina Witt of East Germany, winning the silver instead. Sumners became a professional skater shortly after the Games, performing in ice shows, television specials, and competitions held for professional skaters during the eighties and nineties.

Superbowl of the Sexes (See Battle of the Sexes; King, Billie Jean; Tennis)

Surfing

In surfing athletes "ride the waves," either on specially designed boards, in surf boats or canoes, or with their bodies (known as body surfing). The phases of surfing include paddling out to catch a breaking wave, sliding at an angle to the swell, and adopting the position needed to ride the wave.

Surfing originated with the Polynesians, and especially skilled surfers could be found in the Hawaiian Islands where the sport had been known since ancient times. Surfers used different kinds of boards, based on their social class. For royalty, there were large, thick surfboards, while other surfers used shorter, thinner boards called planks. There were also strict rules about where different classes could surf. Boards were carefully carved from certain trees, then dried and oiled each time they were used.

The popularity of the sport declined after religious missionaries arrived on the islands during the 1800s, insisting that the native peoples wear large, baggy dresses rather than the brief traditional clothing that had been more amenable to sports. Interest in surfing was revived during the 1900s, though, and the sport spread to the mainland. The United States Surfing Association was developed in 1961, when the sport reached new heights of popularity.

Women compete at local, national, and international surfing championships in standing races, paddling races, and style competitions, as well as tandem (pairs) events. World-class events are held in such places as Australia, the Cook Islands, and Bali. Hawaiian surfers of both genders dominated world and U.S. championships for decades, but in 1958, mainlander Marge Calhoun of Santa Monica, California, won the national women's title. A top woman surfer during the early 1990s was Jessica Little, who won the U.S. amateur title in 1993 when she was only 17 years old. In 1994, Frieda Zamba of Ormond Beach, Florida, won the national title at the Ocean Pacific Women's Pro Tournament.

Sutton Bundy, May (1887–1975)

In 1905, May Sutton became the youngest woman tennis player (by three months) ever to win the national women's singles tennis title. She caused a furor at Wimbledon in 1904 by shunning the usual tennis shirt for one of her father's shirts, rolling back the cuffs so that her wrists showed, something heretofore banned. In 1904, she won the U.S. women's crown, again displaying a strong serve and forehand and skill in volleying at the net.

Playing as May Sutton Bundy after her marriage, she became the first American woman to win the Wimbledon crown in 1905. She captured that title again in 1907. That same year, she was crowned queen of the Tournament of Roses, an annual event preceding the Rose Bowl football game in Pasadena, California. Bundy also

won the women's singles tennis title in southern California for many years and was still competing in her forties. She taught tennis until the 1950s.

May Sutton was one of the famous Sutton sisters who grew up playing tennis at a court on their property. The five Suttons, particularly May and her sister Florence, dominated the game of tennis in California both as children and adults. During the early 1900s, a popular slogan went "It takes a Sutton to beat a Sutton." In 1956, Sutton was inducted into the International Tennis Hall of Fame.

Swarthout, Betty (See Shooting)

Swimming

Swimming dates back thousands of years, as revealed by pictures inside ancient caves and references in ancient texts such as the Bible. Early swimming began as part of military training and was used in warfare, as men swam away in self-defense or to take an enemy by surprise. But people also found that swimming was enjoyable. Imitating animals that were natural swimmers, people used their hands, arms, and legs to propel their bodies through the water. During the Middle Ages, however, Europeans shunned outdoor swimming for fear of catching various plagues that were killing people by the thousands. It was believed that diseases were spread in the water, as well as other places.

A revival of water sports took place in the nineteenth century, primarily in Great Britain. Swimming pools were built throughout England, and clubs for aquatics were organized. The breaststroke was widely used by swimmers. Competition may have first started in London, during the 1830s. The National Swimming Society oversaw these contests. In 1875,

Captain Matthew Webb became the first person to swim across the English Channel, covering the distance between Dover and Calais in 21 hours and 45 minutes.

The first strokes may have been dog-paddling, then the breast stroke, followed by the side stroke. In the mid-1800s, some Native Americans demonstrated their way of swimming, a crawl stroke that was also being used in Australia. As competitions became more common, swimmers adopted the sidestroke in order to swim faster. While visiting other countries, travelers learned new swimming strokes to bring back to their native lands. It was the crawl stroke that Gertrude Ederle used when she swam the English Channel in 14 hours and 31 minutes, setting a new record for speed.

A former director of the International Swimming Hall of Fame, Buck Dawson, once said that the history of women's liberation can be traced by looking at the swimsuits that have been worn through the decades. During the 1800s, women bathers wore costumes that covered their whole bodies. In 1915, the Amateur Athletic Union (AAU) permitted women to swim in competition for the first time, and they wore knee-length suits made of thick wool.

The first woman in the United States known to have appeared in public in a one-piece bathing suit was Australian Annette Kellerman. On Revere Beach, in 1907, Kellerman was arrested for "indecency." (Kellerman also tried to swim across the English Channel, but did not succeed. Her story was later made into a motion picture called *Million Dollar Mermaid*, which starred swimming champion and actress Esther Williams.) Another woman, Olympic medalist Ethelda Bleibtrey, was arrested for "nudity" on the beach when she removed her woolen

stockings before a swim. But as time went on, attitudes changed. Gradually women swimmers were allowed to alter suits to improve their speed in competition. A short skirt that had been worn around the hips for reasons of modesty was also dropped during the later 1900s.

Women have competed in swimming events for more years than in most other sports, and swimming was one of the first Olympic events for women. Swimming and diving events were added at the 1912 Games, and the Amateur Athletic Union (AAU) began sponsoring indoor and outdoor title swim meets for women in 1916. Standard swim competitions for women feature races in the freestyle, backstroke, breaststroke, and butterfly for distances ranging from 40 yards to 1,500 meters. There are individual events and relays.

American woman have done well in international competitions for swim events from the time of the first Olympics. The first woman to swim 100 yards in 1 minute flat was Helene Madison of Seattle, Washington. At some Games, U.S. women swimmers have won the majority of events, as in 1964 when a group of teenagers the press called "Water Babies" won seven of the ten women's swimming and diving events. At the 1972 Olympic Games, three U.S. women swept all three medals in the 200-meter butterfly event, as Karen Moe Thornton won the gold, Lynn Colella won the silver, and Ellie Daniel took home the bronze. Thornton was the first U.S. woman to win first place in that particular event.

See also Amateur Athletic Union; Babashoff, Shirley; Belote, Melissa; Bleibtrey, Ethelda; Caulkins, Tracy; Chadwick, Florence; Cohen, Tiffany; Curtis, Ann; de Varona, Donna; Ederle, Gertrude; Evans, Janet; Hogshead, Nancy; Holm, Eleanor; Madison, Helene; Martino, Angel Meyers; Meagher, Mary; Meyer, Deborah; Norelius,

Martha; Nyad, Diana; Rawls, Katherine; Riggin, Aileen; Sanders, Summer; Stouder, Sharon; Van Dyken, Amy; von Saltza, Chris; Wainwright, Helen; Williams, Esther

Swimming, Distance

Long-distance, or marathon, swimming involves covering distances measured in miles. Among the great U.S. champions in this sport are Gertrude Ederle, Florence Chadwick, and Diana Nyad.

One of the outstanding woman marathon swimmers worldwide was Denmark's Greta Anderson, who won a gold medal in the 1948 Olympics for the 100-meter sprint and swam 25 miles around Atlantic City, New Jersey, in 10 hours and 17 minutes in 1956. As of 1977, she had swum the English Channel more than any other woman—five times. She also once held speed records for swimming the Channel: from France to England in 11 hours 1 minute; from England to France in 13 hours 10 minutes. Cindy Nichols of Canada broke that record, and in 1975, swam the Channel nonstop in 19 hours and 55 minutes.

See also Chadwick, Florence; Ederle, Gertrude; Nyad, Diana

Swimming and Diving Hall of Fame (See International Swimming and Diving Hall of Fame)

Swimming, Racing

In swimming races, women have historically been able to equal times achieved by men. In 1922, New Yorker Ethel McGray swam 440 yards in 6 minutes, 24.4 seconds, faster than champion male swimmer Harold Kruger. His time had been 6 minutes and 28 seconds. Newspapers recorded this historical event with headlines such as "Woman Breaks Man's Record for First Time in Swim History."

Swimming, Synchronized

Synchronized swimming involves the performance of swim strokes that blend with music or with the movements of other swimmers—or both. These performances have been compared to dance routines in the water. During the moves, swimmers must keep their heads high enough above water to hear the music and observe their fellow performers, and they need strong legs to keep propelling themselves through the water while their arms move gracefully. Elaborate arm and hand movements are often part of the synchronized routines, which are done in front-layout or back-layout positions. Other acrobatic moves such as somersaults are also performed. Popular world champion and entertainment swimmer Esther Williams was known for her synchronized routines, which were also the main attraction at the Aquacade shows.

Gail Johnson dominated the sport during the 1970s, winning 11 national titles (including four consecutive outdoor solo titles between 1972 and 1975). In 1975 Johnson won the world solo title and a gold medal in the solo event at the Pan American Games. Johnson also won outdoor and indoor duet titles in 1972 and 1973 with partner Teresa Anderson and the outdoor duet title in 1974 with Sue Baross.

Synchronized swim events became part of the Olympics starting with the 1984 Summer Games. Competitors were required to complete both a compulsory section of required movements and a 4-minute performance of their choice. American Tracie Ruiz-Conforto won both the solo and, with partner Candy Costie, the duet competitions. U.S. swimmers continued to dominate this sport in the 1990s. The U.S. team won the 1994 world synchronized swimming title. National champion Becky Dyroen-Lancer, of Campbell,

Defying the rule that prohibited women from running in the Boston Marathon, Kathy Switzer (261) entered and finished the 1967 marathon—and even managed to avoid officials the entire 26 miles.

California, won the solo competition and the figures event, then teamed with Jill Sudduth of Morgan Hill, California, to win the duet competition.

At the 1996 Summer Olympics in Atlanta, a new eight-member synchronized event was added. The U.S. women's team won the gold medal, scoring several perfect 10s for technical merit and artistic presentation at the final competition.

See also Aquacades; Ruiz-Conforto, Tracie; Williams, Esther
Reference Hickok, *A Who's Who of Sports Champions* (1995); Markel et al., *For the Record* (1985).

Switzer, Kathrine (b. 1948)

As K. Switzer, a name she often used, Kathy Switzer registered to run in the (all-male) Boston Marathon in 1967. At the time, she was training with members of the men's track team at Syracuse University in New York. When officials realized Switzer was a woman, they tried to physically remove her from the group of racers, but at that point, Switzer was outrunning a number of male competitors. Her boyfriend, a strongly built athlete, kept angry officials from reaching her.

Switzer completed the 26-mile run, defying the long-held assumption that women could not run more than a mile and a half. Since she had registered and been issued a number, she became the first numbered woman to complete the marathon. However, her run was not officially recognized, and the Amateur Athletic Union (AAU) suspended her for violating rules governing the length of races that women were allowed to run. Switzer went on to enter numerous contests that women had previously not entered. Her trademarks were neon green sneakers and hair ribbons to match.

A public outcry helped to change the rules, and women were legally allowed into marathons beginning in 1972. Switzer later said that when she entered that first Boston Marathon, she had not realized that women were not allowed in the race: "I thought that other women just weren't interested." As a result of her historic run, she received several awards, including a national honorary award from the President's Council on Physical Fitness and Sports.

Later, Switzer worked for Avon Products, Inc. as manager of sports promotions and director of media affairs and sports programs. Avon promoted women's sports throughout the world, even in countries like Brazil and Japan, where women athletes were not common. Avon Inc. organized the Avon International Running Circuit in 1979, in which women from 24 countries competed. Avon also played a key role in developing an annual London Marathon and joined those asking the International Olympic Committee (IOC) to include a women's marathon in the Olympics.

See also Boston Marathon; Marathon Running
References Cahn, *Coming On Strong* (1994); Kaplan, *Women and Sports* (1979)

Table Tennis (Ping-Pong)

It is not clear where table tennis originated or who invented the game, but in Great Britain it has been played since at least the twelfth century. In the United States, it became known as indoor tennis, or the "miniature indoor tennis game." Eventually, the name Ping-Pong caught on, reminiscent of the sounds the ball makes during play. In table tennis, players rely on speed, reflexes, good eye-hand coordination, and skillful footwork to play well. The simplicity of the game and the readily available, lightweight equipment have made table tennis a popular sport for people of different ages and income levels. It ranks second to soccer in terms of worldwide popularity.

In 1926 players around the world met in Berlin, Germany, for a world table tennis conference. They founded the International Table Tennis Federation, which set out to standardize the rules and equipment used in the game and during competition. By 1939, there were more than 30 nations in the federation. Great Britain led the pack, with more than 250 table tennis leagues. In international competition, Great Britain, the United States, Czechoslovakia, and Hungary have won most top honors. Historically, matches have offered equal prize money for men and women table tennis champions.

In 1936, Ruth Hughes Aarons became the first (and, as of 1996, only) American of either sex ever to win a world singles title in the sport. Leah Thall Neuberger was the dominant woman singles player during the national competitions held during the late 1940s and 1950s. During those years, she won the national title seven times, winning her eighth in 1961. The 1994 women's U.S. national champion was Amy Feng of Wheaten, Maryland. With partner Lily Yip of Metuchen, New Jersey, Feng also won the doubles crown that year.

See also Aarons, Ruth Hughes

Taekwando (See Martial Arts)

Team Sports (See Baseball; Basketball; Football; Soccer; Softball)

Team Tennis (See World Team Tennis)

Television

Television has had a great impact on women's sports, at the same time, women have helped reshape television sports coverage. Coverage of women's sports, especially during the Olympics, has increased people's exposure to certain sports, encouraged more participation by girls and women, and popularized numerous women athletes. Among the most popular women's Olympic events are figure skating, gymnastics, diving, and track and field. Women's tennis and golf gained a devoted TV following, and during the 1990s, women's basketball also began to attract large viewing audiences.

The earliest televised sports event featuring women, along with men, was the popular "Roller Derby" show that first aired in 1948. This rough-and-tumble sport, in which men and women on roller skates raced around a track, pushing and tripping each other to gain an edge, shattered many people's ideas about femininity and sports. Roller derby remained popular into the early 1970s.

Coverage of other women's sports events, however, remained scant during these years. Some women bowlers and golfers could be seen, along with some female tennis players. Although the major networks broadcast an average of 310 hours of sports events a year, only a few of those hours showed women competing. For example, NBC offered 366 hours of sports coverage between August 1972 and September 1973, but only one hour was devoted to women athletes—the final match at the Wimbledon tennis tournament. During the early seventies, women athletes never received more than about 2 percent of the time networks devoted to sports coverage.

Many critics blame this situation on the lack of women sportswriters and sportscasters, as well as the fact that broadcasting executives were predominantly male. Mariah Burton Nelson, author of *Are We Winning Yet?* and *The Stronger Women Get, the More Men Love Football*, found that only 8 percent of the nation's sportswriters and broadcasters were women as of 1994, though there was a trend toward hiring more women in these fields.

Change came slowly. On September 20, 1973, the famous "Battle of the Sexes" tennis match between Billie Jean King and Bobby Riggs at the Houston Astrodome drew more than 28,000 paying fans and 48 million television viewers. Networks also began to televise more of the early women's matches at major tennis tournaments and feature more women's bowling and golf matches. During the mid-seventies, one major network broadcast the annual "Women Superstars" contest, which featured top athletes from a variety of sports competing against each other in several events. The rise of new cable television stations after the 1970s made it possible to televise more women's team and individual sports and broadcast documentaries about women's sports and women athletes.

Basketball was particularly popular. In 1978, a women's college basketball final was broadcast for the first time. The day after the tournament was held, NBC's "Sportsworld" featured this game between UCLA and Maryland. The next year, NBC paid $7,500 for the rights to televise women's basketball championships and they featured a live broadcast of the finals between Old Dominion and Louisiana Tech. By 1994, there were 64 teams in the NCAA tournament. CBS began telecasting the Women's Final Four (the final matches played among the top four college teams) in 1991.

On April 2, 1995, the University of Connecticut Huskies and University of Tennessee Lady Volunteers played in the final game of the NCAA Division 1 women's basketball championship. The game, televised by CBS that Sunday afternoon, attracted more viewers than had the National Basketball Association (NBA) games on NBC. Realizing the women's basketball was attracting so many fans, ESPN agreed to pay $19 million for the sole rights to broadcast the women's NCAA tournaments from 1996 through 2002.

ESPN and ESPN2, two cable networks devoted to sports, and local stations that can broadcast sports events of regional as well as national interest have continued to bring more women's sports events into homes. More sports and more kinds of sports, such as archery, soccer, body-building, jump-roping, and rodeo, were telecast.

Coverage may vary with the sport. Tennis and golf have regular tournaments, which are covered on television. Olympics gymnastics and figure skating events get a great deal of coverage because they attract so many viewers. The women's figure skating competition at the 1994 Olympics attracted the third largest television audience in U.S. history, after two Super Bowls. Aside from men's team sports, figure skating is one of the only sports covered on TV during prime time viewing hours (8–11 p.m.). Beach volleyball, with a number of attractive players including model Gabriella Reece, has received more coverage in the 1990s. On the other hand, women's softball, soccer, and volleyball received far less coverage, even though, as happened in 1994, the U.S. women's team won the soccer World Cup, while the U.S. men did not.

A number of women have become sports commentators, and some have created their own shows. Dana Torres, a swimmer who set national and world records, then won four medals in three Olympic Games (1984, 1988, 1992), embarked on a career as a sports commentator and television reporter. After retiring from competition at age 25 and moving to New York City, Torres developed her own show for the Discovery Channel, reporting about sports like sky diving that use special technology.

As producers, women have devel-oped shows about women and sports as well as taking charge of general sports programming. ABC-TV producer Amy Jill Sacks (1955–1994) won 13 Emmy Awards during her career, some for her contributions to sports programming on that network. She oversaw coverage of the 1984 Summer Olympics and produced two specials during the 1988 Winter Olympics. Praised for her innovative use of music during sports telecasts, Sacks is regarded as a pioneer in her field. As vice-president of programming at ABC sports, Lydia Stephans developed a well-received documentary about women's sports called *A Passion to Play*. It was aired from 1994 through 1996 and new episodes were scheduled for production.

Women have also made inroads as commentators on men's sports. In July 1995, Suzyn Waldman, an experienced sports reporter, became the first woman to call a major-league baseball game for a major TV network. Waldman provided commentary for ABC during a game between the New York Yankees and Texas Rangers.

Critics charge that coverage of women athletes and sports remains inequitable and inadequate. Author Madeleine Blais found that during the early 1990s, local television stations devoted about 92 percent of their sports time to men's athletics. Daily newspapers gave about 3.5 percent of their space to women's sports. NBC was also criticized for failing to give enough coverage to women's team sports, especially softball and soccer, at the 1996 Olympics. The U.S. women's teams both won gold medals in these sports. Sportswriter Richard Sandomir called the scant coverage of the championship games "Not just unfair. Insulting." But changes are taking place. For example, in 1995, Liberty

Sports, owner and operator of regional sports cable channels, announced it would develop a women's sports channel.

References Blais, *In These Girls, Hope Is a Muscle* (1995); Guttmann, *Women Sports: A History* (1991); Sandomir, "Women's Sports Gets a Boost," *New York Times*, April 9, 1995, p. 7; Sandomir, "Not All (Women's) Sports Created Equal on NBC," *New York Times*, August 5, 1996, p. C7; "Sport and Television: Swifter, Higher, Stronger, Dearer," *Economist*, July 20, 1996, pp. 17–19; Whitten, "Dana Torres Basks in Post-Olympic Glory," *Swim*, January/February 1996, p. 25.

Temple, Ed (b. 1927)

The coach of women's track and field at Tennessee State University for 44 years, Edward Stanley Temple developed numerous world champions and Olympic medalists. His internationally famous Tigerbelles are regarded as the most successful women's track team in U.S. history. The team won many national events, including 34 Amateur Athletic Union (AAU) titles, 30 Pan American Games medals, and 23 Olympic medals.

Among his most famous protégées were May Suggs, Wilma Rudolph, and Wyomia Tyus Simberg, the only Olympic sprinter ever to successfully defend her sprint title in a subsequent Olympiad. Temple spotted Rudolph while he was scouting local basketball games for talented female athletes, and Rudolph went on to win three gold medals in the 1960 Olympics in Rome.

A native of Harrisburg, Pennsylvania, Temple began coaching at Tennessee State, where he was also a professor of sociology in 1950. He had earned his bachelor's degree and a master's degree in health and physical education, with a minor in sociology, at Tennessee State. He scouted track meets in Tennessee and the surrounding area for promising athletes. In addition to heading the women's track team program during the academic year, Temple operated a summer track and field program for talented high school students. Those high school students chosen to become Tigerbelles were offered work aid scholarships to the university. Besides training rigorously and achieving their best in athletics, the Tigerbelles were expected to maintain high standards in their coursework and personal conduct. Temple's track athletes recalled that academics came first with him. He believed students should look ahead to the future, since they were not going to be athletes all their lives, and urged them to take advantage of their opportunity to get a college education. Of the 40 Olympians he coached, 39 completed college and earned one or more degrees.

Temple organized his team carefully and expected strict discipline. Team members who did not arrive promptly for practice sessions were required to run an extra lap around the track for each minute they were late. He explained, "Suppose one of them comes down and warms up, then a second one comes down and warms up. Well, what's the first one going to do while the second one is warming up? I can't be in two places at once." He also trained his team to run in different kinds of weather and under a variety of conditions, to prepare them for whatever might happen in competition.

Temple believed that one of the major reasons his students were so successful was that they had such strong competition from their fellow Tigerbelles. He once said that Wilma Rudolph had benefited from "the tremendous competition from her teammates, the three next fastest girls in the country. Take Barbara Jones.

She ran a world record 10.3 hundred yards at Randall's Island in 1958. Jones would sometimes beat Rudolph. Lucinda Williams would sometimes beat Rudolph. Martha Hudson would give her competition." These four Tigerbelles teamed up for the gold medal in the 400-meter relay at the 1960 Olympics.

Temple coached both the 1960 and 1964 U.S. Women's Olympic Track Teams and several Pan American Games teams and AAU teams. He was a member of the U.S. Olympic Committee in 1960, 1964, 1968, 1972, 1976, 1980, and 1984. He was inducted into the National Track and Field Hall of Fame, the Tennessee Sports Hall of Fame, the Pennsylvania Sports Hall of Fame, and the Black Athletes Hall of Fame. Of her beloved coach, Wyomia Tyus later said, "He was very strict, and he was very tough. . . . When I look back on it, I sometimes wonder how I made it, but I also know that he was very good for us as women. . . . He was always there to lend a helping hand."

In 1994, Temple retired from coaching and teaching. In his honor the National Collegiate Athletics Association (NCAA) gives the Edward S. Temple Award each year to the top female track-and-field athlete.

References Biracree, *Wilma Rudolph* (1988); Carlson and Fogarty, *Tales of Gold* (1977); Tennessee State University, "Edward Stanley Temple" fact sheet (1995)

Tennis

The game of tennis, played with racquets and a ball, dates back hundreds of years. Thousands of years earlier, some form of game with a ball and sticks was a fertility rite in Egypt and the Middle East. The word "tennis" may have come from the French word *tenez*, which means to hold; a town along the Nile called Tinnis in Arabic; or the Latin verb *tenere*, which means "to catch." The word racquet came from the Arabic word *rahat*, which means "palm of the hand." The word "deuce," the score when two more points are needed to win the game, may have come from the French *deux*, meaning "two."

In twelfth-century France, knights played tennis, called *jeu de paume* (palm game) on large, walled courts outdoors. The clergy also apparently played a version of the game, and it became a popular pastime among royalty. Women, too, were playing tennis in France as long ago as the 1400s. For a while, King Charles V banned the game after spectators began placing bets on matches.

From France, tennis spread to the British Isles. In 1874, American Mary Ewing Outerbridge was vacationing in Bermuda, an island in the Atlantic Ocean that had been a British colony. She learned to play tennis from British army officers and brought the game back to the United States. With the net, rackets, and balls she obtained on the island, she played with friends in Staten Island, where she lived. One of Outerbridge's brothers was a director at the Staten Island Cricket and Baseball Club, and the first tennis court on U.S. soil was built there in the spring of 1874.

In 1881, the U.S. Lawn Tennis Association (USLTA) was formed, and the first national championships were held, with men competing. Ellen Hansell became the first women's national champion in 1887, while Bertha Washington won the crown during the next two years. At that time and for several decades, women played a more delicate and restrained version of tennis than female players today. In her book *Tennis for Women*, Lou Eastwood Anderson wrote, "A woman's game does not include prolonged training on volleys and fancy strokes that make huge drafts on energy, but rather emphasizes accuracy in placement." According to Anderson, a woman who played an aggressive game, moving in to the net or exerting herself to serve hard was likely to "incapacitate herself and to limit her possible advancement and ultimate joy in the game."

Teenager Lottie Dod of Great Britain is credited with having introduced the volley and smash shots. She won the Wimbledon title for the first of five times in 1877. An all-around athlete, Dod competed in the sports of archery (Olympic silver medalist, 1908), figure skating, golf (British national ladies' champion, 1904), hockey, and tobogganing. In 1904, May Sutton Bundy became the first American woman to win at Wimbledon, a victory she repeated in 1907. French player Suzanne Lenglen liberated women from wearing corsets with their tennis dresses in 1919. She appeared at Wimbledon in a one-piece cotton dress—calf-length, short-sleeved, and minus petticoats—to the shock of the tournament. During these years, women began to play a more assertive, hard-hitting style of tennis during these years.

In the United States, tennis became quite popular during the 1960s. President John F. Kennedy, from a sports-loving family, encouraged Americans to become more physically fit and to take part in sports. Tennis clubs sprang up around America, some with indoor courts for year-round play. The game also moved beyond the country club setting and became less exclusive. Traditional tennis whites gave way to more individual, even colorful clothing. The game gradually lost its elite status and

was embraced by people of all socioeconomic levels. Between 1970 and 1982, the number of women playing tennis rose from 3 million to 11 million. Clubs sprang up in large towns and small ones, offering lessons and clinics for women and leagues for various levels of play.

In 1968, two major championships, the U.S. National and British National—Wimbledon—became "open" so that both professionals and amateurs were allowed to enter. A year later, the United States Lawn Tennis Association (USLTA) changed its rules to permit nonprofessional players to accept prize money. Still, male tennis players received priority. Women's matches were often scheduled early in the day, while men played on the main courts at times spectators were more likely to watch. Men's tournaments drew more fans, and men received more prize money for their matches. The press also covered men's tennis much more than women's.

The seventies began a new and more lucrative era for women's tennis. Thanks to such dynamic players as Billie Jean King and Chris Evert, women's tennis grew more exciting and gained stature. Gladys Heldman, editor of *World Tennis* magazine, helped to organize women players, and they developed their own tours. Fans now came out to see the women as well as the men.

King and others said women deserved equal prize money. She pointed out that they were entertaining and gratifying fans just as male players were. Besides, said King, "Technically, women play sounder tennis because we're not as strong physically. Things [men] can do with a flick of the wrist we have to do with technique and execution. What men do with power we do with finesse and dexterity. With us, everything has to be a little surer." Some spectators prefer to watch women, since points may last longer. (Men's points can end quickly if a player is serving exceptionally well.) In women's tennis, a ball might cross the net literally dozens of times before one player wins the point. Tactics play a great role in success.

Some male players supported women's claims; others frankly disagreed. Bobby Riggs, a men's champion during the thirties and early forties, said, "Women's tennis? I think it stinks. They hit the ball back and forth, have a lot of nice volleys and you see some pretty legs. But it's night and day compared to men's tennis." Nonetheless, the women did make gains. From 1970 to 1972, prize money for women tennis players rose from about $50,000 to over $1 million. Top players of the 1990s could expect to earn millions during their careers from prizes and endorsements.

Tennis is an Olympic sport. In 1996, at the Atlanta Games, Californian Lindsay Davenport won the gold medal in the women's singles competition, while Mary Joe Fernandez and partner Gigi Fernandez won the women's doubles competition, as they had four years earlier at the Olympics in Barcelona, Spain.

See also Austin, Tracy; Battle of the Sexes; Betz, Pauline; Brough, Louise; Capriati, Jennifer; Connolly, Maureen; Evert, Chris; Garrison-Jackson, Zina; Gibson, Althea; Hart, Doris Jane; Heldman, Gladys; International Tennis Hall of Fame; King, Billie Jean; Marble, Alice; Navratilova, Martina; Palfrey, Sarah; Prize Money; Shriver, Pam; Sutton Bundy, May; United States Lawn Tennis Association; Wightman, Hazel Hotchkiss; Wills, Helen; Wimbledon; World Team Tennis
References Collins and Hollander, eds., *Bud Collins' Modern Encyclopedia of Tennis* (1994).

Tennis Championships, U.S.

The first men's tournament was held in Newport, Rhode Island, and moved to the West Side Tennis Club in Forest Hills, New York, in 1915. The women's tournament moved to Forest Hills in 1921 from the Philadelphia Cricket Club, where it had been held since 1881. In 1968, the tournament became an "open," so that both amateurs and professionals are eligible to compete. The U.S. Open moved to Flushing, New York, in 1978.

Among the early women's champions were Ellen Hansell (1887) and Bertha Washington, who won in 1888 and 1889. One memorable match took place in 1930, when May Sutton Bundy slipped and broke her left leg on the court. She insisted on finishing the set, while using a crutch.
See also Hansell, Ellen

Terwillegar, Erica (b. 1963)

As a teenager, Terwillegar lived near enough to Lake Placid to have access to a refrigerated luge track built for the 1980 Olympics. She took up the luge at 13, one of a handful of Americans who learned this sport in childhood. By age 19, she had won the silver medal at an international junior luge event—the first time any American had won a medal in world luge competition. In 1983, Terwillegar again achieved a "first" for Americans, male or female, when she finished in fifth place in the world luge championships. She also won the gold medal in the North American competition.

Thaden, Louise McPhetridge (b. 1906)

Thaden won the first Women's Air Derby, also called the Powder Puff Derby, in 1929. A native of Pittsburgh, Pennsylvania, Thaden flew from Santa Monica,

California, to Cleveland, Ohio, in 20 hours, 19 minutes, and 10 seconds. That same year, she set a record for consecutive flight when she stayed in the air for more than 22 hours, as well as a speed record for women—156 miles per hour. In 1928, Thaden had set a women's altitude record by flying at an altitude of 25,400 feet. She went on to set a women's endurance record in 1932 during a flight that lasted 8 days, 4 hours, and 5 minutes.

Thaden continued to race after the 1929 derby. In 1936, flying with Blanche Noyes as copilot, she won the $7,000 first prize for the Bendix Race. The two women piloted a Beechcraft Staggerwing craft from Los Angeles to Cleveland. That year, Thaden was honored with the Claude B. Harmon Trophy, given to the most outstanding woman flier of the year. In 1938, her book *High, Wide, and Frightened* was published, an account of her adventures in the air.

Thomas, Debi (b. 1967)

With powerful jumps and dynamic footwork on the ice, Thomas became the first African-American to gain world recognition as a figure skater. She won the U.S. women's figure skating championship in 1986 and 1988 and was world ladies' champion in 1986.

When she was three years old, Thomas, a native of Poughkeepsie, New York, became fascinated with figure skating after seeing the Ice Follies. She took up skating because it looked like fun, beginning with group lessons at a local rink, where she won her first contest at age 9. Showing great promise, she began training at the Redwood City Ice Lodge, in northern California. Thomas impressed her coach Alex McGowan by completing a triple jump when she was just 11 years old. The next year, she reached the na-

tional finals in the novice category and took home the silver medal.

Thomas then began a rigorous training program, traveling many miles each day to and from school and the rink. She usually practiced six hours a day, six days a week. For a while, she quit school and took correspondence courses in order to devote more time to skating but soon realized she did not want to sacrifice her education and everything else in her life for skating. In 1985 Thomas placed second in the national and fifth at the world championships. She won the women's figure skating event at the National Sports Festival (now called the Olympic Festival). Steadily improving her performance, she had managed to move up from thirteenth place in the United States to second, in only two years' time.

Despite her success on the rink, Thomas had other important goals. She was accepted at the University of Colorado–Boulder, where she began premed studies with a major in microbiology. With a rigorous academic schedule, Thomas had little time to practice for the 1986 national championships. Even so, her strong, athletic performance brought her the U.S. women's title for the first time. During her long free skating performance, she completed an amazing five triple jumps.

She crowned that victory by winning the world championship six months later. There she faced the 1984 and 1985 world champion, Katarina Witt of Germany. Witt had trouble with her jumps during the competition in Geneva, Switzerland, falling during a double loop in her short program. Thomas won both the short and long programs, landing four triple jumps during the latter performance. Spectators were thrilled with her triple–double jump combination.

Thomas had trouble maintaining her

Dividing her time between medical school and training, Debi Thomas was still able to win the 1986 World Women's Figure Skating Championship and a bronze metal at the 1988 Winter Olympics.

momentum in 1987. Studying limited her practice time severely. She also pulled muscles in both calves shortly before the nationals and developed tendinitis when she rushed to train before her muscles had healed. In pain during the competition, she lost the title to Jill Trenary. At the world championships, Witt regained her world title from Thomas.

Thomas finally agreed with her coach to leave school for a year in order to prepare for the 1988 Olympic Games. She worked hard to develop a more artistic program, studying ballet movements and working with a talented choreographer to help her blend skating with music. At the end of the short skating program of the Olympics, Thomas was in first place. During her long program, she skated well but did not complete two of her triple jumps and made a small error on another triple. Witt won the gold medal, and a Canadian skater named Elizabeth Manley took the silver after earning higher scores than both Witt and Thomas in the long program.

Thomas's third-place finish was a disappointment, but others pointed out that to be rated third-best women's figure skater in the world was an enormous achievement. At the world championships held shortly after the Olympics, Thomas again finished in third place. Moving forward in other areas of her life and newly married, Thomas retired from competitive amateur skating but skated as a professional on weekends. She graduated from college in 1991 and went on to Stanford University medical school in 1993 to pursue her dream of becoming an orthopedic surgeon.

Thomas inspired many people with her example. Through hard work, she achieved success in two demanding areas of life at the same time.

References Hilgers, *Great Skates* (1991); Swift, "There's No Doubting Thomas," *Sports Illustrated*, February 17, 1986, 22ff.

Tickey, Bertha Reagan (b. 1925)

For 13 years, Tickey was star pitcher for the Raybestos Brakettes of Stratford, Connecticut, one of the greatest fast-pitch softball teams in history. During her 20 years as a player, Tickey won 757 games and lost only 88.

Born in California, Tickey first played on another top fast-pitch team, the Orange, California, Lionettes (1950–1955). Playing against other U.S. teams and some from Canada, the team won four national championships: 1950, 1951, 1952, and 1955. During the first championship season, "Blazing Bertha" won 65 of 73 games and achieved 143 scoreless innings in a row. Opposing batters managed only 143 hits against Tickey, and she "fanned"—struck out—795 of them. At the 1950 championships in San Antonio, Texas, Tickey hurled 26 innings in the last two games. A fellow softball player, M. Marie Wadlow, later recalled, "She was knocked to the ground by a vicious line drive to the stomach in one of the games, only to get up and finish the game and the tournament."

Tickey then played with the legendary Brakettes, who won the national title in 1958, 1959, 1960, 1963, 1966, 1967, and 1968 while Tickey was part of the team. At eight of these national championships, Tickey was voted most valuable player.

During a career that continued into her forties, Tickey pitched 735 winning games, 161 of them no-hitters. In 1967, when Tickey was 42 years old, she pitched a no-hitter during a 13-inning game. She retired the next year, and lived in Clovis, California, with husband Ed Tickey, an outstanding fast-pitch catcher, until his death in

1993. In 1972, Tickey was inducted into the National Softball Hall of Fame.

References "Bertha Tickey," biographical sketch from National Softball Hall of Fame; "M. Marie Wadlow," biographical sketch from National Softball Hall of Fame.

Tigerbelles

This famous women's track and field team at Tennessee State University rose to prominence during the mid-1900s under coach Ed Temple. Among the most famous Tigerbelles were Wilma Rudolph and Wyomia Tyus, both of whom won Olympic gold medals. Numerous other Tigerbelles won national and international titles. They include Mae Faggs, Madeline Manning, Edith McGuire, Willye White, and Chandra Cheesborough.

See also Rudolph, Wilma; Temple, Ed; Tyus Simberg, Wyomia

Title IX

Designed to prevent sex discrimination, this federal law was drafted by the Department of Health, Education, and Welfare and passed as part of the Educational Amendments Act of 1972. It requires that people of both sexes have equal opportunities in educational programs, including athletics. Title IX reads: "No person in the United States shall, on the basis of sex, be excluded from participation in, be denied the benefits of, or be subjected to discrimination under any educational program or activity receiving federal financial assistance." In other words, schools that practice sex discrimination may not receive federal funds. Before Title IX was passed, U.S. colleges and universities often allocated amounts as small as 1 percent of their total athletic budgets to women's sports. They devoted much more space and staff to men's programs.

Opposition to Title IX came from individuals and from groups, including the National Collegiate Athletic Association (NCAA), which governed men's college sports. Women were not permitted in the NCAA until 1974. Many male athletes and male college administrators complained that Title IX would cut into their funds and damage their programs. After the law was passed, some schools declared varsity cheerleading a sport, in order to have a current activity qualify as a women's sports program. Rather than implement new women's athletic programs at their schools, they gave additional money to cheerleading squads.

In the years immediately following the passage of Title IX, courts were asked to consider cases in which males wished to play on all-female teams. A 1979 U.S. Supreme Court case (*Cannon v. University of Chicago*), which involved a nurse who wished to be admitted to a medical school, established the right of individuals to sue federally funded schools and colleges for alleged violations of Title IX.

But in most high schools and colleges, athletic programs for female students were developed. By 1978, there were about 2,083,000 girls taking part in high school sports, compared to 317,000 in 1972 and 294,000 in 1970–1971 (a year during which 3,666,000 boys had participated in high school sports programs). By 1991, that figure had risen to about 2 million. Also as a result of Title IX, more money was made available to women athletes in the form of college scholarships. The number of women competing in athletics at the college level rose from about 8,000 in 1967 to more than 60,000 in 1974. From 1970 to 1976, the number of school members in the Association for Intercollegiate Athletics for Women (AIAW) rose from 301 to 843. By the late seventies, the AIAW was larger than the

NCAA. Expenditures for women's sports in the NCAA's Division I rose from $27,000 in 1973–1974 to $400,000 in 1981–1982.

Still, critics complain that Title IX has not solved all the problems it was meant to address. According to Madelaine Blais, as of 1994, women college athletes were still only receiving about a third of all available scholarship money, and only about a fourth of all college sports' operating budgets was allocated for women's sports. Critics also point out that men still hold most of the administrative and coaching positions in schools, colleges, and universities, thus wielding more control over sports programs. For 1972, about 90 percent of the coaches for women's teams were women, but that percentage declined to 50 percent by 1987.

Individuals and groups who want to report a violation of Title IX may complain to the director of the U.S. Office of Civil Rights.

See also Association for Intercollegiate Athletics for Women; National Collegiate Athletic Association
References Guttman, *Women's Sports: A History* (1991); Kaplan, *Women and Sports* (1979); Nelson, *Are We Winning Yet?* (1991).

Todd, Jan (See Weight Lifting)

Torrence, Gwen (b. 1965)

Torrence, who grew up in Atlanta, Georgia, won the gold medal in the 200-meter sprint at the 1992 Summer Olympics in Barcelona, Spain. She also competed in the 100-meter race but finished fourth, after American Gail Devers, who won the gold medal during that competition.

At the Grand Prix meet in 1994, Torrence placed second in the 100-meter and lowered her career-best time to 10.82 seconds. In June 1995, she won the 100-meter event at a meet in Sacramento. Her husband and coach, Manley Waller, had urged her not to compete, because Torrence had been injured on a trampoline while doing a photo shoot in May, then aggravated the injury in the national championship heats.

Racing at the 1995 world championships in Göteborg, Sweden, in August 1995, Gwen Torrence finally won the 100-meter for the first time in international competition, with a time of 10.85 seconds. Torrence said, "The 100 is every sprinter's favorite race. We all want to be the world's fastest woman." She completed the 200-meter race by setting a new world record of 21.77. Before the race, Torrence had been upset to find that her favorite spikes were missing, perhaps stolen. She ran in an old pair instead.

When the track judges reviewed tapes of the 200-meter race, they found that Torrence had stepped across her lane while rounding a curve. Disqualified, Torrence filed a protest, saying she had not realized that she stepped on the line, but the committee ruling stood. Some onlookers said that Torrence would have won the race even if she had not stepped on the line. Women's team coach Teri Jordan commented, "It's obvious that she won by a decisive margin." A disappointed Torrence said, "I can't worry about it. I will just have to beat them at the Olympic Games." In a television interview in January 1996, Torrence said she was training hard for the upcoming Olympics, where she was favored to win one or more events. In Atlanta, Torrence won a bronze medal in the 100-meter race.

References Interview, "The CBS Morning Show," January 25, 1996; Longman, "Disqualification in 200 Stings Torrence," *New York Times*, August 11, 1995, B7, B10; Longman, "Go Home? Torrence Gets Home in First," *New York Times*, June 20, 1995, B16; Longman, "Torrence Wins Race, but Not

Popularity Contest," *New York Times,* August 8, 1995, B9, B13.

Torres, Dara (See Television)

Track and Field

Track and field events can be traced back to ancient Greece and were probably popular before that. At the first Greek Olympic Games in 776 B.C., the only event was a 200-yard foot race. The javelin throw was another early event. Events that required running, jumping, or throwing were important to the warriors of that era, and only men were allowed to compete or be spectators at these Games held every four years. Women were regarded as unfit for this kind of activity and had low status in Greek society.

The first track meets for women may have been held in Germany starting in 1904. American E. MacBeth is believed to have set the first track and field record when she ran the 50-yard dash in 6 seconds. In the United States, women's and girls track teams were less common than men's and tended to receive less funding for coaching or equipment. Notable exceptions were the Tigerbelles of Tennessee State University and women's athletics at the Tuskegee Institute.

As the modern Olympic Games continued into the 1900s, different track and field events were added. In the running events, athletes participate in sprints that include the 100- and 200-yard dash and 100-meter and 200-meter. Middle distance runs go from a quarter mile (440 yards or 437.5 meters) to 880 yards (800 meters or 875.9 yards). Distance races were once confined to men, since it was thought that women were not capable of endurance racing or marathons. To back up this belief, men pointed out that during the London Olympics in 1948, some women had fainted during the 800-meter race. Others said these women had been improperly trained but were not inherently unfit for endurance runs. The rules were changed so that the Olympics featured 1,500-meter, 3,000-meter, and 10,000-meter races as well as a marathon race for women competitors.

Among younger track-and-field competitors, those ages 12 to 14 can compete in the mile run, those 15 and over are eligible for a 2-mile run, and in college and other competition, the 3-mile or 5,000-meter run is allowed. Cross country running has also become more popular, and the length of such races depends on age. Girls 9 to 11 compete in 1-mile runs, moving to the 2–5-mile races in college. Cross country running is often done in teams of 5 to 12 runners. In relay races, each person on the team runs a leg of the race, and runners exchange a baton (stick) as smoothly and quickly as possible during the changeover.

There are two kinds of jumping events in track and field. In the high jump, athletes leap over a bar held by two upright poles called "standards." In 1975, Joni Huntley of Oregon State University jumped 6 feet, 2.75 inches to set a new U.S. record. Other Olympic gold medalists in high jumping include Jean Shiley (1932), who cleared 5 feet 5.25 inches; Alice Coachman (1948) who cleared 5 feet 6.125 inches; and Mildred L. McDaniel (1956), who cleared 5 feet 9.25 inches. No U.S. woman won the gold medal in the high jump between 1956 and 1988. In 1988, American Louis Ritter won the gold and set a new Olympic record with a jump of 6 feet, 8 inches.

In the long-jump event, Jodi Anderson won the national title in 1978 with a jump measuring 22 feet, 7.5 inches. Kathy

A competitor clears a hurdle during a practice run at the 1992 Barcelona Olympics.

McMillan won the U.S. event in 1976 with a jump of 22 feet, 3 inches, and Willye White was U.S. long-jump champion in 1964 with a jump of 21 feet, 6 inches. The long jump became an Olympic event for women in 1948. As of 1995, the only U.S. woman to win an Olympic gold medal in the long jump was Jackie Joyner-Kersee (1988). Joyner-Kersee won the bronze medal in that event in 1992 and also in 1996, when she competed with an injured leg.

In hurdling, runners sprint down a track and jump over a series of hurdles in their path. The sport requires speed, power, and agility. Hurdling events range from 50 yards to 400 meters in length and may include from four to ten hurdles along the length of the track. They can be low hurdles (30 inches high) or high ones (33 inches). Runners must not knock over the hurdles.

The discus itself, which has been compared in appearance to two pie pans connected facing each other, measures about 7 inches in diameter and weighs slightly more than 2 pounds. It must be thrown in a certain direction and is thrown with one hand after the thrower whirls in a circle to create momentum. In 1976, Jan Svendsen became the first American-born woman to throw the discus more than 180 feet. Her throw was 180 feet, 11 inches. The next year, Lynne Winbigler of California set a new record for U.S. women by throwing the discus 187 feet, 2 inches. As of 1995, the only U.S. Olympic gold medalist for the discus was Lillian Copeland (1932).

The javelin is a seven-foot spear that weighs about one and one-half pounds. The athlete runs down a thirteen-foot wide lane that must measure at least 98 feet long and ends in a scratch line of wood or metal. The javelin is thrown over the shoulder and must land tip first on the ground. American women who have thrown more than 200 feet are Kate Schmidt (227 feet, 5 inches in 1977); Sherry Calvert (207 feet, 11 inches in 1978); and Karin Smith (203 feet, 10 inches in 1976). As of 1995, only one American woman had won an Olympic gold medal in this sport—Babe Didrikson Zaharias, with a throw of 143 feet, 4 inches in 1932.

See also Coachman, Alice; Didrikson Zaharias, Babe; Joyner-Kersee, Jackie; Marathon Running; Pentathlon; Shiley, Jean; Shot Put; Tigerbelles; Triathlon; Tuskegee Institute; White, Willye B.
References Condon, *Great Women Athletes of the Twentieth Century* (1991); Hollander, *100 Greatest Women in Sports* (1976); Kierens et al., *The Story of the Olympic Games* (1977); Knudsen, *Babe Didrikson* (1985); Sullivan, *Track and Field* (1980).

Trainer, Athletic

Athletic training is among the fields that have expanded for women since the 1970s, especially as women's sports programs increased after the passage of Title IX. Athletic trainers aim to get and keep an athlete in good shape for training and competition. They monitor the athlete's condition, giving first aid or advising medical care when necessary, and help athletes recover after an injury. Trainers work in school and college sports programs, as well as with professional athletic teams and individuals, and at sports medicine centers. They may also be certified teachers. Many trainers are athletes themselves.

College preparation for trainers involves studying anatomy and physiology, kinesiology, exercise, nutrition, and methods of life-saving and first aid, among other related subjects. A certain number of hours of clinical experience is also required for certification by the National Trainers Association.

See also Title IX

Trason, Ann (b. 1959)
During the early 1990s, Trason, who lived in California, broke new ground in the endurance races known as ultra marathons, also called ultra running. As of 1996, Trason held most women's ultra running records and had sometimes finished within minutes of men competing in the same races. From 1988 to 1995, she won the women's title at the Western States 100-Mile Endurance Run. In the Netherlands in 1995, Trason set a new women's world record for the 100-kilometer race (slightly more than 62 miles). She finished in 7 hours and 47 seconds. She also won the Sri Chinmoy TAC/USA 24-Hour Race in 1989, becoming the first woman to win an open national championship, setting a national record of 143 miles.

Trason has said that she is pleased to see the progress women have made in various sports, such as basketball, during the 1990s. However, she still sees inequities, pointing out that after her 1995 marathon race in the Netherlands, "The men all got metal trophies, the women all got flowers."

See also Ultra Running; Western States 100-Mile Endurance Run

References Negron, "Form chart: Our Look at the Top Contenders in the Men's and Women's Olympic Marathons," *Runner's World,* August 1992, 74; Nelson, *Are We Winning Yet?* (1991); Walsh, "Fueling Secrets of the Fast and Famous," *Women's Sports and Fitness,* April 1995, 85–87.

Trenary, Jill (b. 1970)
The Minnesota native began skating in 1973 on the pond at her grandparents' farm in Minnetonka at age three. In 1984, she began training under Carlo and Christa Fassi in Colorado Springs, Colorado, and won the U.S. Junior Ladies' figure skating title the next year. Later in 1985, a collision on the ice caused a deep gash on Trenary's left leg, cutting muscles

and veins. Doctors feared she might have to quit skating, but with hard work, she was back on the ice and won the U.S. Senior Ladies' crown in both 1987 and 1989. At the 1988 Olympics, Trenary came in fourth.

Retiring from amateur competition, Trenary skated as a professional and competed in numerous pro events. In 1995, she married British champion ice dancer and choreographer Christopher Dean, who, with partner Jayne Torvill, had won European and world titles and the Olympic gold medal in 1988.

Reference Trenary, *The Day I Skated for the Gold* (1989).

Triathlon
This three-event track and field competition requires athletes to complete a 100-meter dash, high jump, and javelin throw. The first triathlon competitions began in Europe during the late 1920s. At the 1964 Olympic Games, two more events—the long jump and shot put—were added, forming the pentathlon. New forms of the triathlon have been developed, including the Ironman championship, which requires competitors to complete a swim, road-cycling race, and marathon. In the Ironman, men and women complete the same events and start at the same time. Paul Newby-Fraser of Zimbabwe is among the top women to complete this triathlon. She finished eleventh overall in 1988, first among women contestants.

Triathlon, Women's
The first women-only triathlon was held in June 1990, in Long Beach, California. It was sponsored by the Danskin company, a manufacturer of women's dance and exercise wear. More than 2,000 women competed in the three events, which included a marathon run (26.2 miles), 2.4 mile ocean

swim, and a 112-mile bicycle race. The winner of the triathlon was Lisa Lahti.

Tuskegee Institute

In 1929, Tuskegee, a university founded and run by African-Americans, started the first highly competitive women's track and field team. The Tuskegee Relays held at the university offered black women the first chance to compete in a college setting. The institute also developed training programs and scholarships for talented high school students. Under director Clive Abbott the program expanded and was known around the country as an excellent training ground for champions. Many Tuskegee athletes earned advanced college degrees and worked in the field of athletics as coaches and directors. Abbott's daughter Jessie set up the first permanent track and field program at Tennessee State University in 1945.

See also Coachman, Alice; Jackson, Nell
References Ashe, *A Hard Road to Glory* (1988); Biracree, *Wilma Rudolph* (1988); Cahn, *Coming On Strong* (1994); Smith, ed., *Notable Black American Women* (1992).

Twigg, Rebecca (b. 1963)

This top cyclist became the first American woman ever to win the gold medal in the pursuit event at a world championships. A native of Seattle, Washington, Twigg was a child prodigy who started college at age 14, the same year she entered her first cycling races. She won third place in the road race and came in fifth in the intermediate track event. To win her first senior pursuit title in 1981, she defeated Connie Carpenter-Phinney, with whom she would race again on many occasions. She won the senior pursuit and senior time trials in 1982.

Twigg went on to win the 1983 Coors International Classic and a silver medal at the world road race championships.

That year, *Cycling USA* named her Rider of the Year for the second time. At the 1984 Olympic Games, Twigg captured the silver medal for the 79-kilometer road race, narrowly defeated by winner Connie Carpenter-Phinney. Twigg won four national titles in 1984: the 1-kilometer, the points race, the individual pursuit, and the match spring. She was national individual pursuit and points race champion in 1985, and she set a world record of 30.642 seconds in the 500-meter race the next year.

Reference Hickok, *A Who's Who of Sports Champions* (1995)

Tyler, Dorothy (b. 1893)

Tyler may have been the first girl to win as a jockey in a race featuring prizes and professional competition. Growing up in Joplin, Missouri, Tyler had a reputation as the strongest teenager in town, male or female. A horse-lover, she decided to become a jockey. At age 14, she won a quarter-mile long race in 1907, riding a horse she had raised and trained herself. The other jockeys in the race, all male, were more experienced and one was a professional.

See also Jockey, Professional

Tyus Simberg, Wyomia (b. 1945)

Growing up in Griffin, Georgia, Wyomia Tyus was a natural runner. She later said that she ran fast in order to keep up with her three older brothers and so that she would be able to play team sports with the neighborhood boys. As a teenager, Tyus was told to stop being a "tomboy." She later said, "I enjoyed the idea of competing and being out in the fresh air. I also had a lot of encouragement from my father who believed there was nothing wrong with a girl playing sports." Mr. Tyus also urged his children to study hard in school and did not let them work at jobs when they were children, even though the family could have used more money.

In high school, Tyus excelled on the track team. A highly respected college track coach, Ed Temple, saw her at a state track meet when she was 14. Temple had developed an outstanding women's track team, the Tigerbelles, at Tennessee State University. Among his famous runners was Wilma Rudolph, winner of three gold medals in the 1960 Olympics. Impressed by Tyus's speed and determination, Temple asked her to spend the summer at Tennessee State University training with other women athletes. She attended the program in both 1962 and 1963 and later said that Coach Temple was "very strict and very tough," but he helped her develop a stronger, more efficient running style. The intense training paid off when Tyus won three events at a 1963 Amateur Athletic Association (AAA) meet.

Tyus won a scholarship to Tennessee State, where she joined the women's track team. She took part in a rigorous training program, running at least 6 miles a day as well as many shorter runs. At the trials for the 1964 Olympic team, Tyus placed third in the 100-meter dash, then competed in Tokyo and won that same race with a time of 11.2 seconds, tying a world record. She earned a silver medal as part of the U.S. 4 x 100–meter relay team. In 1965 and 1966, she set a new world record for the 100-meter dash (11.1 seconds).

Although Tyus had doubted she would compete in another Olympics, she trained again for the 1968 Games in Mexico City. She later said that as she got ready to race, she was thinking, "I'll be glad when it's over with." As usual, she focused on doing her best and tried not to think of success or failure. Running the 100-meters in just 11 seconds, Tyus set yet another world record and became the first sprinter of either gender ever to win the same event at two successive Olympics. She capped that victory with another gold medal as a member of the winning 4 x 100–meter relay team.

That same year, she graduated from college. In 1969, Tyus married Art Simberg, a representative for Pima, a German company that made track shoes and athletic clothing. While rearing two children, Tyus competed in professional track events and worked as a television commentator. In 1973, she was a featured star in International Track Association (ITA) professional meets, where she thrilled spectators with her speed and grace. She won 8 of the 18 women's events she entered. Determined to do better in 1974, she won all 22 of the races she entered on the ITA tour. For the second year, she was the top earner among the women.

As a teacher in Los Angeles, Tyus encouraged young people to work hard in school as well as in athletics. Pointing to her own experience, she said, "We [Tigerbelles] got our degrees and became teachers, lawyers, and many other things." To Tyus, developing a sound character and becoming educated, contributing citizens was more important than winning.

See also Olympics; Temple, Ed; Tigerbelles; Track and Field
References Carlson and Fogarty, *Tales of Gold* (1977); Condon, *Great Women Athletes of the Twentieth Century* (1991); Lanker, *I Dream a World* (1989); Litsky, *Superstars* (1975); Stambler, *Women in Sports* (1975).

Uber Cup

This prize for the top women's badminton team in the world was first offered in 1957, with the first championships taking place in England. Men had had their own international competition, the Thomas Cup, since 1948. Betty Uber of Great Britain, winner of eight All-England titles in singles and doubles play, donated the cup. Uber played competitive badminton for 25 years and competed on the Uber Cup team for her country.

See also Badminton; Devlin Cup

Ultra Running

Also called ultra racing, this is an extended version of marathon running. A typical marathon is 26 miles, but ultra runners go two, three, even four times that distance up to several hundred miles. In addition to covering great distances, runners may have to endure harsh weather conditions and difficult terrain, such as hills and mountains, facing whatever natural hazards or wildlife occur in these settings.

The number of ultra races has been increasing since the 1980s. The Doc Holliday R.I.P. 34-mile Trail Race is all uphill. The Swiss Alpine Marathon covers a 42-mile course through difficult slopes in this mountain range. The Mad Dog 50-Mile Run takes runners on a looped path through deserts in Arizona. The Leadville Trail Run across the Sky race covers 100 miles in the Rocky Mountains, going uphill 12,600 feet on rocky, snow-covered ground. The United States Association of Track and Field (USATF) 100-kilometer national championship was won by Donna Perkins of St. Francis, Wisconsin, in 1994.

Among the top women in this sport are Ann Trason and Randi Bromka. Bromka was the U.S. national champion in 1993, having run 138.3 miles in 24 hours. Bromka has faced danger during her races, as when she encountered a coiled rattlesnake, ready to strike.

See also Raid Gauloises
References Negron, "Form chart: Our Look at the Top Contenders in the Men's and Women's Olympic Marathons," *Runner's World,* August 1992, 74.

Unified Sports

A program run by Special Olympics that unites athletes with mental retardation and other handicaps with their nonhandicapped peers—also called mainstream athletes. Many Special Olympians reach a level of skill such that they are able to compete on such teams. The Unified Sports program has been growing rapidly since the early 1990s. Some schools and communities sponsor a variety of unified teams. The teams are also eligible to compete in Special Olympics Games.

See also Special Olympics

Uniform (See Dress Code; Femininity)

U.S. Badminton Association (See Badminton)

United States Field Hockey Association (USFHA) (See Field Hockey Association, U.S.)

United States Figure Skating Association (USFSA)

The USFSA governs amateur figure skating in the United States and aims to maintain high standards in the sport. Throughout the nation, many local rinks belong to the USFSA. To enter a competition, a skater must either belong to the organization as an individual or be a member of a club that belongs to the USFSA.

Member clubs sponsor testing, competitions, and ice carnivals. By passing tests at a certain level—juvenile, intermediate, novice, junior, and senior—skaters earn the right to compete at that level. Tests increase in difficulty at each level. Violations of major rules set by the USFSA may result in suspension or permanent exclusion from amateur competition.

United States Lawn Tennis Association (USLTA)

Founded in 1881, the USLTA became the governing organization for tennis in the United States. At that time, tennis matches were played on grass courts—lawns. The first national sports organization of its kind, it was founded to standardize rules for the game and such matters as ball size in order to avoid disputes at tournaments. The new USLTA proceeded to organize national championships that year at Newport, Rhode Island. For a while, it was known as the United States National Lawn Tennis Association (USNLTA), then it returned to the name USLTA. In 1975, the organization decided to become the United States Tennis Association (USTA).

See also United States Tennis Association

U.S. Ski Association (USSA)

Founded in 1904 in Ishpeming, Michigan, the USSA (formerly the National Ski Association), is the official organization for amateur skiing in America. It is based in Colorado Springs, Colorado.

The USSA was instrumental in setting up national championships in skiing, the first of which (a downhill competition) was held in Warren, New Hampshire, in 1933. The first U.S. slalom competition took place two years later in Seattle, Washington. The first U.S. downhill races for women were held in 1938 at Stowe, Vermont.

To encourage skiing excellence, the USSA has established various ski programs and has set standards for skiing schools, as well as organizing competitive events throughout the nation. It also sets rules for and monitors Junior National Ski Championships. Many ski clubs throughout the nation are members of the USSA.

The USSA selects, trains, equips, and transports U.S. teams when they engage in international competitive events, including the Olympic games. It works with the Federation of International Ski (FSI) and the United States Olympic Committee to promote the sport on a worldwide basis. In addition, the USSA coordinates its efforts with the Amateur Athletic Union, National Collegiate Athletic Association, and the National Ski Patrol. The USSA has been instrumental in setting up shelters in isolated mountain areas.

Besides competitive skiing, the USSA promotes the sport for people of all ages and skill levels.

United States Olympic Committee (USOC)

The USOC is the governing body of Olympic sports and sporting events in the United States. Through the years, a few women athletes and other women have served with the committee.

By 1995, only one woman, Anita DeFrantz, was on the executive board of the USOC, and only seven women were among the 106 members of the committee. The USOC directed the various Olympic bodies governing the different sports to make sure that at least 10 percent of the decision-makers in their organizations are women. The USOC said this should be done within five years, and that the percentage of women should reach 20 percent by the year 2005. The international Olympic organization was also directed to take actions to reach these percentages itself within the same five- and ten-year time frames.

See also DeFrantz, Anita
References "U.S.O.C. Making a Call to Enlist More Women," *New York Times*, September 27, 1995, B13.

U.S. Open (tennis tournament) (**See** Tennis Championships, U.S.)

United States Tennis Association (USTA)

The USTA was formerly the United States Lawn Tennis Association (USLTA). In 1975, the word "lawn" was eliminated, since tennis matches had moved away from grass courts to clay, concrete, and other surfaces. Besides organizing regional and national championships, the USTA ranks players throughout the year, using a point system. Until 1972, USTA rankings included only amateur players, but after tournaments became "opens," welcoming both amateurs and professionals, all players were ranked together.

Van Dyken, Amy (b. 1973)

A native of Denver, Colorado, swimmer Van Dyken won four gold medals at the 1996 Olympics in Atlanta. Her two individual golds came in the 50-meter freestyle and 100-meter butterfly. She also won gold as part of the 4 x 100–meter freestyle relay and 4 x 100–meter medley relay teams.

The Games had not begun well for Van Dyken, who was carried out after her first race with severe cramps. She was advised to withdraw from the 100-meter butterfly race but decided to compete after all, winning her first individual gold at the Olympics.

Known for her warm, exuberant personality, Van Dyken has also been a role model as an athlete who achieved success in spite of her battle with asthma. She appeared on many television interview shows after the Games and endorsed various commercial products, including Wheaties cereal. A serious competitor, Van Dyken said that she might continue training for the next Olympics, in the year 2000.

References "After the Gold Rush," *People*, August 19, 1996, p. 44; Lupica, "Butterfly Is Golden," *New York Daily News*, July 24, 1996, p. 60.

Vare Trophy

Named for champion Glenna Collett Vare, this trophy is given to women golfers who have the lowest average score for that year on the women's professional golf tour. The trophy was first awarded in 1952, donated by golfer Betty Jameson.

See also Berg, Patricia Ann; Carner, JoAnne Gunderson; Collett Vare, Glenna; Jameson, Betty; Lopez, Nancy; Rankin, Judy; Rawls, Betsy; Whitworth, Kathy; Wright, Mickey

Vinson Owen, Maribel (1911–1961)

Like many champions, Vinson was quite young, just three years old, when she first donned a pair of ice skates. At age 16, she succeeded champion Theresa Weld (Blanchard) as America's top women's skater. Vinson eventually won the national title nine times. She also earned a silver medal at the 1928 world competition and a bronze medal for third place in 1929. At the 1932 Olympics she won the bronze.

Vinson was also a distinguished pairs skater. With her partner Thornton L. Coolidge, she won the national junior championship in 1927, and they won the senior title for the next two years. She and George E. B. Hill won the pairs championship in 1933 and from 1935 to 1937. In 1937, she turned professional and toured with her own ice show.

After her marriage, as Maribel Vinson Owen, she wrote about women's sports for the *New York Times*, authored instruction books about figure skating, and became a top coach. Among her students was Tenley Albright, who won two world titles and an Olympic gold medal. Vinson Owen also coached her own daughters,

Laurence and Maribel. Laurence became the National and North American ladies' champion, receiving praise for her style and individuality. She was expected to win a medal at the 1964 Olympics. Tragically, Vinson and both of her daughters died in 1961 when a plane carrying the U.S. figure skating team and some coaches crashed in Belgium, killing all aboard. In 1976, she was elected to the U.S. Figure Skating Association Hall of Fame.

See also Albright, Tenley; Weld Blanchard, Theresa
References Hilgers, *Great Skates* (1991); Hollander, *100 Greatest Women in Sports* (1976).

Virginia Slims

This popular women's tennis tour began in 1970, due to the efforts of top women players, notably Billie Jean King and Rosie Casals, and Houston businesswoman and tennis-lover Gladys Heldman. Interest in women's tennis had risen during the late 1960s, and women called for more prize money and playing opportunities. In 1970, a group of top women players, led by King, threatened not to enter the annual Pacific Southwest Championships, in which the ratio of prize money was $12,500 for men and $1,500 for women. The male officials at that tournament refused to distribute the prize money more equitably, so the women withdrew.

Heldman, the publisher of *World Tennis* magazine, helped to set up the first all-women's professional tournament at the Houston Racquet Club. The Philip Morris Company, which manufactured Virginia Slims cigarettes, agreed to invest $40,000 in the tour that first year. Billie Jean King and seven other top players signed contracts agreeing to play on the Slims circuit. At the Houston tournament, prizes totaled $7,500, with Rosie Casals winning the $1,600 first prize.

The Slims tournament grew in stature and prize money each year. At times, it was criticized for promoting cigarettes in an athletic context and for its ads, which used the slogan, "You've come a long way, baby." Many feminists protested at the use of the word "baby." Nonetheless, the tournament offered professional women tennis players improved visibility and earning opportunities. In 1971, the tournament was held in 19 cities and offered $309,000 in prize money. Another city was added the next year, and prizes topped $500,000. By 1973, 22 cities featured Virginia Slims events, and women competed for $775,000. The tour continued for more than 20 years. In 1995, the name Virginia Slims was dropped, as the tournament was phased into the women's professional tennis tour.

See also Casals, Rosie; Heldman, Gladys; King, Billie Jean

Vodon, Vicki (See Wrestling)

Volleyball

The game of volleyball was invented in Holyoke, Massachusetts, in 1895 by William G. Morgan. He thought the sport would be appropriate for older men who did not have the stamina for basketball, but women soon took up the sport, too. The original players used a basketball but soon changed to a lighter and smaller ball. Through the U.S. armed services, the game spread to other countries, where it became more developed and even more popular than it was in the United States.

Japan introduced volleyball into Olympic competition in 1964. The Japanese women's team had won five world titles from 1960 to 1964, and Japanese athletes had developed a strategic style of play. They won the gold medal at the Games.

Before 1976, a U.S. volleyball team only qualified once at the Olympics. But athletes from the United States were instrumental in setting up professional volleyball competition among teams around the world. They developed the International Volleyball Association in the 1970s and helped the sport become an entertaining and dynamic sporting event for spectators. The U.S. Olympic Committee set up a regional training center for American women volleyball players in Colorado Springs, Colorado. Here the women on the Olympic team trained during the late 1970s preparing for the 1980 Games.

Early in 1987, the Major League Volleyball organization (MLV) was set up for professional women court volleyball players. However, it did not summon enough sponsorship, fans, or television exposure to survive economically. In March 1989, the MLV folded.

Volleyball continued to become more popular with women athletes. The U.S. women's team won the gold medal at the 1996 Summer Olympics.

See also Hyman, Flo; Peppler, Mary Jo; Woodstra, Sue

References *Guinness Book of World Records, 1986*; Peppler, *Inside Volleyball for Women* (1977).

Volleyball, Beach

Beach volleyball has become a popular televised sport and is now also part of the Olympics. Pairs of players compete against each other.

One of the strongest women's teams in the early 1990s was that of Karolyn Kirby and Liz Masakayan, both of San Diego. The two played on the Professional Volleyball Association tour for years. Masakayan played on the national indoor team from 1986 to 1990, while Kirby played college volleyball at Utah State then also professional volleyball on indoor teams. Teaming up in 1993, Kirby and Masakayan won 12 of 13 events they entered on the beach volleyball circuit. In 1994, they won the world women's beach volleyball title.

Volleyball Hall of Fame

Among the players honored in the hall are Lou Sara Clark McWilliams, Jean K. Gaertner, Carolyn Gregory Conrad, Lois Ellen Haraughty, Linda Murphy, Zoann Neff, Nancy Owen, and Mary Jo Peppler.

von Saltza, Chris (b. 1944)

Born in San Francisco, Susan Christine (Chris) von Saltza began swimming training at age eight in Saratoga, California, where her family then lived. As a ten-year-old, she impressed onlookers by easily winning a race at the local swimming club. A well-known coach named George Haines invited von Saltza to train with his group at the Santa Clara Swimming Club.

In 1956, when she was only 12 years old, von Saltza just missed becoming a member of the U.S. Olympic swim squad. Looking forward to the next Games, she trained hard and competed in numerous regional and national events. At one meet, she broke four national records for her age group. She was also an A-student at Los Gatos High School and served as a class officer and cheerleader.

In Rome at the 1960 Olympics, von Saltza was part of a young squad that included swimmers and divers ranging in age from 13 to 18. The press called them "Water Babies," and they won more medals than any women's Olympic swim team since 1932. Von Saltza won three gold medals, setting a world record in the 400-meter freestyle race. Two more golds came to her as part of the 400-meter medley and 400-meter freestyle relay teams. Von Saltza was anchor for the two relay teams, which set world records. In the 100-meter freestyle race, she won a silver medal, losing first place by only six-tenths of a second to the outstanding Australian swimmer Dawn Fraser. After leaving competition and graduating from college, she served with the Peace Corps.

References Laklan, *Competition Swimming* (1965); Stambler, *Women in Sports* (1975).

Wade Trophy

This trophy is awarded annually to the woman judged the most outstanding basketball player of the year. The award has been given since 1978, when the first Wade Trophy was awarded to Carol Blazejowski.

Margaret Wade, for whom the trophy is named, played basketball at Delta State University in Mississippi from 1928 through the 1931–1932 season. That year, basketball was dropped from the women's sports programs at the school because officials thought the game had become "too rough for young ladies." Wade became director of women's intramural sports at Delta State in 1973 when women's basketball was reinstated.

See also Blazejowski, Carol; Lieberman, Nancy

Wadlow, M. Marie (1917–1979)

A talented softball pitcher from Missouri, Wadlow began playing in 1929 with the St. Louis Tabernacle Baptist Church team. By the time she retired in 1950, Wadlow had a record of 341 wins and only 51 defeats, with 42 of those wins no-hitters.

In 1943, Wadlow joined the Caterpillar Dieselettes, a team based in Peoria, Illinois. During her seven years on that team, the Dieselettes won 103 games and lost only 18. Wadlow would later recall the 1950 Amateur Softball Association (ASA) championships as the most thrilling event in her career. Although the Dieselettes lost that tournament, Wadlow struck out 26 batters and enjoyed the intensity of the games, which involved 43 innings in 11 hours. The Dieselettes' team manager called Wadlow "one of the greatest competitors I've seen anywhere." She retired from competitive softball in 1950 and became an accountant for the Caterpillar Tractor Company, from which she retired in 1977.

In 1957, Wadlow became the first woman chosen to enter the National Softball Hall of Fame. In a tribute from her hometown, Wadlow was also the first woman elected to the St. Louis Metropolitan Hall of Fame (1969).

See also National Softball Hall of Fame
Reference "M. Marie Wadlow," biographical material from the American Softball Association Hall of Fame.

Wainright, Helen (b. 1906)

Wainright won a silver medal in springboard diving at the 1920 Olympics; four years later, she won bronze in the 400-meter race, making her one of only a few athletes to have won Olympic medals in both swimming and diving events.

The versatile Wainright was among the top U.S. women swimmers during the early 1920s, winning the national outdoor 100-yard, 880-yard, and 1-mile freestyle races in 1922 and the 440-yard freestyle in 1924. She also won the 100-yard indoor event (1923, 1924) and the 220-yard indoor (1922, 1925). She captured the women's national indoor 1-meter diving title in

1925. The next year, Wainright left amateur competition to tour in professional swim shows, then married an Army officer. During World War II, she donated her numerous trophies and medals to be melted and used in the war effort.

Walsh, Stella (1911–1980)

Polish-American track and field star Stella Walsh had one of the longest careers of any athlete, male or female. During her forties, a time when most sprinters have retired, she won five consecutive U.S. pentathlon championships. This rugged event required her to achieve skill at running, jumping, the discus throw, and the shot put. Walsh set nearly 100 records in U.S. and world track events and won races ranging in length from 60 yards to 1 mile.

Growing up in Cleveland, Ohio, Walsh was an athletic child. At age 19, she won both the 100- and 220-yard sprints at the Amateur Athletic Union championships held in Dallas, Texas. In the broad jump, she squeaked past top athlete Babe Didrikson by a fraction of an inch. Walsh topped off her 1930 achievements by setting a world record, running the 50-yard dash in only 6.1 seconds at the annual Millrose Games, held at Madison Square Garden in New York City. She was named outstanding performer at that event, which had previously been open only to men.

In 1932, Walsh represented the Polish team in the Olympic Games, since she was not yet a U.S. citizen. Running the 100-meter dash in 11.9 seconds, she became the first woman to break the 12-second mark in that race and easily won the gold medal. In the years that followed, Walsh amassed title after title, winning the U.S. Outdoor 100-meter race four times, the 200-meter 11 times, the 220-yard six times, the 50-yard twice, and the broad jump ten times. From 1926 to 1942, she held the world record for the 200-meter race. When Walsh finally retired in her fifties, she had more than one thousand major track and field titles to her credit.

A bizarre controversy swirled around Walsh after her death in 1980. When Walsh was accidentally shot and killed on the street during a bank holdup in downtown Cleveland, the coroner performed an autopsy. In a report issued by the Associated Press on January 22, 1981, the county coroner's office said that Stella Walsh "had male sex organs . . . [and] no female sex organs."

Reference Hickok, *A Who's Who of Sports Champions* (1995)

Waples, Debra (See Fencing)

Warner, Bonny (b. 1962)

A top field hockey player, Warner watched the 1980 Winter Olympics in Lake Placid and decided to train for the luge. She perfected her skills in West Germany and became part of the U.S. luge team. In 1983, she gained seventh place in the world event, while earning the top spot in the U.S. competition. During the 1984 Olympics, an accident during the event made her drop from a likely sixth place to fifteenth.

Water Polo

A relatively young sport, water polo, often referred to as football or soccer in the water, was invented in Great Britain in 1869. The sport became popular around the world after 1890, especially in eastern Europe and Russia. In 1926, the first European water polo tournament was held in Budapest, Hungary. An International Water Polo Board was set up in 1950 to develop rules for the game that could be applied consistently all over the world.

Because it is a vigorous, demanding sport, male players doubted that any women could pursue water polo, but women have successfully entered the sport. Players most often use the front crawl but must also learn to perform expert turns and excel in the breaststroke and scissor-kicking. They control the ball, throw it, lob it, and make shots. The object is to get the ball through the opponent's goal and at the same time prevent the opposing team from scoring. Goalkeepers tread water and lunge to push away the ball.

Various swim clubs around the country have women's water polo teams, and women's water polo was included in the Fifth Aquatic World Championships for the first time. One of the best players on the United States National women's team in the 1990s was Susie McIntyre of California, a competitive swimmer with 14 years experience. She played the defense for the Seal Beach Club.

Waterskiing

The sport of waterskiing probably originated in the United States or in France sometime during the early 1920s. The availability of speedboats may have inspired individuals to see how they could skim across the water on skis. Someone may also have tried riding a surfboard across the water while holding onto a boat. Various individuals tried adapting snow-skis for use on the water or making waterskis from different types of wood.

In 1939, the American Water Ski Association was founded to promote the sport, increase opportunities for competition, and educate the public about safety measures. The sport grew rapidly so that by the 1960s, more than 6 million Americans were waterskiing. Competitions involved jumping, slalom, and trick riding events, as well as marathons in which the skiers covered hundreds of miles.

The first national waterskiing competition for women was held in Long Island, New York, in 1939, three years after the first U.S. tournament for men. Esther Yates was named top all-around water-skier. In 1945, after World War II ended, water-skiers from around the world formed the International Water Ski Union (IWSU). The IWSU sponsored the first international championship on the southern coast of France in 1949.

Women and girl water-skiers compete in the same four divisions as men— jumping, slalom, tricks, and the overall. Among the top U.S. water-skiers were Jeannette Brown of Tampa, Florida, who won a number of waterskiing titles in different events during the 1960s. In 1963, she won the world women's overall title. Liz Allan Shetter won the national title six years in a row, from 1970 through 1975. In 1977, a 13-year-old, Kris Carroll, was named Outstanding Female Eastern Water Skier.

Junior competitors on the U.S. team performed brilliantly at the 1994 world championships. They swept all four events—the slalom, tricks, jump, and overall. Rhona Barton of Canyon Lake, California, won the women's title.

See also Shetter, Liz Allan
References *Lincoln Library of Sports Champions*, vol. 16 (1989); Pratt and Benagh, *The Official Encyclopedia of Sports* (1964).

Watson, Lillian Debra (Pokey)
(b. 1950)
In 1968, Watson became the first woman to win the Olympic 200-meter backstroke event. A native of Long Island, New York,

Watson had also been a member of the 1964 women's Olympic swim team. During those Games, she was a member of the winning 4 x 100–meter freestyle relay team. In 1965, she won the U.S. national outdoor freestyle women's title, and the next year captured the 200-meter title.

In 1967, at the Pan American Games, Watson placed third in the 100-meter event and fourth in the 200-meter race. She trained hard and was able to improve on that performance for the 1968 Olympics. At the first Olympic 200-meter backstroke event for women, Watson's winning time was 2 minutes, 24.8 seconds.

Wecker, Kendra (b. 1983)

At age 12, in January 1995, Wecker became the first female to qualify for the National Football League (NFL) annual Pass, Punt, and Kick competition. Wecker, from Marysville, Kansas, threw the football 133 feet at the competition held in San Diego. Prior to the competition, Wecker had honed her skills playing flag football in a city recreational program in her hometown.

Reference Interview, "CBS This Morning," January 9, 1995.

Weight Lifting (Power Lifting)

Clearly a sport of strength and power, weight lifting was associated with male attributes and manly accomplishments for centuries. Nonetheless, women tried their skill and began to build up their strength. During the 1940s, Abbye Stockton of Santa Monica, California, performed in weight-lifting exhibitions. At 5 feet 1 inches and 118 pounds, Stockton astonished spectators when she could press 110 pounds, snatch 100 pounds, and clean-and-jerk 140 pounds. Stockton also could hold up her 185-pound hus-

band Les on one hand for as long as 30 seconds while they performed a stunt in which he stood upright on her shoulders then flipped into a handstand, using his wife's hands as a base.

During the 1970s, women began entering weight-lifting competitions and women's championships (with different weight divisions) began to develop throughout the country. Among the top American female weight lifters was Jan Todd. An English teacher and farmer, Todd won the U.S. Women's National Championship in power lifting in 1978, as well as numerous other weight-lifting titles. She was able to lift nearly 500 pounds, which was more weight than 95 percent of male pro football players could lift at that time.

Aside from competitive weight lifting, women have turned to weight training to promote fitness and for cross-training purposes to improve their performance in other sports. Among the athletes who has said that lifting weights improved her performance in her major sport is tennis player Martina Navratilova.

References Duffy and Wade, *Winning Women* (1983); Letter from John Grimek to *Strength and Health Magazine,* June 10, 1968, quoted in Benagh, *Incredible Athletic Feats* (1969).

Weiss, Alta

At age 14, the baseball-loving Weiss began pitching for local boys' teams around her hometown of Ragersville, Ohio. Two years later, she became a pitcher for a men's semiprofessional team, the Vermilion Independents. As 1,200 people watched her pitch her first game, Weiss gave up only four hits and one run in five innings. Newspaper reports praised her skill, saying that she could hold her own with male players, and Weiss continued to make headlines. Finding a long skirt cumbersome, she adopted a set of ex-

Donna Mayhew hefts 154 pounds in the clean-and-jerk portion of the National Weight Lifting Championships in 1986. Although international women's weight lifting competitions have become increasingly prevalent since the 1940s, women's weight lifting is still not included in the Olympic Games.

tremely full bloomers that looked like a skirt. Large crowds gathered to watch her play at Cleveland Naps' park.

A doctor's daughter, Weiss used her baseball earnings to finance her medical education. While practicing medicine, she continued to play baseball and later became the first woman to own and manage a professional men's team.

Weld Blanchard, Theresa (1899–1978) A pioneer in American figure skating, Weld earned many honors and the gratitude of skaters and lovers of the sport. A tribute written to Weld in a 1953 issue of *Skating* magazine said, "I do not know anyone in our skating family who has

worked with such efficiency, prudence and fine taste for the benefit of skating and has rendered such outstanding service to our sport."

Weld's skating career began in 1911, when the Skating Club of Boston first opened, with its fine outdoor rink. Young Theresa, whose father had helped to found the club, was one of its most devoted patrons. As often as possible, she drove her pony cart three miles to the club to skate.

In 1914, Weld became the first American ladies' champion at a competition in New Haven, Connecticut. She won that title again five times, from 1920 through 1924. With partner Nathaniel W. Niles, she also won the waltz title and placed second in the pairs event. Beginning in 1924, Weld and Niles won nine U.S. pairs titles and, in 1925, captured the North American pairs title.

Unlike most other women skaters of her day, Weld tried adding some jumps to her program. Some judges marked her down for doing these "unladylike" moves. A judge at a 1920 competition warned Weld that it was "unsuitable" for women to perform jumps, since it would cause their skirts to rise up around their knees. Nonetheless, Weld completed a small Salchow jump. She won the free-skate part of the competition, coming in third overall to take home a bronze medal. In 1920, Weld also won a bronze medal at the Olympics in Antwerp, Belgium, and received enthusiastic cheers from many U.S. servicemen still stationed in Europe after World War I.

That same year, she married Charles Blanchard. After her marriage, Weld continued to compete and then to officiate at several Olympic Games. In 1923, she became the editor of *Skating*, the official magazine of the U.S. Figure Skating Association, which she and her former pairs' partner helped to found. She continued as editor for 50 years, promoting the development of figure skating in America. In 1976, she was elected to the U.S. Figure Skating Hall of Fame.

Western States 100-Mile Endurance Run

This annual race is a prestigious event in the sport of ultra racing, also called ultra running. There are both men and women winners, as well as an overall winner. From 1989 to 1995, Ann Trason dominated the women runners, winning the run for seven years in a row. Trason came in third overall in both 1992 and 1993. In the 1994 race, she arrived 5 minutes be-

hind the male winner of the race. Many thought Trason had a good chance to be the overall winner in 1996.

See also Trason, Ann

White, Cheryl

Jockey White became the first African-American to become prominent in this profession. As a teenager during the early seventies, White rode the circuit on small tracks throughout the country. Her proficiency caught the attention of trainers, who provided horses for her to ride in the larger races. By that time, jockeys Kathy Kusner and Robyn Smith had already obtained a license (1969), and more women were competing in the sport. White won a major stakes race in Atlantic City in 1971.

See also Kusner, Kathy; Smith, Robyn

White, Willye B. (b. 1939)

Between 1960 and 1972, track and field star White won ten national titles in the outdoor long jump event. She is also the only U.S. woman as of 1996 to have competed in five separate Olympics—1956, 1960, 1964, 1968, and 1972.

White's first Olympic appearance was in 1956, when she was still in high school. At that Olympiad, she captured the silver medal, the only one she would win in her specialty, the long jump. White became a member of the famous Tigerbelles team at Tennessee State University. In 1964, at her third Olympiad, she won a gold medal as part of the women's 4 x 100–meter relay team. White continued to compete in the long jump and set several U.S. women's records in this event. Her best jump was 21 feet, 6 inches.

After retiring from competition in 1972, White studied nursing. She served as a consultant to the U.S. Olympic Opportunity Program and as a member of the President's Commission on Olympic Sports. She was also inducted into the Black Athletes Hall of Fame.

References "Willye B. White" fact sheet from Tennessee State University, 1996.

Whitworth, Kathy (b. 1939)

Golf champion of the fifties and sixties, Kathrynne Ann Whitworth was born in Texas but grew up in Jal, New Mexico. At age 14, she weighed 215 pounds ("I couldn't stay out of the refrigerator," she later said). Her weight continued to rise, and she took up golf partly to reduce through exercise. The challenges of the game intrigued her, and Whitworth spent hours perfecting her strokes.

She played her first amateur tournaments in 1955, doing well in local events. As an 18-year-old on the professional tour among top players, she consistently lost. After about six months on the tour, she finished in sixteenth place in one tournament and won $33. Whitworth quit playing for over a year and lost more weight, becoming a trim 140 pounds, then went back on the tour. She was voted "most improved professional" of 1960 and particularly impressed people with her putting skills.

In 1962, she was on her way, winning the Kelly Girl Open and Phoenix Thunderbird Open. The next year, she won eight championship titles, a record she repeated in 1965 when she was ranked the number one U.S. woman golfer. She kept that status into the 1970s.

One of Whitworth's best weapons remained her putting ability. Competitor Sandra Haynie once said of her, "When she has to putt, she gets it every time." She was also known as a great "scrambler," able to make good shots from a difficult position or from the rough, when necessary. Although Whitworth never won a U.S. Open, she won three Ladies Professional Golf Association (LPGA) titles and the Colgate's Triple Crown tournament in 1975. As of 1988, Kathy Whitworth had won more LPGA victories (88) than any other golfer, with Mickey Wright in second place with 82. She also had earned more than $1.6 million in prizes.

Whitworth has won numerous awards. Each year from 1966 through 1973, with the exception of 1970, she was named LPGA Player of the Year. The Associated Press chose her as their Woman Athlete of the Year in both 1965 and 1967. She also won the Vare Trophy in 1969, the first of seven times she would capture this prize. In 1975, she became the seventh woman inducted into the LPGA Hall of Fame. Golf magazine named her golfer of the decade for 1968–1977 in 1988. She has also been elected to the World of Golf Hall of Fame.

Throughout her career, Whitworth was a staunch advocate for other women golfers and expressed concern that many women athletes had a tough time earning enough to cover expenses. She has said that women contribute a lot to the game, especially by demonstrating techniques that recreational golfers can use. Whitworth has also expressed her appreciation at being able to make a living doing what she loves to do, saying, "It sure beats the eight to five."

References *LPGA Media Guide* (1995); Litsky, *Superstars* (1975).

Wichman, Sharon (b. 1952)

A native of Fort Wayne, Indiana, Wichman was the first woman to win the Olympic gold medal in the 200-meter breaststroke event. She swam the race in 2 minutes, 44.45 seconds at the 1968 Games, where this event was offered for the first time.

See also Olympics; Swimming, Racing

Engulfed in a cloud of sand, golf champion Kathy Whitworth gets herself out of a trap at the Women's International in 1982.

Wightman Cup

This first international competition for women tennis players originated in 1923. Champion player Hazel Hotchkiss Wightman gave the U.S. Lawn Tennis Association (USLTA) a sterling silver vase as a prize for the winner of an event between American and British teams. The victor was to keep the cup for a year. A junior Wightman competition was also introduced.

The first Wightman Cup match was held at a newly built stadium at Forest Hills in Queens, a borough of New York City. Wightman served as captain, and she and her partner, Eleanor Goss, won three doubles matches in the tournament. The American team defeated the British seven matches to zero. Matches were suspended in 1989, because the U.S. team had become disproportionately stronger than the British team. However, in 1991, plans were made to revive the Wightman Cup, with the Americans facing off against a team made up of European women players.

See also Wightman, Hazel Hotchkiss

Wightman, Hazel Hotchkiss

(1887–1974)

Her Olympic tennis doubles partner Dick Williams said of Wightman, "Nothing bothered Hazel. She had marvelous anticipation and coordination—but her concentration was incredible." Born in Healdsburg, California, petite Hazel Virginia Hotchkiss won 48 U.S. tennis titles between 1904 and 1954. In singles, she reaped three U.S. singles titles (1909–1911 and 1919). In 1924, she won the Wimbledon ladies' doubles title with partner Helen Wills. That same year, she was a member of the first U.S. women's tennis team to win a gold medal at the Olympics, and she became the first American woman to win a gold medal in the mixed doubles competition with partner R. Norris Williams. She and Wills won a gold medal at the same Olympic Games playing women's doubles. They paired up to win the U.S. women's doubles in 1915, 1924, and 1928.

A year after graduating from the University of California at Berkeley in 1911, she married George William Wightman, a tennis player and attorney. "Lady Tennis," as she was called, stopped playing for a while to become a mother. But as Hazel Wightman, she won the U.S. doubles and mixed doubles in 1915 and reclaimed her singles title in 1991, at age 32. The durable right-hander continued to win doubles titles and spent many hours coaching U.S. players, free of charge.

Wightman believed that women should have a tournament on par with the men's Davis Cup. In 1923, she founded the Wightman Cup as an international competition for women, held annually between the United States and Great Britain, another nation with a good field of competitive players. Wightman played in five cup matches herself and was team captain 13 times.

Hazel Wightman once called the game of tennis "a channel of intensified life." During her career, she earned 34 U.S. adult titles, the last being the U.S. Indoor women's doubles titles at age 56. In 1957, she was elected to the International Tennis Hall of Fame. Starting in the 1920s, she devoted herself to teaching other players and wrote *Better Tennis*, where she advised players to concentrate and to "cultivate a buoyant spirit." Wightman also began running free tennis clinics, open to all students, in 1922, and she held tournaments at her home. Wightman died in 1974, just before turning 88.

References "From Wimbledon to Forest Hills," *New Yorker*, October 13, 1975; Klaw, "Queen

Mother of Tennis," *American Heritage,* August 1975; Maddocks, "The Original Old Lady in Tennis Shoes," *Sports Illustrated,* April 10, 1972; Scherman and Green, eds., *Notable American Women* (1980).

Wilber, Doreen (b. 1930)

In 1972, Wilber, a housewife from Jefferson, Iowa, became the first woman to win the Olympic gold medal in the individual archery championship. The 1972 Games featured this event for the first time, and Wilber set a world record with her point total of 2,424 points for the two rounds. For each round, she shot 36 arrows from four different distances: 30, 50, 60, and 70 meters. Her scores for the two rounds were 1,198 and 1,226, respectively. Wilber also won the national field archery title in 1967. She was the runner-up at the world championships in both 1969 and 1971.

Williams, Esther (b. 1921)

This California native became known as the Million Dollar Mermaid after she left competitive swimming to appear in swim shows and movie extravaganzas produced at MGM. Williams began swimming at an early age, and by 16 she had won three U.S. national championships in breaststroke and freestyle swimming. After she won the 100-meter freestyle in 1939 with a time of 1 minute, 0.09 seconds, everyone expected her to add Olympic gold to her titles. However, the 1940 Olympics were canceled because of World War II.

Williams's talent and looks brought her attention from showman Billy Rose, who produced the Aquacades, a Broadway musical featuring hundreds of swimmers and divers and stunning special effects. Williams auditioned and became the leading lady, featured first at the San Francisco World's Fair Aquacade opposite Olympic champion Johnny Weissmuller. The two performed many romantic choreographed routines at Aquacade shows. Williams later appeared in successful films with swimming themes, bringing more attention to the sport of synchronized swimming and to her own balletic style. She promoted a line of swimming pools as well as Esther Williams swimwear and promoted swimming as a sport for youth. In 1966, she was elected to the International Swimming Hall of Fame.

During the 1970s, Esther Williams produced instructional films on teaching infants how to swim and appeared on television programs to promote water safety and lessons for infants and toddlers. She continued to swim into her seventies, in a backyard pool equipped with a device that created a three-knot current in the water. Williams told journalist Harald Johnson that swimming "is the only sport you can do from your first bath to your last, without hurting yourself. You are ageless and weightless in the water."

References Johnson, "Esther Williams: America's Swimming Sweetheart," *Fitness Swimmer,* Summer 1995, 32–34; McWhirter, et al., *Guinness Book of World Records: Special Edition, 1986.*

Williams, Linda (b. 1960)

In 1978, a federal court order allowed Linda Williams, then 18 years old, to play as part of the baseball team at her Texas high school. The presence of Williams on the otherwise all-male team brought national publicity, as TV crews filmed the game and interviewed players and coaches.

Williams, Venus Ebonistarr (b. 1980)

At age 14, Williams became one of the youngest tennis players to turn professional. Raised in Compton, California, Williams later moved to Pompano, Florida, where she continued to pursue her sport.

American actress and swimmer Esther Williams gives a neo-Greek underwater performance.

She was viewed as a prodigy with a bright future in tennis. Williams parents were impressed with her ability, and her father called her a "ghetto Cinderella" who would astonish the tennis world.

Williams worked hard. Her role models were American Pete Sampras, ranked as the number one men's player, and Monica Seles, a top-ranked women's player. Like these players, Williams developed a powerful serve, strong volley, and good reflexes on the court. By age ten, she was ranked as number one in southern California in the girls' 12-and-under division. When she was 11, the family moved to Rick Macci's International Tennis Academy in Delray, Florida, where Williams attended public school while receiving tennis instruction. Although players usually compete in the junior amateur circuit until age 16, Williams chose not to do so. In 1994, she faced a hard decision as to whether or not to turn professional. She overcame some parental objections, saying she was ready to compete against top players. (After 1994, new rules established by the World Tennis Association [WTA] would strictly limit the number of events in which women under age 18 could compete.)

In the first round of her first pro tournament, the Bank of the West Classic, she defeated Shaun Stafford, a professional with six years of experience. The willowy, 6-foot 1-inch Williams was praised for her serve and a skillful backhand drop shot that allowed her to break her opponent's serve in the first set. In the second round, she played the world's second-ranked woman player, Arantxa Sanchez Vicario. Williams managed to win the first set and break Vicario's serve before losing the match two sets to one.

Williams played several tournaments during the 1995 season. She said that she hoped to compete on the pro circuit for ten years before going to college to study paleontology.

References Finn, "Only 14, But Groomed and Set To Be a Pro," *New York Times*, October 4, 1994, B12; Jenkins, "Venus Rising," *Sports Illustrated*, November 14, 1994, 30ff; Kirkpatrick, "Great Names, Great Games," *Newsweek*, January 2, 1995, 114–115; Kirkpatrick, "Tennis Life Begins Gloriously at 14," *New York Times*, November 2, 1994, B9, B10; Kirkpatrick, "Waiting Impatiently for Venus to Rise," *Newsweek*, September 12, 1994, 70–71.

Wills, Helen (b. 1905)

Tennis champion Helen Wills was born in Berkeley, California, on October 6, 1905. A recreational player as a child, she began to study the game seriously at age 14, while attending a Vermont boarding school. She reached the finals of the U.S. Open tournament when she was only 16.

By her late teens, Wills had become one of the top women players in the world. In 1924 she won both the U.S. ladies' singles title and the ladies' singles title at the 1924 Olympics, where she also captured the doubles' title with her partner Hazel Hotchkiss. Wills was the first American woman to win gold medals in both events at the same Olympics. During that time, she was an art major at the University of California and later graduated with high honors.

A strong hitter, Wills patterned her winning forehand stroke on that of a male champion named William Johnston. Wills was also known for her intense concentration and her lack of emotional displays during a match. She was sometimes called "Queen Helen" or "Little Miss Poker-Face." Wills explained, "When I play, I become entirely absorbed in the game."

As a champion athlete, Wills moved in high social circles. Once she was presented to Queen Mary at Buckingham Palace. Wills was also known for her sketches of tennis players, some of which were featured in magazines, and she also sold her fashion designs and drawings. In her leisure time, Wills painted and visited museums. She married stockbroker Frederick Shander Moody, Jr., in 1929. After they divorced ten years later, she married polo player Aidan Roark.

In all, Wills won seven U.S. singles titles, eight Wimbledon singles titles, and two doubles titles at each of those tournaments. She also won the French Open four times. In 1937, at age 32, Wills retired from professional tennis and pursued art and other activities, including writing her autobiography. In 1958, she was inducted into the International Tennis Hall of Fame.

References Condon, *Great Women Athletes of the Twentieth Century* (1991); Frayne, *Famous Women Tennis Players* (1979); Litsky, *Superstars* (1975); Wills, *Fifteen-Thirty* (1937).

Wimbledon

Called the All-England Tennis Tournament, the matches take place in Wimbledon, a small town outside of London. This prestigious annual international tennis tournament, which began as an amateur event in 1877, is one of four major tournaments a player must win during a year in order to achieve a Grand Slam.

The All-England Lawn Tennis and Croquet Club is one of the oldest existing lawn tennis sites. Courts at Wimbledon have a grass surface, which is fast-playing, and may favor players with an aggressive serve-and-volley game over those who prefer to hit groundstrokes from the baseline. The surface can also turn dry or bumpy, changing the bounce of the ball and other playing conditions—a factor that makes Wimbledon a particularly challenging tournament. Australian tennis great Roy Emerson once commented, "Wimbledon is fast and hard, but Wimbledon is sometimes a little slippery."

In 1968, the tournament became an "open," which meant that professionals could compete as well as amateurs. Events for women include the singles tournament and women's doubles and mixed doubles. Final matches and those of the top players are scheduled on the legendary Centre Court. There are 17 courts in all.

A number of American women have won titles at Wimbledon. As of 1995, the female player with the most Wimbledon victories was Martina Navratilova, with a total of 21 singles, doubles, and mixed doubles titles. Prior to 1990, Billie Jean King held that honor with a total of 19 titles.

See also Grand Slam; King, Billie Jean; Navratilova, Martina

References Collins and Hollander, *Bud Collins' Modern Encyclopedia of Tennis* (1995); McPhee, *Wimbledon* (1972).

Windsurfing

Some of the top U.S. women in the sport were from the Swatek family. Susie Swatek became the world champion, while her sister Lori won the American Championships, and Cheri became Junior Champion.

Winston World Championship (See Muldowney, Shirley)

Withington, Gerane (See Roller Skating)

Woman Bowler of the Year

This title is awarded annually to an American woman by the Bowling Writers Association of America. The record-holder for the honor was Marion Ladewig, who won the title nine times during the fifties and early sixties.

Women in the Martial Arts (WIMA)

Spearheaded by California martial artist Beth Austin, WIMA was founded in the

Five-time Wimbledon champ Billie Jean King crouches to reach the ball at the 1975 Wimbledon tournament. Begun as an amateur tournament, Wimbledon opened the competition to professionals as well as amateurs in 1968.

early 1970s. Austin, who was teaching women at the Venice California Women's Center, realized that women in the martial arts should be able to know each other. She sent letters to martial arts schools across America inviting interested women to contact her. Thirty women from different fields of martial arts became the first group, setting up a newsletter and meetings as well as some ongoing projects. WIMA organized demonstrations and workshops, which were attended by hundreds of interested women.

Women's Basketball League (WBL)
(**See** Basketball; Joyce, Joan; Lieberman, Nancy)

Women's Bowling World Cup (See Bowling)

Women's Golf Hall of Fame (See LPGA Hall of Fame)

Women's International Bowling Congress (WIBC)
The WIBC developed from the first women's bowling association, the Women's National Bowling Congress, which was formed in November 1916. Ellen Kelly of St. Louis, Missouri, was the major organizer and had gathered together about 40 women for a national championship in St. Louis. After the tournament, Dennis J. Sweeney, proprietor of the bowling center where the championship was held, suggested to the women that they form a national group as male bowlers had done.

The WIBC helps to organize groups of women bowlers throughout America. Along with the American Bowling Congress and American Junior Bowling Congress, it is regarded as one of the "Big Three" organizations governing the sport

of bowling. The three make up the largest ruling body for any sport in America and distribute about 2 million bowling awards, large and small, each year.

The WIBC was active during World War II, when it sponsored numerous exhibitions for military personnel and raised funds for wartime use. It purchased the *Miss WIBC*, a bomber presented to the U.S. Army Air Force on March 23, 1943, as well as an ambulance and some ambulance planes. American women enjoyed the sport of bowling during the war, and membership in the WIBC doubled during those years, to reach 252,540 by 1945. The WIBC continued to grow during the 1950s, as more middle-class women took up bowling and joined leagues that played during various times of the day. From 1945 to 1955, the number of leagues in the WIBC tripled, reaching 22,482. Owners of bowling centers said that women made up 40 to 50 percent of their clientele.

Members of the WIBC supply local bowling leagues with information, lists of rules, schedules for tournaments at the local and national levels, and material about the annual convention. Awards may be won for individual and team performance in the areas of high scoring, improved performance, and other achievements. A department of the WIBC is available to help settle disputes. By the 1990s, the WIBC had more than 4 million members.

Women's International Bowling Congress (WIBC) Hall of Fame
Established in 1953, the WIBC Hall of Fame is located in St. Louis, Missouri, along with the National Bowling Hall of Fame and American Bowling Congress Hall of Fame. Those nominated must have competed in at least 15 years of

WIBC tournaments and won at least one WIBC Queens title or one international title. WIBC officials, media representatives, and a 12-member committee made up of Hall of Fame members vote on potential inductees. In addition the athletes, some members are chosen for their meritorious service to women's bowling.

Women's Martial Arts Union (WMAU)

The first organization for women in this sport, the WMAU was founded in New York City by women involved in karate, judo, aikido, t'ai chi, and other martial arts, but attending different schools. One of the main goals of WMAU was to raise awareness of violence against women and to increase women's skills in self-defense. One of the founders, Annie Ellman, said, "Every time we fight back and resist attacks and violence, we help destroy the myth of women as passive and helpless and make the world safer for all women." Toward that end, WMAU published its *Guide to Self-Defense* (1973) and other helpful materials for women.

Members of the union conducted many demonstrations at schools, public events such as street fairs, television shows, and political rallies, among other places. Training sessions were conducted in cities across America. Through these demonstrations, interviews, and articles, they encouraged other women to take part in the martial arts. When WMAU disbanded in the late 1970s, there were thousands of women martial artists across the United States and an organized network of regular conferences and workshops. A number of union members went on to join the National Women's Martial Arts Federation when it was formed in 1981.

Women's Motoring Club (See Motoring Club, Women's)

Women's Olympic Games

In 1922, these Games were held in Paris under the auspices of the Fédération Sportive Féminine Internationale (FSFI). Besides the swimming, diving, tennis, and golf that had been events at other world competitions, the Women's Olympics featured track and field events. Women from the United States, France, and several other European countries took part in the 11 different events, before about 22,000 spectators. Controversy swirled around the inclusion of track and field events. To some physical educators in the United States, these sports were not appropriate for women and required them to dress in unacceptable ways. Also, some people disliked the fact that many working class women had taken up these sports and planned to compete in Paris. American Dr. Harry Stewart, a physical education teacher, asked the Amateur Athletic Association (AAA) and others to help organize the women track and field athletes for the Women's Olympics but they refused. Stewart then organized the National Track Athletic Committee for this purpose.

The name of this event was changed to Women's World Games in 1926. The International Amateur Athletic Federation (IAAF), which governed European men's track and field, decided it would develop rules for women's track as well. It convinced Alice Milliat, who had organized the 1922 women's games, to follow its guidelines for women competitors.

Women's Professional Softball League (WPSL)

In 1976, softball star Joan Joyce and tennis star Billie Jean King organized other athletes to form the WPSL, the first organized league that would pay women to play softball. The women also became team owners. Joyce took charge of the Connecticut Falcons, and King and golfer Jane Blalock also became owners. The league lasted until 1979.

Women's Sports Foundation

The foundation publishes *Women's Sports and Fitness* magazine. It also helps to fund sports teams for girls and provides legal assistance to female athletes fighting against sex discrimination in their schools. Annually it recognizes top athletes with awards such as the Professional Athlete of the Year Award, and it operates the Women's Sports Hall of Fame (see below).

Women's Sports Hall of Fame

Founded in 1980 by the Women's Sports Foundation, the hall honors both contemporary figures and pioneers in women's sports. Among the nine inductees the first year were pioneers Patty Berg, Amelia Earhart, Gertrude Ederle, Althea Gibson, Eleanor Holm, and Mildred "Babe" Didrikson Zaharias. The three contemporary inductees were Janet Guthrie, Billie Jean King, and Wilma Rudolph.

See also Berg, Patricia Ann; Didrikson Zaharias, Babe; Earhart, Amelia; Ederle, Gertrude; Gibson, Althea; Guthrie, Janet; Holm, Eleanor; King, Billie Jean; Rudolph, Wilma; Women's Sports Foundation

Women's Tennis Association (WTA)

In June 1973, at the Wimbledon tennis tournament, Billie Jean King assembled a group of top women players to organize the WTA. She proposed that the women band together to protest unfair playing conditions and unequal distribution of prize money and to negotiate better terms both for tournaments and for television rights and commercial endorsements. King had long been a top player and devoted a great deal of time to feminist causes and to improving opportunities for women in sports.

See also King, Billie Jean

Women's World Judo Championship

Open to women judo experts from around the world, this tournament was instigated by American Rusty Kanokogi. She served as tournament director and president of the organizing committee for the first championship, held in 1980 at Madison Square Garden in New York City. This first event lasted two days, and included women from 27 countries and 5 continents. The tournament made women judo artists more visible and contributed to the decision to add women's judo events to the Olympics in 1988.

See also Kanokogi, Rusty

womenSports

This magazine was founded by tennis champion Billie Jean King and her lawyer-businessman husband Larry King. First published in 1974, its goal was to cover women athletes and their achievements in greater detail than had ever been done by the other sports magazines, which focused on male athletes and male-dominated sports. Ahead of its time, *womenSports* folded within a few years but was the forerunner of a number of later magazines devoted to women's sports and fitness.

Woodard, Lynette (b. 1959)

Basketball player Lynette Woodard was a college superstar, leading the nation's college women in scoring, rebounding, and steals during her years at the University of Kansas. As of 1992, she was still the all-time leading scorer in NCAA women's basketball. The Wichita, Kansas, native racked up 3,649 points (more than star men's player Wilt Chamberlain) and averaged 26.3 points per game during her collegiate career. Her team won three consecutive Big Eight championships, and Woodard won the Wade Trophy as the most outstanding woman player of the year in 1981.

In 1980, Woodard was selected to play with the U.S. Olympic women's basketball team. Then President Carter decided that the United States would boycott the Games that year to protest the invasion of Afghanistan by Russia. Two years later, Woodard played on the American team that defeated Russian players, then captained the gold-medal winning U.S. team at the Olympic Games in Los Angeles in 1984. When the women's basketball league was formed in 1984, Woodard was the first free agent chosen by a team (Columbus, Ohio). In 1985, the Harlem Globetrotters team broke its all-male rule and invited Woodard to try out and then to join them. For two years, Woodard traveled throughout the country with the popular team, playing about 15 to 18 minutes per game. Fellow Globetrotters praised her fake shot, and teammate James Sanders said, "Globetrotters don't just play, they've got to have fun and project that fun into the crowd. Lynette really helps break the monotony. She comes to play, and she comes to have fun." As the only female member of team, Woodard had her own hotel room and a separate place to change into her uniform.

Woodard went on to play in Europe, as part of an Italian women's basketball league. In the early 1990s, she moved on to another continent to become one of Japan's most popular basketball stars.

References Hickok, *A Who's Who of Sports Champions* (1995); Lidz, "Is This Sweet Georgia Brown?" *Sports Illustrated,* January 6, 1986, 44–47.

Woodstra, Sue (b. 1957)

Volleyball player Woodstra distinguished herself as a great all-around player who could serve, set, and hit beautifully. At 16, she was asked to play on the U.S. junior team. In 1980, she was chosen captain of the U.S. women's volleyball team, on which she had played since 1978. In World Cup competition in 1981, the U.S. women came in fourth. She was also part of the North-Central and Caribbean American team that won the gold medal in 1981. With Woodstra on board, the U.S. women won a bronze medal at the 1983 world championships, then went on to capture the silver medal at the 1984 Summer Games in Los Angeles.

World Team Tennis (WTT)

The vision of women's champion Billie Jean King and her husband, lawyer-businessman Larry King, the WTT was developed in 1973 with Larry King as founder and vice president. The first teams began playing matches in 1974, with 16 American cities initially sponsoring teams. The WTT folded in its fifth season, 1978.

The WTT was reorganized and renamed TeamTennis, with Larry King as the chief executive officer. Under the team format, all players played doubles as well as singles. The team events differed from United States Tennis Association (USTA) events in that fans were encouraged to be verbal and noisy if they wished. TeamTennis has a five-week season each year from late June to early September. Top players such as Jimmy Connors, Martina Navratilova, and Tracy Austin have taken part.

See also King, Billie Jean

References Collins and Hollander, *Bud Collins' Modern Encyclopedia of Tennis* (1995); Davis, "World Team Tennis: It's Apples and Oranges for '78," *Tennis,* May 1978, 102; Sullivan, *Great Lives: Sports* (1988).

Wrestling

An ancient form of physical contact between opponents, wrestling was used to subdue an opponent as a means of self-defense or during an attack. Although physical strength was once the major test of a wrestler, athletes learned skills that enabled smaller opponents to defeat heavier, more muscular ones. Wrestling holds and positions can be seen in ancient Greek art and statuary, and wrestlers performed at Greek feasts and sporting contests. In 704 B.C. at the Olympics, wrestling was part of the pentathlon, a five-event competition designed to identify the best all-around athlete at the Games. Forms of wrestling were popular with Native Americans and in Asian countries. Gradually, the sport was refined through the Middle Ages and afterwards.

Despite the idea that this was clearly a man's sport, women have tried their skill at wrestling. In 1911, Bertha Rapp, a passenger on board a ship, announced that she would wrestle anyone aboard who thought they could defeat her. She proceeded to pin several men heavier than herself, with the last match ending in a draw. The secret to her success, said Miss Rapp, was "practice."

Arm-wrestling, a division of the sport, has female competitors. Californian Vicki Vodon gained the women's world arm-wrestling title during the 1970s. She later became a women's athletic trainer at the University of California.

References Gipe, *The Great American Sports Book* (1978).

Wright, Mickey (b. 1935)

A native of San Diego, California, Mary Kathryn (Mickey) Wright is considered one of the all-time greatest women golfers. Wright was an athletic child who reached her adult height of 5 feet 9 inches at age 11. Her father gave her four golf clubs, which she began using at home and on the golf course, and she filled a scrapbook with pictures of famous golfers. By age 12, she played well enough to score 100 on a full-sized course. She won her first tournament in 1949, earning the Southern California Girls' title. A year later, she hit a hole-in-one at a tournament in La Jolla, California. By age 19, Wright was golfing well enough to catch the eye of her childhood idol, champion athlete and golfer Babe Didrikson. Wright became the greatest woman golfer of her day, winning the All American and world amateur titles, among many others. She was known for her smooth, strong swing and calmness under pressure.

In 1954, Mickey Wright turned professional and proceeded to dominate women's golf for more than ten years. In 1958, 1959, 1961, and 1963, she won the U.S. Women's Open. In 1958, 1960, 1961, and 1963, she won the Ladies Professional Golf Association (LPGA) tournament. She also set a new record by winning both titles in three different years. From 1960 to 1964 she won the Vare Trophy. Her 1961 "grand slam" of women's golf included winning the Titleholders, U.S. Open, and LPGA tournaments. Two years later, she achieved the amazing average score of 72.81 strokes.

Wright set a new record in 1963 by winning 13 tournaments. She was named Athlete of the Year in both 1963 and in 1964, a year in which she finished one 18-hole course with a score of only 62, breaking the previous record of 64 set by Patty Berg. That year, Mickey Wright was inducted into the LPGA Hall of Fame.

At age 31, in 1966, Wright left professional golf to finish college at Southern Methodist University. Arthritis in her wrist had hurt her game. Yet three years later, she returned and won the Bluegrass Invitational Tournament. She competed during the early 1970s, after moving to Boca Raton, Florida, where the warm climate enabled her to enjoy her beloved golf year-round. Wright was renowned for her strong drives. She regularly hit drives that exceeded 225 yards, and one of her drives measured 272 yards.

Wright played fewer matches between 1960 and 1973, the year she retired, but she still garnered 82 LPGA titles in her career, giving her second place to Kathy Whitworth, who won her eighty-eighth title in 1988. She and Whitworth were the first to team up to compete in the Legends of Golf tournament.

Wright was named to the World Golf Hall of Fame in 1976 and to the Women's Sports Hall of Fame in 1981. Her talent brought more interest to her sport. In later years, champion Judy Rankin said that Wright "got the outside world to take a second hard look at women golfers, and when they looked they saw the rest of us." As a result, opportunities and prize money for women increased greatly after the 1960s.

References Benagh, *Incredible Athletic Feats* (1969); Hollander, *100 Greatest Women in Sports* (1976); *LPGA Media Guide* (1995); "Wright Hits a 62 for LPGA Title," *Sports Illustrated*, November 23, 1964, 83–85.

Wright, Shannon (See Racquetball)

Yachting (**See** America's Cup; Riley, Dawn; Sailing)

Yamaguchi, Kristi (b. 1971)
A native of Fremont, California, Kristi Tsuya Yamaguchi, a fourth-generation American of Japanese descent, took her first skating lessons at age six. Her family was delighted to see Kristi succeed in a sport, since she had been born with severely clubbed feet, requiring casts and special shoes during her first year of life. By age eight, the determined athlete had entered her first competition. Kristi had been inspired by Dorothy Hamill's exuberant, gold medal–winning performance at the 1976 Olympics, and her favorite toy during those years was a Dorothy Hamill doll. She later said that she dreamed of attaining that kind of success herself as she trained hard on the ice. Her rigorous schedule included rising each day at 4 a.m. in order to skate several hours before school.

At the junior level, Yamaguchi skated both in singles and in pairs competition. She and her partner Rudy Galindo won the world title for their age group in 1988. That same year, she captured the ladies' singles crown, the first time someone had won gold medals in two events at the world junior championships. In 1989, she again competed in both events, this time as a senior. Then 17, she placed second in the women's competition, and she and Galindo won the pairs. Moving on to the world championships in Paris, the two placed fifth, while Yamaguchi was judged sixth best woman skater in the world.

Yamaguchi continued to train hard, her sights set on the 1992 Olympic Games. She feared that at 20 years old, she might be too young to win. She cried out in joy when she received a perfect mark of 6.0 from one judge during the world ladies' competition in 1991, where she won her first world crown as a senior. "She listens and does pay attention," said coach Christy Ness, praising Yamaguchi's concentration. Yamaguchi worked hard to master tricky moves, like the triple-Lutz-triple-toe-loop combination.

In 1992 she achieved the women's triple crown: the U.S. women's title, followed by the Olympic gold medal, then the world title. All of the judges at the Olympics gave her the highest marks for her short program. Yamaguchi's long program included five triple jumps, and at the world championships, she landed an astonishing six. In both programs, she was the only woman skater to do a Lutz-to-toe-loop combination. Her performances were praised for combining athletic feats with artistry. Once again, the United States had a new ice queen as Yamaguchi became the first U.S. woman in 16 years to win the Olympic gold medal.

After the Games, Yamaguchi became a professional skater and appeared in ice shows, televised skating specials, and as a television sports commentator. She endorsed a variety of commercial products, including contact lenses and dairy products. At professional ice competitions, Yamaguchi continued to perform like a champion, winning the women's title at the World Professional Figure Skating Competition in 1995.

References *Current Biography Yearbook: 1992;* Hilgers, *Great Skates* (1991); Swift, "Stirring XVI Olympic Winter Games," *Sports Illustrated,* March 2, 1992, 16–21.

York-Romary, Janice Lee (b. 1928)

Fencing champion York-Romary was a member of six U.S. Olympic teams, from 1948 through 1968, and later worked on the organizing committee that helped plan the 1984 Los Angeles Olympic Games. A native of California, she graduated from the University of California at Los Angeles. In her first year as a member of the U.S. team (1948), it finished fifth at the world championships. In 1952 and 1956, York-Romary finished fourth among all competitors in the individual foil event at the Games.

When she competed at her sixth Olympiad in 1968, York-Romary set a women's record for taking part in that many consecutive Games in any sport. The record was not equaled until 1972, when discus thrower Lia Manoliu of Romania competed in her sixth consecutive Games. Another female fencer, Ellen Muller-Preis of Austria competed over the greatest span of years, from 1932 to 1956. During her fencing career, York-Romary won ten national championships and was a member of seven national championship teams.

At the Mexico City Olympics in 1968, York-Romary was chosen to bear the flag as the team marched into the Olympic stadium, the first woman to do so. She is honored with other top fencers in the Helms Hall of Fame.

References McWhirter, ed., *Guinness Book of World Records, 1988.*

Young, Candy (b. 1962)

Canzetta (Candy) Young amazed sports fans in 1979 when she set a new world record in the 60-yard hurdles, a track and field event. At the time, Young was only 16 years old.

Born in Beaver Falls, Pennsylvania, Young was one of nine children born to a minister and his wife, all of them involved in sports. She enjoyed baseball, basketball, football, softball, and gymnastics. Young later said that her early gymnastics training had been a tremendous help to her as a hurdler, teaching her how to control her body in the air. As a high school freshman, Young impressed her gym teacher by running the 50-yard dash in just 5.7 seconds. She joined the track team and tried the hurdles, quickly showing a natural ability in this event. She won the state hurdling championship at age 15. Since there was no real place to practice hurdling at her school, she and her coach devised a four-hurdle course (the actual course contains five hurdles) in a 50-foot-long corridor.

In 1978 Young attended a track and field development course at the U.S. Olympic Training Center in Colorado Springs, Colorado, and learned ways to improve her technique. At the 1979 Amateur Athletic Union (AAU) national track and field meet, one of Young's opponents was a college student named Deby LaPlante, who held the world record in hurdling. Pushing herself throughout the race, Young managed to finish in 7.50 seconds, a split second ahead of LaPlante. She had set a new world record.

After the meet, Young was invited to important national track and field events. To raise money for her expenses, the local newspaper sponsored a fund-raising drive. At the national outdoor championships that year, Young broke the 13-second barrier in the 100-yard hurdle event. At an international competition, she faced two of the world's top hurdlers, from the Soviet Union. Young crossed the finish line ahead of them both and was timed at 7.3 seconds in that 60-yard event. She was named best high school athlete in the United States in 1979.

Since the United States boycotted the 1980 Olympic Games, Young was not able to compete in track and field that year. She had her choice of scholarships to colleges and selected Farleigh Dickinson University in New Jersey, where one of the coaches was an expert hurdler.

Reference Stambler, *Women in Sports* (1975).

Young, Sheila (b. 1950)

Young became one of the few people to achieve world acclaim in both summer and winter sports. A world-class bicyclist, she also earned Olympic gold as a speed skater. Born in Birmingham, Michigan, she began skating at age two and shed her bike's training wheels at the early age of four. Both parents and her older brother Roger were champion cyclists, so it was natural that Sheila take up the sport. The family, which included four children, often went skating or bicycling together for fun. On weekends, the Youngs competed in races. As a high school student, Sheila won second place in the U.S. National Speed Skating Championships. She decided to train in earnest after graduation and moved to Milwaukee, Wisconsin, near the town of West Allis, which contained the only training rink the size of the official Olympic speed skating rink.

Her intense training paid off when 20-year-old Young won the U.S. National Outdoor and North American Outdoor Speed Skating titles in 1970. The next year, she won the U.S. title again. But at the 1972 Olympics, she was disappointed to barely miss a bronze medal, finishing fourth in the 500-meter race. A few weeks later, she won two 500-meter races at an international race in Sweden.

After that, Young devoted even more time, about four hours a day, to practicing and ran during the summer to build her strength and endurance. In 1973, she won the 500-meter sprint at the U.S. Women's Speed Skating Championship, setting a new world record time of 41.8 seconds. She competed in demanding track racing events for cyclists, too. At the 1973 World Spring Cycling contest, Young was injured when a neighboring cyclist bumped her bike, causing her to hit the cement wall. But after a 20-minute rest, she returned to the race and won— the first time in 50 years an American had won a world cycling event!

Another shot at Olympic glory came at the Winter Games of 1976. Temperatures at Innsbruck, Austria, were below freezing, but Young wore her skates over bare feet, a habit she said allowed her to "feel [her] skates better." In the 1,500-meter race, she won a silver, second-place medal. Then she tore a ligament before the next race began. Her left foot bandaged, Young skated the next day anyway and won the 500-meter race, breaking the previous Olympic record with a time of 42.76 seconds. In the 1,000 meter, she added a bronze medal to her collection. No American had ever won three medals in one Winter Olympics before Sheila Young's triumph.

After the 1976 Olympics, Young moved right on to cycling competitions, winning the U.S. National Sprint Championship and world title in Italy. She retired to marry Jim Ochowizc, and they settled in Wisconsin to raise three children. They enjoyed a variety of sports as a family—cross country skiing, ice skating, cycling, and roller blading. Young continued to stay involved in the world sports scene and worked on the committee that helped plan the Winter Games held in Lake Placid, New York, in 1980. Young has also worked in several capacities for the Special Olympics.

Yurchenko Vault

A complicated gymnastics routine named after Russian gymnast Natalia Yurchenko who developed it over a period of years and performed it at the 1983 world championships, winning the competition. The gymnast sprints down a runway, then does a roundoff onto a springboard placed about 4 feet from a stationary horse. The gymnast must land with both feet on the springboard, back facing the horse. Next, she leaps with arched back, similar to a backward dive, landing on her hands on the horse briefly before pushing off, twisting in the air, and landing on her feet. The Yurchenko may be done with a tucked full—a somersault in the air. It can also be performed with a full twisting layout in which the gymnast rotates in the air with a straight body.

The vault, while complex, became increasingly common at gymnastics meets during the 1980s. Kathy Johnson, a 1984 Olympian, later told journalist Joan Ryan, "Everybody felt like they had to do it, and they rushed it. It's not that hard to do, but if something goes wrong, it's a disaster. You need to be so confident with it and so competent that a mistake on it would only mean you'd land short and jam an ankle or whatever." Possible mistakes include missing the horse after leaping off the springboard or overshooting the board and slipping off the back.

Controversy intensified in 1988 after world-class gymnast Julissa Gomez fell while doing the vault in a competition in Japan. Gomez was paralyzed from the neck down and died a few years later. Yet supporters of this vault claim it may be safer for some gymnasts than certain other vaults, since it adds power they may not be able to generate on their own in the more traditional vaults.

Reference Ryan, *Little Girls in Pretty Boxes* (1995).

Zayak, Elaine (b. 1966)

Zayak, a native of Paramus, New Jersey, lost part of her foot in an accident with a lawnmower when she was just a toddler. But her talent was such that by age 15, she had won the U.S. national senior ladies' figure skating title. Her amazing performance included 18 jumps, 7 of them difficult triple jumps. Another brilliantly executed and challenging program brought her a world title in 1982. Her winning program included six triple jumps, setting a new record for women in competition. Two jumps were triple Salchows, and four were triple toe-loops, two of them in combinations.

A stress fracture prevented Zayak from defending her title at the 1983 world competition. With this injury came months of inactivity, and Zayak placed only third at the 1984 U.S. championships. Through determined hard work, she came back to finish third at the 1984 world competition.

Zayak then turned professional and electrified audiences with her performances in the Ice Capades. She is best known for her triple jumps, now a standard part of women's free skating performances. In response, skating officials established the Zayak Rule, which limits the number of repetitions of triple jumps in a skater's freestyle program. The rule aims to promote a balanced performance with attention to artistic dance movements, as well as more acrobatic ones, in figure skating.

Zayak became reinstated as an amateur so that she could compete in the 1994 championships. She received a standing ovation as she made a comeback, skating to the same music she had used for the 1984 Olympics. Although she had been out of competition for several years, the 28-year-old Zayak earned fourth place.

Zmeskal, Kim (b. 1975)

One of America's top gymnasts, Zmeskal won the world all-around title in 1991. She was expected to win a medal at the 1992 Olympic Games in Barcelona, Spain, but early in the competition, she fell off the balance beam and later made two uncharacteristic errors during her floor exercise. Losing a crucial tenth of a point for briefly crossing the boundary line by a couple inches, she moved down in the standings and finished tenth overall in a field of 36 gymnasts. The U.S. team finished third in that competition and won the bronze medal.

Critics watching the competition said that Zmeskal seemed underweight, tired, and in pain after having injured her left wrist. Commentators noted that the women's gymnastic team in general appeared worn out and overly thin, criticisms that had been surfacing more often during the early 1990s. Young Zmeskal spearheaded an effort to raise money for the medical expenses of fellow gymnast Christy Henrich, who was dying as a result of long-standing, severe eating disorders. In 1994, Zmeskal ended a two-year retirement to resume training with coach Bela Karolyi at his Houston gym.

At age 18, she was part of Karolyi's experiment to see if older gymnasts could successfully compete against the younger teens who had come to dominate women's gymnastics in the eighties and nineties.

References Ryan, *Little Girls in Pretty Boxes* (1995).

TIME LINE

776 B.C.	First Olympian Games: Women are banned from all events and are not permitted to watch the competition
Middle Ages	Women of the lower classes in Europe run footraces and play a game called stoolball at spring fairs; upper-class women ride horseback and sometimes hunt game
	Women also take part in informal archery contests but these are not sponsored by tradesmens' guilds as men's contests are
1800s	More women, mostly in the upper classes, take up croquet, archery, golf, and lawn tennis, sports deemed "suitable" for women
Mid-1800s	Catharine Beecher, director of girls' school in Hartford, Connecticut, advocates physical education/exercise for women; her program becomes a model for other schools
1851	Amelia Bloomer and her supporters suggest women wear wide pants beneath a loose-fitting dress; the "Bloomer Costume" gives many new freedom of movement
1856	Catharine Beecher publishes *Physiology and Calisthenics*, regarded as the first fitness book written for women
1866	Vassar Resolutes becomes the first women's college baseball team
1868	Women enter cycling races held in Bordeaux, France
1875	Teenage Agnes Beckwith creates public sensation by swimming six miles of the Thames River in London
1876	In New York City, marathon walker Mary Marshall defeats Peter Van Ness by winning two of three 20-mile races
1879	Women compete in the National Archery Contest, the first time American women take part in any national athletic competition
1880s	Women's baseball teams, the "Blues" and "Reds," (also called Blondes and Brunettes) play exhibition games in New York City, Philadelphia, and Newark, New Jersey

Time Line

1885	Mrs. M.C. Howell becomes the first U.S. women's archery champion, winning the first of her 16 national titles
1892	College women begin playing organized basketball, physical education teacher Senda Berenson of Smith College develops official set of rules for women's basketball
1895	First U.S. women's amateur golf championship is held, at Hempstead, New York
	Feminist Frances Willard publishes her bestseller, *A Wheel within a Wheel*, describing how she began riding a bicycle
1896	The first women's college basketball game is held, between teams from Stanford University and the University of California at Berkeley
Summer, 1896	Modern Olympic Games begin, in Athens, Greece; women are again barred from all competition, but a Greek woman, Melpomene, runs the 40-kilometer marathon unofficially
1900	At the Olympic Games in Paris, 19 women compete in tennis and golf events. Margaret Abbott of Chicago becomes America's first gold medalist, winning the golf competition
1901	Annie Edson Taylor, age 43, of Bay City, Michigan, becomes the first person to go over Niagara Falls in a barrel
1904	At the Olympic Games in St. Louis, women compete in archery as well as tennis events; all archery events are then dropped, to be reinstated in 1972
	Bertha Kapernick is the first woman to ride a bronco at the nation's top rodeo, Frontier Days in Cheyenne, Wyoming
1907	First women's bowling leagues are started in St. Louis, Missouri
1908	Thirty-six women compete at the Olympics in gymnastics, tennis, archery, and figure skating. Madge Syers of Great Britain wins first women's gold medal in figure skating
1910	Australian-born swimmer Annette Kellerman causes scandal by wearing a one-piece swimsuit, called "indecent," in Boston Harbor
1912	Swimming and diving events for women are added to the Olympic Games, held that year in Stockholm
1913	Georgia "Tiny" Broadwick becomes first woman to free-fall parachute from an airplane
1916	In St. Louis, Missouri, the first national women's bowling tournament is held
1917	Lucy Diggs Slowe wins women's American Tennis Association (ATA) championship, the first African-American woman to win a national title in any sport
1920	Women's 400-meter freestyle event is held at Olympics for first time; Ethelda Bleibtrey becomes America's first female swimming champion and the first person to win all swimming events at one Olympics

Time Line

	First women's springboard diving event is held at Olympics; U.S. women win all springboard diving medals from 1920 through 1948
1921	The first all-women Olympics, Jeux Feminins, is held in Paris; Alice Milliat and members of Femina Sport organize the Fédération Sportive Féminine Internationale (FSSI)
1922	FSSI sponsors international track and field competition for women in Paris
	Professor Constance Applebee helps to found the United States Field Hockey Association (USFA) in Philadelphia
1924	Winter Olympics debut in Chamonix, France, with events for women in figure skating (individual and pairs)
	Fencing is added to women's events in Summer Olympic Games
1926	Gertrude Ederle becomes first woman to swim English Channel (France to England), setting a new record for speed: 14 hours and 39 minutes
1927	Floretta McCutcheon, age 39, defeats top men's bowler Jimmy Smith in an exhibition match held in Denver, Colorado
1928	Women's track and field events featured for the first time at Olympic Games, held that year in Amsterdam, Holland
	American Betty Robinson wins the 100-meter dash, becoming the first women to win a gold medal in track and field at the Olympics
	Martha Norelius becomes first woman swimmer to win gold medals in two different Olympics (1924 and 1928)
1932	A women's speed skating exhibition is held at the Winter Olympics at Lake Placid, New York
	Mildred "Babe" Didrikson becomes the first woman to win medals in three events at the Olympics, held that year in Los Angeles
	Lillian Copeland wins discus throw, the first and only U.S. woman to win that event as of 1996
	Amelia Earhart becomes first woman pilot to fly solo across the Atlantic
	Two black women, Tidye Pickett and Louise Stokes, win spots on the Olympic track and field team but do not get to compete
1936	Women's alpine skiing is added to the Winter Olympics
	Sonja Henie of Norway becomes the first (and, as of 1996, the only) woman ever to win three Olympic gold medals in individual figure skating competition
	Track and field star Tidye Pickett, a hurdler, becomes the first African-American woman to compete in the Olympic Games

Time Line

1937	U.S. women compete in national cycling championships for the first time
1938	Tennis champion Helen Wills Moody wins a record eighth ladies' singles title at the Wimbledon tournament
1940	Californian Belle Martell becomes the first woman boxing referee, officiating eight matches in San Bernadino on May 2
1943	The All-American Girls Professional Baseball League is organized (1943–1954)
1944	Ann Curtis wins the James E. Sullivan Award, the first woman and first swimmer to receive this honor
1945	Associated Press (AP) names Babe Didrikson Zaharias "Woman Athlete of the Year," the first of four times she receives this honor; in 1951, the AP will name her "Sportswoman of the Half-Century"
1946	U.S. Ladies Professional Golfers Association (LPGA) is formed
1948	Gretchen Fraser becomes the first American to win a gold medal in an Olympic skiing event
	Alice Coachman becomes the first African-American woman to win a gold medal at the Olympics (in the high jump event)
1950	Althea Gibson becomes the first African-American woman admitted to the United States Lawn Tennis Association
1951	Florence Chadwick becomes the first person to swim the English Channel from England to France
1952	Winter Olympics: Andrea Mead Lawrence becomes the first American to win two gold medals in alpine skiing
	Summer Olympics: equestrian events are opened to women competitors for the first time
	American Pat McCormick wins a gold medal in both platform and springboard diving and will become the first to win a "double-double" after repeating this performance in 1956
	Patricia McCormick enters a fight in Juarez, Mexico, as the first woman bullfighter in North America
1952–1953	Maureen "Mo" Connolly becomes the first woman to win the Grand Slam of tennis
1953	African-American Toni Stone becomes the first woman to play on top-level professional mens' baseball team
1955	Women's basketball becomes part of Pan-American Games
1956	Tenley Albright becomes the first U.S. woman to win an Olympic gold medal in women's figure skating

Time Line

Girl's ice hockey becomes a high-school varsity sport in Minnesota

The Colorado Silver Bullets, an all-female professional baseball team, begins playing against men's semipro and minor league teams

1995   American skydiver Cheryl Stearns has now broken three world records: number of jumps in a 24-hour period, highest number of dead-center jumps in a 24-hour period, and highest number of jumps for women in a 24-hour period

An amateur women's soccer league is organized with 19 teams from across the United States

1996   An all-female team of commentators—Billie Jean King, Martina Navratilova, and Mary Carillo—covers women's matches at the All-England Tennis Championship (Wimbledon)

Summer Olympics, Atlanta, Georgia: Women's softball becomes an event for the first time; U.S. women's team wins the gold medal

U.S. women's gymnastic team wins first-ever Olympic team gold medal; Gymnast Shannon Miller becomes first U.S. woman to win gold medal in balance beam event

Women's soccer becomes part of the Olympics; U.S. team wins gold medal

Team synchronized swimming for eight swimmers replaces solo and duet events; U.S. team wins gold medal

Mary Ellen Clark wins her second consecutive bronze medal in platform diving; at age 34, Clark becomes the oldest American diver to win an Olympic medal

Beach (sand) volleyball, played by two-person teams, becomes a medal sport for both men and women

BIBLIOGRAPHY

Aasong, Nathan. *Florence Griffith Joyner: Dazzling Olympian*. Minneapolis, Minn.: Lerner, 1989.

_____ . *The Locker Room Mirror : How Sports Reflect Society*. New York: Walker and Company, 1993.

Anderson, Charles. *The New York News*, 21 August 1919: Editorial (From the Tuskegee Institute Archives, News Clippings).

Andersen, Gail Myers. *A World of Sports for Girls*. Philadelphia: Westminister Press, 1981.

Anderson, Dave. *The Story of Basketball*. New York: Morrow, 1988.

Appleton, Nancy. *Healthy Bones*. Garden City, N.Y.: Avery Publishing Group, 1991.

Ashe, Arthur. *A Hard Road to Glory: A History of the African-American Athlete Since 1946*. New York: Warner Books, 1988.

Associated Press Sports Staff. *The Sports Immortals: Fifty of Sports All-Time Greats*. Englewood Cliffs, N.J.: Prentice Hall, 1972.

Atkinson, Linda. *Women in the Martial Arts: A New Spirit Rising*. New York: Dodd Mead, 1983.

Austin, Tracy. *Beyond Center Court*. New York: William Morrow, 1992.

Baker, William J., and S. A. Mangan, eds. *Sport in Africa*. New York: Africana, 1987.

Banta, Martha. *Imaging American Women*. New York: Columbia University Press, 1987.

Barnes, Mildred J. *Women's Basketball*. Boston, Mass.: Allyn & Bacon, 1980.

Barrett, Norman. *Dragsters*. New York: Franklin Watts, 1987.

Bass, Howard. *The Love of Ice Skating and Speed Skating*. New York: Crescent, 1980.

Bateman, Hal. *United States Track and Field Olympians, 1896–1980*. Indianapolis: Athletics Congress of the United States, 1984.

Bellamy, Rex. *Game, Set, and Deadline*. London: Kingswood, 1986.

Benagh, Jim. *Incredible Athletic Feats*. New York: Hart, 1969.

Benoit, Joan, with Sally Baker. *Running Tide*. New York: Knopf, 1987.

Benoit, Joan, with Gladys Klufelt. *Running for Life*. Rodale, Pa.: Rodale Press, 1995.

Berke, Art, ed. *Lincoln Library of Sports Champions*. Columbus, Ohio: Frontier Press, 1989.

Berliner, Don. *The World Aerobatics Championships*. Minneapolis, Minn.: Lerner, 1989.

Bike World Magazine. *All About Bicycle Racing*. Mountain View, Calif.: World Publications, 1975.

Biracree, Tom. *Wilma Rudolph*. New York: Chelsea House, 1988.

Blais, Madelaine H. *In These Girls, Hope Is a Muscle*. New York: Atlantic Monthly Press, 1995.

Blue, Adrianne. *Grace under Pressure: The Emergence of Women in Sport*. London: Sidgwick and Johnson, 1987.

_____ . *Faster, Higher, Further: Women's Triumphs and Disasters at the Olympics*. London: Virago, 1988.

Boehm, David A., et al. *Guinness Sports Record Book 1989–90*. New York: Sterling, 1990.

Boggan, Tim. *History of U.S. Table Tennis*, vol. 1., 1996.

Bontemps, Arna. *Famous Negro Athletes*. New York: Dodd, Mead, 1964.

Boothroyd, John, et al. *The Book of Windsurfing*. New York: Van Nostrand, 1980.

Bibliography

Bortstein, Larry. *After Olympic Glory: The Lives of Ten Outstanding Medalists.* New York: Frederick Warne, 1987.

Boutilier, Mary A., and Lucinda SanGiovanni. *The Sporting Woman.* Champaign, Ill.: Human Kinetics, 1983.

Brasch, R. *How Did Sports Begin?* New York: David McKay, 1970.

Brooks-Pazmany, Kathleen. *United States Women in Aviation 1919–1929.* Washington, D.C.: Smithsonian Institution, 1983.

Brown, Fern G. *Special Olympics.* New York: Franklin Watts, 1992.

Brown, Gene. *The Complete Book of Baseball.* New York: Arno Press, 1980.

Bulger, Margary A. *The Sporting Image.* New York: University Press of America, 1988.

Burek, Deborah M., ed. *Encyclopedia of Associations.* 3 vols. 27th ed. New York: Gale Research, 1993.

Cahn, Susan K. *Coming On Strong: Gender and Sexuality in Twentieth-Century Women's Sport.* New York: Free Press (Macmillan), 1994.

Campbell, Gail. *Marathon: The World of the Long Distance Athlete.* New York: Sterling, 1977.

Campbell, Malcolm. *The Random House International Encyclopedia of Golf.* New York: Random House, 1991.

Carlson, Lewis H., and John J. Fogarty. *Tales of Gold: An Oral History of the Olympic Games As Told by America's Gold Medal Winners.* Chicago: Contemporary Books, 1987.

Carruth, Gordon, and Eugene Ehrlich. *Facts & Dates of American Sports.* New York: Harper & Row, 1988.

Casewit, Curtis W. *The Complete Book of Mountain Sports.* New York: Messner, 1978.

Cavallo, Dominick. *Muscles and Morals: Organized Playgrounds and Urban Reform: 1880–1920.* Philadelphia: University of Pennsylvania Press, 1981.

Chambliss, Daniel F. *Champions: The Making of Olympic Swimmers.* New York: William Morrow, 1988.

Chew, Peter. *The Kentucky Derby: The First 100 Years.* Boston, Mass.: Houghton, 1974.

Clark, Judith Freeman. *Almanac of American Women in the 20th Century.* New York: Prentice Hall, 1987.

Coffey, Wayne R. *Comeback: True Stories of Incredible Determination.* Middletown, Conn.: Weekly Reader Books, 1985.

Collet, Glenna. *Golf for Young Players.* New York: Harper & Row, 1926.

_____ . *Ladies in the Rough.* London, New York: A. A. Knopf, 1928.

Collins, Bud, and Zander Hollander, eds. *Bud Collins' Modern Encyclopedia of Tennis.* Detroit, Mich.: Gale Research, 1994.

Collins, Patricia Hill. *Black Feminist Thought.* Boston, Mass.: Unwin Hyman, 1990.

Condon, Robert J. *Great Women Athletes of the Twentieth Century.* Jefferson, N.C.: McFarland, 1991.

Cook, Jeff. *The Triathletes: A Season in the Life of Four Women in the Toughest Sport of All.* New York: St. Martin's Press, 1992.

Coombs, Charles. *Drag Racing.* New York: Morrow, 1970.

_____ . *Auto Racing.* New York: Morrow, 1971.

Cooper, Courtney Ryley. *Annie Oakley: Woman at Arms.* 1927.

Cooper, Michael. *Racing Sled Dogs: An Original North American Sport.* New York: Clarion, 1988.

Cotton, Henry. *A History of Golf, Illustrated.* Philadelphia, Pa.: Lippincott, 1975.

Dannett, Sylvia G. *Profiles of Negro Womanhood.* Yonkers, N.Y.: Educational Heritage, 1966.

Dater, Judy, and Carolyn Coman. *Body and Soul: Ten American Women.* Boston, Mass.: Hill, 1988.

Davis, Mac. *101 Greatest Sports Heroes.* New York: Grosset and Dunlap, 1954.

Davis, Marianna. *American Women in Olympic Track and Field: A Complete Illustrated Reference.* Jefferson, N.C.: McFarland, 1992.

Davis, Michael B. *Black American Women in Olympic Track and Field.* Jefferson, N.C.: McFarland, 1992.

de Koven, Anna. "The Athletic Woman," *Good Housekeeping,* August 1912; 151–152.

Dickey, Glenn. *Champs and Chumps: An Insider's Look at Today's Sports Heroes.* San Francisco, Calif.: Chronicle Books, 1976.

Didrikson Zaharias, Babe, with Harry Paxton. *This Life I've Led.* New York: A.S. Barnes, 1955.

Dolan, Edward F. *Dorothy Hamill: Olympic Skating Champion.* New York: Doubleday, 1979.

_____ . *Great Moments at the Indy 500.* New York: Doubleday, 1982.

Dolan, Edward and Richard Lyttle. *Janet Guthrie.* Garden City, NY: Doubleday, 1978.

Dorsey, Frances, and Wendy Williams. *Creative*

Bibliography

Ice Skating. New York: Contemporary Books, 1980.

Duffy, Tony and Paul Wade. *Winning Women.* New York: Times Books, 1983.

Durant, John. *Highlights of the Olympics from Ancient Times to the Present.* New York: Hastings House, 1977.

Durant, John, and Otto Bettman. *Pictorial History of American Sports from Colonial Times to the Present.* New York: A.S. Barnes, 1952.

Earhart, Amelia. *The Fun of It.* New York: Brewer, Warrer & Putnam, 1932.

Elliott, Jill, and Martha Ewing, eds. *Youth Softball: A Complete Handbook.* Dubuque, Iowa: Brown and Benchmark, 1992.

Engelmann, Larry. *The Goddess and the American Girl: The Story of Suzanne Lenglen and Helen Wills.* New York: Oxford University Press, 1988.

Fitzgibbon II, Herbert S., and Jeffrey N. Bairstow. *The Complete Racquet Sports Player.* New York: Simon and Schuster, 1980.

Flint, Rachel H., and Netta Rheinberg. *The Story of Women's Cricket.* London: Angus and Robertson, 1976.

Forsee, Alylesa. *Women Who Reach for Tomorrow.* Philadelphia: Macrae Smith, 1960.

Frayne, Thomas. *Famous Tennis Players.* New York: Dodd, Mead, 1977.

Froissard, Jane, and Lily Powell Froissard, eds. *The Horseman's International Book of Reference.* New York: Metheun, 1980.

Gallico, Paul. *Farewell to Sport.* New York: Knopf, 1938.

Garfield, Elizabeth A. *The Wilson Report: Moms, Dads, Daughters and Sports.* Los Angeles, Calif.: Women's Sports Foundation, 1988.

Gattey, Charles Nelson. *The Bloomer Girls.* New York: Coward-McCann, 1967.

Gault, Frank, and Clare Gault. *Stories from the Olympics.* New York: Walker, 1976.

Gault, Jim, with Jack Grant. *The World of Women's Gymnastics.* Millbrae, Calif.: Celestial Arts, 1976.

Gelman, Steve. *Young Olympic Champions.* New York: Norton, 1964.

Gerber, Ellen W. *Innovators and Institutions in Physical Education,* Philadelphia: Lea Fabiger, 1971.

_____ , ed. *The American Woman in Sport.* Lexington, Ken.: Addison Wesley, 1974.

Gibson, Althea. *So Much To Live For.* New York: Putnam, 1968.

Gilbert, Dave. *The American Bicycle Atlas.* New York: Dutton, 1981.

Gipe, George. *The Great American Sports Book.* Garden City, N.Y.: Doubleday, 1978.

Glenn, Rhonda. *The Illustrated History of Women's Golf.* Dallas, Tex.: Taylor, 1991.

Gluck, Berna. *Rosie the Riveter Revisited: Women, the War, and Social Change.* New York: Rawson, Wade, 1979.

Goerner, Fred. *The Search for Amelia Earhart.* New York: Doubleday, 1968.

Golf Magazine editors. *Golf in America: The First Hundred Years.* New York: Harry N. Abrams, 1981.

Green, Carl R. *Jackie Joyner-Kersee.* New York: Crestwood House, 1995.

Green, Tina Sloan, et al. *Black Women in Sport.* Reston, Va.: American Alliance for Health, Physical Education, Recreation, and Dance (AAHPERD), 1981.

Greenberg, Stan. *The Guinness Book of Olympics Facts and Feats.* Enfield, Middlesex, England: Guinness Superlatives, 1983.

Gregorich, Barbara. *Women at Play: The Story of Women in Baseball.* New York: Harcourt Brace & Company, 1993.

Gregory, Howard. *Parachuting's Unforgettable Jumps.* Rolando Beach, Calif.: Howard Gregory Associates, 1986.

Grimsley, Will. *Golf: Its History, People, and Events.* New York: Prentice-Hall, 1966.

_____ . *Tennis: Its History, People, and Events.* New York: Prentice, 1971.

_____ . *101 Greatest Athletes of the Century.* New York: Crown, 1987.

Gutman, Bill. *Modern Women Superstars.* New York: Dodd, Mead, 1978.

_____ . *More Modern Women Superstars.* New York: Dodd, Mead, 1979.

Guttman, Allen. *From Ritual to Record: The Nature of Modern Sports.* New York: Columbia University Press, 1979.

_____ . *The Games Must Go On.* New York: Columbia University Press, 1984.

_____ . *A Whole New Ball Game.* Chapel Hill: University of North Carolina Press, 1988.

_____ . *Women's Sport: A History.* New York: Columbia University Press, 1991.

_____ . *The Olympics: A History of the Modern Games.* University of Illinois Press, 1992.

Haley, Bruce. *The Healthy Body and Victorian Culture.* Cambridge, Mass.: Harvard University Press, 1978.

Bibliography

Hamill, Dorothy, with Elva Clairmont. *Dorothy Hamill On and Off the Ice*. New York: Knopf, 1983.

Hamner, Trudy. *The All-American Girls Professional Baseball League*. New York: Macmillan, 1995.

Haney, Lynn, and Bruce Curtis. *Show Rider*. New York: G.P. Putnam's, 1982.

Harris, Barbara J. *Beyond Her Sphere: Women and the Professions in American History*. Westport, Conn.: Greenwood Press, 1978.

Havighurst, Walter. *Annie Oakley of the Wild West*. Lincoln: University of Nebraska Press, 1992.

Haycock, Kate. *Gymnastics*. New York: Crestwood House, 1993.

Haylett, John, and Richard Evans. *The Illustrated Encyclopedia of Tennis*. New York: Exeter Books, 1989.

Helmer, Diana. *Belles of the Ballpark*. Brookfield, Conn.: Millbrook Press, 1993.

Henderson, Edward B. *The Negro in Sports*. rev. ed. Washington, D.C.: Associated Publishers, 1939.

Henie, Sonja. *Wings on My Feet*. New York: Prentice Hall, 1940.

Hickok, Ralph. *Who Was Who in American Sports*. New York: Hawthorn Books, 1971.

_____ . *New Encyclopedia of Sports*. New York: McGraw Hill, 1977.

_____ . *A Who's Who of Sports Champions, Their Stories and Records*. Boston, Mass.: Houghton Mifflin, 1995.

Higden, Hal. *Boston: A Century of Running, Celebrating the 100th Anniversary of the Boston Marathon*. Emmaus, Pa.: Rodale Press, 1995.

Hilgers, Laura. *Great Skates*. Boston, Mass.: Little Brown, 1991.

Hollander, Phyllis. *American Women in Sports*. New York: Grosset and Dunlap, 1972.

_____ . *100 Greatest Women in Sports*. New York: Grosset and Dunlap, 1976.

Hollander, Zander, ed. *The Modern Encyclopedia of Basketball*. Garden City, N.Y.: Doubleday, 1979.

Hoose, Philip M. *Necessities: Racial Barriers in American Sports*. New York: Random House, 1989.

Hovis, Ford, ed. *Tennis for Women*. New York: Doubleday, 1973.

Howell, Reet, ed. *Her Story in Sport*. West Point, N.Y.: Leisure Press, 1982.

Huey, Linda. *A Running State*. New York: Quadrangle Books, 1976.

Hult, Joan S. and Marianna Trekell, eds. *A Century of Women's Basketball: From Frailty to Final Four*. Reston, VA: American Alliance for Health, Physical Education, Recreation, and Dance, 1991.

Humiston, Dorothy, and Dorothy Michel. *Fundamentals of Sports for Girls and Women*. New York: Ronald Press, 1965.

Jacobs, Helen Hull. *Beyond the Game*. London: J. B. Lippencott Company, 1936.

Jacobs, Linda. *Wilma Rudolph: Run for Glory*. St. Paul, Minn.: Eric, 1975.

Jarrett, William. *Timetables of Sports History: The Olympic Games*. New York: Facts On File, 1990.

Jenner, Bruce. *Bruce Jenner's Guide to the Olympics*. Kansas City, Mo.: Andrews and McMeel, 1979.

Johnson, Arthur T., and James Frey, eds. *Government and Sport*. Totowa, N.J.: Rowman and Allenheld, 1985.

Jones, Tim. *The Last Great Race*. (Iditarod) Seattle: Madrona Publishers, 1982.

Kaplan, Janice. *Women and Sports: Inspiration and Information about the New Female Athlete*. New York: Viking, 1979.

Keane, Christopher, and Herman Petras. *Handbook of the Martial Arts and Self-Defense*. New York: Harper, 1983.

Keeley, Steve. *The Complete Book of Racquetball*. Northfield, Ill.: DBI Books, 1976.

Kidwell, C., and V. Steele, eds. *Men and Women: Dressing the Part*. Washington, D.C.: Smithsonian Institution Press, 1989.

Kierens, John, et al. *The Story of the Olympic Games*. New York: Lippincott, 1977.

Killanin, Lord, and John Rudd. *The Olympic Games*. New York: Macmillan, 1976.

King, Billie Jean, with Frank Deford. *Billie Jean*. New York: Viking, 1982.

Kircksmith, Tommie. *Ride Western Style: A Guide for Young Riders*. New York: Macmillan, 1991.

Knudsen, R. R. *Babe Didrikson, Athlete of the Century*. New York: Viking, 1985.

_____ . *Martina Navratilova: Tennis Power*. New York: Viking, 1986.

Krone, Julie. *Riding for My Life*. Boston: Little, Brown, 1995.

Krout, John Allen. *Annals of American Sport*. New Haven, Conn.: Yale University Press, 1929.

Ladies Professional Bowlers Tour. *1994 LPBT Guide*. 1994.

Ladies Professional Golf Association. *LPGA 1996 Player Guide*. Daytona Beach, Fla.: LPGA, 1996.

Ladies Professional Golf Association. *LPGA Media Guide*. Daytona Beach, Fla.: LPGA, 1995.

Bibliography

Laklan, Carli. *Competition Swimming: The Training Way to Championship.* New York: Hawthorn Books, 1965.

Lanker, Brian. *I Dream a World: Portraits of Black Women Who Changed America.* New York: Stewart, Tabori, & Chang, 1989.

Lardner, Ring. *The Legendary Champions.* Toronto, Canada: McGraw Hill, 1972.

Lawrence, Andrea Mead. *A Practice of Mountains.* New York: Seaview Books, 1980.

Leamer, Laurence. *The Kennedy Women: The Saga of an American Family.* New York: Villard, 1994.

Leder, Jane. *Grace and Glory: A Century of Women at the Olympics.* Washington, D.C.: Multi Media Partners, 1996.

Lee, Mabel. *A History of Physical Education and Sports in the United States.* New York: John Wiley and Sons, 1983.

Lenskyj, Helen. *Out of Bounds: Women, Sport, & Sexuality.* Toronto: Women's Press, 1986.

Lerch, Harold A. *History of American Physical Education and Sport.* Springfield, Ill.: Charles C. Thomas, 1981.

Lerner, Gerda. *The Woman in American History.* Menlo Park, Calif: Addison Wesley, 1971.

Levine, Susan, and Harriet Lyons, eds. *The Decade of Women: A Ms. History of the Seventies in Words and Pictures.* New York: Paragon, 1980.

Lichtenstein, Grace. *A Long Way, Baby: Behind the Scenes in Women's Pro Tennis.* New York: William Morrow, 1974.

Liebers, Arthur. *The Complete Book of Sky Diving.* New York: Coward McCann, 1968.

Litsky, Frank. *Superstars.* Secaucus, N.J.: Derbibooks, 1975.

_____ . *Winners on the Ice.* New York: Franklin Watts, 1979.

Litsky, Jim. *The Winter Olympics.* New York: Franklin, Watts, 1979.

Littlefield, Jim. *Champions: Stories of Ten Remarkable Athletes.* Boston, Mass.: Little, Brown, 1993.

Livingston, Bernard. *Their Turf: America's Horsey Set and Its Princely Dynasties.* New York: Arbor, 1973.

Lobo, Ruth Ann, and Rebecca Lobo. *The Home Team: Of Mothers and Daughters and American Champions.* New York: Kodansha America, 1996.

Longrigg, Roger. *The History of Horse Racing.* New York: Stein & Day, 1972.

Lucas, John. *The Modern Olympic Games.* New York: A.S. Barnes, 1980.

Lucas, John, and Ronald Smith. *Saga of American Sport.* Philadelphia, Pa.: Lea and Febiger, 1978.

Lundgren, Hal. *Mary Lou Retton: Gold Medal Gymnast.* Chicago: Children's Press, 1985.

Lynn, Janet. *Peace and Love.* Carol Stream, Ill.: Creation House, 1975.

McCane, Fred, and Cathrine Wolf. *Winning Women: Eight Great Athletes and Their Unbeatable Stories.* New York: Bantam, 1995.

_____ . *The Worst Day I Ever Had.* Boston, Mass.: Little, Brown, 1991.

McPhee, John. *Wimbledon: A Celebration.* New York: Viking, 1972.

McWhirter, et al. *1986 Guinness Book of World Records*, 1986.

Macy, Sue. *A Whole New Ball Game.* New York: Henry Holt, 1993.

_____ . *Winning Ways: A Photohistory of American Women in Sports.* New York: Henry Holt, 1996.

Mallon, Bill, and Ian Buchanan. *Quest for Gold: The Encyclopedia of American Olympians.* New York: Leisure Press, 1984.

Mandell, Richard D. *The Nazi Olympics.* New York: Macmillan, 1971.

_____ . *Sport: A Cultural History.* New York: Columbia University Press, 1984.

Manning, Madeline Jackson. *Running for Jesus.* Waco, TX: Word Books, 1977.

Marble, Alice. *The Road to Wimbledon.* New York: C. Scribner's Sons, 1946.

Markel, Robert, et al. *For the Record: Women in Sports.* New York: World Almanac Publications, 1985.

Marshall, John L., and Heather Barbash. *The Sports Doctor's Fitness Book for Women.* New York: Delacourte, 1981.

Mendenhall, Thomas C. *A Short History of American Rowing.* Boston, Mass.: Charles River, 1980.

Menke, Frank G. *The Encyclopedia of Sports.* New York: A.S. Barnes, 1963.

Meserole, Mike, ed. *The 1995 Information Please Sports Almanac.* Boston, Mass.: Little, Brown, 1995.

Meyer, Gladys C. *Softball for Girls.* New York: Scribner, 1982.

Michener, James. *Sports in America.* New York: Ballantine, 1976.

Minton, Robert. *Forest Hills: An Illustrated History.* New York: Lippincott, 1975.

Moffett, Martha. *Great Women Athletes.* New York: Platt and Munk, 1974.

Bibliography

Mohr, Merilyn Simonds. *The Games Treasury.* Shelburne, Vt.: Chapters Publishing, 1993.

Murray, Tom, ed. *Sport Magazine's All Time All-Stars.* New York: Atheneum, 1977.

Myers, Gail Anderson. *A World of Sports for Girls.* Philadelphia, Pa.: Westminster, 1981.

Navratilova, Martina, with George Vecsey. *Martina.* New York: Knopf, 1985.

Navratilova, Martina. *Tennis My Way.* New York: Scribner, 1983.

Needham, Richard. *Ski: Fifty Years in North America.* New York: Harry N. Abrams, 1987.

Nelson, Mariah Burton. *Are We Winning Yet? How Women Are Changing Sports and Sports Are Changing Women.* New York: Random House, 1991.

Nielsen, Nicki J. *The Iditarod: Women on the Trail.* Anchorage, Alaska: Wolfdog, 1986.

1995 Fact Book: United States Olympic Committee. New York: United States Olympic Committee, 1995.

Norris, Ty, ed. *1994 Winston Cup Media Guide.* Winston-Salem, N.C.: NASCAR Winston Cup Series, 1994.

Noverr, Douglas A. and Lawrence E. Ziewacz. *The Games They Played: Sports in American History: 1865–1980.*

NWO: A Directory of National Women's Organizations. New York: National Council for Research on Women, 1992.

Nyad, Diana. *Other Shores.* New York: Random House, 1978.

Oates, Joyce Carol. *On Boxing.* New York: Doubleday, 1987.

O'Brien, Andy. *The Daredevils of Niagara.* New York: Ryerson Press, 1964.

Oglesby, Carole A., ed. *Women and Sport: From Myth to Reality.* Philadelphia. Pa.: Lea & Febiger, 1978.

Okrent, Daniel, and Harris Levine, eds. *The Ultimate Baseball Book.* Boston, Mass.: Houghton Mifflin, 1979.

Olney, Ross. *The Young Sportsman's Guide to Surfing.* New York: Thomas Nelson, 1965.

_____. *Modern Drag Racing Superstars.* New York: Dodd, Mead, 1981.

Olney, Ross R., and Chan Bush. *Roller Skating!* New York: Lothrop, Lee, and Shepard, 1979.

Olsen, James T. *Billie Jean King: The Lady of the Court.* Mankato, Minn.: Creative Education, 1974

Pachter, Marc, et al. *Champions of American Sport.* New York: Harry N. Abrams, 1981.

Page, James. *Black Olympian Medalists.* Englewood, Colo.: Libraries Unlimited, 1991.

Parsons, Terry. *Canopy Relative Work.* DeLand, Fla.: Skydiving Book Service, 1983.

Peppler, Mary Jo. *Inside Volleyball for Women.* Chicago, Ill.: Henry Regnery, 1977.

Peterson, Robert P. *Only the Ball Was White.* Englewood Cliffs, N.J.: Prentice-Hall, 1970.

Peterson, Susan Goldner. *Self-Defense for Women.* New York: Scribners, 1984.

Pizer, Vernon. *Glorious Triumphs.* New York: Dodd, Mead, 1980.

Podhojsky, Alois. *The Art of Dressage.* New York: Doubleday, 1976.

Postema, Pam, with Gene Wojciechowski, *You've Got to Have Balls to Make It in This League: My Life as an Umpire.* New York: Simon and Schuster, 1992.

Poynter, Dan. *Parachuting: The Skydiver's Handbook.* Santa Barbara, Calif.: Para Publishing, 1989.

Pratt, John Lowell, and Jim Benagh. *The Official Encyclopedia of Sports.* New York: Franklin Watts, 1964.

Quercetani, Roberto. *Athletics: A History of Modern Track and Field, 1860–1990.* Milan, Italy: Vallardi & Associati, 1990.

Rader, Benjamin G. *American Sports: From the Age of Folk Games to the Age of Televised Sports.* 2d. ed. Englewood Cliffs, N.J.: Prentice Hall, 1990.

Randolph, Blythe. *Amelia Earhart.* New York: Franklin Watts, 1987.

Rapport, Ron, ed. *A Kind of Grace: A Treasury of Sportswriting by Women.* Berkeley, CA: Zenobia Press, 1994.

Read, Phyllis, and Bernard L. Witlieb. *The Book of Women's Firsts.* New York: Random House, 1992.

Reeder, Amy L., and John R. Fuller. *Women in Sport.* Carrollton, Ga.: West Georgia College, 1985.

Reno, Ottie W. *The Story of Horseshoes.* New York: Vantage Press, 1963.

Riegel, Robert Edgar. *American Feminists.* Lawrence: University of Kansas Press, 1963.

Riviere, Bill. *Pole, Paddle, and Portage.* New York: Van Nostrand Reinhold, 1975.

Roggensack, David. *The Wonderful World of Roller Skating.* Everest, 1980.

Ross, John M., et al., eds. *Golf Magazine's Encyclopedia of Golf.* New York: Harper, 1979.

Rothman, Sheila M. *Woman's Proper Place.* New York: Basic Books, 1978.

Rudolph, Wilma, with Martin Ralbovsky. *Wilma:*

Bibliography

The Story of Wilma Rudolph. New York: New American Library, 1977.

Rush, Cathy, with Lawrie Mifflin. *Women's Basketball*. New York: Hawthorn Books, 1976.

Rust, Edna, and Art Rust. *Art Rust's Illustrated History of the Black Athlete*. New York: Doubleday, 1985.

Ryan, Joan. *Contributions of Women: Sports*. Minneapolis, Minn.: Dillon Press, 1975.

_____ . *Little Girls in Pretty Boxes: The Making and Breaking of Elite Gymnasts and Figure Skaters*. New York: Doubleday, 1995.

Saunders, William. *Parachuting Complete*. Santa Barbara, Calif.: Para Publishing, 1966.

Savage, Jeff. *Kristi Yamaguchi: Pure Gold*. Columbus, Ohio: Dillon Press, 1993.

Scarff, ed. *Golf Magazine's Encyclopedia of Golf*. New York: Harper & Row, 1970.

Schaap, Richard. *An Illustrated History of the Olympics*. New York: Alfred Knopf, 1963.

_____ . *The Official USOC Book of the 1984 Olympic Games*. New York: Random House/ABC Sports, 1984.

Scherman, Barbara, and Carol Hurd Green, eds. *Notable American Women: The Modern Period*. Cambridge, Mass.: Belknap Press, 1980.

Schultz, Jeff, and Bill Sherwonit. *Iditarod, The Last Great Race*. Bothell, Wash.: Alaska Northwest Books, 1991.

Scott, Tom, and Geoffrey Cousins. *The Golf Immortals*. New York: Hart, 1968.

Sellick, Bud. *The Wild, Wonderful World of Parachutes and Parachuting*. New York: Prentice, 1981.

Shangold, Mona, and Gabe Mirkin. *The Complete Sports Medicine Book for Women*. New York: Simon and Schuster, 1985.

Shields, Mary. *Sled Dog Trails*. Fairbanks, Alas.: Pyrola Publishing, 1984.

Sicherman, Barbara, Carol Hurd Green, Ilene Kantrove, and Harriette Walker, eds. *Notable American Women: The Modern Period*. Cambridge, Mass: Harvard University Press, 1980.

Silver, Caroline. *Eventing: The Book of the Three Day Event*. New York: Collins, 1976.

Silverstein, Herma. *Mary Lou Retton and the New Gymnasts*. New York: Franklin Watts, 1985.

Ski Magazine editors. *Ski Magazine's Encyclopedia of Skiing*. New York: Harper, 1979.

Smith, Beatrice S. *The Babe: Mildred Didrikson Zaharias*. Milwaukee, Wisc.: Raintree, 1976.

Smith, Beverly. *Figure Skating: A Celebration*. Toronto: McClelland & Stewart, 1994.

Smith, Dick. *Inside Diving*. Chicago, Ill.: Henry Regnery, 1973.

Smith, Jessie Carney, ed. *Notable Black American Women*. Detroit, Mich.: Gale Research, 1992.

Sparhawk, Ruth M., et al. *American Women in Sport: 1887–1987*. Metuchen, N.J.: Scarecrow Press, 1989.

Spear, Victor, M.D. *Sports Illustrated Racquetball*. New York: Lippincott, 1979.

Spivey, Donald, ed. *Sports in America*. Westport, Conn.: Greenwood Press, 1985.

Sports Illustrated editors. *Sports Illustrated Horseback Riding*. New York: Lippincott, 1971.

_____ . *Sports Illustrated 1996 Sports Almanac*. New York: Prentice-Hall, 1996.

Stambler, Irwin. *Women in Sports: The Long, Hard Climb*. Garden City, N.Y.: Doubleday, 1975.

Stanek, Carolyn. *The Complete Guide to Women's College Athletics*. Chicago: Contemporary, 1981.

Stanton, Elizabeth Cady. *Reminiscences of Elizabeth Cady Stanton*. London: T. Fisher Unwin, 1898.

Steel, Donald. *The Guinness Book of Golf Facts and Feats*. New York: Abbeyville Press, 1992.

Steiner, Andy. *A Sporting Chance: Sports and Gender*. Minneapolis, Minn.: Lerner, 1995.

Strandemo, Steve. *The Racquetball Book*. New York: Pocket Books, 1977.

Styles, Showell. *On Top of the World: An Illustrated History of Mountaineering and Mountaineers*. New York: Macmillan, 1967.

Sullivan, George. *Queens of the Court*. New York: Dodd, Mead, 1974.

_____ . *Better Basketball for Girls*. New York: Dodd, Mead, 1978.

_____ . *Track and Field: Secrets of the Champions*. Garden City, N.Y.: Doubleday, 1980.

_____ . *Better Basketball for Girls*. New York: Dodd, Mead, 1981.

_____ . *Better Field Hockey for Girls*. New York: Dodd, Mead, 1981.

_____ . *Superstars of Women's Track*. New York: Dodd, Mead, 1981.

_____ . *Great Lives: Sports*. New York: Scribners, 1988.

Taylor, Rich. *Indy: 75 Years of Racing's Greatest Spectacle*. New York: St. Martin's Press, 1991.

Taylor, Robert Lewis. *Center Ring*. Garden City, N.Y.: Doubleday, 1956.

Thoroughbred Racing Association of North America, *1994 Directory and Record Book*

Trenary, Jill. *The Day I Skated for the Gold*. New York: Simon & Schuster, 1989.

Bibliography

Twin, Stephanie, ed. *Out of the Bleachers: Writings on Women and Sport*. Old Westbury, N.Y.: Feminist Press, 1979.

Twombly, Wells. *200 Years of Sport in America*. New York: McGraw Hill, 1976.

U.S. Olympic Committee. *Athens to Atlanta: 100 Years of Glory*. Salt Lake City, Utah: Commemorative Publications, 1993.

U.S. Lawn Tennis Association, ed. *Official Encyclopedia of Tennis*. New York: Harper & Row, 1972.

Van Steenwyk, Elizabeth. *Dorothy Hamill: Olympic Champion*. New York: Harvey House, 1976.

_____ . *Women in Sports: Figure Skating*. New York: Harvey House, 1976.

Vecchione, Joseph J. *The New York Times Book of Sports Legends*. New York: Simon and Schuster, 1991.

Vecsey, George. *The Way It Was: Great Sports Events from the Past*. New York: McGraw Hill, 1974.

Verbrugge, Martha H. *Able-Bodied Womanhood*. New York: Oxford University Press, 1988.

Vertinsky, Patricia. *The Eternally Wounded Woman: Women, Doctors and Exercise in the Late Nineteenth Century*. New York: Manchester University Press, 1979.

Voy, Robert, with Kirk D. Deeter. *Drugs, Sport, and Politics*. Champaign, Ill.: Leisure Press, 1991.

Wade, Mary Dodson. *Amelia Earhart: Flying for Adventure*. Brookfield, Conn.: Millbrook Press, 1992.

Wade, Paul, with photographs by Tony Duffy. *Winning Women: The Changing Image of Women in Sports*. New York: Quadrangle, 1983.

Wallechinsky, David. *The Complete Book of the Olympics*. New York: Penguin Books, 1984.

Walsh, Loren. *Inside Softball*. Chicago, Ill.: Henry Regnery, 1977.

Ward, Geoffrey, and Ken Burns. *Baseball*. New York: Knopf, 1994.

Ware, Susan. *Holding Their Own: American Women in the 1930s*. Boston, Mass.: Twayne, 1982.

Watson, Mary Gordon. *The Handbook of Riding*. New York: Knopf, 1982.

Waugh, Carol Ann, and Judith LaBelle Larsen. *Roller Skating: The Sport of a Lifetime*. New York: Macmillan, 1979.

Weiskopf, Herman. *The Perfect Game: The World of Bowling*. Englewood Cliffs, N.J.: Prentice Hall, 1978.

Whipple, A.B.C., et al. *The Racing Yachts*. New York: Time-Life, 1980.

Wills, Helen. *Fifteen-Thirty: The Story of a Tennis Player*. New York: Scribner & Sons, 1937.

Wolff, Rick, ed. *The Baseball Encyclopedia*. 9th ed. New York: Macmillan, 1991.

Woolum, Janet. *Outstanding Woman Athletes: Who They Are and How They Influenced Sports in America*. Phoenix, Ariz: Oryx Press, 1992.

Works, Pat, and Jan Works. *The Art of Freefall Relative Work*. DeLand, Fla.: Skydiving Book Service, 1988.

Wright, Shannon, with Steve Keeley. *The Women's Book of Racquetball*. Chicago, Ill.: Contemporary Books, 1980.

Wynne, Brian, and Jerry Cotter Wynne. *The Book of Sports Trophies*. New York: Cornwall Books, 1984.

Yannis, Alex. *Inside Soccer*. New York: McGraw-Hill, 1980.

INDEX

Index

Index

Index

Index

Index

Index

Index

Index

Index

Index

Index

Index

Index

Index